Organization and Management

A Critical Text

Organization and Management

A Critical Text

Edited by

Jim Barry
John Chandler
Heather Clark
Roger Johnston
David Needle

Organization Studies Research Group
East London Business School
University of East London

Australia • Canada • Denmark • Japan • Mexico • New Zealand • Philippines
Puerto Rico • Singapore • South Africa • Spain • United Kingdom • United States

Organization and Management

Copyright © 2000 Thomson Learning

Business Press is a division of Thomson Learning. The Thomson Learning logo is a registered trademark used herein under licence.

For more information, contact Business Press, Berkshire House, 168–173 High Holborn, London, WC1V 7AA or visit us on the World Wide Web at: http://www.itbp.com.

British Library Cataloguing-in-Publication Data
A catalogue record for this book is available from the British Library

ISBN 1–86152–193–6

First edition published 2000 by Thomson Learning

Typeset by LaserScript, Mitcham, Surrey
Printed in the UK by TJ International, Padstow, Cornwall

Contents

Preface

The idea for this book originated in the Organisation Studies Research Group (OSRG) based in the University of East London's Business School (ELBS). Drawing on a long tradition of critical and scholarly thinking in ELBS this group has attracted a number of academics who independently, over the years, have been teaching and researching into organization and management.

The work of the group has benefited enormously from links established in recent years with like-minded academics from a number of universities including Staffordshire, Portsmouth, Central Lancashire, Keele and Bolton Business School, who are all part of the expanding *Organisation Studies Network* (OSN). Our regular seminars have encouraged the sharing of knowledge in a critical but *supportive* scholarly environment and have seen the development of a number of perspectives and ways of seeing organization and management.

Whilst most of the authors in this book are associated with the OSRG we are delighted that some of our friends and colleagues from the OSN have contributed. We hope that future volumes will better reflect their profound influence on our own intellectual development through joint publication.

Acknowledgements

In many ways this book has been a long time coming. It has certainly been a labour of love for us as an editorial group. It has also left us with a debt of gratitude to our contributors who responded speedily and with good humour to editorial feedback. We are also grateful to Elaine Allen and Judi Westfallen in the ELBS Research Office who struggled valiantly with the manuscript and to our families who, like us, have lived with this book for some time. We are also thankful to our editors at Thomson Learning, in turn Steve Reed, Nicholas Edwards, Maggie Smith and not least long-suffering Jenny Clapham who has heard, tolerated and sympathized with a considerable number of apologies and justifications for delay. The understanding, patience and trust of all these people, who have above all encouraged and supported us, should not go unacknowledged. We hope that they, and you the reader, will not be disappointed with the result.

Contributors

Andy Adcroft is a Senior Lecturer and Programme Manager in the Corporate Programmes division of the East London Business School at the University of East London. He also teaches in the Industrial Relations Department at the London School of Economics and Political Science. His current research interests are focused on the political implications of globalization but in the past he has published on a wide variety of issues such as strategies in the early twentieth century, American manufacturing, the global automotive industry, foreign direct investment in the UK and the USA, the role of industrial strategies in the renewal of the Labour Party and the late capitalist crisis of cost recovery.

Rod Allen, is Head of the Department of Journalism at City University, London. Prior to entering academic life he was a magazine editor and publisher; a producer for factual television programmes at London Weekend Television; an international television co-production executive at LWT and at HTV; a CD-ROM and World Wide Web pioneer as editorial director of Harper Collins Publishers' interactive division; and media consultant with the Henley Centre's Media Futures programme. His research interests include media: he is co-editor (with Nod Miller) of a series of books on broadcasting policy.

Jim Barry is a political sociologist, a Reader at the University of East London and currently Co-Director of the University's Organisation Studies Research Group in the East London Business School. He is involved in two long-term projects: one into the gender and urban governance and another into gender and organizations with particular reference to higher education. He has published on gender and politics, gender and public services, gender and organizations, gender and business ethics and lone parenting and employment.

Joanna Brewis has recently moved from the University of Portsmouth Business School to the Department of Accounting, Finance and Management at the University of Essex. Her research interests centre around the use of Foucault to explore organizing processes through the lens of gender, sex, sexuality and identity. These interests are reflected in recent publications including 'Unpacking Priscilla: Subjectivity and Identity in the Organisation of Gendered Appearance (with Stephen Linstead and Mark P. Hampton (1997), *Human Relations*, 50 (10)); 'Time After Time; The Temporal Organization of Red-collar Work' (with Stephen Linstead, (1998), *Time and Society*, 7 (2)); and 'Who Do You Think You Are? Feminism, Work, Ethics and Foucault' (1998), in M. Parker (ed.) *The Ethics of Organisations*, London: Sage.

John Chandler is a sociologist teaching Organisation Studies in the East London Business School at the University of East London. His current research interests are gender and managerialism in higher education and in personal social service organizations with particular reference to the understanding of individual identities and life histories. He is currently Co-Director of the Organisation Studies Research Group in the East London Business School.

Heather Clark is a sociologist who is currently Co-Director of the University of East London's Organisation Studies Research Group in the East London Business School and is involved in a long-term research project into gender and organizations with particular reference to Higher Education. She has published on gender and organizations, gender and business ethics, and lone parenting and employment.

Peter Fenwick is a Senior Lecturer in Human Resource Management who was an executive in the car industry before he became an academic. He teaches undergraduate, professional and postgraduate students and his research interests centre on the formation of human resource strategies and their relationship with organizational performance goals. He has also published on developments in industrial relations.

Roger Johnston is Senior Lecturer in Organisation and Management at the University of East London. He holds degrees in social anthropology and sociology from the University of Edinburgh. Since 1996 he has been Business Studies co-ordinator running East London Business School courses at Queen Mary and Westfield College, University of London. He is currently working in the area of labour process and accountancy.

Nod Miller is Professor of Innovation Studies and Assistant Vice-Chancellor (Lifelong Learning) at the University of East London. Her research interests include learning from experience and the use of new media technologies for learning and teaching. She describes herself variously as media sociologist, experimental educator, T-group enthusiast, lifelong learner, autobiographer and fan of popular culture.

Adrian Murton is a Principal Lecturer in Human Resource Management and HRM Subject Group Leader in the East London Business School where he has taught and researched for the past ten years. His main teaching and research interests lie in the area of employee relations and employment regulation. Within this he has undertaken research into changing patterns of strike activity in post-war Britain which formed the basis of his Ph.D. thesis, and work on the operation and effectiveness of the National Dock Labour Scheme. His current research is concerned with assessing and evaluating the impact of new employment legislation on employee relations and patterns of employment in the UK and the Irish Republic.

Alan Neale combines a part-time Senior Research Fellowship at the East London Business School with being a full-time carer. The main focus of his current research is environmental policy and corporate 'greening'. His work on this topic has been published in the *Journal of Environmental Planning and Management*, the *International Journal of Urban and Regional Research, Business Strategy and the Environment*, and *Environment Politics*, and he has contributed to *Environmental*

Futures (Macmillan, 1998) and *Greener Marketing* (Greenleaf, 1999). He is also co-author of *Economics in a Business Context* (Chapman & Hall, 3rd edition forthcoming).

David Needle is currently Head of Corporate Programmes in the East London Business School, where he has taught for 23 years on undergraduate and postgraduate programmes. Before that he was engaged in management training. He has taught regular classes at the London School of Economics and has acted as a consultant to a number of small and medium sized companies. In 1989–90 he completed a period of attachment with Ford Motor Company. His main academic focus is Comparative Management and he has carried out research in Britain, Germany and more recently Korea and Japan. He developed courses in Comparative Management at both MBA and undergraduate levels and teaches each year on the University of East London's MBA programme in Singapore and Kuala Lumpur. He devised the Business in Context model and is the author of a popular textbook of the same name and is joint editor of the series based around the model.

Martin Parker is Senior Lecturer in social and organizational theory at the University of Keele. He holds degrees in anthropology and sociology from the Universities of Sussex, London and Staffordshire and previously taught sociology at Staffordshire. His writing is usually concerned with organizational theory and the sociology of culture. His most recent books are *Ethics and Organisation* (Sage, 1998), *The New Higher Education* (with David Jary, Staffordshire University Press, 1998) and *Organisational Culture and Identity* (Sage, 1999).

Ian Pirie is a Principal Lecturer and Subject Area Co-ordinator for Politics at the University of East London. He has over 30 years' teaching experience, originally in 'Liberal Studies', and more recently in political philosophy. The social responsibility of business (and of technologists) has been one of his main interests since starting up a course – probably one of the first of its kind – on the social responsibilities of business in 1976. This course has always been popular with students, and as part of their assessment they undertake a 'social audit' of a company or an industry. Observing how student attitudes to these issues have changed over the years – from the early 1970's radicalism through the Thatcher era, when it was often quite rare for students to want to criticize business, to the current mix of new radicalism with old cynicism – was one stimulus to the thinking behind this chapter.

Robert Willis is the Tutor of Doctoral Programmes at the East London Business School at the University of East London. His main research interests lie in strategic and change management, globalization, entrepreneurship and innovation. As well as publishing widely in these areas, over the past five years he has also published on a wide variety of other issues including new perspectives on management accounting, the global automotive industry, innovation and regulation in the pharmaceuticals industry and the late capitalist crisis of cost recovery.

Sally Wyatt is a Principal Lecturer in the Department of Innovation Studies at the University of East London. She is the author of Technology's Arrow, Developing Information Networks for Public Administration in Britain and the USA (University Pers Maastricht, 1998). She is currently doing research about the future of the Internet, under the auspices of the ESRC's Virtual Society? programme.

Introduction

The days when it seemed possible to study the likes of industrial sociology, organizational behaviour, personnel management and industrial relations as independent subjects are long gone. It hit home recently when a respected academic, who will remain nameless, reflected on the papers he and his colleagues were presenting at a conference and said, 'look at us, fifteen years ago we were all doing papers on trade unions and strikes, now we're all studying management!'. These comments can of course be interpreted in different ways. Maybe he felt a sense of loss. Or perhaps he was acknowledging a need simply to take account of the most recent fashion or fad – and was already beginning to wonder what will come *after management*. But one thing this pained comment does seem to signal is a sense that disciplinary walls, which have for so long represented the academic division of labour, have been coming down. Or perhaps that academics, like those who found themselves in Berlin in 1989, have been scaling walls, to peer nervously over the top to see just what is happening on the other side.

However this may be, in recent years the area of organization and management studies has seen an outpouring of work which is broadly critical and goes beyond the managerialist and prescriptive approaches of the past. In journals such as *Organization Studies, Organization*, the *Journal of Management Studies, Critical Perspectives on Accounting* and *Gender, Work and Organization*, and at conferences like the Standing Conference on Organizational Symbolism (SCOS), the Labour Process Conference and the Colloquia of the European Group for Organizational Studies (EGOS), academics from within Schools of Business and Management as well as 'traditional' social science disciplines, have been looking at organization and management from a variety of critical perspectives. These have included neo-marxist, feminist, Foucauldian and postmodern perspectives which collectively represent an emerging academic sub-field of critical organization and management studies.

Yet in the midst of this intellectual ferment the very area of study which deals centrally with organization and management, *Organizational Behaviour* or *OB*, seems to have gone largely untouched.[1] Indeed as a group of lecturers who have been engaged in teaching and research in the field of organization and management for some time, what has struck us most has been the *dominance* or *orthodoxy* of OB, with its formulaic prescriptions for a fairly clearly defined area of study which has changed little in recent years. In part this is a reflection that the vast tomes of OB, written for mass consumption by a growing number of business and management students, suffer from time lags. Text books take a long time to write and publish. Yet it is also more than this. It reflects a concern on the part of OB textbook authors to offer building blocks, to those who are new to the subject, which can be learned and (re)presented to examiners for approval in discrete, often descriptive, chunks. It is also indicative of a concern to limit consideration of a wider view; after all if we admit too many other disciplines and contextual variables it all becomes rather unwieldy. But there is a danger here that the complexities of the 'real world' of organization and management, and the intellectual attempts to understand and make sense of it in all its rich complexity, may get lost in the process.

Accordingly each contributor to this volume has been asked to take full account of historical legacy, key issues and ideas, applications and alternative approaches to their chosen area of concern – to reflect recent developments in the field. In addition they have been asked to do what so many texts on OB fail signally to do, address fundamental issues, uncover underlying agendas, explore assumptions and engage critically with the complex and contradictory realities of organizational life: in short to help re-orient the field of OB and demonstrate the significance of the social, economic, political and global context of which organization and management are a constitutive part. And to do this in a challenging, critical, reflective and *accessible* way that engages the scholarly imagination and whets the appetite to know and to read more. This book is the result.

While the book is wide-ranging in its coverage our aim has not been to provide a complete overview of the area but to reflect the diversity of critical perspectives on organization and management and to explore possibilities for a re-orientation of the field. We wanted to focus on particular topics and themes which are of contemporary relevance, to show how they are rooted in historical context and a product of particular social, political and economic circumstances. The study and practice of organization and management does not occur in a vacuum, intellectual or otherwise, which is why we asked contributors to offer a range of perspectives and critical thoughts in their examination of the theory and practice of organizational life. Our concern has been to demonstrate the importance of context and perspective and to challenge those who are or who would be managers to face and reflect on the social and personal implications of what they do.

The book itself is organized into four sections with each section preceded by its own introduction. The section introductions are an important part of the book. They provide a brief summary of each chapter and some comment on the rationale for their inclusion in the section. They identify theoretical perspectives and make links with other sections and chapters.

The book opens by offering a series of challenges to the conventional wisdom of OB. The implications of this are then developed in subsequent sections. Here examples from the literature, seen from a variety of perspectives and embedded in context, are used to open OB to the wider developments taking place in the field of organization and management.

The first section, *Unsettling Orthodoxy*, explores the taken for granted assumptions of texts on OB. The chapters challenge the prevailing orthodoxy of OB by locating individual organization members, and the organizations in which they work, within wider social structures based on factors such as class and gender, about which the conventional wisdom is all too often silent. They also unsettle the stability of OB by locating them in contexts characterized as constantly changing, where the certainties of the past are increasingly questioned. Raising issues of identity, labour process and post-modernism/postmodernism, these chapters show that the way in which the subject matter is approached has profound implications for how we see and understand organizations and those working within them.

The second section, *Organizational Lives*, extends the discussion of the individual within the organization, showing how the play of historical forces impact on and shape the experience of work. The chapters deal with issues of work stress, sex at work and the role of information and communication technologies (ICTs). Drawing on concepts such as anomie and alienation, as well as the work of the French philosopher Foucault and his notion of 'discourse', these chapters underscore the importance of contextual factors in our understanding of organizational life and the opportunities and constraints surrounding individual action.

Section three, *The Limitations of Management*, develops the theme of constraint through a consideration of a number of topical issues: corporate and organizational culture; human resource management (HRM); flexibility; and globalization. What these chapters have in common, perhaps above all else, is an interest in the global economy and the interconnections of an increasingly international environment in which organizations and management operate. What they also share is a concern to look beyond popular (mis)conceptions and the simplistic mystifications, nostrums and panaceas of management gurus to an understanding of the powerful forces at play in the wider global arena.

Finally section four, *The Politics of Organization and Management*, comprises just two chapters which highlight the relationship between business and politics. One deals with the issue of business ethics, the other the social responsibility of business. They were selected as a conclusion to the book because, by questioning and exploring in their different ways the values of contemporary business, they challenge much of what is taken for granted in the study of OB. And they offer alternative visions of the future. They bring centre stage that which is all too often marginalized or ignored and make explicit the challenge, implicit or explicit in other chapters, to think otherwise.

The chapters in this book seek to move us beyond the conventional wisdom of OB texts. Taken together they represent an approach to the study of organization and management which is concerned with setting OB in its social, political, economic and global context, covering a range of different theoretical perspectives. The chapters invite the reader to engage with current debates about organization and management and will, we hope, enliven the imaginary worlds of OB.

The Editors
Organisation Studies Research Group
East London Business School
University of East London
June 1999

Notes

1 We note the honourable exception of Thompson and McHugh (1995).

REFERENCES

Thompson, P. and McHugh, D. (1995) *Work Organisations: A Critical Introduction* (2nd edn) London: Macmillan.

Section 1
Unsettling Orthodoxy

While organization and management is of interest to academics from a wide range of subject disciplines and perspectives, a field of enquiry known as Organizational Behaviour, or OB, has emerged in recent years. OB can be seen as an academic specialism in its own right, with dedicated texts and an assured place on courses in business and management. But there is a dominant orthodoxy within OB that the chapters in this introductory section seek to question, from different critical perspectives: Chandler in social constructionist terms, Johnston from a broadly neo-marxist, labour process approach, with Parker exploring the value of postmodernism in re-orientating the field. What they share is a desire to move beyond a managerialist and prescriptive approach and explore challenges to orthodox thinking on organization and management as represented in conventional OB courses and texts.

In the first chapter Chandler identifies inadequacies in the treatment of the individual in conventional texts on OB. He argues that the components of the individual have been treated in a fragmented way with no coherent view of individual identity. Without this, he argues, we can have no conception of social actors, no idea of agency with our understanding and explanation of organizational behaviour remaining flawed as a result.

Chandler argues that identity and emotion are largely ignored in OB literature, possibly because they are in a sense too 'real' to fit within the limited theoretical conceptions of the subject currently on offer. But this means that for us, as participants in organizations, the most vital part of ourselves – our emotions and identity – are suppressed or silenced. Similarly it is argued that the conventional literature gives scant and unsatisfactory attention to moral issues, ignoring, for example, feminist contributions to the debate.

Chandler's main concern is that the conventional OB literature treats the individual as essentially *asocial*, denying a fundamental notion found in social science that both individuals and organizations are socially constructed. This frequently leads writers on OB to ignore the issue of the exploitation of individuals as 'human resources', conceptualized as somehow separate from the organization itself. This reinforces a depoliticized view of organizations, for to recognize the politics involved would mean acknowledging the legitimacy of other perspectives and interests.

This concern with different competing perspectives on organizations is taken up by Johnston. Noting that existing OB texts say little or nothing about the nature of capitalism, he explores the contribution of labour process analysis which looks closely at how production actually works and relates these processes to their capitalist context. In drawing on Karl Marx's analysis of capitalism this body of thought constitutes a challenge to conventional thinking about organization and management.

Johnston outlines the basic structural elements of capitalist organization of production. The tendency of capitalist organizations to reduce costs by intensifying work is the key explanation of how organizations are structured and changed, from this perspective. The writer who is acknowledged as inspiring the large body of contemporary research in the labour process tradition is Harry Braverman (1974). Johnston examines one of Braverman's original main theses that, in the course of intensifying the labour process, work has become progressively more degraded in terms of the skill involved. Whether this is true or not (and it is hotly disputed on various grounds), we have here an alternative explanation for some of the characteristic responses to work which OB literature tends to conceptualize as problems for managers to 'solve' through analyses of motivation, leadership, group performance and management by objectives. Johnston goes on to discuss two linked major developments from labour process analysis in particular, those of control and resistance, and of the nature of subjectivity within organizations.

Whilst Johnston considers the capitalist context of organization and management as the key issue, Parker in the next chapter focuses on postmodernism. As a challenge to modernism – one of the dominant ideas of the twentieth century, with its core concept of rationality, and consequent prescriptive and systemic approach to organizational analysis – postmodernism raises a number of contentious issues. In considering this important set of ideas, however, it is helpful if we distinguish between two different meanings of the term. On the one hand, 'post-modern' as signifying a particular epoch or period marked by different organizational characteristics and, on the other hand, 'postmodern' as a theoretical perspective, with a particular interest in the use of language which questions how we come to 'know'.

This distinction is related to two main questions posed by Parker: first, what might be the characteristics of post-modern organizations; and second, what use can be made of postmodern analysis? To begin with, he argues, the rational modernist approach has evidently not lived up to expectations, either in terms of internal operations or in meeting the challenges of rapidly changing market conditions. Questions have accordingly arisen about the extent to which contemporary organizations have adapted to changing conditions by adopting new post-modern forms of organisation. These forms are supposedly flexible, de-centered in terms of power, and non-bureaucratic. Although the evidence for new forms of organization is weak, there is a recognition that functionalist bureaucratic forms no longer offer a valid response to market conditions: rationalism is under attack from the inside.

The second and possibly more profound challenge to modernism, however, is seen as related to how we *think* about organizations. Again the key concept of rationality associated with modernism is central, but this time the focus is on meaning and language – found also in other fields of intellectual inquiry, particularly that of culture. Problematizing language invites us to *reflect* on what we do: particularly as language is the medium through which we constitute or comprehend what we come to understand as, and call, reality. Here, by deconstructing the notion of 'organization' into its various component parts, we see it more clearly as a social construct rather than a 'thing', a supposedly concrete reality to which we are subject. Parker traces the arguments by reviewing work which looks at how the notion of organization as an efficient monolithic entity has given way to a view of organization as a 'process'.

From this perspective the emphasis is on how organizations are produced and sustained.

This, in turn, raises questions about subjectivities and power. Language it is argued plays a key role in bringing into being our ideas about organization, questioning the way in which we equate social processes like 'organization' and 'management' with more definite forms of reality. From this perspective we may even see organizations as shaping the language and perceptions used within them. This, Parker argues, provides valuable insight into what constitutes 'organization'.

From differing social constructionist, labour process and postmodernist perspectives the chapters in this introductory section thus share common ground in questioning the current ways of conceiving organization and management found in the literature of OB. Taken together they offer fundamental challenges to the prevailing orthodoxy as well as to our own ways of seeing and thinking about individuals, organization and management.

Organizational behaviour and the individual: critique of a consensus

1

John Chandler

INTRODUCTION

Organizational Behaviour texts typically look at the human aspects of organizations at three different 'levels' of analysis – the individual, the group and the organizational. As far as the individual level is concerned there is a remarkable degree of homogeneity in what these books offer the student (e.g. Buchanan and Huczynski 1997; Mullins 1996; Robbins 1998). All of them examine the individual from an exclusively psychological perspective as a collection of unrelated processes or phenomenon such as perception, learning, motivation, attitudes and 'individual differences'. The treatment seems thorough and comprehensive and the student is not invited to reflect on the ways in which this may be a partial view of the individual. However, the argument in this chapter might be summed up, if in slightly exaggerated fashion, by saying that the way in which conventional Organizational Behaviour texts represent the individual is as an emotionless, amoral, asocial subject without agency. Furthermore the treatment is ahistorical and apolitical. These deficiencies are explored and some alternatives examined in the following sections.

THE EMOTIONLESS INDIVIDUAL?

Despite the appearance of comprehensiveness in the investigation of psychological dimensions Organizational Behaviour texts say remarkably little about the emotions or feelings that people who work in organizations experience on a day-to-day basis and which one might expect a predominantly psychological perspeetive on organizational behaviour to deal with. The silence is not total – texts do usually deal with the issue of job satisfaction and, increasingly, with anxiety and stress. However a curiously limited range of emotions are dealt with despite the actual experience of work, for various individuals, running the full emotional gamut – joy, fear, disappointment, anger, pride, amusement, etc.

In this underplaying of emotion academics in the Organizational Behaviour field are, perhaps, reproducing a view of organizational behaviour as part of a public realm where 'reason' prevails, while emotions are private matters – something the employee takes home with them. One of the few texts dealing with people at work that does deal with emotion directly – not an Organizational Behaviour text but one dealing with work psychology – is David Statt's (1994) *Psychology and the World of Work*. While pointing out that 'books on the way organizations work usually tip-toe quietly round this whole area' (Statt 1994:108) he points out that organizations themselves do so, too:

> Because organizations, and especially work organizations, find the expression of emotions so difficult to handle they usually act as though people didn't have any; a denial of reality with which people themselves collude. So behaviour that expresses things like fear, anger, love, jealousy, joy, hatred or general anxiety is either separated from its underlying emotion and treated as though it suddenly appeared for no good reason, or simply ignored. It is as though there was an unspoken, universal assumption that common behaviour in organizations is entirely conscious, controlled and rational (Statt 1994: 109).

There are echoes here of the work of a number of sociologists who see the suppression of emotion in the public realm as characteristic of modernity. Foremost amongst these, perhaps, was Max Weber who, in analysing bureaucratization, talks of how it offers:

> above all the optimum possibility for carrying through the principle of specializing administrative functions according to purely objective considerations. . . . The 'objective' discharge of business according to *calculable* rules and 'without regard for persons' . . . [Bureaucracy's] specific nature, which is welcomed by capitalism, develops the more perfectly the more completely it succeeds in eliminating from official business love, hatred and all purely personal, irrational and emotional elements which escape calculation. This is the specific nature of bureaucracy and it is appraised as its special virtue (Gerth and Mills 1948: 215–16).

Of course, if sociologists such as Weber recognize the importance of emotion it is in part because of a sociological imagination that sees human behaviour as always set within a particular historical and social context. It is precisely because they are concerned with what is new and different about modern organizational and social life that they see the salience of emotion: they 'see' what is invisible because suppressed. They hear the silence. Psychology, on the other hand, tends to abstract human subjectivity from its historical and social context. But, paradoxically, the more the context is denied the more it tends to take its hold. Psychology is apt to explore questions raised by the conventional wisdom and practical concerns of the time, ignoring other possible questions. The silences of the time become its silences. The biases of the time become its biases.

If individuals and institutionalized practices do conspire to suppress emotion in modern work organizations this may provide some justification for neglecting them. However any critical account of organizational life should, presumably, draw attention to such processes of suppression. This should be done, as Statt's analysis suggests, because it is important to draw attention to the individual and organizational costs of such suppression; costs, for example, in terms of 'mental illness' for the individual and 'turnover' for the organization. But it is also important for a more radical re-thinking of organizational possibilities. For example Patricia Lunneborg (1990), in a study which celebrates ways in which women 'do work differently than men', draws attention to the transformation that can be brought about if feelings are expressed and dealt with at work:

Take the case of a landscape architect, age 40 (she occasionally gets called Mama but that's all right), who said she is not only valued for her superb design work but because she keeps an eye on, and an ear open, to the nuances of people's feelings: 'I read between the lines when people tell me things and smooth over conflicts between people in the office. One of the bosses was having emotional problems and taking it out on all the other employees. The other two bosses were totally unaware. I brought it to their attention and said, "We've got to find some way to deal with this." They do not listen; they do not pick up on cues. . . . A couple of people had left because of it, and the business was in a slump. Everyone knowing that this person was on the edge of a nervous breakdown helped, and the bosses are much more sensitive now' (Lunneborg 1990: 52).

The thesis that emotions are typically suppressed at work can, however, be pushed too far. Hochschild (1983) shows, for example, how in some jobs the use and management of emotion is an essential feature of the work. She looks, for example, at how flight attendants and bill collectors are expected to use the expression of emotion to do their jobs. These jobs, she argues, involve 'emotional labour' which she defines as:

> the management of feeling to create a publicly observable facial and bodily display; emotional labor is sold for a wage and therefore has *exchange value* (Hochschild 1983: 7).

This 'management of emotion' is something the individual can often do spontaneously themselves, but it is also something others can 'train' the employee to do for commercial ends. As Hochschild puts it:

> In the case of the flight attendant, the emotional style of offering the service is part of the service itself . . . seeming to 'love the job' becomes part of the job; and actually trying to love it, and to enjoy the customers, helps the worker in this effort (Hochschild 1983: 5–6).

One example of how workers are trained in emotion management is as follows:

> 'How', the instructor asked the class [at Delta's Stewardess (sic) Training Center], 'do you alleviate anger at an irate?' (An 'irate', a noun born of experience, is an angry person). Answering her own question, she went on:
> 'I pretend something traumatic has happened in their lives. Once I had an irate that was complaining about me, cursing at me, threatening to get my name and report me to the company. I later found out his son had just died. Now when I meet an irate I think of that man. If you think about the *other* person and why they're so upset, you've taken attention off of yourself and your own frustration. And you won't feel so angry.'
> If anger erupts despite these preventive tactics, then deep breathing, talking to yourself, reminding yourself that 'you don't have to go home with him' were offered as ways to manage emotion. Using these, the worker becomes less prone to cuss, hit, cry, or smoke (Hochschild 1983: 24–5).

Such work illustrates how 'emotions' can be central to understanding the individual at work. Arguably, though, Hochschild does not go far enough in that she considers emotional labour to be called for in only approximately one-third of jobs. However, while there are many jobs in which the management of emotional labour is not as central to job performance as they are in, say, that of the flight attendant, it is present in *all* jobs – even those not primarily involving much interaction with customers, clients or co-workers. The management of emotion occurs in every job partly because work organizations embody discipline and co-operation – requiring rage or anger, for example, to be controlled. But the management of emotion is also involved in individual and collective attempts to make work at least bearable if not enjoyable and satisfying.

If, however, it is accepted that emotion is an issue worth exploring it remains to be seen how this can be accomplished. In the space available here only the beginnings of an exploration can be provided. It is clear, though, that while the psychoanalytic approach utilized by Statt (1994) is interesting and useful, it is not sufficient. It is important, too, to draw on cognitive approaches to emotion, stressing, as they do, the importance of subjective interpretation and (in some cognitive approaches at least) the ways in which individuals are not passive recipients of emotions generated by unconscious physiological 'instinctive' processes but are, through processes involving interpretation, memory and language, actively constructing and reworking their emotions (Strongman 1996, provides a useful account of different theories). But the work of Hochschild which we refer to above also suggests that we need to look at emotions not just as 'private', 'individualized' phenomenon but as influenced by, if not created through, *social* processes. This could be done by making reference to 'social-constructionist' theory within social psychology (e.g. Harre 1986) as well as by using sociological work – for example Albrow has advocated a specifically Weberian approach to the study of emotions in organizations (Albrow 1997, see also Fineman 1993). There is also a body of feminist work to draw on which shows how emotions are of enormous personal and political significance and are both 'individual' and 'social' phenomenon. (Crawford 1992; Griffiths 1995).

THE AMORAL INDIVIDUAL?

If Organizational Behaviour texts say little about emotion, until recently they were silent about morality. Again this might be seen as reflecting or colluding with a view that denies the relevance of morality in the workplace. Organizations are, perhaps, to be seen as places where people do what is necessary or most efficient or profitable. Right and wrong in the moral sense does not enter the picture. And yet, again, the experiences of individuals in organizations could be said to be very different. Whether they see themselves as making 'moral' decisions or not, people are often faced with choices that can be seen as moral – whether to steal from or defraud the 'organization', whether to lie to fellow workers, managers or customers and so on. When we evoke the notions of 'fairness' or 'rightness' in, say, the way people are selected for promotion we can also be said to be making moral judgements.

At least some recent texts have shown some belated recognition of ethics as a topic worthy of discussion (e.g. Robbins 1998). But in doing so they have ignored psychological work which one might have expected Organizational Behaviour texts to draw upon. It is true that much of this work originates in the field of developmental psychology and might be seen as a long way removed from the concerns of students of Organizational Behaviour. However just as Organizational Behaviour can usefully draw on learning theory, even though it does not originate in work psychology, so, too, it might usefully draw upon this literature on moral development. In doing so we can move beyond the – at best – limited approaches to business ethics found in some texts and relate individual ethical and moral decisions to wider social and political concerns. Such an approach is consistent with Ian Pirie's arguments elsewhere in this volume.

The work of Lawrence Kohlberg makes a useful starting-point. Building on Piaget's work, Kohlberg (1968: 489) developed an account of moral development which has individuals progressing through six stages of moral development including:

- Level I Pre-moral:
  - Stage 1. punishment and obedience orientation;
  - Stage 2. naive instrumental hedonism.
- Level II Morality of conventional role conformity:
  - Stage 3. good-boy [sic] morality of maintaining good relations, approval by others;
  - Stage 4. authority maintaining morality.
- Level III Morality of self-accepted moral principles:
  - Stage 5. morality of contract, of individual rights, and of democratically accepted law;
  - Stage 6. morality of individual principles of conscience.

How might this be related to understanding the individual at work? One way might be to argue that in the workplace there is an interesting if perhaps reprehensible tendency to regress to an infantile moral order resting on principles of conformity and avoidance of punishment. There are echoes here of Argyris's (1957) suggestion that workers are too frequently expected to be child-like at work – dependent and obedient rather than independent and controlling. This kind of analysis also suggests a way of criticizing existing forms of work organization and suggests positive ways of 'moralizing' organizations by moving from the lower to the higher stages of Kohlberg's hierarchy. While having some sympathy with such arguments they run the risk of ignoring the ways in which people in work organizations often do act and react as 'fully-developed' moral agents in Kohlberg's sense. Indeed this is what may motivate individuals to *resist* dominant organizational forms and practices. It is precisely because individuals *apply* notions of a social contract and 'universal ethical principles' and find organizations wanting that explains why many workers have become, for example, trades union activists or whistle-blowers, or why women have resisted male domination through, say, forming women's groups. However Kohlberg's analysis while interesting and relevant is not, of course, the last word. Even more interesting and relevant to students of Organizational Behaviour is that of Carol Gilligan (1982).

Gilligan's work is a feminist reaction to Kohlberg's. She points out that according to Kohlberg women tend to be morally 'less developed' than men, tending not to exhibit fully the application of universal ethical principles which Kohlberg sees as the highest stage of moral development. Based on her initial research, which involved interviews with about 200 females and males, she concluded that it is not that women are morally inferior to men – they just tend to respond to moral dilemmas in different ways. She suggests that women are more likely to exhibit an 'ethic of care' and men a 'logic of justice'. That is, while men tend to apply abstract principles (e.g. 'justice' or 'freedom'), women tend to see moral choices as involving a response to, and reconciliation of, the needs of people. One of the examples Gilligan gives is the following.

Two eleven year old children, a boy called Jake and a girl named Amy were presented with one of a series of dilemmas devised by Kohlberg to measure moral development in adolescence. In this dilemma a man named Heinz considers whether or not to steal a drug which he cannot afford to buy in order to save the life of his wife. Jake sees the dilemma, as Kohlberg did, as a conflict between the values of property and life. He sees life as having priority and uses this as a logical justification for his choice. As Jake puts it:

> For one thing, a human life is worth more than money, and if the druggist only makes $1000, he is still going to live, but if Heinz doesn't steal the drug, his wife is going to die. (*Why is life worth more than money?*) Because the druggist can get a thousand dollars later from rich people with cancer, but Heinz can't get his wife again. (*Why not?*) Because people are all different and so you couldn't get Heinz's wife again (Gilligan 1982: 26).

The boy sees the moral dilemma as 'sort of like a maths problem with humans'. Amy's response to the dilemma is very different. Asked if Heinz should steal the drug she replies in a way that seems evasive and unsure:

> Well, I don't think so. I think there might be other ways besides stealing it, like if he could borrow the money or make a loan or something, but he really shouldn't steal the drug – but his wife shouldn't die either (Gilligan 1982: 28).

From the standpoint of Kohlberg's developmental theory, Jake seems more advanced than Amy. He is able to apply deductive logic to moral dilemmas and provide a confident, independent judgement. Amy on the other hand presents, as Gilligan puts it, 'an image of development stunted by a failure of logic, an inability to think for herself' (Gilligan 1982: 28). But Gilligan goes on to argue for a different interpretation of Amy's response. One that is not inferior to Jake's, just different.

> The world she knows is a different world from that refracted by Kohlberg's construction of Heinz's dilemma. Her world is a world of relationships and psychological truths where an awareness of the connection between people gives rise to a recognition of responsibility for one another, a perception of the need for response. Seen in this light, her understanding of morality as arising from the recognition of relationship, her belief in communication as the mode of conflict resolution, and her conviction that the solution to the dilemma will follow from its compelling representation seem far from naïve or cognitively immature. Instead, Amy's judgements contain the insights central to an ethic of care, just as Jake's judgements reflect the logic of the justice approach. (Gilligan 1982: 30).

There is an obvious danger of this analysis serving to reinforce stereotypes of 'male' and 'female' behaviour. However, Gilligan emphasizes that such differences are gender-related but not gender specific. We may, therefore, use her distinction between the application of a 'logic of justice' and an 'ethic of care' to understand within-gender, as well as between-gender differences in how people respond to the dilemmas of organizational life.

THE ASOCIAL INDIVIDUAL?

Another way in which Organizational Behaviour texts present a partial view of the individual is by playing down the social influences on individual psychology. The attentive reader of Organizational Behaviour texts will, it is true, notice that motivation may be subject to social influences, with McClelland's (1967, 1987) work, in particular, suggesting that the 'needs' for achievement, power and affiliation are affected by social factors, including the culture in which the individual is brought up. Even in drawing on social psychology, however, it is rare to find reference to the 'social constructionist' school which shows how various psychological phenomena – emotions, attitudes, personality – are socially constructed. Psychologists in this tradition have shown how social interaction not only affects, say, emotions (as when someone makes us angry), but also supplies the very categories we use to make sense of our experiences and structure our response. From this perspective, then, individual behaviour and individual thoughts and feelings are in large measure to be explained with reference to social processes. Of course some varieties of social constructionism suggest that it may be possible to separate out, for analytical purposes at least, those parts of the individual that have social determinants from those that do not. Some social psychologists, that is, do not wish to attack conventional psychology 'head on' but suggest that a social-constructionist view is complementary. Thus social psychology can be seen as attending to, and seeking an understanding of, our 'social selves' leaving conventional psychology to deal with the non-social or personal self. Tajfel (1982: 2) for example, defines 'social identity' as 'that part of an individual's self-concept which derives from their knowledge of their membership of a social group (or groups)'. This suggests that individuals are *partly* social creations, but that there are parts of the person that are immune from social influence. Some, however, would go further arguing as Burkitt (1991: 90) does, for example, that the self is formed within social relations and 'the idea that there is a basic division, between society and the individual' is a 'nonsense' (Burkitt 1991: 189).

Of course it would be wrong to portray conventional texts as ignoring social influences entirely. Most texts devote a considerable amount of space to social aspects in their consideration of group behaviour and leadership, drawing on a long tradition of 'Human Relations' writing to do so. But whereas the classic writers in the Human Relations school, (such as Mayo 1946) were, despite their limitations, willing to link their discussion of the group and social influences to wider debates about the nature of industrial society and the search for 'good' forms of organization, these connections have disappeared in the contemporary literature. Individual psychology has been separated from social psychology and social psychology from sociology and politics.

There may be a variety of reasons for Organizational Behaviour texts ignoring a range of 'social constructionist' positions on the nature of the 'individual'. It may reflect the training and expertise of the authors, or it might reflect a desire to keep things simple and avoid what might be seen as the rather misty and boggy territory of the nature/nurture controversy and competing perspectives on the self (symbolic interactionist, phenomenological, post-structuralist, humanist, Marxist, etc.). The consequence, however, is the reinforcing of a view of the individual as an object, juxtaposed to the 'organization' which is now a 'common-sense' view. It also fits well with a managerial view that seeks ways in which to utilize 'human resources'.

It presents knowledge that can simultaneously be used to enhance managerial control of human resources – through selection, training, motivation, etc. – and makes such attempts legitimate (all we are doing is trying to achieve a good individual–job–organization ' fit' – either by fitting the worker to the job or the job to the worker). It renders invisible the ways in which individuals are constructed by the social practices occurring within organizations and it depoliticizes organizational life. Achieving a good organizational–individual fit is seen as involving individual decisions (Do I take this job or that?) and technical problem-solving (How do we devise a training programme to get employees to do this?). The purposes of organizations are taken as unproblematic 'givens', with forms of domination ignored and residual 'problems' (e.g. 'stress') individualized (cf. Clark *et al.* 1999 in this volume). Authors of Organizational Behaviour texts thus become what Baritz (1974), in an earlier attack on the use of social science in industry, called 'servants of power'.

Those adopting a Foucauldian perspective might wish to go further and argue that Organizational Behaviour, in allying itself to work psychology, becomes a technology of power – not just being used by one group to oppress or exploit another but providing the knowledge and language through which (in part at least) we constitute our subjectivity and our selves (Hollway 1991; Rose 1989; see also Brewis 1999 in this volume). Our knowledge of motivation theory, for example, may begin to dictate how we think and feel about our needs and goals at work. However this may be to exaggerate the potential for Organizational Behaviour to influence our thinking. Indeed perhaps the strongest criticism of conventional Organizational Behaviour texts is that they encourage a superficial approach to learning in which the student learns lists and 'facts' which can be used in examinations and assignments before being promptly forgotten. They singularly fail to inspire critical reflection and resistance.

LOSS OF INDIVIDUAL AGENCY

If the treatment of the person in Organizational Behaviour texts is highly individualized and asocial this can be seen as in accordance with dominant Western conceptions of the self which see the individual self as separate from both the social and natural world and which also places enormous importance and value on the 'individual' (see Morris 1991). And yet those who approach Organizational Behaviour texts expecting to find an exploration of the subjective experience of organizational life are likely to be disappointed. The individual of the Organizational Behaviour text is not the 'I' who works within the organization. Elias (1991: 30) has spoken of a situation, common in the modern age, whereby

> it often seems to the individual that his or her true self, his [sic] soul, is locked up in something alien and external called 'society' as in a cell. He has the feeling that from the walls of this cell, from 'outside', other people, alien powers are exerting their influence on his true self like evil spirits, or sometimes benign ones.

This is no doubt an accurate portrayal of how many of us experience organizational life and Organizational Behaviour texts might be expected to say something about it. But if the 'I' is often conscious of its separateness it is also an *active* participant in organizational life – working and interacting with others in the process. Even when

'I' feel alienated from what is going on around me 'I' cannot help but be a part of it (even 'doing nothing' has consequences). Organizational Behaviour texts fail to comment on this kind of experience. Instead we find a representation of the individual as a set of unrelated parts and processes – motivation, personality, perception, learning. 'Behaviour' is then 'explained' with reference to any *one* of these psychological variables. What is missing is an analysis of the ways in which – through interaction with others, through the use of language, through memory and 'emotion work' – the self is created and continuously re-created; a process through which the self makes itself but not in conditions of its own choosing (see Griffiths 1995 and Giddens 1991); a process involving moral and political choices and consequences.

Consider, for example, the case of Teresa as recounted in Marshall (1995: 133). As a manager in a construction company Teresa experienced many obstacles and much hostility from others. Reflecting on her experience she said:

> I didn't like myself very much, I actually acquired more what I see as masculine traits in order to cope. And these were the more hostile and aggressive ones, where I had to make myself more unreasonable to gain a particular foothold on occasions.

She later left the organization. One might expect Organizational Behaviour texts to analyse such personal reflections – to examine how they come about, what they mean and what the consequences are. This can be done, moreover, in ways that stress the political and social aspects. What, for example, does this say about 'masculinity'? How can and do women and men respond to such situations? Does leaving the job do anything to change the organization, making it less likely for such a path to be trodden by others? Is this a unique situation or does it represent a common reaction of women working in organizations?

It is this sense of an 'I' as a self constructed and re-constructed in and through processes of social interaction, a self imbued with moral and political agency, that is missing and needs to be recovered. Of course it might be objected that such an approach gives too much attention to the 'individual' and reinforces simplistic 'common sense' views which post-structuralists and others would wish to attack. Perhaps it is time we made a radical break with this obsession with the elusive individual (see Shotter and Gergen 1989 for a sustained attack on the conventional notion of the individual from a variety of authors). There are, however, pressing pedagogical and political reasons for holding on to the idea of exploring the individual in organizations. The pedagogical reason is that students are interested in people. To deal with people they can get to know is to draw them in, to engage them. This need not necessitate turning away from post-structuralist writings which might be seen as hostile to individualism – indeed post-structuralism may be used to move beyond and question some taken for granted assumptions concerning the 'individual' in organizational life (see, for example, Rose 1989). Politically, too, a focus on individuals makes sense. The personal is political and identities are not simply ascribed. Let us explore the choices others make and how others construct themselves (under conditions which are not of their own choosing). This can then inform our own choices. As Giddens (1991) and others have explained, there is a connection between politics and self-identity and its construction – seen clearly, but not exclusively, in the case of feminism.

CONCLUDING REMARKS: SOME ALTERNATIVES

There are many different ways in which the limitations of existing Organizational Behaviour texts could be overcome and greater diversity in the way texts deal with people in organizations would be welcome. There are already some texts which depart from the consensus characterized above – in particular those by Hollway (1991) and Thompson and McHugh (1995), both of which provide welcome critical alternatives to the more conventional treatments. Another approach which might, however, be fruitful would be to take a range of 'individuals' from different organizational contexts and analyse their 'identities' and actions.

There are, of course, enormous differences between social scientists in how the term 'identity' is used. The early work of Erikson (1963) which is rooted in psychoanalysis and explores the development of individual 'identity' as a social process is very different from Goffman's analysis of identity management (Goffman 1968). And both of these approaches are very different from the more recent literature on the 'politics of identity' which focuses on various social 'identities' (or aspects of identity?) such as male/female; gay/lesbian/heterosexual; black/white; able-bodied/disabled; and different national identities. This latter body of work is itself a very diverse and lively one (Jenkins 1996 provides an accessible introduction to the literature on identity; see also Rutherford 1990; Calhoun 1994).

There is of course the danger that the notion of 'identity' is so confused and confusing as to be useless. However its attraction lies precisely in its ability to be used to make sense of the individual in society as at once 'individual' and 'social'; the same as others and different; a construction of the self and socially constructed.

One could, for example take the story of Teresa introduced in the previous section and explore issues of masculinity/femininity (and where these notions come from) as well as those of emotion, learning, motivation and personality. It would of course be necessary to look at a number of individuals with different characteristics (gay/heterosexual, black/white, etc.) and in a range of organizational settings ('professional', managerial, manual and clerical labour; in factories, offices and the home; in the UK and other countries; in big and small organizations, etc.). It would also be desirable to examine a range of individual and collective responses to situations (from leaving the job to engaging in informal and organized forms of collective resistance). To adopt this approach might enable the reader to connect the abstract 'theories' of the psychologists of learning, motivation, etc. with the experiences of those labouring within organizations (including the reader's own personal experience). Such an approach would also move beyond a managerial perspective and encourage a critical look at what happens to people in organizations. It would provide a starting point for making moral and political choices which can find expression in individual and collective forms (compare Pirie 1999 in this volume). This might make the study of Organizational Behaviour part of a project to change the nature of organizational life rather than to reproduce existing forms of domination.

REFERENCES

Albrow, M. (1997) *Do Organizations Have Feelings?* Routledge, London.

Argyris, C. (1957) *Personality & Organization,* Harper & Row, New York.

Baritz, L. (1974) *The Servants of Power: A History of the Use of Social Science in American Industry,* Greenwood Press, Westport.

Buchanan, D. and Huczynski, A. (1997) *Organizational Behaviour: An Introductory Text* (3rd edn), Prentice Hall International, Hemel Hempstead.

Burkitt, I. (1991) *Social Selves: Theories of the Social Formation of Personality,* Sage, London.

Calhoun, C. (1994) *Social Theory and the Politics of Identity,* Blackwell, Oxford.

Crawford, J. (1992) *Emotion and Gender: Constructing Meaning from Memory,* Sage, London.

Elias, N. (1991) *The Society of Individuals,* Basil Blackwell, Oxford.

Erikson, E.H. (1963) *Childhood and Society* (2nd edn), Norton and Co., New York.

Fineman, S. (1993) *Emotion in Organizations,* Sage, London.

Gerth, H. and Mills, C.W. (1948) *From Max Weber,* Routledge and Kegan Paul, London.

Giddens, A. (1991) *Modernity and Self-Identity: Self and Society in the Late Modern Age,* Polity, Cambridge.

Gilligan, C. (1982) *In A Different Voice: Psychological Theory and Women's Development,* Harvard University Press, Cambridge, MA.

Goffman, E. (1968) *Stigma: Notes on the Management of Spoiled Identity* Penguin, Harmondsworth.

Griffiths, M. (1995) *Feminisms and the Self: The Web of Identity,* Routledge, London.

Harre, R. (1986) *The Social Construction of Emotions,* Basil Blackwell, Oxford.

Hochschild, A. (1983) *The Managed Heart: The Commercialization of Human Feeling,* University of California Press, Berkeley, CA.

Hollway, W. (1991) *Work Psychology and Organizational Behaviour: Managing the Individual at Work,* Sage, London.

Jack, D. and Jack, R. (eds) (1988) Women lawyers: archetype and alternatives, in Gilligan, Carol, *Mapping the Moral Domain: A Contribution of Women's Thinking to Psychological Theory and Education,* Harvard University Press, Cambridge, MA.

Jenkins, R. (1996) *Social Identity,* Routledge, London.

Kohlberg, L. (1968) Moral Development, in *International Encyclopedia of Social Science, Vol. 10,* 482–94 Macmillan, New York.

Lunneborg, P. (1990) *Women Changing Work,* Bergin and Garvey, New York.

Luthans, F. (1992) *Organizational Behaviour* (8th edn), McGraw Hill International, Boston, MA.

Marshall, J. (1995) *Women Managers Moving On: Exploring Career and Life Choices,* Routledge, London.

Mayo, E. (1946) *Human Problems of an Industrial Civilisation,* Macmillan, New York.

McClelland, D.C. (1967) *The Achieving Society,* The Free Press, New York.

McClelland, D.C. (1987) *Human Motivation,* Cambridge University Press, Cambridge.

Morris, B. (1991) *Western Conceptions of the Individual,* Berg, Oxford.

Mullins, L. (1996) *Management and Organizational Behaviour* (4th edn), Pitman, London.

Robbins, S. (1998) *Organizational Behaviour: Concepts, Controversies, Applications* (4th edn), Prentice Hall, New Jersey.

Rose, N. (1989) *Governing the Soul: the Shaping of the Private Self,* Routledge, London.

Rutherford, J. (1990) *Identity: Community, Culture, Difference,* Lawrence & Wishart, London.

Shotter, J. and Gergen, K. (eds) (1989) *Texts of Identity,* Sage, London.

Statt, D. (1994) *Psychology and the World of Work,* Macmillan, Basingstoke.

Strongman, K. (1996) *The Psychology of Emotion: Theories of Emotion in Perspective,* (4th edn), Wiley, Chichester.

Tajfel, H. (ed.) (1982) *Social Identity and Intergroup Relations,* Cambridge University Press, Cambridge.

Thompson, P. and McHugh, D. (1995) *Work Organizations: A Critical Introduction* (2nd edn) Macmillan, Basingstoke.

2 Hidden capital

Roger Johnston

INTRODUCTION

This book deals with critical management. A major – perhaps the dominant – theme in management training is that of organizational behaviour. This chapter offers a critique of organizational behaviour, using a contrast with recent work in the labour process to do so.

Pick up a copy of a standard American textbook on Organizational Behaviour, say, Luthans (1995), which would be a representative and established one. Look up 'Capitalism' in the index. Found it? No? Found 'Capital'? Ah yes, an indication that firms will need to deploy capital in managing their affairs. So a few lines in a 600 page book on Capital. Not a hint in the text therefore of what organizational behaviour and management is *about*.

It might be objected that it is self-evident that management must involve capital: that of course we live in a capitalist economic system. Yet if we never examine it – find only profit and loss in Accounting textbooks, only allusions to the workings of the market, presumed to work mysteriously to allocate goods and services in economics and marketing textbooks, then surely we are making a dangerous assumption that we *do* understand our economic system. This is especially so since we are happy to accept anthropological accounts of small-scale non-literate societies or even historical accounts of medieval Europe which emphasize the connections between the economic system and the social system. But we do not even make a start (in initial mainstream courses in Business and Management) in discussing the nature of management, about the nature of what they are managing, and how that relates to the wider society. 'Capital' and its management would appear from many standard management textbooks, not to be mentioned. Yet if it is not mentioned, it cannot be properly understood: the student is left to rely on ill-formed perceptions of the subject matter of their professional life. (We do of course acknowledge that many business and management courses do seek to discuss the interrelationships between the economic and social systems: we are concerned with the absence of such discussions in main texts – for us in the areas of organizational behaviour and management.)

We are impelled to ask the question: why the silence? Why the taboo? Is this really a god whose nature or perhaps even existence cannot be openly declared? There is perhaps a moderately common-sense way into the problem. During the Cold War, which virtually coincides with the dominance of American capitalism worldwide, *and* the simultaneous growth of 'management' schools and textbooks, it was perhaps enough to declare the simultaneous virtues of both capitalism and the 'American Way' in contradistinction to the 'other' – the alien Soviet-dominated world.

With the radical change in the Soviet Union's economic system and hence its political form and much of the way of life it is perhaps the time to re-examine capitalism itself, to see what and how political, social and economic systems are affected by and founded on capitalism.

Because a full examination would be too extensive, I propose to take just one part – but a very important part – the Capitalist Labour Process (CLP), and see how using it helps us to understand both capital and our society. Labour process analysis looks at what happens at the point of production and claims that we can thereby understand wider processes.

One thing we can clear up at the start. The fundamental purpose of a capitalist enterprise is to expand the capital itself. 'Making a profit' is difficult to deal with. Accountants can count some twenty-odd different kinds of profit, depending on what you are looking at, and in what time period. But the essential is that a capitalist process must generate a surplus overall. If it does not, then the enterprise will fail. It is a curious feature of management texts, and in particular organizational behaviour texts, that they do not explicate either this simple fact, nor how the material they deal with serves this aim – perhaps there is an unspoken doubt that it does?

LABOUR PROCESS BASICS

Let us try to sketch the fundamental process a little more fully. We trace the analysis of capitalism back to Marx: sometimes it is best to use a critique of a system to get to the core of a subject. We can also use this alternative model to see what analysis is used in current 'OB'.

The Marxist model proposes these elements. First, that capitalism needs a technology – materials, artefacts, tools, machines, and land, to deploy: the 'means of production'. But the capitalist – the owner or entrepreneur who owns these means of production, does not use them directly him- or herself. Secondly, production is *socially* organized. Labour has to be employed to produce goods. This means that there has to be a category of people available to work for the capitalist. Most commonly such people have no alternative means of subsistence, so there is an imbalance of power. Certainly the employee is subject, during working hours, to the organizational requirements of production, as directed by the capitalist or his or her agents. Employees contract time to the employer. Their efforts are organized by the employer. Essentially this is a form of domination, of lack of freedom. Usually some form of hierarchy of organization is implemented – the pyramid shape of the classic bureaucracy is a good example of the social organization aspects. In such an organization there is an explicit statement of position in a hierarchy with highly specified duties, responsibilities and the authority (of the capitalist) to direct the activities of the labour which constitutes the organization. The particular shape or structure of the hierarchy of organization has of course constituted a significant element in management literature.

So capitalist industrial production requires both means of production and some form of organization of labour – social relations of production – in order to make goods (we will ignore the production of services in the interest of simplicity). The labour involved in production, how it is done, is the locus of the Capitalist Labour

Process. Such goods must then be sold – and here the market comes into play – with market conditions, including the market for labour, feeding back into the labour process. For a capitalist to succeed, they must sell goods in the market at greater than the cost of production. Out of the surplus the capitalist takes a portion as manager of the enterprise, as director of production: a portion also goes to those who financed the setting up of the operation, even where that is the manager/capitalist. Shareholders therefore derive their income from their financing of the means of production, and the initial costs of setting up the organizations. They continue to be paid, usually in the form of dividends after the initial financing has been met, but how much they get at any one time is not entirely within their control, unless they are also direct owners of the firm. Note that labour does *not* share in this surplus: labour is treated as a cost, not a beneficiary of success.

However the process is very much influenced by taking place in a competitive market. Others will, in the simple terms and models we are using here, be producing the same goods. Competition takes place in terms of such factors as quality, price, availability and quantity.

Price would seem the most obvious form of competition, but it is in practice not one that can succeed long term. Every drop in price affects the size of the surplus that must be achieved in a capitalist system. And none of the competitors can be secure that a drop in price will not be instantly matched. Since price wars will tend to lower the surplus in an industry they are the least preferred option.

This means that quality may be improved. But manufacturers may find that there is no necessary benefit from higher quality (a tin can that lasts 50 years is of high quality but the requirement is for a much shorter term than that). Quality also tends to require higher skill and/or more expensive means of production with probably higher costs and lower output. The lower output means higher unit costs since all the costs of the enterprise are divided by each unit of production.

So the inevitable answer to competition is to lower costs. This can be done by increasing output, which will usually mean intensifying the labour process, or paying less for raw or input materials (which may involve intensifying the labour process of the supplier). Lower costs may also be achieved by technical improvements either to the means of production – higher output machines working to higher quality or faster standards, for instance – or by reorganizing the labour process, or by paying labour less, or by making it work longer for the same wages – the preferred option in the early days of capitalism. Naturally, it is possible to do all of these simultaneously.

Since the inevitable outcome is that labour will probably, in the long term, be earning less and working more intensely, some degree of lack of consent or resistance or on occasion political action might reasonably by expected. There may of course be a general rise in living standards which conceals the fact that the share of labour in any particular industry falls. The cost of maintaining the population is spread more generally. But each industry has further downwards pressure on labour costs to meet the costs of the 'social settlement' (Williams *et al.* 1994).

It can also be expected that management – the handling of people – will be concerned to limit the effects of such resistance or overt conflict, at least to secure compliance: we will come back shortly to the curious situation that management textbooks do not mention this as a source of the tension that management undoubtedly has to deal with.

So far we have been following a rather well-known Marxist analysis which we can represent diagrammatically as in Figure 2.1. (Further accounts may be followed up in Braverman 1974, Burawoy 1979 and Thompson, 1983.)

Although this is a simple model, and the situation becomes more complicated with the growth of industry and its importance in modern societies, with other elaborations of how capital is circulated and appropriated, the essential characteristics hold true.

BRAVERMAN AND LABOUR PROCESS ANALYSIS

At this point we can explicitly pick up Harry Braverman's analysis in *Labour and Monopoly Capital* (1974). (n.b. we will be using the English spelling throughout) This book is credited with establishing the corpus of work which now constitutes labour process analysis, and with making a decisive break with the dominant framework of organizational behaviour. Braverman is concerned to show how the dynamics of this model of capitalist production and wealth distribution work in such a way as to progressively degrade the worth and work of the worker in the conditions of twentieth-century monopoly capitalism (that is the domination of the economy by large firms).

The degradation of work is an essential feature of Braverman's analysis. Essentially he has in mind a view of work as potentially an expression of the fullest nature of being human. Capitalist labour processes are seen as progressively degrading of this potential, as capitalism attempts to deal with its own survival. This idea may be familiar through the cognate idea of alienation.

But Braverman does not place the notion of degraded work in the context of machinery or inanimate, supposedly neutral, technology, somehow associated with

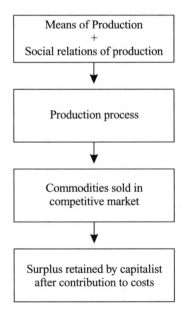

Figure 2.1

necessary technical advance, but in specific capitalist purposes, i.e. an outcome of social *intent*, not determinate technological necessity.

Let us look at his argument, taking industry around 1900 as a convenient starting point. Recall that capitalists – monopoly or not – meet market conditions of pressures to maintain a surplus which is best met by reducing costs. But much of the costs of land and materials will be substantially determined by the markets from which they are bought, and continuous downwards reduction in costs from these sources will be difficult to achieve.

This leaves labour as a cost. Wages may be reduced, but there is a level of subsistence that must in general (although not for any specific capitalist) be met and this level of subsistence or indeed the going rate for wages may be unrelated to the capacity of the business to move into surplus. The working day may be extended, and this was what happened in early capitalism. But this may be self-defeating in terms of worker productivity (which increased when working hours were cut during the First World War in Britain). And the improvement in 'quality of life' has led to successful pressure, largely from trades unions, to limit hours of work in advanced countries.

So two options are left as responses to competitive pressures. One is to innovate technically – to introduce faster, more efficient machinery and techniques, such as the Ford assembly lines. The other is to intensify work – to organize the work and the pace of work such that output is increased.

Of course the greater the output, the lower the unit cost, allowing either a greater potential surplus, or a true reduction in price to enable price-cutting. Any such move might well be copied by competitors, so the process has no end resolution unless monopoly emerges as the result of competition.

Intensifying the labour process inevitably means working at a greater pace or making more effort to achieve greater output. Again there are fatigue limits to physical and mental effort (although note the interest by psychologists and work study engineers in just what these limits are).

A key point to note here is that capitalists do not employ or buy in a specific amount of labour. What they buy is the labourer's time, during which they direct the labourer's effort. But the potential output remains essentially the labourer's: typically the capitalist does not know the optimum output of the employee for the potential remains the employee's, as does the effort.

It is the employee's effort, physical and mental faculties, that are being bought: but these remain essentially the employee's, they cannot be divorced from the self of the employee. Unlike other sources of power, labour is conscious and has its own purposes. Thus the market for labour is different from that of commodities. Commodification of labour may be attempted, but will inevitably raise conflicts. Understandably the employee in general seeks to limit the degree of effort.

A core part of Braverman's argument and those of subsequent commentators is that the twentieth century has seen a significant change in the use and control of labour, much of it combining intensification of output with an overcoming of resistance to greater effort by the workforce.

In early capitalism, labour and labour skills were bought in as a whole. The capitalist had an interest in extending the time worked, and could set targets which implied intensified work, but outside of some areas such as cotton spinning, had little control of or indeed interest in *how* the work was done: often it was devolved to a system of sub-contractors (see Littler, 1982 for a full discussion).

However forces such as 'Fordism' and the application of 'Scientific Management' helped to change this and increasingly management took a closer and closer interest in the immediate control and disciplining of work.

This process was accompanied by technical changes some of which superseded labour (e.g. hydraulic pressing machines for shaping steel). But probably the bulk of significant changes were directed to controlling labour. Thus Ford's assembly line at Highland Park contained little that was technically innovative if the use of machinery is considered. But if we include organizational changes (the social relations of production) as part of the labour process (and hence 'technical') then we get a very different view. The extreme division of labour employed not only speeded up the task through repetition but saved time through specialization – each worker had but one task, ultimately a similar-sized and similarly timed subdivision of the whole time for a product being assembled. And the worker was *subordinated*, not to the machine but to the organization.

But it was not just that the specification of what was to be done and when that was now subject to the capitalists design. The control of a standard time for a standard task enables the capitalist accurately to cost labour, and identify further elements necessary to increase output. But note that the assembly line and its offshoots is not a technical/machine artefact, it is essentially a new form of organization of labour in which the design of the labour process, down to the minutest detail, passes into the control of the capitalist. The worker has little latitude as to choice in any of the elements of work, except to continue resistance to control at the micro level of effort/output. It is this which reduces the worker by eliminating skill and mental requirements – degrades, as Braverman argues.

The complexity of this process, the transfer of knowledge, the application of skill and judgements, from the workers to the employers brings into being whole strata of administration to deal formally with the decision-making involved, while further layers of book-keepers and accountants are involved in tracking costs and values – a paper shadow of the basic production process in Braverman's view (it is ironic that 'management science' does not examine this aspect of its own existence). Yet it is not a matter of technical choice. It firstly serves a particular social purpose, that of the capitalist, which in turn is the outcome of the imperatives of another social relationship, that of the market.

Braverman does argue that deskilling is an essential part of industrial processes, including white-collar work. As we shall see, this aspect has been much disputed. The process is ultimately self-defeating, since the increased output achieved by these means has to be sold at lower prices to induce purchase, which reduces the surplus gained, thus keeping up the pressure for improvements in the 'efficiency'. So in our own times Ford with a two-minute maximum cycle time for each task in assembly, looks enviously at Nissan's one minute thirty-seven seconds.

Since we want to see how this approach compares with other, perhaps more familiar approaches to management, it is worth reflecting that in labour process analysis we see that capitalism's drive for innovation in machinery and methods, and its constant pressure to reduce costs, are not in the interests of efficiency or are simply what management is about. They are not even a result of 'efficiency', however defined. Rather they are a response to the imperatives of capitalism. Yet this is not an abstract system, there are definable social purposes and real beneficiaries. Capitalism is extraordinarily efficient at wealth accumulation through the organization of labour, but much less so at wealth distribution – the two processes separate out after the accumulation of the surplus by the enterprise.

We can also see that well-known 'problems' such as alienation or even the type of subjugation of Man to Machine hilariously satirized in Chaplin's film *Modern Times*, should not be seen as inevitable if rather unfortunate outcomes of the twentieth century's drive for progress, or as technically necessary, or that the detailed monotonous routine of bureaucratized industry and commerce is somehow required, but that they are all related to these particular purposes, most often broken down into particular tasks and duties. The key is that each order, command, duty, rule or technical task is a subdivision of ownership: commonly we see it as authority, as if it were the same as the state's authority, but it is really dependent on ownership or rather our overall consent or compliance with the idea of personal ownership of property.

We could even say that labour process analysis serves as a meta-theory, and indeed that this is its attraction. Without embroiling ourselves in academic discussion, we can think of a meta-theory as an overall explanation that encompasses other theories and ideas (see Thompson in Knights and Willmott 1990).

Labour process analysis works this way in positing that we can best understand business and commerce, their structures, organizations, management and behaviour in them through the key features of its analysis of capitalism: that indeed the core argument of labour process analysis is that connections can be traced from the point of production to the forms of the organization to wider social and economic factors.

Thus work practices, forms of supervision and management and structures of organization are related to economic imperatives and class structures. Braverman's *Labour and Monopoly Capital* is about making these kinds of connections.

From it we get explanations of what we would, from other perspectives, see as technical factors, even factors not thought to figure highly within management, such as work study. We have many explanations of the derivation and functions of management, the perceived necessity for hierarchies, the form of supervision and tracking of values through 'paper shadows' themselves forming minutely regulated bureaucracies requiring supervision and management. We also see the pattern of capital flows and can generate further hypotheses about movements of capital and labour.

Subsections of management thought which draw on the wider context and concepts of sociology and other social sciences such as power in organizations can now be located in terms of labour process analysis. Power in organizations is seen to be deployed in general terms in line with the underlying imperative of the expansion of capital rather than explored as simply a concept in itself, or to 'maintain organization'.

It is its status as meta-theory, the achievement of a radical break with the prevailing but rather stalled organizational analysis of the early 1970s, which accounts for its popularity and the significant body of work produced within the general framework of labour process theory. But although labour process analysis was a breakthrough, we still have some important ideas to consider.

What *was* the orthodoxy in Organizational Behaviour? Why was it seen by many – particularly in Britain – as having little more to contribute, and, most intriguingly of all, why does it still continue, markedly so in management texts in the USA? And does the claim of labour process to be a meta-theory also allow it to offer an explanation of these phenomena?

THE ORTHODOXY

We cannot produce a full critique of 'orthodox' OB here: in line with other chapters of this book we merely offer some initial ideas for discussing the subject, but we can plot the general outcomes.

We can be certain that labour process analysis runs counter to conventional Organizational Behaviour texts and assumptions.

If we locate current Organizational Behaviour as being founded on the human relations movement and its developments, then we would see Organizational Behaviour as at best an attempt to 'humanize' the workplace – a case passionately argued by, say, Michael Rose (1975).

But this liberal–humanist concern fails to acknowledge the more massive economic forces of capitalism. So current Organizational Behaviour is largely silent over pay, lay-offs, de-layering, unemployment and conditions of work. Motivation for instance is seen as securing the commitment of the worker to the firm, without exploring the fundamental and obvious issues of why there is resistance to be 'overcome'. Such intellectual difficulties are highlighted when labour process analysis is used to explain work situations.

In addition to OB texts ignoring the core of capitalism itself, they perversely ignore the source of their own central themes, namely control. What labour process analysis draws our attention to is that capitalists buy labour power – the capacity to labour of the direct producers. But the capacity is inherent, not a given amount. Hence the main aim of the capitalist (or the managers of the enterprise), is to transform the capacity for work into actual labour – essentially a problem of control of labour.

From this perspective, it is clear that the underlying thrust of OB texts is about control of workforces, essentially substituting a language of social psychology for analysis of politics and economics and social relations other than that of the small group – a social psychology from which most of the 'social' has been removed. OB still ends at the factory gate. This means that OB texts essentially depoliticize the class relations within the workplace, emphasizing a supposedly humanist means of social control and consensus in the practice of capitalism. The outcome is an intellectual cul-de-sac for conflicts and contradictions. These conflicts and contradictions find a central role in labour process analysis.

It has also been evident that OB has been in intellectual difficulties. There have been few new directions in research – perhaps a little addition of organizational power, but the key issues of the time – the civil rights movement, feminism, the radical rejection of war, the crises of capitalism, even industrial strife – all live political issues affecting work, all passed by the world of OB which still continued to use the ferment of ideas produced by the Neo Human Relations School in the early 1950s. The curious thing is that OB has still not moved on: some of the research has progressed, undoubtedly, but along the same lines. The development, such as it has been, has been to introduce more 'case studies' which move further and further from the political, social and economic realities of organizations.

In contrast Braverman's work effectively provided a means of explaining what happens at the traditional focus of much of industrial sociology – the nature of work and the experience of it – and linked it to wider political and class concerns (even though some have accused Braverman of omitting such considerations from his own analysis). The core idea of labour process analysis is to make the links clearer.

We can learn to understand these same factors through consideration of the social relations at the point of production. For it is, arguably, a central tenet of labour process analysis that it is possible to connect an analysis of the point of production to an understanding of the structural relations of society. This wide scenario partly explains the range and power of some of the work undertaken in the area.

It might be thought that this central tenet would lie behind most of the work done in the area. But this is not the case. A major division lies between those who advocate the 'back to the roots' approach and those who see the usefulness of the analysis in the developments that took place from 1980 onwards. Both interpretations have produced formidable research (see Knights and Willmott 1990).

DEVELOPMENTS

The first development stemming from Braverman's work was that of the Brighton Labour Process Group (BLPG). The work produced by this group pursued the specifically Marxist applications of the core of Braverman's book, and gave an intellectual background to Edwards's *Contested Terrain* (1979), and set the ground for the Labour Process Conferences held from the mid-1980s.

A second and possibly more popular development deriving from the publication of Braverman's work was the debate on deskilling. Braverman does subtitle his work 'The degradation of work in the twentieth century', so it does seem reasonable to examine the evidence for his claim. Braverman argues that the logic of capitalism leaves few long-term options other than reducing cost in meeting competition. The main means of doing so is to reorganize production methods in order to do away with craft skills. This has the dual effect of reducing wages for what is now designated as unskilled work, and increasing output through the subdivision of labour. This subdivision of labour takes control out of the hands of the workforce and transfers it to a greatly increased management function. The work itself, being subdivided into small repetitive tasks, becomes diminished.

It is central to Braverman's work as a Marxist, that work should be of prime concern for life and humanity. From this follows the judgement that work which allows little personal involvement or creativity or skill degrades the worker's humanity.

Braverman makes great use of the introduction of scientific management at the turn of the century to explore his proposition that work in the twentieth century has become progressively more subject to this form of detailed work organization, and thereby progressively more degraded.

This aspect of Braverman's work generated a great deal of discussion, arguably diverting attention for many away from issues of class, power and the nature of work in a capitalist system. Work such as that of Littler (1982), despite a concern with locating labour process analysis within a wider framework, readily initiated discussion about the nature of scientific management/Taylorism and the extent to which it applied in different industries and locations. Although the intention was to expand on Braverman, it is arguable that the debate on historical patterns moved the focus from understanding analysis of contemporary capital/labour relations to one of debate about the extent of Taylorism as a form of control historically and notions questioning the degradation of work rather than the creation of new forms of skills and controls in old and new industries – a point that Edwards (1979) claimed Braverman overlooked. Littler also criticizes Braverman for taking a linear developmental view of capitalism – from a supposed independent craft control of work, deemed to be intrinsically satisfying for the worker, transformed to an unskilled proletariat, dominated by economic calculus and successful internal organizational political domination.

None the less, the criticism of Braverman's use of Taylorism prompted a number of questions and allowed the development of other lines of enquiry, including an exploration of the *varieties* of capitalist controls of labour (Littler 1982).

Littler reviews the patterns of rationalization and bureaucratization in Britain, the USA and Japan in the twentieth century. While Taylorism as a force is questionable, other issues of economics and politics are not.

This inevitably raises a question mark over the treatment by Braverman of issues of control and resistance. Since Braverman is a Marxist it might be thought that class struggles play a central part in his analysis. But this is not quite so, the general interpretation being that Braverman is so intent on developing the themes of degradation and deskilling that he over-emphasizes the determinism and omnipotent success of scientific management and control (see Thompson and Ackroyd 1995).

Much subsequent writing was concerned to show the extent of resistance to management practices and extensions of control as being widespread. Burawoy (1979), for instance, shows that workers respond by evolving a set of games around production. Johnston (1980) shows the ways in which work is a setting for resistance and struggles for control over work and the use of labour power: and how the organization itself can provide the means of resistance to exploitation.

But whatever the criticisms one might make about Braverman's treatment of issues of control and resistance, they are at least implicit, especially in his discussion of the nature of work and humanity and in his view that work patterns in the twentieth century have led to a degradation at least of the potentialities of labour.

Braverman does not stop his analysis with what happens to the production worker at the point of production. Central to his book is the idea of management control – indeed the development of management itself. He locates the growth of management in the planning, co-ordination and control functions which follow on the fragmentation of the tasks of labour, taking over the control of work formerly held by labour. This control and planning function lead to the emergence, not just of the direct management functions, but of the 'paper shadow' that mimics and monitors the production process, essentially tracking value. This process is itself the generation of the expansion of clerical jobs. Further monitoring – accounting for and tracking of the value of other operations leads to a further expansion of management functions.

So what constitutes much of 'modern organization' for Braverman is based on the overriding of the employee's control over labour by a management function. Braverman produces this account of the genesis of the subject matter of 'management studies' – and of Organizational Behaviour within that – as a vivid picture of management structures being poised like an inverted triangle on the point of the workforce.

In this sense the worker is not just subject to the employment contract but is subordinated also to management structures of control – his or her work and lived experience is subordinated to the whole capitalist process, which is designed to secure a surplus from the worker's labour – what Marxists call 'real subordination of labour'. This real subordination is placed by Braverman firmly in the area of the implementation of scientific management in the early 1900s. Other writers would make the process more general. Braverman's view is seen as unnecessarily narrow here.

He argues that there is a distinction between historic social division of labour and technical division of labour – and between management of large numbers of people engaged in activities and management consequent upon the technical division of labour. The technical division of labour is used not only to gain efficiencies in production due to task specialization, but also to de-skill the task so that lower skilled labour may be used at cheaper rates: it is against this that recent notions of 'empowerment' have to be placed. Such moves do little to restore previous worker craft control.

In chapter 6 of *Labour and Monopoly Capital* Braverman argues that it is the function of various bodies and agencies to take over the 'habituation' of the worker to the new order – essentially he has in mind the practitioners of Organizational Behaviour, although wider political agencies and culture also play a part. This is a criticism widely enough known to occasion some surprise that it has not been answered, further increasing the suspicion that the function of OB is to reflect management's values, rather than to examine what these values are and where they are derived from.

Braverman does supply his own answer: no matter how humanistic and genuinely concerned individuals might be they remain subject to the demands and exigencies of capital.

> As it presents itself to most of the sociologists and psychologists concerned with the study of work and workers, the problem is not that of the degradation of men and women, but the difficulties raised by the reactions, conscious and unconscious to that degradation . . . their task is not the study of the objective conditions of work, but only of subjective phenomena to which these give rise: the degrees of 'satisfaction' and 'dissatisfaction' (Braverman 1974: 141).

For Braverman, breaking the unity of thought and actions – conception and execution – is a 'catastrophe of the human essence' . . . 'the subjective factor of the labour process is removed to a place among its inanimate objective factors' . . . (Braverman 1974: 171).

To ignore the main factors shaping the experience of work while claiming to be seeking to understand it is perverse: the suspicion must be that OB seeks to provide a way of capitalism offering a supposed humanitarian concern while pursuing its main goals in other arenas.

Braverman argues (1974: 175ff) that workers have been increasingly subjected to being treated as machines in a 'rational' system devised by management. In engineering production this process is furthered by removing control of machinery entirely from the worker. The worker in effect becomes dominated by the machine but Braverman is careful to emphasize that machines serve the entirely human purpose of capital accumulation: the machine does not have a purpose, and to treat it so is to reify it. Braverman then argues that the social purpose could conceivably be changed, the work could be socialized to serve labour's ends.

In the last part of the book Braverman argues that occupations that used to be 'white-collar' have become progressively 'proletarianized' as their work has become subject to the routinization and fragmentation characteristic of scientific management. Management itself is increasingly subject to controls and deskilling.

He lastly examines both the working class and the 'middle layers', drawing our attention to the class dimension derived directly from work, in particular capitalism's continual shedding of labour, typically into lower paying and more exploited areas (forming a 'reserve army of labour'). Even for fully employed workers more than one wage earner is required for a family income, with consequent strains on social maintenance and care arrangements.

Much of Braverman's work has been dealt with briefly here. Braverman is concerned to make the point that labour process as a concept argues for a link between the means of production and the social relations of production and the specific organizational forms of capitalism. These organization structures themselves both form and dominate capitalist societies.

Braverman's critique of monopoly capitalism has attracted little further explicit work, perhaps because his perspective is part of a long-standing and recognized critique. But Braverman is evidently offering a powerful counter-argument to the paradigms offered by Organizational Behaviour. Clearly he sees Organizational Behaviour practitioners as being a part (although very much a lesser part) of the organizational apparatus which habituates the worker to the disciplines and drudgery of the workplace. And that OB has a part to play in this habituation of the worker within capitalism.

Braverman's argument specifically challenges the *unacknowledged* meta-theory of Organizational Behaviour which is of course to depoliticize the class relations of capitalism by providing a supposedly humanistic means of social control and consensus in the practice of capitalism.

NEW DIRECTIONS

But labour process analysis has not developed quite in the expected way as a simple counter culture or school of thought and investigation. Although much literature has been generated, the analysis has arguably not just developed Braverman's arguments but also generated other concerns that some argue are ancillary or even contradictory to the original line of argument.

We will now look briefly at some of these developments. The first to emerge from Braverman's publication was the work of the Brighton Labour Process Group (BLPG), which essentially outlined the specifically Marxist framework, in particular drawing attention to the ways in which value is realized from the labour process and surpluses accumulated. Both Elger (1979) and the BLPG argue the dominance of capital over labour but emphasize the failure of Braverman to emphasize *resistance* to this domination, particularly in the form of class struggle, focused on the point of production as the working class seeks to control its own labour power.

The emphasis is on the increasing control of labour at the point of production as industrial enterprises become locked into a competitive system. This approach emphasizes *power* relations at work, together with discipline and enforcement. The approach also draws attention to class relations in capitalism. For this reason Elger (1979) argues that deskilling is not a necessary part of the degradation of labour. He emphasizes that labour processes change with different phases of capital accumulation, and changes in capital beyond production. Yet the 'deskilling debate' in a sense is what happened in the development of labour process analysis.

It can be argued both that deskilling is a diversion from the thrust of labour process analysis, but is also a necessary direction to explore, given Braverman's emphasis on it, especially in the context of scientific management – undoubtedly a deskilling process for the labour involved. Despite the work of writers such as Elger (1979) and the BLPG which sought to place Braverman's work within its wider Marxist tradition, and the eagerness of writers who thought they were able to move organizational sociology from the sterility of the 1970s into the areas of class politics and political economy, much of the 'labour process debate' centred round the notion of whether Braverman's thesis on deskilling was in line with actual developments in industry. This raised a whole set of problems which arguably moved the debate off the main thrust of Braverman's work, which was about power and class, and into rather more definitional concerns.

The exploration of issues such as whether deskilling is central, the extent to which scientific management was implemented (particularly comparing different countries and periods – cf. Littler 1982), and the nature of skill itself (and whether new skills had emerged), initiated comparative studies, which at least had the merit of examining production processes in general. In part the debate was tapping the work of Nichols, Armstrong and Beynon (jointly and severally) which had examined the real skill-based occupational changes in critical sectors of British industry.

This was a welcome refocusing on the empirical situation of workforces and the organization of production (see Burawoy's 1979 analysis of machine shops). There had been a tendency prior to this for sociologists to differentiate out as separate areas the experience of work and the organization of work, particularly from a production point of view. This did give rise to work such as Friedman's (1978), which argued that employers tended to keep the workers they designated as skilled as core workers – thus uprating the importance of skill while highlighting why employers might well seek to shed such skilled labour in the long term. However, the down side was a concentration on essentially definitional problems and the problems associated with validating research which can be both cross-cultural and historical. This is not to disparage this kind of research, but to acknowledge a shift in focus. Labour process analysis did introduce a note of scepticism into the supposed freeing or upgrading of workers in new technologies.

Closely associated with this direction of research has been that of *flexibility*. The main ideas here can, in one sense, be seen as an expansion of the deskilling debate, pointing out that skilled workers may be functionally flexible, thus overriding some of the rules and hierarchies established in the workplace. This is not entirely separate from issues of new technology, where new jobs and tasks are created. Here work has explored the degree to which the process of deskilling is initiated after the first creative phase. Computing is a good example, with a progressive division of labour and a relative drop in pay for operatives. Certainly the notion that flexible specialization and new technology represents a shift, requiring new theoretical perspectives, is argued to be misplaced. Thompson (1989: 224ff) argues that the research shows that flexible technology is limited in scope (see also Pollert 1991), and that so too is flexible specialization. The factories which feature such systems also use predominantly familiar techniques, while of course their goal of accumulating growth in capital remains unchanged. What is happening is the flexible use of labour over a number of linked tasks, which requires a greater degree of involvement in some respects from employees, but which remain none the less thoroughly routinized.

The intensive nature of work associated with Taylorism is still with us. Self-disciplining of workers is still a significant part of current labour processes, most evident in TQM (cf. Ackers *et al.* 1996).

BRAVERMANIA

So Braverman's book initiated a great deal of work. So much so that by 1982 Littler and Salaman were already calling for a reassessment under the title 'Bravermania and Beyond'. The crux of their argument is to note that much work had claimed to use a labour process analysis, without adequately questioning Braverman's work, thus threatening a closure of research. The main flaws in Braverman's argument they see as a lack of interest in actual organizations and structures, with a tendency to see labour as a category, rather than as social actors. This is a theme taken up later in a different guise by Knights and Willmott in particular.

Littler and Salaman also see (1982: 255ff) blockages in Braverman. The first is that the treatment of class conflict is too abstract – that it is assumed somehow that workers are already disposed to oppose capitalist authority. This ignores both general societal and cultural forms of resistance and specific forms of shop-floor resistance. Littler and Salaman also argue that Braverman's general approach ignores wider features of the capitalist labour process and ways of creating a surplus other than through intensification of the labour process. In itself this argument alerts us to the consideration of how capitalism works and the various fractions of capital along with their own specialist workforces – a feature ignored by most Organizational Behaviour text books, which tend to assume a centrality of production (though increasingly of commerce) without problematizing the area of study. Littler and Salaman extend Braverman's focus into cognate areas such as consent, legitimacy, ideologies of technocracy, the questioning of the overall structures and operation of capitalism including 'Four hundred years of surveillance, coercion and moralising (which) have inculcated the legitimacy of property rights' (1982: 258), together with the management function, rule based structures of formal hierarchies and the limits of formal rationality with *the legitimization* of perceived 'efficiency'.

It could be countered that Braverman's delineation of the labour process within monopoly capital enabled the incorporation of these and cognate concepts into the study of organizations from their previous more diffuse places in industrial sociology and political economy: that the power of Braverman's study was the bringing together of previously disparate elements within one coherent conceptual framework. Although Littler and Salaman do validly point to limitations, most of these, apart from resistances and consciousness, can be unproblematically incorporated within labour process studies. Their main criticism, that Braverman's (and Marx's) approach does away with labour as a conscious force has remained a theoretical problem.

Littler and Salaman (1982), in arguing for a wider appreciation of work than that configured in *Labour and Monopoly Capital* are acknowledging a shift in the study of work, which in very general terms, seeks to incorporate political and sometimes economic analysis into the study of work. These themes are perhaps best represented by Paul Thompson's *The Nature of Work* (1989). Although firmly committed to a core of labour process analysis, Thompson reviews areas such as new technology, management control and skill, gender, the politics of production (looking at the possibilities of transforming political processes through changing the nature of work), and what he calls high theory (Thompson 1989: 274ff).

These themes are very much part of wider concerns in the study of work and organizations, and reflect current changes in wider society. They are reflections of social change both within and without work. They are not confined to 'working class' subjects but increasingly look at managerial work and change in the structure and operation of capitalist enterprises (including changes consequent upon the demise of the USSR and its associated political and economic system). Although this diversity of 'labour process' work might be construed as a weakness, it does indicate a position that sees work as interrelated with wider factors, and not confined to narrow managerialist concerns, nor the manipulation of workers in the interests of supposed efficiencies (see, for instance, Smith *et al.*, 1991; Smith and Thompson 1992).

SUBJECTIVITY

However, the introduction of 'high theory', and its appearance in 'labour process theory' does raise one of the most contentious debates in labour process.

Willmott, and particularly Knights, (jointly and individually) have sought to address the 'problem of the missing subject' which Thompson highlighted (Thompson 1989, 1990). In doing so, they appear often to be in direct conflict with those who claim, like Thompson, that there is a core of labour process research and theory which should remain distinct from wider considerations in the sociology of work. The core of the idea is that while it is possible to delineate the structural features of capitalism, and argue its oppressive and exploitative nature, it is difficult to compare such analyses with actual political movements or transformations based on perception of such exploitations by those involved, that is by labour itself. Conversely, there is interest in how labour perceives its own situation – it being common to both positions that some consciousness is necessary for action.

The nature of *subjectivity* – how people are made subject within work organizations (and wider social structures) and how they themselves perceive their situation and consequently act on it, has emerged as a significant area in labour process studies. The connection with organizational behaviour is in the shift to the level of analysis of the self and action based on perceptions. However, the direction taken is distinct from organizational behaviour's essentially psychologistic approach, for here the intent is to see how workers seek to control their own involvement in work and the possibilities within it, with particular emphasis on resistance to managerial control.

The arguments have perhaps seemed persuasive because of their appeal to the generalities of human existence. Connections with basic sociology and indeed psychoanalysis are common. Perhaps for this reason some commentators see the work produced as straying too far from the core of labour process concerns (which they identify as specifically capitalist political and economic frameworks). The result of the recent studies in subjectivity are seen from this perspective as prioritizing of issues of identity, with the result that the focus becomes rather small-scale studies of specific workplaces – a regressive step to the limited workplace studies which Braverman's work helped to break up.

Warhurst argues that the concentration on subjectivity is at the expense of ideas about exploitation and that objective factors such as managerial authority or the disciplines of the market are suppressed (Warhurst 1995: 5).

New directions in studies of subjectivity can be traced to interest in the work of French philosophers, notably Michel Foucault (1977a), particularly the notion of surveillance in *Discipline and Punish* (Foucault 1977a). The notion of the 'panopticon' – a total surveillance system – was seen to be a tendency within managerial control systems, both in terms of organizational design with inherent systems of accountabilities and in terms of techniques of electronic control allowing a minute control of work without direct supervision. So a line of thought which emphasized the role of surveillance and especially surveillance at a distance could easily become part of the critical approach to labour process analysis.

However, Foucault's arguments extended also into issues of identity and power. The core of his argument is that people are party to their own situation – that rules and controls are not simply devised and imposed but are also accepted: that to become subject implies an acceptance. This idea has resonances within industrial sociology in issues of compliance at work, and also in basic sociology as the idea of human society being both a cage and a framework for action.

The idea of identity is thus an idea which has existing connections within the field of study and is indeed connected with Marx's ideas on the essential nature of humankind ('species being'), although it does not imply acceptance of Marx's ideas on the nature of man being bound into work. Unfortunately, in a sense, identity is a focus in other fields of study such as philosophy and psychoanalysis. While such areas provide material that can be used they do so from contexts which do not translate directly into a labour process, or indeed wider political societal framework.

Knights and Willmott (1989) attempt a summary of the justification for the interest in these developments. They start by noting that subjectivity and power are central to labour process analyses in general, and that Foucault's approach might help in understanding the relations between the two, especially noting the argument that for Foucault subjectivity or self-consciousness is a product of involvement in relations of power through which conceptions of identity are generated. Identity is then used to tie subjects into power relations. They become dependent on them, so subjectivity has both positive and negative aspects: resistance is possible because subjects are only partially tied to power relations for confirmation of their identity. Knights and Willmott are fully aware of the dangers of losing sight of objective structures through concentrating too much on subjective consciousness (Knights and Willmott 1989: 537) and are intent on using the approach to emphasize resistance and control at work.

Knights and Willmott argue accordingly that a consideration of subjectivity serves to overcome the split between objective analyses of class and the way that class relations are inter-subjectively reproduced, doing away with elements of determinism that might be detected in Braverman's model, and allowing for pluralism and diversity in the analysis of the labour process together with power–knowledge relations that encompass both technological and environmental factors (cf. Knights in Knights and Willmott 1990).

Notably Knights (in Knights and Willmott 1990: 553) argues that forms of power are exercised through the individual's own identity and are not to be thought of as the direct operation of mechanisms of the forces of production, class struggle or ideological structures: subjectivity is a mediator, itself the product of disciplinary mechanisms or techniques of surveillance and power–knowledge strategies (see also Knights and Willmott 1990: 320).

Willmott tries to develop a more adequate materialist theory of subjectivity (Knights and Willmott 1990: 337ff). Key ideas are the ways in which self-consciousness has become individualized in the process of capitalist self-development, which differs from Marx's conceptualization of class relations and interests, although incorporating a re-working of Marx's own ideas on subjectivity. Willmott emphasizes (Knights and Willmott 1990: 354) the symbolic aspects of workers' existence, while recognizing the ways in which identity is constituted by institutions – and that these identities may be treated as commodities within the capitalist labour process. Willmott argues that capitalist labour processes are also the 'outcome of, and are conditional upon, the efforts of workers and managers to organize their respective identities' (Knights and Willmott 1990: 358)

This focus on subjectivities and identities has been extended by Knights, in particular, into a post-structuralist approach to the labour process, which seeks to problematize the terms of the debate itself.

O'Doherty and Willmott (1998) raise a series of problems with Knights' position, essentially arguing that his 'anti-realist' position, and the terms and concepts used to explore it, only serve to obscure the topic, making it difficult to see what use might be made of thinking derived from this position: that an uncluttered reading and exposition of post-structuralist ideas is what is required to inform labour process debates.

O'Doherty and Willmott (1998) propose a post-structuralist approach which explores issues which surely have a strong claim to appear in Organizational Behaviour textbooks, since they deal with the formation of self-identity, primarily in work situations, but which form no part of current organizational texts (with the notable exception of Clark *et al.* 1994). They argue for consideration of a post-structuralist approach but one incorporating attempts to theorize subjectivity. They argue (1994: 12ff) that their approach implies a 'critique of humanistic psychology, which sees the potential for fulfilment of those at work as essentially unproblematical and that of post-humanistic psychology which problematizes the idea of a unified sovereign subject whose potential for fulfilment is simply impeded by oppressive structures'.

Essentially the human being is seen as undetermined, and therefore not able to fit into the carefully devised schemata of Organizational Behaviour as well as conventional management text approaches. In addition the subject – worker, employee or manager – is seen not simply to be resisting because of the commodity status of labour, but as a result of more diffuse and complex social processes, which may very well be contradictory. For instance, the social relations of capitalism pre-suppose a free autonomous subject to enter into labour exchange relations. But this particular subjectivity and its contradictions will affect the relations found in capitalist labour processes. The worker can see themselves as free and use such freedom to achieve aspects of self-identity. Such self-identities allow for transformational opportunities which post-structuralist positions do not allow for. O'Doherty and Willmott (1998) argue that such contradictions and transformations are primarily social and not based in the psychology of the individual, and that the senses of self are located in the particular capitalist structure of production.

This kind of thinking requires a look again at the basics, having explored some of the contemporary labour investigations and conceptualizations inspired by or influenced by, or focused on, the capitalist labour process. For while current research has raised intellectual and practical research issues, we cannot ignore the arguments that such interests have drifted too far from the initial focus and concerns.

Our aim here has been to contrast the critical approaches to organizational behaviour and management generated by labour process analysis with the, at best, partially humanistic approach of traditional Organizational Behaviour textbooks, in particular to point to conflicts, contradictions, exploitation, hierarchies, power and resistances as well as the sources of consent and self-identities and to point to the essentially limited and prescriptive nature of current organizational behaviour writing.

But it may be that the reader feels that we have moved too much into the realms of obscurity or high theory, so we end with a review of the basic propositions of the analysis of the capitalist labour process and some arguments for its continuing relevance.

CONCLUSION

Organizational Behaviour textbooks in essence try to present a humanistic psychology as applied to the world of (Western, capitalist) work. This is itself no mean feat, since it has been a long battle to have this kind of thinking accepted as part of management thinking, and it has to some extent mitigated the worst effects of capitalism up until say the mid-1980s when ideas of corporatism receded politically. But this approach has adopted the language and assumptions of the management that it seeks supposedly to understand and study. It is essentially unquestioning of the political and economic as well as wider aspects of the social framework in which it operates. It does provide insights into areas of social psychology, but it is limited in terms of its basic assumptions. It has a method of enquiry, based largely on observation and/or contrived quasi-experiments. Increasingly the subject is put across by means of limited case studies which purport to show the operation of particular principles. Yet such case studies are frequently open to unacknowledged challenging or contradictory interpretations. It is plausible now to see organizational behaviour no longer as an independent enquiry, but as part of the ideological apparatus of management. And increasingly *management* forms the focus: the workers, like capital itself, have largely ceased to appear on the agenda.

Of even greater concern is the lack of critical inquiry into what the subject itself is doing. There is little critique of the practices or accumulated findings of the subject and of course few new ideas. An inspection of texts such as Luthans (1995) finds many inventive and informative situations described, and frequently analysed, but little change in the content or basic ideas between the first and latest editions.

Work in the labour process tradition stands in contrast. Debates, arguments and critiques are inherent in the area. Indeed the variety of arguments and directions can mean a degree of confusion for those new to the subject: the subject does not just offer a critique of the subject matter, but often a critique of its own practices, approaches and assumptions – it is a reflexive subject.

It challenges or asserts many notions – that organizations consist of managers only, that workers engage in resistances. It looks at the realities of lack of motivation, rule formation and breaking, negotiations over control, compliance and non-compliance, core and peripheral workers, wages, skill and deregulation, and more recently, identity and subjectivity. It not only reflects current movements in Western capitalism (with an emphasis on labour) but also seeks to introduce ideas, explanations and factors from social, political and economic frameworks.

Yet it has to be conceded that perhaps the diversity of concerns has weakened the focus. This is a position strongly argued by Thompson (1990), who pleads for a re-focusing on the core of labour process work (see also Warhurst 1995: 22). Thompson's points may not fairly reflect the range of subject matters now current but they can still be thought of as constituting a core of labour process thought. In essence these are that a capitalist system necessarily exploits labour through paying it less than the surplus achieved through selling the products: that this process is resisted, although this resistance is complex in its forms: that the process of capitalist competition requires progressive exploitation of labour (in various ways, including deskilling) and that the whole process of production produces movements at political and social levels.

Organizations can then be interpreted in terms of these basic assumptions in a way that strips away the rhetoric employed by capitalist societies to justify the social structures which result from its production methods.

REFERENCES

Ackers, P. *et al.* (1996) *The New Work Place Trade Unionism*, Routledge, London.
Braverman, H. (1974) *Labor and Monopoly Capital*, Monthly Review Press, New York.
Brighton Labour Process Group (1977) The Capitalist Labour Process, *Capital and Class*, No. 1, Spring.
Burawoy, M. (1979) *Manufacturing Consent*, University of Chicago Press, Chigaco.
Clark, H., Chandler, J. and Barry, J. (eds) (1994) *Organisations and Identity*, Chapman and Hall, London.
Edwards, R. (1979) *Contested Terrain: The Transformation of the Workplace in the Twentieth Century*, Basic Books, New York.
Elger, A. (1979) Valorisation and deskilling: a critique of Braverman, *Capital and Class*, No. 2, Spring.
Foucault, M. (1977a) *Discipline and Punish*, Penguin, Harmondsworth.
Foucault, M. (1977b) *The Birth of the Prison*, trans A. Sheridan, Pantheon, New York.
Friedman, A.L. (1978) *Industry and Labour*, Macmillan, London.
Johnston, R. (1980) Bus Crews: a Labour Process Analysis, Ph.D. thesis, University of Edinburgh.
Knights, D. and Verdubakis, T. (1994) in J.M. Jermier, D. Knights and W.R. Nord (eds), *Resistance and Power*, Routledge, London.
Knights, D. and Willmott, H.(1989) Power and subjectivity at work: from degradation to subjugation, *Social Relations*, 123 (4), 535–58.
Knights, D. and Willmott, H. (1990) *Labour Process Theory*, Macmillan, London.
Littler, C.R. (1982) *The Development of the Labour Process in Capitalist Societies*, Heineman, Oxford.
Littler, C.R. and Salaman, G. (1982) Bravermania and Beyond: Recent Theories in the Labour Process, *Sociology*, Vol. 16, No. 2, 251–69.
Luthans, F. (1995) *Organizational Behavior* (7th edn) McGraw Hill, New York.
O'Doherty, D. and Willmott, H. (1998) 'Recent Contributions to the Development of Labour Process Analyses', 16th Labour Process Conference, Manchester.
Pollert, A. (1991) *Farewell to Flexibility*, Basil Blackwell, Oxford.
Rose, M. (1975) *Industrial Behaviour*, Allen Lane, Middlesex.
Smith, C. and Thompson, P. (1992) 'When Harry met Sally', 10th Labour Process Conference, Aston.
Smith, C., Knights, D. and Willmott, H. (1991) *White Collar Work: the Non-manual Labour Process*, Macmillan, London.
Thompson, P. (1983) *The Nature of Work: An Introduction to Debates in the Labour Process*, Macmillan, London.
Thompson, P. (1989) *The Nature of Work: An Introduction to Debates in the Labour Process*, Macmillan, London.
Thompson, P. (1990) 'Crawling from the Wreckage Labour Process Theory' in D. Knights and H. Willmott (eds) *Labour Process Theory*, Macmillan, London.

Thompson, P. and Ackroyd, S. (1995) All quiet on the workplace front? A critique of recent trends in British industrial sociology, *Sociology*, 29 (4).

Warhurst, C. (1995) 'Flawed but not Floored: Labour Process Analysis in the 1990s'. 13th Labour Process Conference, Blackpool.

Williams, K., Haslam, C., Williams, J., Johal. S., Adcroft, A. and Willis, R. (1994) Defend the social settlement: A memo for Labour, *Renewal*, Vol. 1, No. 3.

Willmott, H. (1990) 'Subjectivity and the Dialectics of Praxis: Opening up the Core of Labour Process Analysis' in Knights, D. and Willmott, H., *Labour Process Theory*, Macmillan, London.

3 Postmodernizing organizational behaviour: new organizations or new organization theory?

Martin Parker

INTRODUCTION

> Why do we find it congenial to speak of organizations as structures but not clouds, systems but not songs, weak or strong but not tender or passionate? Is it because organizations physically resemble one but not the other, that we somehow discern through the clamorous hurly burly something that is structural, but not cloudlike, systemic rather then rhapsodic, strong but not tender? What kind of 'structure' could we have in mind that the continual movements of eyeballs, arms, legs, words, papers, and so on should bear a physical resemblance? And are those who think they observe structure simply blind to systemic 'process', and those who spy 'strength' insensitive to obvious signals of 'tenderness'? (Gergen 1992: 207).

Over the last decade there have been a number of attempts to push the study of organizations towards issues that it has tended to marginalize. Indeed, this book illustrates that organizational behaviour in particular is beginning to develop an engagement with gender, power, control, culture, ethics and so on. Another term which is often mentioned in this context is 'postmodernism', and quite a few writers are making claims for its importance that deserve careful scrutiny (see, for reviews of this literature, Hassard and Parker 1993, Boje *et al.* 1996, Chia 1996, Alvesson and Deetz 1996, and Calas and Smircich 1997). This chapter will sympathetically outline some of these claims and then attempt to evaluate them in terms of the difference between thinking about 'post-modern' organizations, or studying organizational behaviour in a 'postmodern' way. That is to say, are we looking for new kinds of organizations, or are we studying organizations with new methods?

But first, where did the word 'postmodernism' come from? Though it had been used before, it was popularized in the late 1970s as an architectural term which referred to a reaction against monolithic modernist brutalism – the tower block for example – in favour of architectures that employed 'reflexivity, irony, artifice, randomness, anarchy, fragmentation, pastiche and allegory' (Ryan 1988: 559). At roughly the same time it was being applied in literary criticism to less linear modes of writing, and quickly entered English-speaking social science via those interested in European writings on philosophy and culture. Whilst the work of the post-structuralist philosophers Jacques Derrida and Michel Foucault is central here, Jean-Francois Lyotard's *The Postmodern Condition* (1984) is probably one of the most widely cited texts in recent social theory. Since then, and most particularly in the last 10 years, postmodernism has moved into areas of interest to organization theorists with increasing rapidity. The term is now widely used in writing about culture in sociology and cultural studies, and much debate has been stimulated about its usefulness, or otherwise, as a tool for explaining emergent features of contemporary societies (Lash and Urry 1987; Connor 1989; Harvey 1989; Lash 1990, Giddens 1990, Cahoone 1996).

In some ways, this connection between postmodernity and culture helps to explain its importation into organization studies. Though those working in the area have been interested in the 'climate', 'atmosphere' or 'personality' of organizations for many years, the publication of Peters and Waterman's *In Search of Excellence* (1982) heralded an explosion of literature on explicitly 'cultural' issues. Whilst much of it has predictably been of the managerial 'quick fix' variety there have also been a number of attempts to avoid normative prescriptions and focus attention on language, myth, symbolism, ritual and so on. Given these developments it was hardly surprising that postmodernism began to be discussed by those who were interested in alternative perspectives on organizations. After all, if our culture is being transformed then perhaps our theories need to change too. A second theme has undoubtedly been the increasing concern with the flexible firm, virtual organization, post-Fordism and so on. The suggestion that organizations are being transformed has led to a huge literature which seeks to describe and understand the nature of that transformation and the new times we find ourselves working in.

Now these two lineages – culturalism and new organizations – seem to have led to the raising of two kinds of question. First, can we use a postmodern analysis to think about organization in a different way? Second, what are the characteristics of a postmodern organization, postmodern job, postmodern economy and so on? Though these questions are related, I think that they should be seen as analytically distinct. To collapse them, as some writers do, will lead to confusion on both counts. However, before I get to this argument, I want to begin by outlining some of the uses (and abuses) of postmodernity from within recent writing on organizing and organizations.

POSTMODERNISM

To define postmodernity, postmodernism or postmodernization would appear to be a futile task. It is not one school of thought and since many of its adherents refuse the language and logic of 'definition' in the first place it is difficult to throw around definitions to their or my satisfaction (Alvesson 1995). I shall instead simply try to indicate some of the concerns raised under the umbrella of postmodernism as they seem relevant to organizational behaviour. Initially it seems important to focus the distinction on what postmodernism claims to reject – the 'modernist' or 'enlightenment' project. The enlightenment is usually taken to mean the historical period during which the light thrown by rationality begins to banish pre-modern superstition and myth. Modernism can hence be characterized as a belief system which has elevated a faith in scientific reason to a level at which it becomes equated with progress. For modernists, the world is seen as a system which comes increasingly under human control as our knowledge of it increases. The common terms for this kind of belief system are positivism, empiricism and science – all sharing a faith in the power of the rational mind to understand nature, that which is 'out there'. There are, of course, many versions of modernism with divergent politics and methodologies but at their core is a rationalism that is essentially unchallengeable and a faith that it is ultimately possible to communicate the results of this kind of enquiry to other rational beings.

In contrast the postmodernist suggests that this is a form of intellectual imperialism that ignores the fundamental uncontrollability of meaning. The 'out there' is constructed by our linguistic conceptions of it and these conceptions are collectively sustained and continually re-negotiated in the process of making sense. The consequence of this is that we are advised to stop attempting to 'systematize', 'define' or impose a logic on events and instead recognize the limitations of all our projects. The role of language in constituting 'reality' is central and all our futile attempts to capture 'truth' should be seen for what they really are – forms of discourse. Further to this, it is often suggested that society, culture and politics are actually in transformation. New forms of social and organizational being are emerging that have little relation to the capitalist or industrialist systems that have constituted human beings throughout the last century. Connecting these ideas is an assumption that new times need new methodologies, novel ways of looking at social processes. If the world is changing, then our theories need to change too.

Prompted by these challenges to social 'science', there are a growing number of writers who claim that these ideas have application to the theory and practice of organization studies. The most numerically common theme in the literature is to claim that there is clearly a new kind of organization emerging which differs from classic organizations in most aspects. In this regard Heydebrand (1989) has suggested that we are witnessing the birth of a post-bureaucratic organizational form. He refers to

> a thoroughly intentional, conscious postmodern strategy of increasing the flexibility of social structures and making them amenable to new forms of indirect and internalized control, including cultural and ideological control (1989: 345).

This argument is echoed in Cooke – the author suggesting that bureaucratic methods of structuring are being replaced by the 'post-modern corporation' (1990: 143). An organizational structure that is numerically and functionally flexible, with no clear centre of power or spatio/temporal location would therefore be an example of the class 'postmodern'. Aronowitz (1989: 47) similarly suggests that the dispersal and deterritorialization of production is one of the features of society that has led to the postmodern 'shift in sensibility' and Gephart (1996) connects these developments to the decline of the modern bureaucratic state. Finally, on a rather different level, Alvesson (1990) notes the coincidence between postmodernist forms of thought and the increasing importance of corporate identity statements, images and marketing in understanding contemporary organizations. It seems that the decline of the modernist bureaucracy might result in an increased emphasis on managing the 'surface', rather than the structure, of the organization.

Many of these themes are reiterated in Stewart Clegg's book *Modern Organizations* (1990). Subtitled *Organization Theory in the Postmodern World*, it is a clear attempt to ground the notion of a postmodern organization in empirical data. He argues that there are forms of organization emerging that bear little or no relation to modernist variations on the theme of bureaucracy. These new organizations are 'de-differentiated' (see Lash 1990), flexible, niche marketed and have a multi-skilled workforce held together through information technology networks and sub-contracting (Clegg 1990: 181). He backs up this assertion with international evidence on the development of organizational forms with high labour responsibility, process variability and product innovation (1990: 218). Clegg clearly sees postmodern organizational forms as arenas that are, as yet, relatively unexplored but bring with them the possibility of progressive developments for the development of industrial democracy and the skill enhancement of labour – as in Sweden for example. There is, however, also the possibility of postmodern organizations being seductive but essentially repressive and exclusive. These organizations would rely on a segmented labour force with a clear stratification of privilege – like Japan. However, against the 'there is no Alternative tendency' of organizational developmental logic he argues that there is a choice to develop new forms that best suit the needs of a postmodern world (Clegg 1990: 58, 235). As he puts it: 'Postmodernity requires management. Organization does not simply fade away' (1990: 17).

On a more self-consciously theoretical level, in 1988 Robert Cooper and Gibson Burrell began publishing a series of papers in *Organization Studies* which were an explicit attempt to show the relevance of postmodernist concerns to the study of organizations. To date four have appeared and I will examine the first three in chronological order. In the first paper Cooper and Burrell (1988) begin by outlining the nature of the modernist–postmodernist debate. A central feature of their argument is that it reflects a return to Weber's concerns about the 'iron cage' of rational bureaucratic organization. Whilst they see Weber as expressing the processual and fragile nature of organizational life his writings have been reread by organization theorists through most of the century as a description of a system that is discrete and subject to control. The notion of an observer who is capable of constructing a meta-language is central to this kind of modernist project. By gaining knowledge we get power over organizations, we can design them, be experts on them. From Comte's systems theory onwards, they see a continued attempt to produce prescriptions for a scientifically designed organization. The aim of this expertise is framed in terms of the grand narrative of progress which is manifested within organizations as a concern for 'efficiency', 'minimization of conflict', 'profitability' and so on. The increasing complexity and unpredictability of industrial societies is placed under control by 'ordering social relations according to the model of functional rationality' (1988: 96). Thus for the system to control inputs and outputs it must be able to structure the world, both in terms of its employees and its environment. The modernist project facilitates this control – it allows predictive and prescriptive statements about organizations to be made with confidence.

By contrast, if we rule out the possibility of an objective standpoint or form of explanation that is superior to any other, then interpretation becomes central. Any study of organizations is thus as good as any other, the main difference is in motivation, in the interests of the observer-participant. The objective of the postmodernist is hence not to 'totalize', to express a trans-historical truth, because that is a futile endeavour. Instead she or he recognizes the fundamental instability of organization, the sense in which language and action are never final but only moves within a game that lead to further possibilities. Postmodernism instead attempts to disrupt our sense of normality – to make strange what is familiar by questioning everyday assumptions about the relations between terms.

Answers to problems about organizational systems should thus get turned into problems about answers. Language is evidently central here, but it is no longer simply a bare object language that communicates facts about the world. Instead it is seen as a discourse that constitutes our sense of the world in order to exercise power over it. The postmodernist must attempt to reveal these power relations – to expose the fragility of organizational life and the mythical nature of its stability.

Cooper and Burrell then draw on these characterizations to suggest that much of the writing on organizations has been prompted by a reaction to problems defined by the modernist project. Organizations, workers and managers are defined as bounded entities with certain functional characteristics. In contrast postmodernity would focus on 'the production of organization rather than the organization of production' (Cooper and Burrell 1988: 106). The implication of this strategy is that we must rid ourselves of the notion that organizations are created and then themselves go on to structure relationships. Instead the analysis should continually recognize its own role in creating a discourse on organization as a verb. The formal/informal, official/ unofficial distinctions commonly made by organization theorists become clear for what they really are, moral imperatives that presuppose objects in order to capture them and hence exclude other 'immoral' activities. For postmodernists the informal, small-scale and continual attempts at making meaning work within organization become all that we can really observe and participate in. A further implication is that academic work must be recognized for what it is – more words in a competing babble of voices with no particular claim to priority over any others.

Burrell's paper (1988), the second in the series, attempts to suggest areas in which Michel Foucault's writings may be of use to organization studies. He suggests that it might be fruitful to consider the sense in which the disciplining effect of organizing constructs the individuals within them. However, this is not simply a version of the dominant ideology thesis but a far more embracing formulation. Expanding the metaphor of the prison, organizations are sites within which power constitutes all subjects and subjectivities. Moreover, we cannot simply step outside this institutional discipline since our social world is productively constituted in this way. We are all always members whether we like it or not. For Foucault, organizations are 'prisons' in the sense that the prison is what gives us both our individuality and our sameness. The use of decision theory, information technology, human resource management and so on simply refines the process of capture, we are watched and we watch ourselves. From the factory to the university, the capillaries of power structure our meanings and our actions. As a result, any simplistic distinction between coercive and liberal organizations should therefore be treated with extreme caution.

The third paper in this series, Cooper's (1989) paper on Jacques Derrida, explores a theory of language that underlies much of postmodernism. Derrida's conception of language as inherently undecidable suggests that our attempts to reduce it to uncomplicated 'communication' are highly suspect. In the name of a grand narrative we attempt to halt the endless flows of meaning in containers like organizations. Writing, formalizing, administrating are ways to manage language but they contain within themselves contradictions that can be opened through the process of deconstruction. Again, this is no simple strategy of revealing a false consciousness, but a continual process of evading the concrete. When we write 'organization' we must see it as a process/verb that needs disorganization in order to exist. Thus things 'out there' like the market, employees and customers are called into being by language and are not pre-existing objects in a relation to the observer and each other that simply needs to be understood by 'science'. Most writing on organizations evades this problem by misrecognizing the model and the method for organization itself – the fallacy of misplaced concreteness, or the metaphysics of presence. If you look for a system you will find one. So, writings on 'bureaucracy', for example, summon up an object of study but also invoke subjectivities which are subordinated to it. Once we use any term as our frame of reference it becomes dominant and unquestioned, but always brings with it its opposite which can be used deconstructively to undermine its concreteness. In terms of power there are clear parallels with Foucault in this account. The professions of organization, management, accountancy, personnel and so on invoke their objects of control through their writing. Divisions of labour and institutional logics are made self-justifying through discourse. Deconstructing these discourses, or questioning the common sense of taken-for-granted language, can reveal the power relations and hierarchies that produce our everyday understandings. 'Within the specific context of organizational analysis (. . .) this means that the "writing of organization" must be overturned in favour of the "organization of writing"' (Cooper 1989: 501).

Whilst Cooper's and Burrell's papers consciously avoided being programmatic, a chapter by Kenneth Gergen (1992) is much less circumspect. He argues that organization theory has up to now been shaped by the twin discourses of romanticism and modernism, but that these discourses are beginning to be exhausted. Replacing them is the emergent discourse of postmodernism and he suggestively outlines the possibilities that this new language opens up within organization theory. For Gergen, the romantic discourse is centrally constituted around the notion of a 'deep interior' to the individual. This 'soul' is what generates our needs for creativity, self-expression, sociability and a moral attitude towards other unique persons. Within organization theory it is reflected in the work of the human relations movement, psychoanalytic approaches, hierarchy of need psychology and writings on management and leadership that stress creativity and commitment. In contrast, the modernist discourse gains its sustenance from a central belief in the power of reason to produce a meta-language for predicting what the world will do next. Intellectual work is progressive in that, if done scientifically, it brings us ever closer to the truth and thus the possibility for control. Within this discourse there is also a great reliance on machine metaphors – descriptions of the world that put forward systematic causal connections between events. For organization behaviour this has resulted in scientific management, systems theory and a psychology that assumes individuals have predictable patterns of behaviour which can connect with organizations in productive ways.

For Gergen both these discourses are still alive, particularly the modernist one, but they are coming under increasing challenge from the margins. Wittgensteinian philosophies of language, ethnomethodological approaches, feminist critiques, semiotics and deconstructionism have all combined to make these older discourses look increasingly dogmatic. Gergen is careful not to suggest that postmodernity therefore has greater explanatory power. He simply says that it resonates more closely with 'the intellectual and cultural *Zeitgeist*' (1992: 208). This postmodern spirit of the times is one that brings representation, not reality, to the fore and acknowledges that it is not possible to rectify or avoid the problem of language. Moreover, there is a stress on the collectiveness of representational practices. The discrete individual is a fiction that we can better do without. The final, and perhaps most contentious, part of Gergen's formulation of postmodernity is the importance of reflexivity and self-criticism. He suggests that since we can no longer pretend that we are persuing truth, we recognize instead that what we are engaged in is 'serious play'.

> The view of knowledge making as a transcendent pursuit, removed from the trivial enthralments of daily life, pristinely rational, and transparently virtuous, becomes so much puffery. We should view these bodies of language we call knowledge in a lighter vein – as ways of putting things, some pretty and others petty – but in no sense calling for ultimate commitments, condemnations, or profound consequences. We should be rather more playful with our sayings. (Gergen 1992: 215).

In other words, the only criteria for judgement of a theory is whether we feel it lends itself to patterns of social life that we like or dislike, whether we feel that it has positive or negative consequences.

With respect to organizational theory Gergen feels that there is some writing that is beginning to move in a postmodern direction and he cites (among others) Gareth Morgan's *Images of Organization* (1986) as an example. His own substantive contribution, towards the end of his paper, draws on Cooper and Burrell (1988) and attempts to formulate a theory of power in organizations which is indebted to Foucault. This involves stressing that the rationalities deployed within an organization are relative and collective. There is no absolute criteria for truth and wisdom inside or outside any given organization and those 'truths' that are utilized are continually subject to re-negotiation and re-encoding by others within the negotiation. Given this continual state of flux, power becomes a matter of constraining signifiers to agree on acceptable organizational aims. One of the key organizational problems that this leads to is the increasing solidity of local rationalities – accounting, marketing and so on – and their increasing incapacity to speak outside their locally agreed languages. This results in organizations, and departments within organizations, becoming increasingly powerless to achieve control over that which is outside their rationality. To restore power, to prevent this attempt at capturing meaning, requires that organizations must be more open to the spillages of meaning that language contains. Their members must become less a part of an organization, and more participants in the process of organizing, continually bringing new rationalities to bear on the process. The ability to continually speak new languages, to use new rationalities is therefore a pre-requisite for postmodern organizing.

ORGANIZATION OR ORGANIZATION THEORY?

The writings of Clegg, Cooper, Burrell, Gergen and others are clearly pointing the way forward to a theory, method and object of organizations that looks very different to the discipline as it is currently taught and researched – even in a 'critical' text like this one. In this section I wish to evaluate the possibilities and problems of this programme from a broadly sympathetic standpoint. As I've already indicated, the distinction which underlies my critique is the difference between post-modernity as a historical period and postmodernity as a theoretical perspective. This is similar to Zygmunt Bauman's distinction between 'a sociology of postmodernity' and 'a postmodern sociology' (1988a, 1988b). From here on I will insert a hyphen in the term when I wish it to be understood as the former – and it should be noted that I have not employed this device in the chapter so far.

So, the first use of the term that I distinguish is as a periodization, 'post-modernity', after the period of the modern. The ground here is epistemologically fairly stable and involves a search for features of the external world that can confirm the hypothesis that our society is moving into a different epoch. It is important to note that this is an ontology, a theory of what exists, which assumes some kind of realist epistemology, a theory of how we can know the world. In other words, the world is out there and we simply need to find the right way of describing it. There is a sense in which this 'post' is related to a proliferation of other terms which refer to specific features of post-modern society. Post-Fordism, post-capitalism, post-industrialism and information society are the most common (Bell 1973; Piore and Sabel 1984; Harvey 1989) but Callinicos lists 15 others that share this naming of a new era (1989: 25). A common theme is disorganization, untidyness, flexibility, globalization – the structures that we have been used to since the industrial revolution are fragmenting into diverse networks held together with information technology and underpinned by a 'postmodernist *(sic)* sensibility' (Lash and Urry 1987: 285). These 'New Times' are seen to require explanation and codification (see Hall and Jacques 1989). If we can understand them we may be able to exercise some control over them, and this holds true for those of the political left just as the managerialist right.

For organization theory the implications of post-modernity are fairly clear: find evidence for a radical shift in organizational structure and functioning and document it. In its essence this approach becomes a process of organizational design – the aim being to provide a set of prescriptions for the organized world to survive in the post-modern era (Gephart *et al.* 1996). Texts will be written that suggest methods for achieving this kind of organization and be taught on MBA courses as the latest and best method for achieving organizational competitiveness and efficiency. The culturalist movement reflects a move in this direction – at its boldest it is a suggestion that structure is simply a reflection of the built commitment of individuals. Get a good flexible culture and change will become an opportunity for excellence and not a problem. The grand (modernist) narrative is still haunting these arguments – science will help us find methods for organizing in an increasingly turbulent, globalizing and complex society.

I contrasted the post-modern periodization with postmodernism – without a hyphen. My understanding of the postmodern perspective relies heavily on post-structuralist philosophy – the writings of Derrida, Foucault and Lyotard – and is essentially epistemological in nature. It is an approach to the question 'how can we know the world?' Since the world is seen as constituted by our shared language the answer is that we can only know it through the particular forms of discourse that our language creates.

Moreover, this language, these symbols, are continually in flux. Meaning can never reside within one term but is continually slipping beyond our grasp. The task of the writer is therefore to recognize and expose this slippage but never with the aim of creating a meta-discourse that can explain all other forms of language. If we are to look at organization (as a verb) in this way we must be continually recognizing the impossibility of the formal structure. The myth of structure is simply one of the ways in which social life is continually constituted. Instead the postmodern organization theorist must be attempting to uncover the messy edges of the mythical structure, the places where the organizing process becomes confused and defies definition by the discourses that are used within it. As Power suggests

> the postmodernist perspective flows from a denial that there is any single, ultimate or deep language game that is uniquely determinative of organizational stability. The organization theorist must be sensitive to the diversity and fluidity of the 'life' of organization and no one model will suffice to orientate research (Power 1990: 121).

What might writing like this look like? First, it could be of no obvious practical use to instrumental organizers since it would be aimed at illustrating the limits of any of their projects. This would include conventional organizational behaviourists, whose attempts at codification and sytematization are just as prone to the myth of the grand narrative of the enlightenment. Secondly, it would be writing that would seek to undermine all the conventions of administrative/academic discourse. It would have to be as disruptive and difficult as possible, continually seeking to evade the ground on which it might stand. Once the descent into the maelstrom of indeterminacy has been made there is no looking back, and no raft of logic to climb on to. Thirdly, it would make no claim to be any more than another language game. This kind of writing could assume no prior place as more 'accurate' or 'truthful' than other accounts of organizational life.

If this distinction between epoch and epistemology is accepted then the implications are severe. The key point is that writers on organizations must be clear when they are trying to find post-modernity and when they are being postmodern. If the social world is no more than colliding discourses, variations on empiricism are simply going to re-produce the fictions of the world under the name of facts. To be postmodern is a task that requires teachers and students to radically rethink their relation to the subject, as it is presently constituted. Even chapters like this one, that rely on a linear logic backed up by reference to a shared discourse, would have to be replaced by something altogether more disruptive. Gergen's paper does attempt to display a more rhetorically elegant version of organizational writing (see the quotation that begins this chapter for example) but none of the other texts I have covered move away from a recognizably social scientific discourse. For someone who wanted to write a postmodern text this would have to be unacceptable. Radical doubt would require that their textual strategies and their motivations for wanting to write at all would be called into close scrutiny, an uncomfortable task for authors at the best of times.

However, if we are looking for post-modernity then much of the institutional and rhetorical apparatus that serves us now may be useful in the future. We should be able to decide when a particular organization or process is post-modern and when it is modern and this will require a belief in the power of rationality that may be flexible but is still at base 'scientific' in the broadest sense of the term. Our language may require 'cleaning up' but it will not need a radical re-constitution (see for example Sandelands and Drazin 1989). Furthermore there would be no compelling reason to move away from writing within the rules of social science – and publishing these writings in textbooks and journals that find a ready home in the library classification system.

Now, as I have presented them, neither of these alternatives looks particularly attractive, though for rather different reasons. The postmodern epistemology is certainly theoretically watertight and provides a bastion from which to ward off dangerous criticism. Terry Eagleton commented that the advantage of this relativist position

> is that it allows you to drive a coach and horses through anybody else's beliefs while not saddling you with the inconvenience of having to adopt any yourself. Such deconstruction is a power game . . . the winner is the one who manages to get rid of all his cards and sit with empty hands (Eagleton 1983: 144, 147).

All competing positions are ruled out by an all-embracing meta-theory. Power notes that if we take this position to its conclusion it would 'outlaw all talk of organization in any sense' (1990: 123). The problem is whether this is not any more than a retreat into the sophistry of academic speculation. If the real world does not exist in anything other than discourse then is writing one interpretation of some texts a worthwhile pursuit? The problems of (fictional) individuals in (mythic) organizations are safely placed behind philosophical double-glazing and their cries are treated as interesting examples of discourse. Many commentators, particularly those of a Marxist disposition, have problems with this position. Harvey suggests this is at base a version of nihilism (1989: 116), Callinicos characterizes postmodernists as fiddling while Rome burns (1989: 174) and Thompson (1993) suggests that this is a 'fatal distraction' from the problems and politics of the real world.

The post-modern periodization fares much better on this count since new organizational and economic forms are seen as 'real' entities with 'real' implications for 'real' people. The theorist has both a reason and a method for investigating the new world we are living in, but only as long as the full implications of the 'hard' postmodern epistemological critique are not accepted. If they are, then post-modernity becomes another example of the grand narrative of 'history' – naming moments in a seamless web of time and then arguing over the distinctions thereby produced. How, after all, are we to know whether our times are post-modern or not? What kind of evidence could be used to support such a grand claim? It could be argued that, for 'new times' post-modernists, the postmodern critique had simply been incorporated and that, though the language might be different, the underlying discourse of knowledge and progress has not really changed at all.

How are these difficulties negotiated by Clegg, Cooper, Burrell and Gergen? Clegg, as the most developed representative of the post-modern organizations school, clearly stands within a broadly rationalist framework. He uses Bauman's (1988a, 1988b) distinction to develop a sociology of post-modernity that effectively marginalizes the post-structuralist heritage in favour of a post-Fordist one. This is, as I have argued, quite coherent on its own terms but brings with it assumptions (grand narratives) that are unquestioned in most of his book. Clegg is clear that his stress on choice and a broadly conflicting pluralist politics 'augments' modernist conventions and does not seek to disrupt them:

> Rather than constructing a distinctive postmodern organization studies on the basis simply of analytical style, one might instead be engaged in developing a study of postmodernist (sic) organization and management practice. (Clegg 1990: 21).

One might indeed, but I doubt whether a post-modernist would concede that analytical style is a 'simple' distinction that can be so easily brushed aside. His reading of post-modernity is therefore entirely circumscribed by his very modernist assumptions about the place of social science and the theorist. His reading of Foucault is a case in point. He uses Foucault's writings about power but does not embrace Foucault's insistence on the undesirability of meta-languages. The epistemological 'baggage' is left behind and the modernist project continues unhindered. Of course this can be seen as Foucault's problem rather than Clegg's but my point is that modernism does not 'solve' post-modernism. Instead it incorporates parts of it and leaves others on the shelf whilst the assumed integrity of the author's project is not challenged.

Cooper and Burrell, however, are careful not to argue that there is a post-modern organization and instead focus on sketching a postmodern epistemology. The difficulty I see with their writings (and to a lesser extent with Gergen as well) is that, though they take the deconstruction of organizational narratives very seriously, they do nothing to explore the nature of the relation between author, text and reader that is so central to anyone who aspires to write from within a distinctively postmodern world view. As Burrell beautifully demonstrates in his later work (1997), the notion of an expert writing from within an institution in social scientific language is one that cannot be sustained if postmodernism is accepted. If it is stripped of this absolute condition of reflexivity then it loses its uniqueness – it begins to look as if it is not that different from other 'radical' perspectives such as ethnomethodology, critical theory, hermeneutics or a generalized form of social constructionism.

In terms of the distinction between epistemology and periodization Gergen appears not to recognize a difference. He moves seamlessly between applying postmodernism to suggesting that organizations need to find new ways of working in the postmodern age. The problem with this kind of jump is illustrated in his notion of 'serious play'. If he wishes to argue that what he suggests about organizational survival is important then he is participating in a serious grand narrative whether he likes it or not. His work would have to stand within a tradition of organizational design, even if it does look and sound radical. Can a writer avoid responsibility for the consequences of his writings simply by suggesting that they were only 'vehicles for public amusement' (Gergen 1992: 216; Parker 1995)?

In terms of the distinctions I have constructed, Clegg and others sit in the post-modern camp, Cooper and Burrell with the postmodernists and Gergen glides between them. All of the works are interesting, challenging and raise critical issues for organizational behaviour. However, the implication of my commentary would be that there are central epistemological, and therefore also textual, issues that are not yet being addressed. Post-modernists simply sideline these issues since they are not seen as relevant to the debates they are concerned with. That is entirely coherent but subject to all the critiques of meta-narratives that postmodernists deploy. On the other hand postmodernists cannot afford to ignore the textual issues that Gergen begins to raise since they are central to, and constitutive of, the new understanding of organization that they seek.

For all of the authors, the Foucauldian (1977) notion of 'discipline' would seem to have some helpful application here. In accepting, or constructing, a disciplinary area such as organizational behaviour the author disciplines their writing, and the student their reading, to re-produce certain forms of knowledge. To extend the pun, they also become disciples to a heritage of writing. For a postmodernist this closure would be unacceptable since it erects the barriers they wish to dissolve. Given instead a space for the play of language without discipline the postmodernist could then claim theoretical purity and consistency. Taking this logic to its limit, the stark choice left would therefore appear to be a flawed grand narrative which gives us reasons for writing about organizations, or a comprehensive critique of all reasons for writing about anything. The idea that 'discipline is necessary in order to write' sounds like a piece of stern pedagogic morality but may have wider application in this context. It is as if the presence or absence of the hyphen leaves the organizational behaviourist in different worlds that can never really meet if their internal logics are followed to the limit (Hebdige 1985). Having taking the reader to this questionable dualism, I am (of course) unable to deliver a neat solution, and instead can only offer a few closing speculations on the implications of these ideas.

POSTMODERNIZING ORGANIZATIONAL BEHAVIOUR?

There is certainly a sense in which 'post-modern', or 'postmodern' organizational theory is jumping on a bandwagon. The distinction gained by 'new' language provides the user with a sense that they are themselves pushing forward the boundaries of their discipline – a quest for novelty itself connected to the modernist project (Bourdieu 1984; Alvesson 1995). This would seem to be particularly important for management and organizational behaviour in order to give it an image and sense of excitement that it often lacks at present within the academic community. So perhaps this is just a question of management academics desperately trying to become as fashionable as those in cultural studies? Perhaps there is no guarantee that these ideas are actually as radical as many of their proponents may like to think. As Featherstone observes

> one strategy for outsider intellectuals is to appear to attempt to subvert the whole game – postmodernism. With postmodernism, traditional distinctions and hierarchies are collapsed, polyculturalism is acknowledged . . . kitch, the popular and difference are celebrated. Their cultural innovation proclaiming a *beyond* is really a *within*, a new move within the cultural game which takes into account the circumstances of production of cultural goods, which will itself in turn be greeted as eminently marketable by the cultural intermediaries (Featherstone 1987: 69).

In a similarly cynical vein John Rajchman suggests that postmodern theory '. . . is like the Toyota of thought: produced and assembled in several different places and then sold everywhere' (in Connor 1989: 19).

We might thus expect more management gurus to be writing books for managers on the use of postmodernism for management practice – 'In Search of Difference', 'Postmodernism for Pleasure and Profit', and so on.

At the same time, it might also be argued that my clinical distinction between postmodern epistemologies and the post-modern epoch is altogether too glib. It runs the danger of preventing any exchange between challenging theoretical currents and the everyday practice of those interested in organization(s). This middle ground may not be acceptable in terms of complete theoretical consistency but it does push organizational behaviourists towards some new and interesting ways of looking at their subject, both as discipline and substance. As I pointed out at the beginning of this chapter, this is certainly what is already happening in many areas – power, culture, symbolism, change, ethics are all being problematized. In general terms, qualitative and critical approaches are challenging the core assumptions that many have held about the process of producing organization. Perhaps this is simply reflective of a long-term rise of interest in the constitution of the area as a whole.

> The body of knowledge that constitutes administrative science is an artifact generated from the a priori constructs of predefined theoretical models. Such constructs do not just describe the world by classifying it into analytical categories, they define its epistemological constitution. Rather than approach organizations as unbiased observers of the facts who passively record events in neutral theoretical descriptions, we already harbour conceptions of what is to be studied; our theories determine what will count as a fact in the first place (Astley 1985: 498).

Whilst not all of this work necessarily gives post(-)modernism a central place, much of it is inspired by the current that Gergen describes as 'language losing its role as functionary in the realm of reality' (1992: 214). Given such a generalized interest in the implications of the linguistic turn it might be foolish to dramatize postmodernism in particular as a Pandora's box that will entirely change the way the world is, and the ways that writers and readers might think about it too. It is, after all, only another word.

So, the distinction I have made may be altogether too stark and the possibilities for cross fertilization far more productive than I have suggested. Indeed it may be argued (Power 1990) that even if we agree with Derrida and others that language is ultimately undecidable, we still do use language pragmatically in everyday organizational life. To 'deconstruct' conventional wisdoms is one thing, to state that we can function without any conventions is quite another. This is one way to state the 'performative contradiction' – 'can anti-foundationalism exist without foundations?' (Turner 1990: 6; see also Clegg 1990: 12). To put it another way, if postmodernists claim there are no truths, then on what basis can they make such a grand claim? In practice much 'postmodern' writing has been aimed at stressing diversity and difference, affirming the possibility of play and resistance within the most oppressive structures (see many of the chapters in Boje *et al.* 1996; Willmott 1994; or Knights 1997 for example). As Foster observes, this is not necessarily a modern nihilism but 'a critique which destructures the order of representations in order to reinscribe them' (1983: xv). This is a characterization of postmodernism as ideology critique to which I feel quite sympathetic, but supporting it does not mean we should neglect consideration of its epistemological and political implications. For postmodernism or post-modernism to be 'useful' in some way they must be considered in depth as both social and philosophical theories and their relationship must be clearly understood. Furthermore, for the postmodernist, questions about the textual responsibility of the theorist must be approached or the integrity of the exercise becomes highly suspect (Parker 1995, 1999). Some kind of 'taming' of post-modernity is evident in several publications which essentially sideline the post-structuralist epistemology in favour of a 'sociological' (Lash 1990; Giddens 1990) or 'materialist' (Harvey 1989; Callinicos 1989) explanation of 'why postmodernity now?' In the terms I have phrased it the question should be 'why write now?' Or even, 'what is writing?' I think that it might be possible that the answers to these questions inform each other, and in that regard I would recommend recent books by Law (1994) and Burrell (1997) as splendid attempts to deliver a theoretical practice of post(-)modern organization theory without worrying too much about labels.

A final note on this chapter. Is it postmodern or post-modern? And, given the undecidability of all words, why should I try to legislate on the use of the term in the first place? I have told you nothing about my reasons for writing and done little to deconstruct social scientific discourse. Neither have I espoused the notion that organizational behavourists should attempt to advise the inhabitants of a new era. Instead I have constructed a meta-narrative in which I have deployed a rationality which attempts to speak for and beyond the texts I have used. For the phantom postmodernist I have created this is clearly a fiction and one that begs for deconstruction in itself. For my phantom post-modernist, it is another retreat into an intellectual ghetto which has little relation to the problems and politics of the real world. What about 'Martin Parker'? I'm not sure where he might fit into this formal strait-jacket of a text at all, but I think that these are the questions that a postmodernist should be asking.

> The Enlightenment is dead, Marxism is dead, the working class movement is dead . . . and the author does not feel very well either (Neil Smith in Harvey 1989: 325).

Acknowledgements

This chapter is a revised and updated version of Parker, M. 'Post-modern Organizations or Postmodern Organization Theory?' published in *Organization Studies* (1992) Vol. 13, 1 pp. 1–17.

REFERENCES

Alvesson, M. (1990) Organization: from substance to image, *Organization Studies*, 11/3: 373–94.

Alvesson, M. (1995) The meaning and meaninglessness of postmodernism: some ironic remarks, *Organization Studies*, 16/6: 1047–75.

Alvesson, M. and Deetz, S. (1996) Critical theory and postmodernism approaches to organizational studies, in S. Clegg, C. Hardy and W. Nord (eds), *Handbook of Organization Studies*, Sage, London, 191–217.

Aronowitz, S. (1989) Postmodernism and politics, in Andrew Ross, *Universal Abandon: The Politics of Postmodernism*, Edinburgh University Press, Edinburgh.

Astley, W. (1985) Adminstrative science as socially constructed truth, *Administrative Science Quarterly*, 30/4: 497–513.

Bauman, Z. (1988a) Viewpoint: sociology and postmodernity, *Sociological Review*, 36/4: 790–813.

Bauman, Z. (1988b) Is there a postmodern sociology, *Theory, Culture and Society*, 5/2–3: 217–37.

Bell, D. (1973) *The Coming of Post-Industrial Society*, Basic Books, New York.

Boje, D., Gephart, R. and Thatchenkery, T. (eds) (1996) *Postmodern Management and Organization Theory*, Sage, London.

Bourdieu, P. (1984) *Distinction*, RKP, London.

Burrell, G. (1988) Modernism, post modernism and organizational analysis 2: the contribution of Michel Foucault, *Organization Studies*, 9/2: 221–335.

Burrell, G. (1997) *Pandemonium: Towards a Retro-organization Theory*, Sage, London.

Cahoone, L. (ed.) (1996) *From Modernism to Postmodernism: An Anthology*, Blackwell, Oxford.

Calas, M. and Smircich, L. (eds) (1997) *Postmodern Management Theory*, Ashgate, Aldershot.

Callinicos, A. (1989) *Against Postmodernism*, Cambridge, Polity.

Chia, R. (1996) *Organizational Analysis and Deconstruction*, de Gruyter, Berlin.

Clegg, S. (1990) *Modern Organizations: Organization Studies in the Postmodern World*, Sage, London.

Connor, S. (1989) *Postmodernist Culture*, Blackwell, Oxford.

Cooke, P. (1990) *Back to the Future: Modernity, Postmodernity and Locality*, Unwin Hyman, London.

Cooper, R. (1989) Modernism, post modernism and organizational analysis 3: the contribution of Jacques Derrida, *Organization Studies*, 10/4: 479–502.

Cooper, R. and Burrell, G. (1988) Modernism, post modernism and organizational analysis: an introduction, *Organization Studies*, 9/1: 91–112.

Eagleton, T. (1983) *Literary Theory*, Blackwell, Oxford.

Featherstone, M. (1987) Lifestyle and consumer culture, *Theory, Culture and Society*, 4/1: 55–70.

Foster, H. (ed.) (1983) *Postmodern Culture*, Pluto, London.

Foucault, M. (1977) *Discipline and Punish*, Penguin, Harmondsworth.

Gephart, R. (1996) Management, social issues and the postmodern era, in Boje, D. Gephart, R. and Thatchenkery, T. (eds), *Postmodern Management and Organization Theory*, Sage, London, 21–44.

Gephart, R. Thatcherenkery, T. and Boje, D. (1996) Conclusion: reconstructing organizations for future survival, in Boje, D., Gephart, R. and Thatchenkery, T. (eds), *Postmodern Management and Organization Theory*, Sage, London, 358–64.

Gergen, K. (1992) Organizational theory in the postmodern era, in M. Reed and M. Hughes (eds), *Rethinking Organization: New Directions in Organization Theory and Analysis*, Sage, London, 207–26.

Giddens, A. (1990) *The Consequences of Modernity*, Polity, Cambridge.

Hall, S. and Jacques, M. (eds) (1989) *New Times*, Lawrence and Wishart, London.

Harvey, D. (1989) *The Condition of Postmodernity*, Blackwell, Oxford.

Hassard, J. and Parker, M. (eds) (1993) *Postmodernism and Organizations*, Sage, London.

Hebdige, D. (1985) The bottom line on Planet One, in D. Hebdige, *Hiding in the Light*, Comedia, London, 155–76.

Heydebrand, W. (1989) New organizational forms, *Work and Occupations*, 16/3: 323–57.

Knights, D. (1997) Organization theory in the age of deconstruction, *Organization Studies*, 18/1: 1–19.

Lash, S. (1990) *Sociology of Postmodernism*, Routledge, London.

Lash, S. and Urry, J. (1987) *The End of Organised Capitalism*, Polity, Oxford.

Law, J. (1994) *Organising Modernity*, Polity, Oxford.

Lyotard, J.-F. (1984) *The Postmodern Condition: A Report on Knowledge*, Manchester University Press, Manchester.

Morgan, G. (1986) *Images of Organization*, Sage, London.

Parker, M. (1995) Critique in the name of what? postmodernism and critical approaches to organization, *Organization Studies*, 16/4: 553–64.

Parker, M. (1999) Capitalism, subjectivity and ethics: debating labour process analysis, *Organization Studies*, 20/1: 25–45.

Peters, T. and Waterman, R. (1982) *In Search of Excellence*, Harper and Row, New York.

Piore, M. and Sabel, C. (1984) *The Second Industrial Divide*, Basic Books, New York.

Power, M. (1990) Modernism, postmodernism and organization, in John Hassard and Dennis Pym (eds) *The Theory and Philsophy of Organizations*, RKP, London.

Ryan, M. (1988) Postmodern politics, *Theory, Culture and Society*, 5/2–3: 559–76.

Sandelands, L. and Drazin, R. (1989) On the language of organization theory, *Organization Studies*, 10/4: 457–78.

Thompson, P. (1993) Postmodernism: fatal distraction, in Hassard, J. and Parker, M. (eds), *Postmodernism and Organizations*, Sage, London, 183–203.

Turner, B. (ed.) (1990) *Theories of Modernity and Postmodernity*, Sage, London.

Willmott, H. (1994) Bringing agency (back) into organizational analysis: responding to the crisis of (post)modernity, in Hassard, J. and Parker, M. (eds), *Towards a New Theory of Organizations*, Routledge, London, 87–130.

Section 2
Organizational Lives

This section of the book focuses on organizational lives, locating individuals and organizations within the immediate social structures and wider context of which they are a part.

The first chapter, from Clark, Chandler and Barry, deals with the topical issue of stress at work. In considering the literature on work stress in historical context the authors undertake a review and critique of the conventional wisdom and its treatment of gender. Their purpose is to demonstrate limitations and offer complementary, sociological, perspectives as a way of helping to enrich our understanding. Their review of the prevailing wisdom, which they argue has been promulgated by 'work psychologists', emphasizes the positivist orientation, managerial bias, reformism and relative gender-blindness of work psychology. The consequence of this, they contend, has been the individualizing of the 'problem' of stress which tends to be seen, experienced and suffered, ultimately at least, alone. In drawing on the work of the sociologist C. Wright Mills, Clark, Chandler and Barry point to the need to consider the degree to which work stress is a 'public' issue. By way of example the authors attempt to show how concepts such as alienation and anomie provide useful frameworks within which to embed study and research into gender and stress at work. Viewed in this way, from a sociological vantage point, they see no easy or ready-made short-term solutions to the 'problem' of work stress which is created for some people by the actions of others – at least until such time as consideration is given to the way life is organized, raising fundamental questions about the very nature of organizations themselves and the vested interests which sustain them. Issues of corporate culture and flexibility, which are discussed in the chapter, reappear elsewhere in this volume in the contributions from Needle and Murton respectively.

The next chapter, from Brewis, offers an alternative way of conceptualizing organizational life, drawing on the work of the French philosopher Foucault. In her chapter, Brewis argues that textbooks on organizational behaviour have largely marginalized sex at work, following the conventional view that sex is somehow antithetical to the smooth running of organizations. It is this 'gap' that she seeks to fill. In order to do this and to help the reader to come to grips with Foucault's contribution to the literature – accounts of which are often absent from textbooks on organizational behaviour and management – the author outlines some of his main ideas. These include the notion that 'truth' is relative to specific historical circumstances and not absolute and that what we 'know' of 'ourselves' is produced by powerful prevailing 'discourses'. Discourses are webs of ideas, arguments, symbols, institutions and practices in operation at any one time in history which represent and sustain particular ways of understanding the world. Brewis uses such insights to help make sense of sex in the workplace through case studies of a financial services organization and a university, both of which operated primarily with understandings of sex at work through the prism of what she calls 'scientific modernism', a discourse that conceptualizes sex as problematic and inimical to organizational efficiency. The critical and radical implications of Brewis' contribution can be appreciated when readers think through their own understandings of themselves and others as sexual beings as well as students and/or workers – and consider the repercussions of thinking, being and doing differently. Related questions of identity are also raised in the chapter from Chandler.

The final chapter in this section, from Allen, Miller and Wyatt, explores the ways in which new technologies affect organizational life. The authors reject what have tended to be the extreme positions adopted in texts on organizational behaviour – on the one hand the (modernist) view that new information and communication technologies (ICTs) are introduced to enhance the quality of working life, and on the other the notion that new ICTs are used as managerial devices to increase profits, reduce wages and deskill workers. Allen, Miller and Wyatt's approach is informed by three theoretical perspectives. First, neo-Schumpeterian work on changes to what have been termed 'techno-economic paradigms'. The emphasis here is on the long processes of adaptation to changes in technology, particularly radical technologies such as ICT, which have the potential for use across a wide range of organizations. Second, a school of thinking which focuses on the social shaping of technology and contends that new technologies emerge through a process of socio-technical negotiation and are not fixed in the ways in which they can be used. Third, following on from this and drawing on recent developments in the critical management literature, the authors argue that, not only are there a variety of factors shaping the development of new technology, there are also a variety of factors shaping their use; these are influenced by managerial strategies as well as local and global conditions, operating in specific industries. Allen, Miller and Wyatt illustrate their arguments through an examination of the ways in which book publishing has changed over the past 20 years, following a day in the life of 'Jane', an editor. In this way the authors consider issues of skill, surveillance and financial control and demonstrate the changes which have occurred in the division of labour between authors, editors, secretaries and typesetters. Interested readers are referred to the chapters from Murton, and Adcroft and Willis in another section of this volume, which develop similar issues in relation to labour markets and globalization respectively.

The issues raised in these three chapters which consider organizational life not only share an interest in the relationships of gender, something considered in the book in the contributions from Chandler and Neale, they also help us to see the connections between individuals and organizations more generally and to understand how each is a part of the other, existing in the wider historical context. The chapters show how forces operating both outside of and within organization members themselves impact on and affect daily life. There are some differences of emphasis, deriving from the use of contrasting theoretical perspectives. Brewis, for example, uses the work of Foucault and the concept 'discourse' to demonstrate how ways of seeing and understanding the world shape our lives, whilst Clark, Chandler and Barry who draw on concepts commonly associated with Marx (alienation) and Durkheim (anomie) focus their attention on the action of people, not just in terms of how the world is understood, but how it is reacted to and changed. Yet both chapters display a sensitivity to the concerns of the other, the first through a discussion of resistance and the second through acknowledgement of the powerful forces at play which constrain action. Allen, Miller and Wyatt are also conscious of context and powerful forces, developed over time, which help to mould the form and direction of technological change as they impact on the processes of socio-technical negotiation. Taken together the chapters in this section suggest that organizational life is perhaps best understood as an interplay between forces in constant flux, as a part of dynamic and ever-changing social structures. 'Organizations' and the people within them do not exist in a vacuum.

Work, stress and gender: conceptualization and consequence

4

Heather Clark, John Chandler and Jim Barry

when *I* use a word, it means just what I choose it to mean – neither more nor less

Humpty Dumpty in Lewis Carroll's
Alice Through the Looking Glass (1872: 274).

INTRODUCTION

Increasing interest is being shown in stress in both academic and popular literature. It has become one of those terms used in everyday conversation. We all think we know what stress is, we have all experienced it, suffered it, coped with it well or badly and seen it manifested in others. Yet stress has different meanings for different people in different situations. It can be 'good', energizing and motivating and it can be 'bad', causing depression and physical ill-health. There appears to be more of it around yet, despite greater awareness of the potential ill-effects, we still suffer in the isolation of our separate lives with no obvious way of knowing if the pain of our own stress is experienced more acutely than someone else's. Our thinking about and experience of stress, however, is influenced by those who claim specialist knowledge, who organize themselves in various professional, academic and journalistic ways, to tell us what it is and who use the word to mean just what they choose it to mean. It is the implications and consequences of this which interest us here.

In order to focus our attention we limit our concern in this chapter to the study of stress as it affects both women and men at work, traditionally the province of a group of academics who, following Hollway (1995: 37; 1991: 6 and 12), we will refer to as work psychologists. These academics have focused on the individual at work, with a number of their practitioners involved in prescribing strategies for individuals and managers interested in the study and alleviation of stress. Whilst acknowledging that work psychologists have advanced our understanding we wish to take issue with what we will argue are the limited definitions and approaches to stress which they have promulgated, paying particular attention to their conceptualization and treatment of gender.

Stress certainly appears to have been increasing in the changing 'flexible' conditions of work with its cost having been counted for some years now by business, concerned about absenteeism, litigation and compensation claims. More is being written about it – even recently as a managerial strategy to control workers (Earley 1994: 11–13; and Murton 1999, in this volume) as interest turns to concerns over efficiency and employee selection in a context which in Britain has witnessed relatively high levels of unemployment and attempts to contain trade union power (Hollway 1995: 45–49; see also Hollway 1984). Yet it is still treated as a 'private' trouble for individuals at work to cope with themselves – albeit with some help – rather than the 'public' issue (Mills 1959: 15) it has become. In this chapter we will argue that researchers might enhance our understanding of stress at work by using sociological concepts such as alienation and anomie in which to embed their studies. This may complicate matters and render 'solutions' less easily workable and attainable but it will, we argue, go some way to widen and enrich our understanding.

If we really want to understand the phenomena that give rise to the social 'problem' of stress we would do well to heed the comments of C.Wright Mills in his seminal text, *The Sociological Imagination*, who refers on the one hand to,

> grand theorists who [never] get down from the higher generalities to problems in their historical and structural contexts . . . [and on the other] . . . abstracted empiricists . . . [who] . . . have not studied what most social scientists consider important problems . . . [t]hey have studied problems of abstracted empiricism; but only with the curiously self-imposed limitations of their arbitrary epistemology have they stated their questions and answers. . . . The details, no matter how numerous, do not convince us of anything worth having convictions about . . . the thinness of the results is matched only by the elaboration of the methods and the care employed (Mills 1959: 42, 65, 63).

What is needed, we argue in this chapter, is an analysis which links the detail of stress to the wider picture, which connects the private troubles of stress to issues of milieux in historical and structural context (Mills 1959: 14–15). We begin by examining the development, orientation and limitations of work psychology before moving on to consider complementary, sociologically-informed, approaches.

STRESS RESEARCH IN CONTEXT: HISTORICAL DEVELOPMENTS AND LIMITATIONS

In their studies of stress, work psychologists have drawn on the discourses of medicine and biology and borrowed, from physics and engineering, concepts such as strain. The term stress itself has a Latin derivation and, according to Davidson and Cooper (1992: 20), was used 'popularly in the seventeenth century to mean hardship, adversity or affliction', being deployed to describe 'force, pressure, strain or strong effort' by the eighteenth century. Early consideration of stress focused on the external pressures affecting individuals whose biological responses were thought to ready them for fight or flight as more and more pressure was brought to bear.

Whilst the likes of Osler (Davidson and Cooper 1992: 20) and Cannon (Newton *et al.* 1995: 19) are among the first names associated with the study of stress and human ill-health, it was Hans Selye MD (1946) who noted a reactive process – something he called the general adaptation syndrome – which started with an alarm reaction, moved on to resistance and finally, where the individual could cope no more, to 'exhaustion'. The potentially damaging consequences of this process could include heart, stomach and lung problems and mental illness.

Yet individuals appeared to vary in their reaction to stressful situations, with some better able to cope than others. To help explain this Rosenman *et al.* (1964) identified two different personality types, A and B, the latter seen to exhibit more laid-back, relaxed, behavioural patterns than the former who were duly labelled as vulnerable to coronary heart problems. Research into this area continues. Some work has questioned the importance of the types in the predisposition to stressful outcomes (Hart 1985: 608; see also Fletcher 1988: 29).[1] Other research continues to point to the *angry, aggressive* and *hostile* components of the so-called type A personality as significant in the aetiology of stress. Since these traits are commonly associated with male behaviour the gender implications of such findings are obvious. Perhaps, as Wilson (1995: 201) has put it, the 'extreme of masculinity . . . can be unhealthy'.[2]

Not all work remained at the level of the individual, however, with Friedman *et al.* (1958: 855) conducting research into an occupational group of male accountants whose stress levels – measured by faster blood clotting times and increased amounts of cholesterol – were found to vary according to time pressures. Their work indicated that the interruption of work routines to meet urgent tax deadlines could lead to what they termed 'socioeconomic stress'; perhaps rather chillingly they report the death of one of their research subjects who 'had been under very severe work stress for at least a week prior to [the] accident'.

Over the years work psychologists – Cary Cooper prominent among them – have developed interactionist models to try and help explain this process. Figure 4.1 illustrates the kind of conceptual model found in use. Here the individual is at the centre of the model, filtering and mediating environmental stressors and suffering 'coronary heart disease', 'mental illness' and ulcers when failing to cope. There is, though, a recognition in this model of social causes and consequences of stress – with the repercussions seen as including 'prolonged strikes', 'frequent and severe accidents' and 'apathy' (Cooper *et al.* 1988: 85).

The implications of such work have not been lost on managers fearful of litigation and compensation claims – noticeable in recent years in the USA which has witnessed an overall growth in stress-related claims particularly in those states which have eased previously 'restricted definition[s] of workplace stress' (Brogmus 1996: 32; see also Murphy 1995: 1 and Cooper 1985). Managers have also faced the possibility of loss of staff, with disruption to the daily flow of organizational routines and concomitant recruitment, replacement and retraining costs.

Nevertheless such approaches retain a conception of the social which ignores the wider structural context. This is in contrast to the work by Eyer and Sterling (1977) which documents the bodily insults resulting from the relentless pressure of a society geared to capitalist production – characterized by booms and slumps, volatile labour markets, flexibility and competitive turmoil into which we all become socialized. This is rarely acknowledged by work psychologists whose reformist orientation seems at one remove from this more radical approach. Easier perhaps to analyse the conflicting

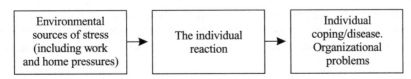

Figure 4.1
Source: after Cooper *et al.* (1988: 85)

pressures of varying work and other roles and offer advice and counselling to distressed individuals than attempt to castigate and seek to remedy the ills of a society whose social relations of production themselves – enticing some individuals to create stress for others – are implicated. The consequence of course is that the 'problem' remains with the isolated organization member who is merely helped to cope with what is in effect their lone suffering. This individualizing of the problem – which essentially blames the victim – renders individual organization members amenable to managerial control, an attractive strategy for managers and consultants eager to apply practical remedies. Work psychologists with their attention on individuals at work facilitate this process by focusing on observable stressors, individual reactions, measurable outcomes and practical 'solutions'. The connection between work psychology and management has been noted by Hollway (1995: 38) who rather tellingly observes that '[m]anagers, not psychologists, are the largest group who practice, and are trained in, work psychology'.

The use of role theory in the hands of work psychologists compounds these difficulties. Their focus on the functional stability of role allocation and effective performance facilitates the conceptualization of choice and change merely in terms of strain, ambiguity and conflict which need to be managed if individual balance and organizational harmony are to be maintained. Whilst undoubtedly role theory helps us to understand some of the pressures that organization members will feel, it serves to divert attention away from the socially and politically constructed – and contested – nature of identity and interaction, away from issues of control, power and domination.

If we now look at the discussion of organizational structure we find it analysed in terms of such factors as work overload, role conflict and supervisor-relations, but with the unquestioned assumption that the structure itself is non-problematic and somehow neutral (cf. Burrell and Hearn 1989: 14–15). Yet organizations are creations which result from the application of knowledge and interests as well as practices and processes built up over time which are reflected in a powerful discourse based on ideas of rationality, efficiency, productivity and control. By ignoring the socially-created, problematic, features of organizational life, research on stress – which is couched in empirical and pragmatic terms – misses the opportunity to consider the deeper level of analysis. What one then also excludes of course is the possibility of understanding a large part of the experience which one is purporting to explain in the first place – particularly the experience of women within organizations.

The research methods typically employed by work psychologists with their emphasis on the systematic comparison of dependent and independent variables, whereby ever-more categories are examined via questionnaire survey for reactions to stress events (Murphy 1995: 9–10), reinforce this conceptualization. As Doyle and Hind acknowledge,

> [q]uestionnaires may be 'blunt instruments' that obscure gender differences and produce misleading findings . . . several authors have noted that psychological measurement instruments are usually developed by men for men and the models underlying such instruments often assume male perspectives and values (Doyle and Hind 1998: 77).

Historically, then, research into stress by work psychologists has tended to be gender-blind. Where, increasingly, women were acknowledged they were invariably subsumed into the more traditional approach which conceptualized women and men alike as individuals – for which read 'men'. Recent research has, it is true, dealt more directly with the question of gender (cf. Davidson and Cooper 1981, 1983, 1992; and Cooper and Davidson 1982), but it remains unclear from the literature whether women actually suffer more from stress than men. Women would seem to be more vulnerable at work to a wider range of stressors, such as discrimination and the potentially stressful double-burden they invariably carry of paid employment and domestic responsibilities, but whether women *suffer* more from their jobs in similar ways to men as a result or are somehow better able to cope is not always entirely clear. Doyle and Hind for example, note from their research into higher education, that whilst female academics

> generally experience higher overall levels of stress in their jobs . . . results indicate that they *may* cope better with the demands placed upon them than their male counterparts (our emphasis) (Doyle and Hind 1998: 67).

Davidson (1997: 66) on the other hand points to the greater predominance of *mental* ill-health found by research into women managers, compared to men who appear to be more vulnerable to *physical* ill-health. This issue was alluded to by Kane (1991: 182–7) when she considered what she referred to as the 'puzzle' of the 'higher levels of women's rates of mental disorder, which appear in hospitals and in the general practitioner reports'. She comments

> there may indeed be unrecognised physical illnesses which affect women. Medicine is still primarily an art, rather than a science . . . The bundle of complaints for which there is no firm diagnosis, and which, depending on the individual doctor, will be categorised either as inexplicable or a sign of mental disorder, may include some genuine sex-specific health disorders (Kane 1991: 182–7).

A great deal is still to be learned. There is also much yet to be understood about the stressful impact of racial discrimination and the effects of prejudice relating to age, disability and other socially refracted variables. Davidson's (1997) recent interest in the relationship between managerial stress, gender and ethnicity is a welcome move historically in opening up a neglected area of enquiry to scrutiny.

These studies, which represent the recent concern to consider gender, do suggest ways of eliminating stress but they are invariably aimed at management training, legislation and counselling. For work psychologists, bounded in the range of concepts and methods of enquiry available, the problem for women is one of roles, occupied by individuals at different times in the life-cycle and occasionally not synchronized or in conflict and as such amenable to intervention. The analysis is thus *useful* to management, failing ultimately to explore the causes of prejudice and discrimination referred to above.

Yet this is precisely the area that needs analysis. Prejudice and discrimination are deep-seated and it will take more than exhortations to politicians, lawyers and managers to 'do' something, although if and when the economic costs of *not* 'doing' become relevant, there may then be direct intervention by management to introduce counselling and fitness regimes. Without tackling causes, interventions of this kind, however well intentioned, are at best reformist and ameliorative.

There has been some research which has looked at structural problems to account for the difficulties faced by women *as* women but we need to go beyond the narrow confines of particular disciplines to find it. Brown and Harris' research into 'vulnerability factors' and the 'provoking agents' of clinical depression in women for example considered the 'possibility of a more direct involvement of the social environment in disorder' (Brown and Harris 1978: 5). Irrespective of the physical or psychiatric basis they were concerned 'with how she perceives and reacts emotionally to these changes . . . [but argued] . . . no one has found it easy to translate [this] into effective research' (Brown and Harris 1978: 5). In a review article some years later, Brown (1986) commented

> It is impossible at the moment to conceive of a way of arriving at true ratio scales to measure phenomena such as degree of stress . . . we have no way of establishing a basic quantum of stress as we have of weight (Brown 1986: 603).

This observation about stress is as relevant today as it was when it was made back in 1986. Witness Doyle and Hind's (1998: 68) recent comment, that, '[e]xperienced work strain is much researched but still relatively little understood'.

The conventional approach to stress thus has its limitations. Perhaps it is time to consider alternative, complementary, approaches to help broaden and enrich our understanding.

COMPLEMENTARY APPROACHES

Our argument here is that a sociological understanding of women's position compared to men would make clear the extra level of permanent ambiguity and ambivalence under which they live – something that has been considered a component of stress by work psychologists. Existing frameworks have not specified where to look for the answers to this gendered element, although raised secondarily by some and alluded to by others. It is not being argued here that all psychologists are the same, or that they assume or accept the conventional paradigm referred to earlier as the norm. What *is* being suggested is that stress has been researched selectively by *work psychologists* who have generally not addressed the structural level, leading them to focus, where they do at all, on *aspects* of individual women's lives without linking them to issues of power and domination. Their approach is accordingly apolitical (or put another way supportive of the status quo), tending to individualize the problem of stress, in that it often blames the victim, as well as 'technical', in that it serves managerial ends. To research and reflect critically – with a sociological imagination – would offer little comfort to the practising manager or the aspiring consultant. As Watson (1995: 17) puts it: '[i]f a management difficulty can be put down to some individual's personality problem you can either sack the individual or send them for therapy . . . [s]ociology does not have a comforting potential in the same way'.

There have, admittedly, been welcome signs that this may be changing. Some recent work has begun on the exploration of *structural* features implicated in the experience of stress but these as yet remain few and far between. Both Clark (1991) and Peterson (1994a, 1994b, 1999) have advocated the contribution of a sociologically informed approach, whilst Newton *et al.* (1995: 7–8) have offered an analysis which draws on the work of Foucault, labour process theory, radical structuralist frameworks and a sociology of emotion. In addition Brown (1996) has developed a discursive approach which demonstrates the contested and constructed nature of 'stress'. Accounts of gender and occupational stress are still, however, scarce, as noted by Doyal (1995: 165); though attempts to remedy this have been started by Hall (1989); Clark (1991); Frankenhaeuser *et al.* (1991); Doyal (1995, and 1979: 93–95) herself; Clark, Chandler and Barry (1996); Davidson (1997) – who has extended the coverage to gender and ethnicity – and Benishek and Lopez (1997; see also Matthews *et al.* 1998).

Two concepts which derive from classical sociological thought and which might be used to locate stress as experienced individually in wider social structures (Mills 1959) are those of alienation and anomie. They are two among many sociological concepts that might be used and both are certainly problematic, remaining essentially contested concepts because of their moral underpinnings. There have also undoubtedly been attempts to de-radicalize them and use them in ways denuded of their original critical potential. They nevertheless provide a useful starting point.

THE 'LEGITIMACY' OF SOCIAL CONTROL

We will use as a basis for our exploration insights deriving from John Horton's seminal text 'The dehumanization of anomie and alienation'. In this text Horton (1964: 283) argues that '[c]ontemporary definitions of anomie and alienation have confused, obscured and changed the classical meanings'. An example of research which effectively de-radicalizes the concept of alienation and one favoured by textbooks on organization and management is that by Blauner (1964) which relates alienation of workers to the objective character of the work process and their subjective feeling-states.

Blauner's research is interesting for our purposes in that his dimensions of alienation, powerlessness, meaninglessness, social alienation or isolation and self-estrangement, are all elements which can be conceptualized as leading to stress (Peterson 1994b: 510).[3] Leaving aside for the present his operationalization of social alienation – which owes much to Durkheim's concept of anomie which is considered further in the next section of the chapter – his research findings, which postulated levels of alienation varying with developments in technology within capitalist society and moving at first upwards before turning inexorably downwards, do not carry the same powerful implications of Marx's (1844; see also Braverman 1974: 125) own use of the concept. For Marx eradication would result in a fundamental change in social, economic and political arrangements, affecting organizational life very directly.

The significance of this is highlighted by Horton (1964: 283 and 285–6) who contends, '[a]lienation for Marx and anomie for Durkheim were metaphors for a radical attack on the dominant institutions and values of industrial society. They attacked similar behaviour, but from opposing perspectives', with problems of power and change for Marx becoming problems about the maintenance of order for Durkheim. 'Anomie concentrates on culture or culture transmitted in social organization; alienation on the hierarchy of control in the organization itself'. There is a strong ethical stance and concern over the, 'social process, values and assumptions about the relation between man [sic] and society'; '. . . [n]either Durkheim nor Marx was interested in abstract historical and psychological definitions', although in modern definitions it is, 'precisely the original radical, historical, and sociological content which has been removed or altered'.

There are problems in operationalizing the concept of alienation but Horton (1964: 285) argues that alienation is a problem of 'legitimacy of social control; it is a problem of power defined as domination'. This is precisely what women are finding at work. How do women identify with the end result of their labours when it is managed, owned and controlled by men, when the apprehension and experience of domination and lack of control gives rise to alienatory stress? The cartoon in Figure 4.2 is but one example of alienation; the underlying stress level is as yet undiscussed.

The concept of alienation is thus of importance for women; they are treated as a commodity and are often part of a reserve army of labour to be called into action as and when required – to work in a variety of insecure jobs. Even where they attain relatively senior positions they are invariably seen as 'tokens' rather than competent individuals who have got where they have on merit. This is part of the double-bind for women, with their responsibility for the domestic sphere still not considered to be really important. Witness the case of lone mothers who, in Britain, comprise nine out of ten one-parent families and whose prospects according to one leading academic commentator, look 'bleak' (Lewis 1997: 72) – and who are now expected to contribute to society as active citizens through *paid* work in circumstances where it is difficult to find secure, well-paid, employment which is compatable with the demands of lone parenthood (Clark *et al.* 1999).

There are clear differences between the concepts of exploitation and oppression – the former concerning wage-labour and alienation, the latter patriarchy, in essence

Figure 4.2 'The job will involve you doing the work and me taking the credit...'
Source: Mary Holland, Moss Street, Dublin 1.
Reproduced with kind permission by Attic Press.

male domination of women. Yet there is a clear overlap between women's private and public lives, even if it appears in different guises. Women occupy many different structural work locations, for example manager (which will be discussed in the next section), factory worker and homeworker. Consider examples of these two latter 'ghettoized' situations. The first, a factory in which a majority of workers are women making clothes (Westwood 1984). A 'domestic' enclave is produced, with men in the majority as managers. Poor wages and conditions are the norm, the camaraderie of the women helping to cover up the exploitation and their lack of power, though failing ultimately to dissipate the effects of sexual harassment and discrimination. The same research, whilst unable to demonstate an indisputable relationship between sexual harassment and health problems, nonetheless highlights women's situations as classically stressful with illness seen as 'a common response to the pressures of the job' (Westwood 1984: 34). Faced with a choice between sexual interference and job loss, women are invariably forced to maintain a 'constant state of vigilance . . . [which] can lead to long-term physical problems such as high blood pressure, ulcers or heart disease [as well as] . . . mental health problems (Doyal 1995: 168).

The second example is the traditional area of home-working and the increased 'flexibility' being introduced there as in other areas of the economy both in Britain and abroad (Huws 1984; see also Murton 1999 in this volume; Proctor *et al.* 1994; Pollert 1987; Atkinson 1984). Although little research exists on the health of homeworkers, the stress they experience may be significant since there are enhanced levels of alienation and stress for workers required to be 'flexible' as we saw when considering the work of Eyer and Sterling earlier. In 'comparison with employed women, homeworkers have fewer opportunities for learning new skills and more monotonous work, although [this may be compensated by the fact that they] are more able to vary the pace of their work and break times' (Matthews *et al.* 1998: 1419–20). Yet the effect of women's inferior position is more keenly felt in isolation, lacking for example the factory women's 'buffer' zone of camaraderie. The stress of isolation is often experienced by so-called 'token women' in managerial positions (Davidson 1997: 64) – unless they have social networks on which to draw.

Of course the concept of alienation is likely to remain difficult to operationalize. What should be kept in mind of the classical definition is the notion of domination - whereby a 'superordinate' group exercises power and control over a 'subordinate' group. There will be various ways in which the consequences or effects of this will manifest themselves, stress being one of them. Such an insight has not been fully incorporated into the orientation of work psychology hitherto, rendering it more amenable to practical manipulation by managers and their consultants, as well as attractive for research funding and academic publication – the implications of the latter not likely to be lost on social scientists in the current pinched financial climate and present obsession with university research ratings (Goode and Bagilhole 1998; see also Kinman 1996; Fisher 1994; Earley 1994).

Use of sociological concepts such as alienation would help us to question the legitimacy of social control by focusing on the similarities of stress experienced by *women and men* in the productive process. In its classical sense the concept of alienation also promises insights into stress felt by *women as women*, as a subordinate group.

THE 'PROBLEMS' OF SOCIAL CONTROL

Anomie appears to offer an even more fruitful area for future research than alienation. John Horton (1964: 285) again: 'anomie refers to the problems of social control in a social system', where the 'values are conflicting or absent . . . or individuals are not adequately socialised to cultural directives'. Where this is the case individuals are suffering from normlessness. This certainly seems to apply to women at work since the culture that exists in organizations has been shown to be gendered and traditionally male-oriented (Gherardi 1995; Coe 1992; Hearn *et al.* 1989). Women suffer stress as a result. The male role models incorporate generalized expectations of men, about men and for men; women are absent from this scheme and, although they are now moving into higher managerial posts, are still seen as 'outsiders' lacking social support. Laurie Taylor's piece, reproduced here in Figure 4.3, makes the point well.

Women have little or no control over male attitudes towards them and where women do reach the higher echelons of organizations they are often to be found in small numbers, or alone. As Kerman (1995: 139), a female academic, explains, illustrating Laurie Taylor's 'fictitional' account,

> As the only woman member of Academic board meeting, Governor's meetings, Finance Committee meetings, interview panels for students, interview panels for staff, Departmental Board meetings, Management Group Meetings, I was accustomed to being made to feel out of place. I recognised as exclusion devices, the opening lewd joke, made with an eye cast in my direction, the detailed discussion of football tactics before we got down to business, the chairman (sic) who began with his feet on the table. They were tiresome, but they did not really bother me as they appeared to confirm that the meeting was changed because of my presence. Certain things could not be said because of my being there, certain other things could be said.

The competitive nature of organizations is invariably stressful for women to operate in. An illustration of this comes from a commercial electrician in Lunneborg's (1990: 129–30) research commenting on her male colleagues, 'they're all keyed to competition [and t]hose competitive work attitudes and ethics lower the quality of their work'. The women in this study had consciously developed coping behaviours to enhance their means of control.

These contradictory situations for women are likely to be the 'norm'. Women may not always exhibit extreme distress because they have learned the ability to both 'accommodate' and 'resist' (Gherardi 1995: 14; see also Anyon 1983). Nevertheless, this juggling of the conflicting messages in a man's world does not eliminate the stress. The capitalist culture of present-day work does not represent or reflect women's experience in the way it does for many men. This has led some women to sense a radical potential. Kleinman (1996: 137) for example comments,

> The person who lives in two worlds can occupy a special position: instead of taking either world for granted, such a person has enough distance to critically analyze both. . . . Feminists have also come to recognize the radical potential of being on the margins. . . . Once we realize that we can never fully belong, we

Laurie Taylor

Universities . . . have been condemned as among the worst discriminators against women; *report by Hansard Society Commission, January 1990.*

So we're agreed that Doctor Cooper should be added to our shortlist?

I must say he looks a very solid sort of chap to me.
Very, very solid.
Solid *and* substantial. That's what I thought.
A nice overall sense of weight.

Excellent. So that's Cooper, Noakes, Sarney, Divott and Perkins. Five solid looking candidates. Should be able to fit them into a morning's interviewing. Any other names? Yes, Professor Fagan?

Well, vice chancellor, although I very much go along with your proposed shortlist. I wonder if we might just spend another couple of seconds on Doctor Sangster.
Doctor Janet Sangster?
That's right. You may remember that she was eliminated in the first round.
Quite so.
I only raise her name again because she does seem to have a very impressive publication record and three excellent references. On paper that rather makes her the equal of all our other shortlisted candidates.

Well, I can't see there being any great harm done if we were to take another peep at this case. Anyone else with strong views on Ms Sangster?

I have to say, vice chancellor, that I did go over her application with the proverbial fine toothcomb, but in the end decided, with some regret – God knows, we could do with some good women at the top – that there was, overall, something distinctly lightweight about her application.

A lack of solidity.

Not quite the degree of depth and gravitas one rather tends to look for in a departmental head.
A certain lack of bottom?
Yes, indeed. She somehow came through as a little too – a little too – insubstantial.
That's right. One would have welcomed a greater meatiness.

Well, gentlemen, how then might we best summarize our thoughts on this candidate?

I think, vice chancellor that we should record our high opinion of this application – our *very* high opinion.
Hear, hear.
But note that it was unfortunately somewhat lacking in – what might one call it?

Masculinity?

The very word.

© THE TIMES SUPPLEMENTS LIMITED, 1990
Published by The Times Supplements Limited. Priory House. St. John's Lane, London EC1M 4BX. England, typeset by ComputerGraphics Ltd.. 37–42 Compton Street. London EC1 and printed by Derby Daily Telegraph. Northcliffe House. Meadow Road, Derby DE1 2DW. Friday. February 2. 1990. Registered as a newspaper at the Post Office. ISSN 0049-3929.

Figure 4.3
Source: Laurie Taylor, 2nd February 1990
Reproduced with kind permission of the *Times Higher Education Supplement*. Copyright: *Times Supplements Limited*, 1996.

might become less invested in playing the game and be able to assess the structure of the organization/institution and the values that underlie it.

This seems unlikely to help alleviate stress in the short term, however. Whether women attempt to adapt to or change the culture of a workplace which reflects male priorities, as demonstrated in a study of lawyers by Jack and Jack (1988), they suffer stress as a result. However adept at 'conjuring' women become, the underlying level of anomie for them is always present, an insight yet to be fully acknowledged in studies of corporate culture (Ray 1986; Needle 1999 in this volume). Attitudes, values and behaviour at work are male (Wajcman 1998) and even where there are many women working together, the expectations of them as women will still prevail. Little wonder that Kinman (1996: 17), in her study of occupational stress for lecturers in further and higher education, revealed that more women than men had 'seriously considered leaving the profession' and that Marshall (1995) found evidence of women managers 'moving on'.

CONCLUDING REMARKS

> Why strive for knowledge of reality if this knowledge cannot serve us in life?
> Emile Durkheim, *The Rules of Sociological Method* (1938: 48).

In this chapter we have argued that the study of work stress has been the province of work psychologists, whose orientation has restricted them from taking the wider view. In this respect we have argued that work psychologists have favoured an approach which is quantitatively based, presupposed a coincidence of managerial and worker interests, individualized the problem of stress often in the service of managerial ends and tended, until relatively recently at least, to be gender-blind. We have also advocated the use of complementary approaches in order to broaden our understanding of the issues involved. The complementary approaches are unlikely to 'succeed' if used alone, however. They simply offer an historical and social structural framework within which other research into stress could be embedded.

We have tried to give some idea of where classical sociological concepts might have relevance. The concepts of alienation and anomie, considered here, offer insights into stress for both women *and* men at work. The power to control their own existence is not yet in women's hands and the increasing number of them in managerial and professional positions has yet to reduce the general sexual stereotyping that exists in the culture of organizations. A sociological framework will encompass critical questions about the group under analysis: '[p]eople who ask questions of this order . . . may be said to share a common perspective . . . the commonality rests in the questions asked and certainly not in the answers that are given' (Eldridge 1971: 139). We would want to know the source of the stressful alienation and anomie that women (and men) suffer and why, how and by whom these processes are sustained. What and where is the evidence that will help shed light on this?

Those researchers into stress, in any discipline, who are interested in the same questions will use structural concepts in historical context in which to embed them. It is the questions that matter – the research, however difficult, will produce results of interest and enhance our understanding of the issues involved.

As things stand we know that work stress can be harmful and we know that it is possible to reduce it and lessen its damaging effects. Even so the approaches and remedies on offer at present from work psychologists are reformist and ameliorative; important in themselves and helpful to some, but likely in our view to have little real impact on the problem of stress at work. What we have advocated as a first step is that we re-think, or re-conceptualize, the problem and ask different kinds of questions, questions which are 'difficult' and to which there are no ready or easy answers since the resolution of the problem may necessitate a radical change in the ways in which we arrange contemporary organizational life. This does not, in and of itself, mean that our analysis is misguided. It may expose the reality of the interest vested in the perpetuation of existing social, economic and political arrangements and lead us to ask awkward questions about power and domination, but this does not render the exercise misconceived. The link between conception and consequence is significant and has rarely been more clearly drawn than in the study of stress and gender at work.

Notes

1   Also interesting in this respect is the work of Marmot *et al.* (1978) whose work on the British civil service found men in the lowest grade 3.6 times more vulnerable to coronary heart disease than men in the highest grade. This calls into question part of the common sense notion that stress is more likely to be found in jobs at the apex of organizations which carry high levels of responsibility and raises issues of social class for stress researchers.
2   Wilson (1995: 201) also notes that 'being too feminine' can be unhealthy as it may lead women to become over-involved in others at the expense of themselves.
3   In a critique of the literature on work stress Peterson (1994b: 501–8) makes reference to the concept of alienation and considers issues of control.

REFERENCES

Anyon, J. (1983) Intersections of gender and class: accommodation and resistance by working class and affluent females to contradictory sex-role ideologies, in Walker S. and Barton L. (1983) (Eds) *Gender, Class and Education*, Falmer Press, Lewis, 19–37.

Atkinson, J. (1984) Manpower strategies for flexible organisations, *Personal Management*, August, 28–31.

Benishek, L.A. and Lopez F.G. (1997) Critical evaluation of hardiness theory: gender differences, perception of life events and neuroticism, *Work and Stress*, 11 (1), 33–45.

Blauner, R. (1964) *Alienation and Freedom: The Factory Worker and his Industry*, The University of Chicago Press, Chicago, IL.

Braverman, H. (1974) *Labor and Monopoly Capital: The Degradation of Work in the Twentieth Century*, Monthly Review Press, New York.

Brogmus, G.E. (1996) The rise and fall? of mental stress claims in the USA, *Work and Stress*, 10 (1), 24–35.

Brown, G.W. (1986) Statistical interaction and the role of social factors in the aetiology of clinical depression, *Sociology*, 20 (4), November, 601–6.

Brown, G.W. and Harris, T. (1978) *Social Origins of Depression: A Study of Psychiatric Disorder in Women*, Tavistock, London.

Brown, S.D. (1996) The textuality of stress: drawing between scientific and everyday accounting, *Journal of Health Psychology*, 1 (2), 173–93.

Burrell, G. and Hearn, J. (1989) The sexuality of organization, in Hearn, J. Sheppard, D.L., Tancred-Sheriff, P. and Burrell, G. (eds), *The Sexuality of Organization*, Sage, London. 1–28.

Carroll, L. (1872) Through the Looking Glass, in Carroll, L. *Alice's Adventures in Wonderland and Through the Looking Glass*, Puffin, Harmondsworth (1962 edn).

Clark, H. (1991) *Women, Work and Stress: New Directions*, University of East London, Occasional Papers on Business, Economy and Society, Paper No 3.

Clark, H.,Chandler, J. and Barry, J. (1996) Work psychology, women and stress: silence, identity and the boundaries of conventional wisdom, *Gender, Work and Organization*, 3 (2), 65–77.

Clark, H., Chandler, J .and Barry, J. (1999) 'I'd like to work full-time but I can't afford to': lone parenting and employment in Britain, in Dent, M., O'Neill, M. and Bagley, C. (eds), *Professions, New Public Management and the European Welfare State*, Staffordshire University Press.

Coe, T. (1992) *The Key to the Men's Club: Opening the Doors to Women in Management*, The Institute of Management, Corby.

Cooper, C.L. (1985) The road to health in American films, *New Statesman and Society*, 6 September, 335–6.

Cooper, C.L. and Cartwright, S. (1994) Healthy mind; healthy organisation – a proactive approach to occupational stress, *Human Relations*, 47 (4), 455–71.

Cooper, C.L. and Davidson, M.J. (1982) *High Pressure: Working Lives of Women Managers*, Fontana, Isle of Man.

Cooper, C.L. and Payne, R. (eds) (1988) *Causes, Coping and Consequences of Stress at Work*, Wiley, Chichester.

Cooper, C.L. and Rousseau, D.M. (eds) (1995) *Trends in Organizational Behaviour: Volume 2*, Wiley, West Sussex.

Cooper, C.L., Cooper, R.D. and Eaker, L.H. (1988) *Living with Stress*, Penguin, Harmondsworth.

Davidson, M.J. (1997) *The Black and Ethnic Minority Woman Manager: Cracking the Concrete Ceiling*, Paul Chapman Publishing, London.

Davidson, M.J. and Cooper, C.L. (1981) Occupational stress in female managers – a review of the literature, *Journal of Enterprise Management*, 3 (2), 115–38.

Davidson, M.J. and Cooper, C.L. (1983) *Stress and the Woman Manager*, Robertson, Oxford.

Davidson, M.J. and Cooper, C. (1992) *Shattering the Glass Ceiling: The Woman Manager*, Paul Chapman Publishing, London.

Doyal, L. with Pennell, I. (1979) *The Political Economy of Health*, Pluto Press, London (1981 edn).

Doyal, L. (1995) *What Makes Women Sick: Gender and the Political Economy of Health*, Macmillan, Basingstoke.

Doyle, C. and Hind, P. (1998) Occupational stress, burnout and job status in female academics, *Gender, Work and Organization*, 5 (2), 67–82.

Durkheim, E. (1938) *The Rules of Sociological Method*, The Free Press, New York (1964 edn).

Earley, P. (1994) *Lecturers' Workload and Factors Affecting Stress Levels: A Research Report from the NFER*, NATFHE, The University and College Lecturers' Union, London.

Eldridge, J.E.T. (1971) *Sociology and Industrial Life*, Nelson, Sunbury-on-Thames.

Eyer, J. and Sterling, P. (1977) Stress-related mortality and social organization, *Review of Radical Political Economy*, 9 (1), 1–44.

Fisher, S. (1994) *Stress in Academic Life: The Mental Assembly Line*, SRHE and Open University Press, Buckingham.

Fletcher, B. (C) (1988) The epidemiology of occupational stress, in Cooper, C.L. and Payne, R. *Causes, Coping and Consequences of Stress at Work*, Wiley, Chichester.

Foucault, M. (1977a) *Discipline and Punish*, Peregrine, Penguin, Harmondsworth.

Frankenhaeuser, M., Lundberg, U. and Chesney, M. (1991) *Women, Work and Health: Stress and Opportunities*, Plenum, New York.

Friedman, M., Rosenman, R.H. and Carrol, V. (1958) Changes in the serum cholesterol and blood clotting time in men subjected to cyclic variation of occupational stress *Circulation*, XV11, 852–61.

Gherardi, S. (1995) *Gender, Symbolism and Organizational Cultures*, Sage, London.

Goode, J. and Bagilhole, B. (1998) Gendering the management of change in higher education: a case study, *Gender, Work and Organization*, 5 (3), July, 148–62.

Greenglass, E.R. (1993) The contribution of social support to coping strategies, *Applied Psychology: An International Review*, 42 (42), October, 323–40.

Guppy, A. and Rick, J. (1996) The influences of gender and grade on perceived work stress and job satisfaction in white collar employees, *Work and Stress*, 10 (2), 154–64.

Hall, E.M. (1989) Gender, work control and stress: a theoretical discussion and an empirical test, *International Journal of Health Studies*, 19 (4), 725–45.

Hart, N. (1985) The sociology of health and medicine, in Haralambos, M. (ed), *Sociology: New Directions*, Causeway Press, Ormskirk, 519–654.

Hearn, J., Sheppard, D.L., Tancred-Sheriff, P. and Burrell, G. (eds) (1989) *The Sexuality of Organization*, Sage, London.

Hollway, W. (1984) Fitting work: psychological assessment in organizations, in Henriques, J., Hollway, W., Urwin, C., Venn, C. and Walkerdine, V. (eds), *Changing the Subject: Psychology, Social Regulation and Subjectivity*, Methuen, London, 26–59.

Hollway, W. (1991) *Work Psychology and Organizational Behaviour*, Sage, London.

Hollway, W. (1995) Industrial (occupational) and organizational psychology, in Colman, A.M. (ed) *Applications of Psychology*, Longman, Harlow, 37–52.

Horton, J. (1964) The dehumanization of anomie and alienation: a problem in the ideology of sociology, *British Journal of Sociology*, 15, 283–300.

Huws, U. (1984) *The New Homeworkers: New Technology and the Changing Location of White-collar Work*, Pamphlet No 28, Low Pay Unit, London.

Jack, D. and Jack, R. (1988) Women lawyers: archetype and alternatives, in Gilligan, C., Ward, V.J. and McLean Taylor, J. with Bardige, B. (eds) *Mapping the Moral Domain*, Harvard University Press, Cambridge MA., 263–88.

Kane, P. (1991) *Women's Health: From Womb to Tomb*, Macmillan, Basingstoke.

Kerman, L. (1995) The good witch: 'advice to women in management', in Morley and Walsh (1995) *op cit*, 131–44.

Kinman, G. (1996) *Occupational Stress and Health Among Lecturers Working in Further and Higher Education*, NATFHE, The University and College Lecturers' Union, London.

Kleinman, S. (1996) *Opposing Ambitions: Gender and Identity in an Alternative Organization*, The University of Chicago Press, Chicago, IL.

Lewis, J. (1997) Lone mothers: the British case, in Lewis, J. (ed) *Lone Mothers in European Wellfare Regimes: Shifting Policy Logics*, Jessica Kingsley, London, 50–75.

Lunneborg, P. (1990) *Women Changing Work*, Bergin and Garvey, New York.

Marmot, M.G., Rose, G., Shipley, M. and Hamilton, P.J.S. (1978) Employment grade and coronary heart disease in British civil servants, *Journal of Epidemiology and Community Health*, 32 (4), 244–9.

Marshall, J. (1995) *Women Managers Moving On: Exploring Careers and Life Choices*, Routledge, London.

Marx, K. (1844) Economic and philosophical manuscripts, in Marx, K (1974) *Early Writings*, Penguin, Harmondsworth, 279–400.

Matthews, S., Hertzman, C., Ostry, A. and Power, C. (1998) Gender, work roles and psychosocial work characteristics as determinants of health, *Social Science and Medicine*, 46 (11), 1417–24.

Mills, C. Wright (1959) *The Sociological Imagination*, Pelican, Harmondsworth (1970 edn).

Morley, L. and Walsh, V. (eds) (1995) *Feminist Academics: Creative Agents for Change*, Taylor & Francis, London.

Murphy, L.R. (1995) Occupational stress management: current status and future directions, in Cooper, C.L. and Rousseau, D. M. (eds), *Trends in Organizational Behaviour: Volume 2*, Wiley, West Sussex.

Newton, T. with Handy, J. and Fineman, S. (1995) *Managing Stress: Emotion and Power at Work*, Sage, London.

Peterson, C. (1994a) Contribution of a sociological approach to the concept of stress: a reference to occupational stress, *Annual Review of Health Social Sciences*, 79–91.

Peterson, C. (1994b) Work factors and stress: a critical review, *International Journal of Health Services*, 24 (3), 495–519.

Peterson, C. (1999) *Stress at Work: A Sociological Perspective*, Amityville, Baywood.

Pollert, A. (1987) *The 'Flexible Firm': A Model in Search of Reality (or A Policy in Search of A Practice)?* Warwick Papers in Industrial Relations, December, No 19.

Proctor, S.J., Rowlinson, M., McArdle, L., Hassard. J, and Forrester, P. (1994) Flexibility, politics and strategy: in defence of the model of the flexible firm, *Work, Employment and Society*, 8 (2), June, 221–42.

Ray, R.C.A. (1986) Corporate culture: The last frontier of control?, *Journal of Management Studies*, 23, 287–97.

Rosenman, R.H., Friedman, M., Straus, R., Wurm, M., Kositchek, R., Hahn, W. and Werthessen, N.T. (1964) A predictive study of coronary heart disease, *Journal of the American Medical Association*, 189 (1), 15–22.

Selye, H. (1946) The general adaptation syndrome and the diseases of adaptation, *The Journal of Clinical Endocrinology*, 6 (2), 117–230.

Thompson, P. and McHugh, D. (1995) *Work Organisations: A Critical Introduction* (2nd edn), Macmillan, Basingstoke.

Wajcman, J. (1998) *Managing like a Man: Women and Men in Corporate Management*, Polity Press, Cambridge.

Watson, T. (1995) *Sociology, Work and Industry* (3rd edn), Routledge and Kegan Paul, London.

Westwood, S. (1984) *All Day Every Day: Factory and Family in the Making of Women's Lives*, Pluto Press, London.

Wilson, F.M. (1995) *Organizational Behaviour and Gender*, McGraw-Hill, Berkshire.

5 Sex, work and sex at work: using Foucault to understand organizational relations

Joanna Brewis

INTRODUCTION

According to Michel Foucault (1986a, 1990), sex has been seen as an important component of the so-called human condition since the earliest years of 'civilization' in the Western world. Importantly, though, Foucault claims that sex did not attain its current status – that is, being perceived as *central* to human existence – until the eighteenth century, roughly the beginnings of the modern era in the West (Foucault 1986b: 340). According to Foucault, then, there has been a historical shift into a widespread understanding of sex as crucial for healthy human existence in the West, so that: 'the [modern] West has managed . . . to bring us almost entirely – our bodies, our minds, our individuality, our history – under the sway of a logic of concupiscence and desire' (Foucault 1979: 78)

An example of this modern preoccupation with sex is the 'sexual liberation' of the 1960s, which Brewis and Grey (1994) argue has produced a state of affairs in which we constantly monitor ourselves to assess the 'healthiness' of our sexual relations, and has also resulted in a proliferation of sex manuals and self-help videos which supposedly enable us to lead fulfilling sex lives. There are, then, certain expectations of us as sexual beings in the contemporary West; for example, O'Connell Davidson claims that we inhabit: 'a world in which it is widely held that the only legitimate sex is between people who love each other and that "money can't buy you love"' (O'Connell Davidson 1995: 9).

This prevalence of what Hollway (1989) calls the have/hold discourse, which privileges mutual affection and fidelity as the only proper basis for sexual exchange, means that prostitutes and their clients are stigmatized because of the commercial nature of, for example, their sexual encounters.

However, despite the importance of sex in our lives, the modern Western discipline of Organizational Behaviour has traditionally paid little attention to sex (Burrell 1984, 1992; Burrell and Hearn 1989; Parkin 1993). The lack of interest in sex at work, which runs counter to the wider social emphasis on sex as so important, seems to be based on the assumption that sex disrupts organizational processes, that organizations are therefore designed to 'keep sex out' and, consequently, that sex at work is not worthy of analysis. This particular interpretation of the relationship between sex and work arguably dominated OB until relatively recently. Since the late 1970s, however, feminist analyses of workplace sexual politics, focusing on sexual harassment and recommending policy to address this abusive behaviour (for example,

MacKinnon 1979; Farley, 1982), and more conceptual analyses of sex at work (for example, Burrell 1984, 1992; Hearn *et al.* 1989; Hearn and Parkin 1995) have sparked interest in the topic as one that merits attention. Consequently, sex at work could now be argued to be on the OB agenda.

None the less, even given the growing interest in sex at work in OB as a whole, it is still the case that few OB *textbooks* pay attention to sex as a dimension of organizational relations. If sex is mentioned at all, it is often only in (brief) reference to sexual harassment – for example, Vecchio (1995: 629*n*), Pettinger (1996: 232) and Robbins (1998: 408–10). One exception to this is Wilson's (1995) *Organizational Behaviour and Gender*, which devotes a chapter to 'Sexuality in organizations' (although this focuses on sexual harassment for most of the discussion). Another is Thompson and McHugh's (1995) *Work Organizations: A Critical Introduction*, in which the connection between common themes in the study of organizations, as influenced in particular by Weber's (1964, 1968, 1970) work on bureaucracy, and the absence of sex in such analysis is made:

> For Weber, the rise of bureaucracy brings with it an instrumental rationality in which impersonal rules, procedures and hierarchies are operated with technical efficiency. . . . Issues of gender and sexuality are thus despatched to a private realm . . . no longer to endanger rational-legal authority in the public sphere (Thompson and McHugh 1995: 147).

Given the above, this chapter is intended to contribute to OB textbook provision examining sex as an important dimension of organizational relations. More specifically, it aims to analyse understandings of the relationship between sex and work amongst a particular group of workers, and to identify the implications of these ways of understanding working life. The chapter, using an analysis derived from the work of Foucault, begins from the premise that there are at present three main discourses – three sets of ideas, arguments, images, practices and institutions – around sex at work (Brewis and Grey 1994; Brewis 1996). The first is scientific modernism,[1] which identifies sex as dangerous and disruptive in the workplace, arguing that it is fit only for the private sphere and that there should be a sustained effort to deny it entry to organizations. It is this discourse, and its position that sex is a threat to organizations which must be designed out of work processes, which, as suggested above, can be seen to have dominated Organizational Behaviour until the late 1970s. The second discourse is the liberal feminist analysis of sexual harassment, which argues that the presence of sex in the workplace disadvantages women because of the historical link between women, sex and irrationality. It is suggested by sexual harassment discourse that sex at work is used as a weapon against women, to degrade and abase them, to remind them of their 'unsuitability' for organizational life (Schneider 1982; Konrad and Gutek 1986; Collinson and Collinson 1989: 99–103, 107–9). Sexual harassment discourse therefore often agrees with scientific modernism that sex should be expelled from organizations, albeit for different reasons. The third discourse, re-eroticization, argues the reverse; that sex is a positive force which can only enrich working life (Burrell 1992). Relevant commentators include Reich (1942, 1969, 1972a, 1972b) and Marcuse (1968, 1969), both of whom argue for the essentially liberating potential of sex – and suggest that this potential should not be denied in the public sphere, and in the workplace specifically. There is also a body of theory which could be labelled postmodernist re-eroticization discourse, which sees sex less as a natural human essence and more as a social construction but, nevertheless, agrees that sex should be re-affirmed in public life because of its liberating effects (see, for example, Cixous 1988; Baudrillard 1990). In both re-eroticization discourses, then, there is a challenge to the 'work is public/sex is private' division which scientific modernism and liberal feminist sexual harassment discourses seek to preserve.

This chapter, however, focuses only on scientific modernism, primarily because the empirical data which forms the basis of discussion here suggests that this is the most powerful and meaningful discourse in the experience of contemporary working subjects (Brewis 1996).

A brief summary of Foucault's work as it is relevant to the chapter follows.

FOUCAULT, DISCOURSE AND SEX

We start with Foucault's (1980) claim that any body of knowledge contains nothing more than a historical and cultural claim to truth. Foucault accepts that human beings, their bodies, their patterns of behaviour and their organizations exist – but does not accept that there is some kind of real, fundamental, ahistorical truth about these phenomena which can be established by scientific exploration. He suggests that the various discourses which currently constitute our ways of understanding our existence are not really 'true' in the conventional sense of truth representing the essence of particular phenomena, because there is nothing stable or solid about human beings which represents such a truth. Foucault argues, instead, that we *believe* that these discourses are truthful and meaningful. This 'buying in' to particular representations of human existence produces our understandings of that existence – and, therefore, our ideas about and images of ourselves, our behaviour towards others, our practices and the institutions that we erect in our social world, such as work organizations. Consequently, Foucault uses the term 'discourse' to refer to the 'nexus of ideas, arguments, symbolic structures and images, social institutions, and specific concrete practices, that combine to support a particular way of knowing the world and to perpetuate it' (Brewis *et al.* 1996: 23n)

According to Foucault, the powerful effects of discourse operate at the level of every human individual who comes, as a result of being exposed to various discourses, to 'know' what it is to be 'human'. They therefore strive to behave in an 'essentially human' way in their everyday lives (Foucault 1979: 94). Power here is not an oppressive force which somehow bends, shapes or distorts our natural human essence. Instead, power actually makes us what we are, it produces our beliefs about ourselves and the ways in which we act towards ourselves and each other. Foucault therefore differs from more conventional analysts of socialization – Freud (1963) is the classic example – who argue that we learn socially acceptable behaviour and at the same time repress our natural instincts. Instead, Foucault emphasizes that:

> The individual is not to be conceived of as . . . inert material on which power comes to fasten or against which it happens to strike, and in so doing subdues or crushes individuals . . . the individual is an effect of power (Foucault 1980: 98).

To summarize, Foucault argues that the discourses which prevail in modern society literally *produce* us – there is no human individual outside of discourse, no human essence which is shaped by specific discursive regimes. For example, Foucault's analysis of sex in the first volume of *The History of Sexuality* (1979) accepts that we are beings who, in certain circumstances, experience particular kinds of physical sensations. However, Foucault does not accept the prevailing understanding of these sensations as making up something called sex – a crucially important human essence which must be carefully managed and expressed only in certain ways (for example, not in return for money) – as any sort of 'real truth' about human beings. As he argues: ' The notion of "sex" [has] made it possible to group together, in an artificial unity, anatomical elements, biological functions, conducts, sensations and pleasures' (Foucault 1979: 154).

For Foucault, modern ideas, arguments, symbols, practices and institutions have produced a powerful image of the human individual as having essential sexual desires, capacities and responsibilities – but he suggests that this is *only* an image, not an essentially truthful portrayal of human existence as such. His analysis is therefore focused on identifying the point at which these 'anatomical elements, biological functions, conducts, sensations and pleasures' became something which we know as 'sex'.

None the less, as the above implies, discourses can only be sustained by the activities of human subjects because we reproduce them through thinking, behaving and doing things in particular ways. If we do not accept a discourse as true – for example, if we reject the have/hold discourse's claim that sex should not be exchanged for money – we do not understand ourselves and behave in ways which reflect and sustain that discourse. For Foucault, we create and sustain our own subjection to the powerful operations of discourse: 'Power is only exercised over free subjects and only insofar as they are free' (Foucault 1982: 221). Therefore discourses are always unstable, and Foucault's analysis places particular emphasis on the ways in which discursive understandings of sex, for example, change and shift over time (Foucault 1979, 1986a, 1990). Furthermore, Foucault also emphasizes that power is: 'in reality an open, more-or-less coordinated (in the event, no doubt ill coordinated) cluster of relations' (Foucault 1980: 199). That is to say, the multiplicity of discourses currently in existence means that the *particular* way in which an individual will come to 'understand' or 'know' themselves is unpredictable – because there are a variety of identities available to us at any one time (also see Hollway 1989). Foucault also suggests it is our constitution as thinking, active human agents, which comes about as a result of our exposure to discourse, that makes us able to reject particular discourses and to 'buy in' to others as more 'meaningful' or more 'true'. He therefore suggests that, wherever there is power, there is resistance. We, as active human agents produced through the operations of discourse, can resist; we can say 'no' to particular discursive regimes. For example, there is evidence that some prostitutes refuse to see the work that they do as morally degrading, and instead find it sexually pleasurable and fulfilling, despite the popular understanding (as generated by the have/hold discourse) that sex ought not to be sold for money (Brewis and Linstead 2000a, 2000b). However, as suggested above, and importantly, Foucault suggests that we choose to buy in to or to reject discourses *on the basis of our perceptions of them as more or less meaningful, more or less true*. Our rejection or refusal of one particular set of discursive understandings, then, always derives from our sense that we 'know a better truth'; it always derives from the powerful effects of *another discourse*. Prostitutes who resist the have/hold discourse can be seen to buy in, instead, to what Hollway (1989) describes as the permissive discourse – which argues that any kind of sex is acceptable as long as it is pleasurable. Resistance does not, therefore, take us beyond power – while we are able to resist specific discourses, we are mistaken to think that this resistance liberates us in any fundamental way.

Consequently, Foucault goes on to argue that our ways of understanding ourselves, occasionally resistant though they are, are unpromising. For him, our preoccupation with being 'truly human' closes off other ways for us to be. This concern leads Foucault (1986a, 1986b, 1988, 1990) to argue that we should develop a new form of understanding ourselves. This (his 'critical ontology of self') rests on a full-scale resistance to there being *any* enduring human truth, on the questioning of *all* knowledge available to us. Within the critical ontology of self, argues Foucault, we become able to *genuinely choose* who we want to be from available interpretations of what it is to be human, rather than being *compelled* to reproduce what we see as meaningful or true. This is a much more reflexive form of relating to ourselves and so Foucault moves towards the conclusion that it is possible for us to try to 'separate out, from the *contingency* that has made us what we are, the possibility of *no longer being, doing or thinking what we are, do or think*' (Foucault 1986b: 46 – emphasis added).

In engaging in this kind of self-reflection, Foucault implies, we learn 'how we suffer from being what we are', we identify what it is that we have not permitted ourselves to be. It is this kind of practice which Foucault advocates we build into our lives. As he points out:

> The critical ontology of ourselves has to be considered as an attitude, an ethos, a philosophical life in which the critique of what we are is at one and the same time the historical analysis of the limits that are imposed on us and an experiment with the possibility of going beyond them (Foucault 1986b: 50).

For Foucault, we become free when we are able to think of the ways in which we live as entirely contingent and so are able to 'get free of ourselves' over and over again.

To conclude, the strengths of Foucauldian analysis are that, first, it is able to unpack the effects of our exposure to a variety of discourses and the consequent complexity (and at times inconsistency) of our beliefs about and behaviour in the world. It also decries essentialism – the notion that human beings have some kind of natural or ideal state to which we should always strive to return. Essentialism is always restrictive, because it sets up one way of living as the ideal – and it should be noted that this 'ideal' is frequently racist, sexist, homophobic, ageist and so on. The origins of the Holocaust, as well as those of more recent attempts at ethnic cleansing, for example, can be seen to lie in essentialist philosophy about what is 'properly' and 'ideally' human (Bauman 1989; Hebdige 1989). Finally, Foucauldian analysis, in refusing to offer utopian promises of an existence without power, forces us to pay attention to our lives as they are currently lived. Foucault is very suspicious of grand political projects like the Marxist revolution, which promise such a utopia, because they rest on ideals of an essentially better future and the notion of power as oppressive. He instructs instead that power matters in our own lives, and that we as individual human agents can begin to make a difference to the ways in which we live and the experiences that we have by reflecting on what it means for us to behave, think and feel in certain ways (Foucault 1980, 1986b, 1988). His analysis thus opens space for all of us to begin to make that difference, on our own terms and in our own lives (Brewis 1998). It is these strengths in Foucault which make him an interesting and useful theorist in terms of understanding – and potentially working to change – organizational relations.

Using Foucauldian analysis as explained above, then, this chapter aims to examine the ways in which a particular group of organizational participants reproduce and resist one contemporary discourse around sex at work – that of scientific modernism – and to ascertain what it means for these men and women to understand themselves in these ways. The ideas, arguments, symbols, institutions and practices which make up this discourse denote its powerful effects in terms of the ways that humans relate to, interact amongst and seek to organize themselves. Scientific modernism is summarized in the section which follows.

SCIENTIFIC MODERNISM, SEX AND WORK

Scientific modernism, which derives from the Enlightenment philosophy of the late seventeenth and eighteenth centuries, defines the ideal state of human existence as consisting of a trade-off – the need for humans to become less instinctive and less 'sexual' and, instead, more rational and more intellectual. It suggests that humans cannot make the best kinds of decisions about how to run their lives if they do not suppress their instincts, the most disorderly of these being sex (Marcuse 1969). This discourse is characterized by 'the fear that the unrepressed human body will turn out to be a wild animal rutting and snarling in the squalor of its own excrement' (Watts 1975: 168). An example of scientific modernist thinking can be found in the work of Freud; particularly his argument that sexual instincts clash with orderly social life. According to Freud, the repression of 'natural' sexual urges is necessary if humans are to achieve 'civilization', to make the world 'beautiful' and 'serviceable' – so civilization is to some degree restrictive and restricted (Freud 1963: 32–3). As Rieff (cited in Watts 1975: 41) suggests, then: 'Not only did Freud employ sexuality to deflate the pride of civilized man, he further defined it pejoratively by those qualities which make the sexual instinct intractable to civilized sensibility.'

Scientific modernism makes us responsible for using reason as the best way of fashioning our social world. Following from this, it suggests that we need to control our instincts, and our sexual appetites in particular.

Ideas, arguments, symbols, institutions and practices characteristic of scientific modernism can be identified in Europe as early as the seventeenth century (Elias 1978; Bauman 1983). More significant here, however, is the division of society into the two realms of public and private, which emerged in particular during the eighteenth century and is usually associated with the onset of capitalism. The public realm was at this time designated as the sphere of rational decision-making – so as to ensure that production, education, health provision and so on were maintained at the optimum level, free from 'irrationality'. The private realm became the sphere of home, family, intimacy, emotions, reproduction and sex (Martin 1989: 16). The instincts here are relegated to the private sphere, at a 'safe distance' from the sphere of decision-making and public policy, of production and progress.

Weber (1970: 204) suggests that the organizational type which began to proliferate across the public sphere at this time was highly and purely bureaucratic, even compared to bureaucracies typical of earlier societies. He summarizes the benefits of the bureaucracy as follows:

> Bureaucratization offers above all the optimum possibility for carrying through the principle of specializing administrative functions according to purely objective considerations. Individual performances are allocated to functionaries who have specialized training and who by constant practice learn more and more. The 'objective' discharge of business primarily means a discharge of business according to *calculable rules* and 'without regard for persons' (Weber 1970: 215 – emphasis in the original).

This proliferation of bureaucracies, rule driven, governed by objectivity and task focused as they are, was seemingly intended to buttress the public sphere against the irrationality of the instincts, and of sex in particular. In bureaucratizing the public sphere, the early moderns seem to have created organizations designed to protect them from themselves; to ensure that, within this sphere, they behaved rationally at all times and did not 'fall prey' to their instincts. Scientific modernism has therefore been extremely powerful historically, constituting subjects to believe in themselves as possessing a sexual capacity and sexual desires which threatened their ability to reason. However, the relevant question at this point is the extent to which scientific modernism *still* informs thinking about, approaches to, relationships at and activities within work. This is the issue which the next section explores.

SCIENTIFIC MODERNISM AND CONTEMPORARY ORGANIZATIONAL RELATIONS

Data from a programme of semi-structured interviews conducted in a university (Smithtown) and a financial services company (Minerva) are used in this section in order to underline how powerful scientific modernism can be seen to have been with regard to individuals in the respondent group, and to ascertain what it might mean for these men and women to understand themselves in these ways. The data used here are intended to render visible 'real life' power effects of, and resistances to, one discourse around sex at work, and therefore to make Foucault's complex argument about power and discourse easier to grasp.

Respondents tended to identify sexual relationships as potentially problematic, even 'absolutely disastrous', in the work context. A Smithtown female technician remarked that:

> I think that's it, work's work and play's play, you know, and I don't go sort of behind filing cabinets and have a go [sex] with somebody. I think that's absolutely disgusting, or the dark room, I mean, the dark room, I could easily go in there . . . I don't think that's right . . . there are limits . . . I think there's a time and a place for everything.

This respondent suggests that there may be opportunities to engage in sex at work – but that these should be resisted, because the 'time and place' for sex is out of work hours, in the private sphere. Furthermore, those respondents who worked in the same organization as their partner were insistent that they made a conscious effort not to see their 'other half' whilst at work. Other couples were described as behaving in similar ways:

I know there's one couple and I said [to the man] 'How do you manage to work on the same section as your girlfriend?'. Cause they're actually engaged now as well, and he said 'We just don't speak to each other during the day. We just ignore each other completely, you know' (female underwriter, Minerva).

There's a lad on our section who doesn't bother really – [he and his girlfriend] sit twenty yards [apart] and I sit in the middle. They sit ten yards either side [of me] and it doesn't bother them much. They come in [to work] together and that's all (male clerk, Minerva).

Both Smithtown and Minerva respondents also talked of problems caused by 'uncontrolled' sexual relationships between colleagues. A female Ph.D. student at Smithtown pointed to two relationships which she thought had affected the judgement of the men involved:

Well, basically, the lecturer in our department who was having a relationship with a student, he threatened to leave if she didn't get the lectureship that came up . . . there's a postdoc[toral researcher] and a Ph.D. student and that's caused problems inasmuch as he [postdoc] kind of has a lot to say about what goes on in the lab and has helped her quite a bit, too much basically.

Similarly disparaging remarks were made by others about the first couple, who were engaged at the time of the interviews. They were described as having a general tendency to let their sexual involvement, their intimacy, spill over into work time.

The difficulties which arise when such a relationship ends were also referred to. The theme here was that the emotionality of the period after a break-up prevented the ex-partners concentrating on work, as well as making it difficult for their colleagues. A female section supervisor at Minerva, for example, told of how one of her staff had absented herself from the section to air differences with her former partner, also a Minerva employee, in another part of the building. She said that the pair were returning to work just as she arrived to separate them, but also that 'I would have felt compelled to do something about that' if they had continued to argue.

On the whole, it seems that Smithtown and Minerva respondents feel that sex and work can co-exist only under certain tightly controlled circumstances – because sex is seen to affect the individual's capacity to work to the best of their ability. Interestingly, however, despite this general theme of the reproduction of the precepts of scientific modernism in respondents' thoughts and reported actions, there was also some evidence of an apparent rejection on the part of some respondents of the need for there to be such a rigid division between sex and work. At Minerva, the clerical staff describe themselves and are described by others to be the most 'sexy' in their organizational conduct. This group apparently spend a proportion of their working day chattering about subjects which could be classified as sexual – employees fancying each other, periods, sexual relationships and so on. For example, a male senior clerk said he was often consulted by female colleagues about their relationship difficulties:

I just speak my mind and obviously I know what's in a lad's mind . . . they won't see it, you know, I have to explain to them, say 'Oh well, you know, they'll do that' and if someone's seeing someone behind his girlfriend's back then that annoys me . . . I'll have to explain . . .

The clerks also claim that it is very unlikely that anyone involved in this 'banter' would be offended. The only instance of such banter (chatter amongst men about a lunchtime visit to a stripshow) reported as having offended another individual was dismissed as an instance of over-reaction on the part of that individual. Otherwise, the banter was noted only as a potential source of mild irritation if the working day had been trying or tiring.

This banter might be seen to indicate that junior members of Minerva staff do not necessarily agree that sex and work are incompatible; that they are to some extent resistant to scientific modernism. It was also noted by higher grade employees that the banter might pose a threat to efficiency. For example:

> I mean, you get the banter on the sections where you get the lower grades and it's just dismissed as a laugh but obviously there has to be an end to that and *if it goes further then you're stepping on thin ice really* . . . (male senior underwriter – emphasis added).

However, the clerks mainly accepted and approved of the banter. One man, for example, had been promoted into a section which in the main consisted of higher grade staff. He said that: 'what I do miss is all my mates downstairs, there was always something happening. The people on our floor are a bit different, they're not like that . . . I feel a bit left out' (male clerk).

At Smithtown, 'sexy' banter seemed less common – perhaps because those members of Smithtown staff occupying positions similar to the Minerva clerical grades tend to work in offices on their own. There are, for example, no secretarial pools at Smithtown. Where banter was seen to exist, however, was amongst the technicians, who are also of a relatively low grade and who share offices within the university. Most respondents commented that they would expect the technicians to display the most 'sexy' forms of behaviour in Smithtown and the technicians themselves supported this:

> You should hear the conversations that I have when the lads are there. Nothing [is sacred], I mean they don't worry, they just say, intimate parts of the body, sexual relations, not particularly their own personal ones but they joke and laugh, you know . . . (female technician).

Certain postgraduate students were also described as having a bantering culture. This group again could be seen to be of low status in the organizational hierarchy. The situation in Smithtown is therefore roughly approximate to the situation at Minerva – what resistance there appears to be to scientific modernism exists amongst groups who occupy the lower hierarchical levels. What is particularly interesting about the banter in both organizations is that it is reported both by those who engage in it and by those who do not – this suggests that it is a well-established behaviour.

What, then, does all of this mean for the individual subjects who are talking here about their beliefs, relationships and practices at work with regard to sex?

Firstly, it is important to note that Weber himself (and others such as Marcuse, 1968, 1969; Habermas, 1972, 1987; and Adorno and Horkheimer, 1979) have criticized the powerful effects of scientific modernism – such as the bureaucracy. Weber asserts that bureaucracy is a formally rational, technically superior way to organize human action. However, he also refers to the 'iron cage' of bureaucracy, and laments what he sees to be its inexorable rise, stifling human freedom, spontaneity and creativity. Weber, then, is a staunch 'critic of the standardization and insensitivity of bureaucratized capitalism . . . a cultural interpreter of the soulless characterology of the modern state' (Turner 1992: 11–12).

Considering the data in terms of these concerns of Weber's, it seems that scientific modernism may have constituted certain Smithtown and Minerva subjects who adhere so religiously to the separation of sex and work that a good deal of meaning in work is lost to them and their colleagues. For example:

> . . . [bureaucracy] doesn't really create an environment in which you can express your view, for example, in the department . . . the extent to which you can is very limited by the sort of formal bureaucratic arrangements (female employee relations officer, Minerva).

> yeah, I mean formally in the company as a whole there's probably a bit more feeling inhibited because of the size of the place and the bureaucracy . . . and I just think 'Well, that's so inhibiting [of] even work taking place let alone any feeling of enjoying what you're doing' (female graduate recruitment officer, Minerva).

This reluctance to voice an opinion, which apparently comes from a sense that to do so would be 'irrational' or incautious, is reported by Smithtown respondents to be stronger in certain situations. Where individuals are subordinate to others, and may also depend on them for career progression and advice, concern about being too outspoken, too irrational, is seen to increase. For example:

> from time to time I smell a little amount of fear among [postgraduate] students where I say 'Well, go and see your supervisor and bloody give him hell' . . . and they're [i.e. students] reluctant 'cause they've [i.e. supervisors] got to sign the report, they've got to pass the thesis, and I detect a little bit of fear in that . . . just the fact that it's student–supervisor and [supervisors have] a little bit of power over them (male head technician).

Moreover, in one department at Smithtown, an atmosphere which seems again to be rooted in scientific modernist understandings of the necessary separation of sex and work was identified as making team work difficult, reducing enjoyment of work and interfering with the flow of information. For example, a secretary told an anecdote about her boss, a professor, which seems to demonstrate how individuals can come to isolate themselves at work as a result of scientific modernist understandings. This professor always asks the respondent to type memos if he wishes to communicate with another member of the department – even if that member of staff occupies the next door office! She also has to announce him on the telephone, no matter who he is ringing. Further to this, a female lecturer commented that this professor is unable to let down his ultra-impersonal guard even at departmental social occasions – she says that, when the group go to the pub, they do not invite this professor: '[he's a] nice bloke, but we can get pissed without him'. However, the most damning criticism of the effects of scientific modernist understandings on workplace relations came from another female lecturer in this department:

> I think people are just expected to get on [with their work here] so any deviation from work seems to be not acceptable . . . I think there is no understanding of

> human relationships in general and that's my feeling. There is very little experience among the management of human relationships in general . . . this is the first place where I have been where they do not have any human relationships, apart from fishing. I would describe that as really extremely boring . . . this is the first place where I didn't make friends.

This woman talked of the lack of sympathy with which she had been treated since coming to Smithtown, also saying that she had recently been seriously ill, which she attributed to her experiences there.

Here a proportion of the respondents describe what it can be like working in an environment where scientific modernist understandings prevail – that it can be frustrating, frightening and could even make one ill.

A further implication of this powerfulness of scientific modernism seems to be a degradation of working women. Scientific modernism has been identified by feminist commentators as very *masculine* (see, for example, Mills and Tancred, 1992; Parkin, 1993). The fact that women traditionally have been considered to be closer to their instincts and to sex in particular, because of their role in carrying and giving birth to children, is argued to mean that what scientific modernism sees as problematic in the public sphere are the supposedly feminine elements of the human condition. Women therefore come to be seen as less fit for organizational life than men – as having 'further to go' in the development of reason, if indeed they are capable of reason at all.

This notion that men and women are naturally different, that women are more emotional, more sexual and thus less suited to organizational life, shows up clearly in the Smithtown and Minerva data. Many respondents implied that women are not naturally made of the 'stern stuff' required for reasoned and objective decision-making. For example:

> Mostly the supervisors are women . . . I think they may give a softer approach if [staff] step out of line. I wouldn't know for certain, it just may appear that way. (male clerk, Minerva).

> I think the women [supervisors] are generally more lenient towards letting customers off paying money whereas a man'd argue down the phone, say 'No, you're not having this, we are going to take you to court', whereas a woman might say, particularly my supervisor would say 'Oh, they can have it.' (male senior clerk, Minerva).

Women are also depicted as less able to make rational judgements of others. Their supposed tendency to be 'bitchy', to criticize colleagues on irrelevant or irrational grounds, appeared in respondent commentary several times. For example:

> there is quite a bit of infighting among the girls upstairs, you know, and they watch each other . . . I don't like it . . . But I think when you get a group of women together you always get that – one watches what the other's got, doesn't like it . . . (female technician, Smithtown).

Interestingly, some interviewees were equally critical of women who were perceived to have stepped too far out of their 'natural' gender role, to be acting 'overly' rationally or 'overly' assertively. For example, a female academic at Smithtown was described by several respondents as 'bolshy', 'pushy', and 'having something to prove'. Moreover, even the more positive evaluations of women appeared to derive from an assumption that women fit neatly into the feminine mould. For example, respondents talked of women's supposed social skills as opposed to men's insensitivity:

> If it's a person problem as I call it, rather than a work issue, I find the women always think about it very very deeply before they're prepared to take any action or consider a conclusion to it. The men are very much to the other extreme – 'Oh, just get it done, tell 'em' (female section supervisor, Minerva).

A female lecturer at Smithtown agreed that men are less able to cope with 'personal' issues:

> I think that men are less sensitive to each other . . . they're all rigid in their approach towards work and they think that if there has been any other problems at work then they expect that it will just drop out of sight.

There was also some criticism of men for what was perceived to be an excessive preoccupation with work:

> Because he liked it all so much it wasn't a contest for him, he wasn't thinking 'Oh God, the kids'll be in bed by the time I get home.' It was his life, he loved it . . . men like having obsessive absorptions (female lecturer, Smithtown – talking about her ex-boss).

Even when contrasts between men and women are being made which favour women, then, there still seems to be a sense that women are not ideally suited to the 'cut and thrust' world of the workplace because they make decisions more slowly, they are more sensitive to other people and they are less concerned with work than they are with private sphere activities. The comments from women that distinguish between the genders' 'natural' capacities are especially interesting, given that they are often (whether explicitly or implicitly) criticizing their own gender here.

Furthermore, comments from Smithtown respondents suggested that these understandings result in a downgrading of women in organizational practice. The female lecturer who had suffered from a stress-related illness described her department as very sexist, and stated that her problems derived at least partly from this sexism. Another female academic said that her male colleagues had not encouraged her to apply for the job which she currently holds – even though at the time she was a researcher in the department and, therefore, a logical candidate. She attributed this failure to their assumption that she would soon be leaving work to start a family. The association of women with irrationality, with the instincts and with sex, then, is seen by these women as frequently producing organizational inequality.

The last issue to be considered here is the seeming resistance among some Smithtown and Minerva staff to the scientific modernist precept that sex and work cannot co-exist. As implied earlier, Foucault (1980, 1988) argues that resistance should not be read as an irrepressible 'humanness' bubbling up against 'repression'. Resistance for him is always localized, specific and has its own implications – because it derives from an alternative discursive understanding of the world, or even from a different level of the same discourse, as is evident in the discussion that follows. This ambiguity of resistance can be identified in the accounts of banter from

Smithtown and Minerva respondents. The fact that the clerical staff at Minerva are very tightly disciplined, so as, seemingly, to ensure that their workplace conduct is irreproachably rational, was mentioned several times. For example:

> Obviously the nature of the [clerical] work is of a less challenging nature . . . if you think about it [the clerks are] actually often timed in their work. They have very little sort of *responsibility or autonomy* in their work, they do one thing and then it goes on to a higher grade (female employee relations officer – emphasis added).

The clerks often expressed a sense that this lack of opportunity to *make decisions, to reason for themselves* at work, and the boredom that results, means that they banter to provide a respite. Such banter seems to represent little more than an attempt to obtain some enjoyment (however minimal) from their working day – an attempt to offset the frustration caused by not being able to use their own reasoning abilities. Furthermore, despite senior staff's concern that the banter might prove disruptive, the clerks frequently made a connection between the banter and their own productivity. For instance:

> Everyone tends to respect someone more that'll speak to them normally and also respect the fact that, you know, you do need to talk during the day, you can't come in for eight hours a day and just sit here doing the job . . . people'll rebel against it . . . you usually find the sections that are [a] lot [more] moody and that's usually 'cause like the supervisor [is] cracking [down] on them all the time so they rebel against it and think 'Oh, I'm doing nothing for him' and [they] carry on talking anyway 'cause they're not going to shut up (female senior clerk).

There is, then, no real subversion of the scientific modernist bureaucratic regime at Minerva as a result of the banter. Indeed, it is quite clear from the comment above that management tolerance of banter may forestall a much more significant form of rebellion. Furthermore, the clerks seem in their *apparent* resistance to reproduce understandings *characteristic* of scientific modernism – that workplace activity should be characterized by the use of reason. It appears to be the resentment caused by their inability to use their reason at work – due to the tight discipline exercised – which gives rise to the 'safety valve' of the sexy banter. Similar arguments can be made with regard to Smithtown, where it is the technicians and postgraduate students who are reported to indulge in this kind of chatter – those staff who, again, are near the bottom of the organizational hierarchy. This analysis of banter bears out Foucault's argument that resistance must always be treated as ambiguous.

CONCLUSIONS

This chapter has, using Foucault, catalogued the power effects of and resistances to one discourse around sex at work with regard to a particular respondent group. The analysis has, in examining scientific modernism as an *interpretation* of what it is to be human which generates particular kinds of effects and resistances and, more importantly, emphasizing that these effects and resistances have certain implications, explored the constraints which Smithtown and Minerva respondents place around their working lives. It is this kind of analysis which Foucault envisages will encourage others to begin to question what they 'know' of 'themselves', to begin the critical ontology of self.

As suggested earlier, Foucault's writings about what he conceives of as freedom differ significantly from those offered by more conventional theorists of social and organizational behaviour – his intention is to create spaces for us to contest our current beliefs about ourselves, rather than to provide us with detailed prescriptions about the nature of that freedom. Foucault therefore offers a radical alternative for understanding the way that we relate to each other in organizations, whilst also allowing us to work to change those relations at the level where we experience them – that of our own personal interactions. Furthermore, he allows us to analyse organizational life as mediated by a variety of *competing* discourses which claim to explain the human condition – enabling us to analyse neglected aspects of workplace relations such as sex.

Notes

1   This label is derived from the work of Geuss (cited in Reed, 1985: 80–1).

REFERENCES

Adorno, T.W. and Horkheimer, M. (1979) *Dialectic of Enlightenment*, Verso, London.

Baudrillard, J. (1990) *Seduction*, Macmillan Education, Basingstoke.

Bauman, Z. (1983) Industrialism, consumerism and power, *Theory, Culture and Society*, 1 (3): 32–43.

Bauman, Z. (1989) *Modernity and the Holocaust*, Polity, Cambridge.

Brewis, J. (1996) *Sex, Work and Sex at Work: a Foucauldian Analysis*, unpublished Ph.D. thesis, UMIST, UK.

Brewis, J. (1998) Who do you think you are? Feminism, work, ethics and Foucault, in Parker, M. (ed.) *The Ethics of Organization*, Sage, London.

Brewis, J. and Grey, C. (1994) Re-eroticizing the Organization: an Exegesis and Critique, *Gender Work and Organization*, 1 (2): 67–82.

Brewis, J., Hampton, M.P. and Linstead, S. (1996) Unpacking Priscilla: subjectivity and identity in the organization of gendered appearance, *Occasional Papers in Organizational Analysis* (4), Department of Business and Management, University of Portsmouth Business School.

Brewis, J. and Linstead, S. (forthcoming 2000a) Placing prostitution, discourse and desire in the analysis of sex and work, *Human Relations*.

Brewis, J., and Linstead, S. (forthcoming 2000b) The worst thing is the screwing: consumption and the management of identity in sex work, *Gender, Work and Organization*, 7 (2).

Burrell, G. (1984) Sex and organizational analysis, *Organization Studies*, 5 (2): 97–118.

Burrell, G. (1992) The organization of pleasure, in Alvesson, M. and Willmott, H. (eds) *Critical Management Studies*, Sage, London, 67–88.

Burrell, G. and Hearn, J. (1989) The sexuality of organization, in Hearn, J., Sheppard, D.L., Tancred-Sheriff, P. and Burrell, G. (eds) *The Sexuality of Organization*, Sage, London, 1–28.

Cixous, H. (1988) Sorties, in Lodge, D. (ed.) *Modern Criticism and Theory*, Longman, London, 286–293.

Collinson, D.L. and Collinson, M. (1989) Sexuality in the workplace: the domination of men's sexuality, in Hearn, J., Sheppard, D.L., Tancred-Sheriff, P. and Burrell, G. (eds), *The Sexuality of Organization*, Sage, London, 91–109.

Elias, N. (1978) *The Civilizing Process: The History of Manners*, Basil Blackwell, Oxford.

Farley, L. (1982) *Sexual Shakedown: Sexual Harassment of Women on the Job*, McGraw-Hill, New York.

Foucault, M. (1979) *The History of Sexuality, Volume 1: An Introduction*, Allen Lane, London.

Foucault, M. (1980) *Power/ Knowledge: Selected Interviews and Other Writings 1972–1977*, Gordon, C. (ed.) Harvester Press, Brighton, Sussex.

Foucault, M. (1982) The subject and power in Dreyfus, H. and Rabinow, P. (eds.), *Michel Foucault: Beyond Structuralism and Hermeneutics*, Chicago University Press, Chicago, 202–226.

Foucault, M. (1986a) *The History of Sexuality, Volume 2: The Use of Pleasure*, trans. R. Hurley, Viking/Penguin, Harmondsworth.

Foucault, M. (1986b) *The Foucault Reader*, Paul Rabinow (ed.), Penguin, Harmondsworth.

Foucault, M. (1988) *Politics, Philosophy, Culture: Interviews and Other Writings 1977–1984*, Kritzman, L.D. (ed.), Routledge, New York.

Foucault, M. (1990) *The History of Sexuality, Volume 3: The Care of the Self*, Penguin, Harmondsworth.

Freud, S. (1963) *Civilization and its Discontents*, Hogarth Press, London.

Habermas, J. (1972) *Knowledge and Human Interests*, Heinemann Educational, London.

Habermas, J. (1987) *The Philosophical Discourse of Modernity*, Blackwell, Oxford.

Hearn, J. and Parkin, W. (1995) *'Sex' at 'Work': The Power and Paradox of Organization Sexuality* (2nd edn) Hemel Hempstead: Prentice Hall/Harvester-Wheatsheaf.

Hearn, J., Sheppard, D.L., Tancred-Sheriff, P. and Burrell, G. (eds) (1989) *The Sexuality of Organization*, Sage, London.

Hebdige, D. (1989) 'After the masses', *Marxism Today*, January, 48–53.

Hollway, W. (1989) *Subjectivity and Method in Psychology: Gender, Meaning and Science*, Sage, London.

Konrad, A.M. and Gutek, B.A. (1986) Impact of work experiences on attitudes towards sexual harassment, *Administrative Science Quarterly*, 31 (3), 422–38.

MacKinnon, C.A. (1979) *Sexual Harassment of Working Women: A Case of Sex Discrimination*, Yale University Press, New Haven, Ct.

Marcuse, H. (1968) *Negations: Essays in Critical Theory*, Allen Lane, London.

Marcuse, H. (1969) *Eros and Civilization: A Philosophical Inquiry into Freud*, Allen Lane, London.

Martin, E. (1989) *The Woman in the Body: A Cultural Analysis of Reproduction*, Open University Press, Milton Keynes.

Mills, A.J. and Tancred, P. (1992) Introduction, in Mills, A.J. and Tancred, P. (eds), *Gendering Organizational Analysis*, Sage, London, 1–8.

O'Connell Davidson, J. (1995) The anatomy of 'free choice' prostitution, *Gender, Work and Organization*, 2 (1): 1–10.

Parkin, W. (1993) The public and the private: gender, sexuality and emotion, in Fineman, S. (ed.) *Emotion in Organizations*, Sage, London, 167–189.

Pettinger, R. (1996) *Introduction to Organisational Behaviour*, Macmillan Business, Basingstoke.

Reed, M. (1985) *Redirections in Organizational Analysis*, Tavistock Publications, London.

Reich, W. (1942) *The Function of the Orgasm*, Noonday, New York.

Reich, W. (1969) *The Sexual Revolution: Towards a Self-Governing Character Structure*, Vision Press, London.

Reich, W. (1972a) *The Invasion of Compulsory Sex-Morality*, Souvenir Press, London.

Reich, W. (1972b) *Reich Speaks Out On Freud*, Higgins, M. and Raphael, C.M. (eds), Souvenir Press, London.

Robbins, S.P. (1998) *Organizational Behavior: Concepts, Controversies, Applications* (8th edn), Prentice-Hall International, Upper Saddle River, NJ.

Schneider, B.E. (1982) Consciousness about sexual harassment among heterosexual and lesbian women workers, *Journal of Social Issues*, 38 (4), 75–98.

Thompson, P. and McHugh, D. (1995) *Work Organisations: A Critical Introduction* (2nd edn), Macmillan Business, Basingstoke.

Turner, B.S. (1992) *Max Weber: From History to Modernity*, Routledge, London.

Vecchio, R.P. (1995) *Organizational Behavior*, (3rd edn), Dryden Press, Fort Worth, TX.

Watts, A. (1975) *Psychotherapy East and West*, Vintage Books, New York.

Weber, M. (1964) *The Theory of Social and Economic Organization*, Free Press, New York.

Weber, M. (1968) *Economy and Society: An Outline of Interpretive Sociology*, Bedminster Press, New York.

Weber, M. (1970) *From Max Weber: Essays in Sociology*, Gerth, H.H. and Wright-Mills, C. (eds) Routledge and Kegan Paul, London.

Wilson, F.M. (1995) *Organizational Behaviour and Gender*, McGraw-Hill, London.

New technologies and organizational behaviour

6

Rod Allen, Nod Miller and Sally Wyatt

INTRODUCTION

New information and communication technologies (ICTs) – which themselves represent one of the largest and highest-growth business sectors – are implicated in changing the face of industrial and institutional organizations in ways which would have been hard to predict even 10 years ago. People no longer need to work in city centres, side by side with their colleagues. Information necessary for work can be communicated across any distance. This opens up possibilities for new forms of organization, as well as the elimination of considerable quantities of paper. On the other hand, ICTs can be used to create working methods which replace or consolidate tasks previously performed by people, and they can be used to monitor the productivity of remaining workers. Management can obtain access to substantial quantities of information about the performance of products, markets and people; so new ICTs are being used to make people redundant, to change the skill mix, to intensify management control over the labour process and to alter divisions of labour within organizations. At the same time, the pervasive diffusion of ICTs, particularly in the office environment, presents a challenge to orthodox organizational behaviour theory. Instead of an ever-increasing division of labour, for instance, it is possible to observe widespread consolidation and recombination of tasks; and the alienation which has long been thought to arise from automation in the workplace does not seem to be manifesting itself widely in the PC-dominated networked office.

In this chapter we set out to make connections between the work of those who study the social relations of technology and issues arising in the field of organizational behaviour. We take the general view that technological change is socially determined, coming about largely because of factors exogenous to the technologies themselves, and that it is important to study the interdependency of social structures (including industrial and business organizations) and technological change. Institutions and organizations are not obliged to adopt new technologies nor to use them in particular ways. Institutions and organizations themselves are inextricably linked with the process of technological change: it is in the context of society's changing behaviours and needs – explicit and implicit – that technologies are developed, exploited, taken up or rejected.

There is sparse mention in the OB literature of new information and communication technologies, their origins or their implications, outside of discussion of computerized automation in the manufacturing sector. For example, Robbins

(1998) makes no mention of computers, telecommunications technologies, groupware or management information systems, even though the latest edition of this volume incorporates a CD-ROM bound into its inside back cover containing the full text of the book (its presence appears to be seen as completely unproblematic, since it is mentioned only on the front cover). Buchanan and Huczynski (1997: 576) do, on the other hand, deal with 'advanced technology and the changing nature of work', but this takes up a mere 10 pages in a book of 744 pages, suggesting they do not attach much importance to it (indeed they have reduced the space devoted to the topic since the previous 1991 edition). Similarly, Fincham and Rhodes (1992) only have a short, though useful, section on technology and the labour process. Kling (1996) examines in particular the replacement of manual record-keeping systems with ICTs.

NEW TECHNO-ECONOMIC PARADIGMS

Electronic computing, the technology at the heart of ICT, has been around for over 50 years. Not all of the promises made by early computer evangelists about productivity gains, abolition of boring and repetitive tasks, and elimination of paperwork have been realized in all of this time. Perez (1983) and others suggest that this is because it takes a long time to adjust to a new 'techno-economic paradigm'. ICTs make it possible to process, communicate and respond to information much more rapidly than previously. Organizations are able to respond more quickly to changes in demand and to customize their product designs, regardless of whether they are selling automobiles, clothing or life insurance. No longer are the techniques of mass production used to achieve economies of scale; now the flexibility offered by ICTs make is possible to achieve economies of *scope*. ICT is not simply a new product nor a new technique radically changing the production process in a single sector; it is a technology that is applicable to all sectors of the economy with the potential for radically altering the way things are done everywhere. Because of this pervasiveness, ICT has been labelled a new techno-economic paradigm (Perez 1983; Dosi *et al.*, 1988).

Changes of techno-economic paradigm do not happen frequently. Previous examples include the host of technical and economic changes associated with the introduction of the steam engine or of electric power. Changes of techno-economic paradigms involve the creation of whole new products and sectors as well as fundamental changes in existing sectors. With a new techno-economic paradigm, there emerges a new factor of production with 'clearly perceived low – and descending – relative costs; unlimited supply for all practical purposes; potential all-pervasiveness; a capacity to reduce the costs of capital, labour and products as well as to change them qualitatively' (Perez 1983: 361). In other words, a new techno-economic paradigm, such as ICT, alters the relative costs of inputs and outputs and thus the conditions of production and distribution for both old and new products. In more qualitative terms, however, it involves the emergence of a new 'common sense', a new best-practice set of rules and customs for designers, engineers, managers and users which differs fundamentally from that established for the previous paradigm. It can take many years for the benefits of the new paradigm to be realized as the process of learning and adaptation takes place in the myriad of economic and social institutions which together constitute economies and societies. The literature on techno-economic paradigms is concerned largely with long-term macro-economic changes. Current research about techno-economic paradigms draws on work earlier this century by Nicholas Kondratiev (1925) and Joseph Schumpeter (1934, 1939, 1943). Both were concerned to explain long-run changes in the relationship between technical change and economic performance. For Schumpeter, this was largely prompted by his experience of the Depression of the 1930s; Kondratiev proposed a long, regular fifty-year cycle of economic change.

In this chapter, we focus on what the new 'common sense' might mean within organizations. There are two possible approaches. The first is informed by the Marxist tradition of labour process theory, in which technology is regarded as one of the major instruments by which capitalists are able to maintain control over workers, by replacing humans with machines, or by imposing a highly detailed division of labour, or by increasing the capacity to monitor the activities and workrates of employees. In arguing that advanced capitalism uses technology to improve management control over workers, Braverman (1974) implies that an important value of new technology for management is that it tends to deskill the workforce, thus increasing the amount of power wielded by a Taylorist management. However, this approach implies that once the technologies are developed, they necessitate a particular form of use. It ignores other considerations at play within capitalism. A second approach recognizes that capitalists use alternative strategies for improving their competitive positions, including the development of new products or of improving quality, both of which require skilled and motivated workers. It also recognizes the possibilities of resistance by trades unions and less formally organized groups of workers. Management is not the only group with clearly defined objectives. The ways in which technologies are actually used can be negotiated at a more local level, shaped by the needs and practices of particular countries, industries or firms; the outcome can tend towards empowerment of the individual worker as well as to less desirable outcomes such as deskilling or job loss. (See the volumes, *Studies in the Labour Process*, arising from the annual labour process theory conferences held in Britain, including Knights and Willmott, 1988, 1990.)

AN EXAMPLE FROM A KNOWLEDGE INDUSTRY

One area which can provide some useful examples of organizational change arising from the increased use of information and communications technologies is that of book publishing. Publishing is itself an information industry and it may be paradigmatic of the expected shifts of power and function implied by the use of ICTs. To illustrate some of the changes which have taken place in the publishing industry we would like to introduce Jane, who has worked as an editor in a London book publishing company for the past 20 years. Our intention is to compare her daily work life today with that of the year in which she first joined the company as an editor. This can help us to understand the processes of change at work, particularly in knowledge-based industries, and to demonstrate that the changes which occur are the result of a complex interplay of social, economic and technological factors.

The changes in the publishing industry have not simply been the result of the arrival of networked personal computers on employees' desks; they have also been affected by changes in the global publishing industry, and by the diffusion of ICTs to other people involved (including authors, printers, retailers and banks). Some of the changes have meant that publishing employees no longer carry out some tasks, but they have also meant that employees have developed new skills, and many of the functions carried out today in a publishing office have replaced functions carried out previously by other groups of workers in other enterprises, thus making significant numbers of people (and skills) redundant over time.

The main work of an editor in the book publishing industry involves selecting ideas for books and persuading management to invest in those ideas by way of publishing contracts and financial advances; liaising with and commissioning work from authors; estimating the production costs and likely sales of individual books; preparing manuscripts for press; seeing work through press; and dealing with the company's sales representatives to ensure that the books are sold effectively into bookstores. An editor also takes part in the day-to-day administration of an editorial department, and may have assistant or associate editors to manage.

PAPER STILL EXISTS

Twenty years ago, Jane's day would have started with the daily post, delivered to her from the company's mailroom. In her mail would be letters from authors, perhaps some direct mail advertising an industry conference, and internal memos from other people in the company. Typically, the letters and memos were typed on manual or electric typewriters, and some of the internal memos consisted of carbon copies (literally, copies made when the memo was being typed by means of the insertion of carbon paper between top and subsequent copies in the platen of a typewriter). Today, she still gets paper-based post, but it is on the whole restricted to formal letters or contracts and advertising matter. Contracts still mainly take written form because of the ease with which electronically-stored text can be altered and because the legal status of an electronic signature has not yet been fully settled. Contracts are the bedrock of much business activity; particularly in areas where intellectual property is concerned, such as publishing and entertainment, it is through the wording of contracts that value is obtained from copyrights. So contracts are still thought to be too important to entrust to intangible forms of communication and reproduction; the risks are too high and the level of trust which can be safely be placed in the scrupulousness of (say) an author's agent not to change contract wording electronically is too low. The written or printed page remains definitive. The production of contracts has been made much easier by the use of word processors which store 'boilerplate' text from which standard forms of contract can be assembled, but for the present, lawyers expect courts only to recognize a handwritten signature on a paper contract. Since in the field of intellectual property the contract remains the most important document of all in relation to revenue generation, management reluctance to automate or digitize the contract itself speaks eloquently about the value which organizations place on technology; the electronically vulnerable digital contract, which addresses the security of a core income stream, has not been adopted. Nevertheless, this reluctance to adopt digital contracts also represents a new determinant for the computer applications industry, which has now seen a market opportunity and created electronic signature systems and text protection protocols which only await testing in a court.

Most of Jane's written communications today come either through the medium of the personal computer on her desk, or (less often these days) by facsimile (fax). The fax started to proliferate in the late 1980s (in Britain, at least partly because a series of postal strikes made traditional business correspondence difficult) despite the fact that the fundamental technology itself was first used at the end of the nineteenth century. It provides an instant means of transmitting written and illustrated material, but the paradigm remains that of the letter; faxes are sometimes dictated by the sender and typed by a secretary (where secretaries still exist), and because the thermal paper on which faxes are sent does not last, incoming faxes are sometimes photocopied (by a secretary) for filing in the traditional manner. Faxes are inherently of low resolution, which means that they are not suitable for transmitting detailed illustrations. And because faxes are effectively graphic objects rather than text objects, material sent by fax cannot be edited or forwarded without rekeying the text and printing it on to paper. By contrast, electronic mail (e-mail), which Jane now uses as her primary communications medium, allows her to type messages directly into her computer, and to send them through local or external computer networks to her correspondents. She can also attach binary files (consisting for example of high-resolution illustrations, word processor documents or spreadsheets) to her e-mail, which her correspondents can view on their screens, or print out, or edit and return, or redistribute.

E-mail appears to be a major factor in a profound change in the division of labour in office work, and it is blurring previously well-defined boundaries between professional and clerical workers. Organizational structures built on a hierarchical pattern in which people are 'protected' by secretaries are flattening out because of the decline in the use of secretarial and clerical staff which has been made possible by the use of personal computers, word processing software, faxes and e-mail. Most people in offices are now expected to type their own mail and maintain their own appointments diaries; the secretarial function, where it is retained at all, is moving to a higher level and the term 'executive assistant' is more likely to be used. This in its turn changes symbolic behaviour in offices; it is harder to use secretaries and outer offices as part of the construction of a 'personal front' (Goffman 1971) if such elements have been eliminated. Whether the reduction of secretarial employment is changing the opportunities available to women in the workforce remains to be seen. Clerical work in offices was originally carried out by men and was taken over largely by women during the 1930s and 1940s (Kling 1996). Fincham and Rhodes (1992) thought that the 2 million women in the workforce who performed clerical and secretarial work were most at risk from what was then being called 'office automation'. Yet in the 1990s there has been no net reduction in the number of women in the workforce; on the contrary, women represent an increasing percentage of the total workforce. According to figures published by the British Council (1997), the economic activity rate for women of working age (16–59) in the UK increased from 63 per cent in 1979 to 71 per cent in 1994, while that for men of working age (16–64) fell from 91 per cent to 85 per cent in the same period. By 1995, the number of women in the British workforce exceeded the number of men. Massive inequities remain, of course, particularly in pay rates (women, on average, received just 73 per cent of the earnings of their male counterparts, excluding overtime, in 1997 (Office of National Statistics, 1998: Table 6.14)); but it appears possible that the release of women from what Kling (1996) calls the 'ghettoised' area of clerical work may have improved women's opportunities for diversity of employment in the way suggested by Friedrichs and Schaff (1982), who predicted that activities which 'creatively occupy' people, such as the professions, management, arts and media, public service, leisure and care, would expand as traditional jobs diminish.

Today, Jane, our editor, is expecting the second draft of a manuscript from one of her authors, who lives in the Scottish Highlands. In 1978, this would have arrived in the mail, typed or handwritten on paper, and Jane would then have gone through the manuscript with a pen, using traditional printers' marks to make corrections and suggestions in the margins of the text. This laborious process would have taken place several times in the production of a manuscript, with an increasingly tattered set of pages shuttling back and forth in the mail between Jane and her author. If the changes required were particularly extensive, the manuscript would probably have been retyped at least once, either by Jane or by a typist, so that further changes could be clearly indicated. Today, the second draft of the manuscript arrives by e-mail from the author as an attached word processor document. During the morning, Jane runs through the manuscript on her computer, using the 'red-line' facility of her word processor to indicate to the author what changes she is suggesting; by lunchtime she has checked the parts of the text about which she is concerned and she e-mails the new version back to the author, who can look at it at once on her computer screen. There are still many authors who write out their copy by hand, or use ordinary typewriters (novelist Melvyn Bragg is said once to have smiled wryly at the suggestion that he might wish to use a laptop), and even today for the most part publishers do not oblige authors to supply their work in machine-readable form; the cost of converting (re-keying) it is still seen to be small by comparison with the income generated by publishing the manuscript, so new technologies cannot be said to be dictating the process in this dimension of the publishing industry. However, national newspapers, on the other hand, now require copy to be filed electronically, and freelance journalists who are not connected to e-mail systems are much less likely to be used than those who are.

EFFECTS OF GROUPWARE ON THE WORKGROUP

It is not merely authors and editors in publishing houses who exchange views on the same written text, or participate in co-operative drafting, by e-mail instead of face-to-face, and the changes in procedure made possible by electronic office communications raise some important questions about social functions in the workplace. The development of 'groupware' such as Lotus Notes over the past few years has taken place as a response to a need for groups to work together on the creation and revision of business documents without constant time-consuming re-typing and redrafting. In the past, such work would have been done across a table in a single meeting-room, with typists in another room working constantly to 'repair' a single text. But today personal 'interactional work' in the workplace (Fincham and Rhodes, 1992) is being replaced by the use of e-mail and groupware; and such aids to communication as gaze (Argyle and Cook 1976) and body language are not readily available over computer networks. This can make it difficult for individuals to make use of the ability to develop 'personal constructs' of others at work (Adams-Webber 1981). Personal construct theory deals with a range of professional social skills which enable people to analyse interactions from different perspectives and make judgements about other people's personalities and meanings; these skills, which can lead to the making of predictions about colleagues, are drawn from previous personal experience of other people. Such experience comes from a wide range of inputs, including appearance, body language and, importantly, small talk about interests, hobbies and pursuits as well as from the content of business interactions. If e-mail and groupware reduce social interaction to terse text, then the likelihood of developing viable personal business relationships and mutual comprehension on the basis of sociality and commonality (Kelly 1955) is diminished; the terseness of e-mail in particular facilitates pre-emption, which leads to the use of stereotypes and ready-made generalizations about the other being constructed (Fincham and Rhodes 1992) and to uncertainty and ambiguity. Video conferencing, by which means people in different locations remain visible to their colleagues in meetings via television cameras and monitors, does not appear to have been generally adopted, and this raises questions about what other ways, if any, might be available for colleagues to construct one another in the workplace.

QUALITY AND/OR QUANTITY OF WORK

A further issue that is highlighted by the swift turnround and terse discourse of e-mail is that of the quality of the work that is done by means of ICTs. Like many people in the cultural industries, Jane derives much of her job satisfaction from the objective characteristics of her job; she has a sense that she is doing her job well and creating a high quality product (Hackman and Oldham 1975). Certainly in terms of the core dimensions of her job – skill variety, task identity, task significance, autonomy and task feedback – there has been a considerable change in the job of an editor in a publishing house as a result of the increasing use of ICTs, and from the perspective of variety and fulfilment many of these changes can be regarded as beneficial. Jane's skill variety has increased; she is required to exercise many more discrete competencies, including copy editing, marketing skills and negotiation ability, than she would have done 20 years ago. Her task identity is stronger, too; having more control over the production of the books for which she is responsible means that she can identify much more closely with the final product when it reaches the bookshops. Her task is clearly a significant one for the outside world; books can have a profound impact, and though not all of Jane's books are world-shaking bestsellers, most of them bring pleasure, insight or knowledge to readers. Jane has much apparent autonomy in her work; she is trusted by management to deal effectively with authors and suppliers, and only when the money she is likely to invest in a book exceeds certain limits does she even have to check with her managers; and she gets clear feedback about her work, not least from the sales figures which appear on her desk every Monday. The effect of new ICTs has been to reduce significantly the number of people involved in the production of a book, and though this results in increased burdens of personal and fiscal responsibility for individual editors, for those who adhere to the job characteristics model of job satisfaction the outcome appears to be positive for the individuals involved.

Nevertheless, Jane sometimes wonders whether the quality of her work, and the time she is given to attend to detail, has not suffered because of the speed with which she can now perform her tasks. Twenty years ago, one of the most tedious jobs Jane (or an assistant) would have to have done was 'casting-off' a manuscript – the printing industry's term for counting the words in a text and then estimating how many pages it would occupy at a given size of type and page. Today, by the time they are ready for press, all manuscripts are held in electronic form, either on the firm's servers or on a floppy disk, and the number of words and extent (number of pages) of the book has been worked out well in advance. In 1978, the manuscript took the form of a typewritten document, many pages long, carefully marked up by a production editor to indicate typographical style. From the production editor, the book went to a specialist typesetter, from whose machine were produced 'galleys' of type – long columns of typesetting which either took the form of rows of cast lead which were physically inserted into a printing machine or photographic prints which could be pasted onto page-sized boards, photographed and transferred to metal offset litho plates and wrapped round the cylinder of an offset press. Before being made up into pages, the material would be proofread against the original author's copy and where necessary new lines of type would be cast for insertion into galleys, or new paragraphs would be photoset to be pasted onto the made-up boards. If illustrations were involved, they were rephotographed either on to negatives for offset litho platemaking or on to metal plates, known as blocks, which were inserted into formes along with the text matter for letterpress printing. This long, complicated, error-prone and labour-intensive process, right up to the point of production of the printing plate, now all takes place inside a computer. The time from delivery of manuscript to final layout has been reduced to days rather than months.

In Taylorist terms, it is the editor's work that has been intensified, and her productivity has been enormously increased. But it has happened in a way that offers a curious contrast to Taylorist principles: instead of her tasks being broken down into their component parts and divided up among different workers, what has actually happened (not only in Jane's job but in jobs throughout the knowledge industries) is that a number of discrete tasks have been concatenated, taken out of the hands of a large number of people and concentrated into the hands of a single person, who has been obliged to become *multi*skilled rather than finding him or herself becoming *de*skilled. There are two important corollaries here: the first, of course, is that a large number of people have been put out of work or have had to retrain; but the second is that for people remaining in work the employee alienation expected to arise from the spread of automation has not in fact occurred. On the contrary, the suggestion by Blauner (1964) that there would be a counter-trend to alienation, as through workplace technology employees 'gain a new dignity from responsibility and a sense of individual function' rather than alienation, is worth revisiting. However, this view should be tempered by the fact that Blauner's work was based partly on a study of the pre-computer hot metal printing industry of the 1960s which has completely disappeared through technological change. And it is also true that outside the knowledge industries there remains much automated process work which fails to generate the integrated job functions which can lead to individual satisfaction; it is likely that there are industries in which little has changed since Nichols and Beynon's (1977) study of a chemical plant where there was much low-grade unskilled work and consequently little job satisfaction or integration. Nevertheless, the integration of ICTs into administrative and office jobs has had the opposite effect to Taylorist atomization of processes, or Adam Smith's 'proper division' of operations (1776/ 1982): productivity has been achieved by the combination rather than the separation of discrete tasks.

THE NETWORK PANOPTICON

But there are prices to pay for the increased autonomy that ICTs have brought to those remaining in employment. Because of the greater speed with which material can be processed, the number of books Jane produces each year has increased substantially. Her personal profitability is now carefully measured by her employers along with that of all the other editors in the house to make sure that it remains acceptably high; it is difficult to make comparisons with her profitability in 1978, because the company's accountants in those days simply did not have the computing tools to enable them to make such measurements in such detail. This acts as a counterpoint to the appearance of autonomy in her job; the network computer system in an enterprise can be thought of as a highly efficient, if invisible, panopticon which allows managers to keep a constant watch on the activities of their subordinates without themselves being visible to those they survey (Foucault 1977). As Foucault suggests, through electronic surveillance of her business activities, the individual can be made the object of information without having to be the subject of communication. Not only are the editor's financial outgoings constantly checked against her budget, but the earnings from her output (book sales) are also constantly checked against agreed forecasts. If there are unexpected divergences she will quickly be called to account.

Like many enterprises whose goods are sold at retail, the publishing house now uses information generated by EFTPOS (electronic funds transfer at point of sale) till systems installed in most bookstores. These systems, using information contained in the barcodes printed on the back of every book jacket, not only record the cash paid by customers, but also report sales title by title via communications links (using modems and telephone lines) to the wholesalers' and publishers' own computers, thus enabling publishers to calculate royalties due to authors and providing information about product performance, and guidance on reprints and future sales strategies. Twenty years ago, these calculations were made on the basis of written returns from wholesalers and distributors, and authors had to wait for many months before accurate sales figures were available on which to base royalty payments (booksellers are entitled to return unsold stock and royalties were generally calculated on the basis of copies sent out minus returns, thus obliging publishers to wait until retailers had physically sent back unwanted copies before being able to calculate royalties); there was a similar wait before management could calculate employee performance on the basis of sales figures. (A useful description of EFTPOS systems and their implications may be found in Furche and Wrightson 1996).

The instant availability of financial outcomes to senior management raises control issues related to the fact that, in financial terms at least, even employees who perform quite complex professional or craft-oriented tasks no longer know more about their work than their managers do, the effect of which is to diminish the employee's negotiating power *vis-à-vis* management. It is not the division of labour that has given rise to management's enhanced ability to exercise control in this instance, but rather their knowledge of the total labour process, another Taylorist principle.

The electronic pantopicon poses a further challenge to employee autonomy: it is possible (and in many firms it is everyday practice) for every one of a worker's electronic transactions through her computer to be noted and recorded by means of the network. So every Web page that worker visits, whether for leisure or for work, and – controversially – every e-mail message she sends or receives may be read by management. Information derived from both activities can be used (and has been used) by management in disciplinary or other action against the employee. Although there are profound civil rights implications, courts in the USA and the UK have upheld management's right to read employees' e-mail. This enables managements who care to take advantage of it to exert powerful control over their employees, although the volume of data may be a deterrent.

In the context of the publishing house there are also important implications for authors, and these implications are similar to those for all suppliers of intellectual property, raw materials and component parts throughout the knowledge and other industries. Publishing (or manufacturing) decisions are much more closely related than they used to be to likely financial outcomes, because information about past performance of similar titles is much more easily available through spreadsheet programs which can model with apparent accuracy the marketplace performance of a given product. (Use of the spreadsheet as the main tool in business decision-making has been said to give rise to 'delusions of accuracy'.) By altering variables such as price, print run, paper quality and extent of a given book proposal on an interactive spreadsheet, the effect of such changes on the profitability of a title can quickly and easily be seen, and detailed decisions can be made swiftly about whether and how it should be published. This makes cost-cutting easy, and it is likely that the physical quality of many new books has diminished, since items like the weight, and hence the cost, of paper, represent easy candidates for reduction at the publishing decision-making stage. To keep extents down, books are sometimes set in smaller typefaces than editors would like, to reduce the number of pages to be printed. It is easy, too, to calculate the cost of the warehouse space taken up by a given number of stock items, and to make calculations about the relative merits of holding stock or reprinting. Historical data about returns and continuing backlist sales also contribute to judging print run numbers more accurately, and since printing, packing, binding and warehousing represent a high proportion of a book's production costs the personal financial performance of employees and of suppliers, watched so carefully by management, and the company's overall profitability, can be controlled through overt (and covert) monitoring and surveillance of operations by networked computer.

CONCLUSIONS

The spread of ICTs throughout the workplace has a wide and complex range of implications. Comparisons with the introduction of automated process control technology in the manufacturing sector, on which much of the organizational behaviour literature has focused, are problematic: the alienation thought to result from the imposition of automation is not a key factor in the use of ICTs in the office environment, and the *integration* of job functions that results from the way in which versatile networked personal computers are being used provides a stark contrast to the division of labour proposed by the classical texts for the production line.

It is important to recognize that the introduction of information and communications technology to the office has taken place slowly and over a long period of time. The first 'automated office', J. Lyons' LEO computer, appeared in the early 1950s; mainframe computers took over a number of tasks such as record-keeping, actuarial work and stock control in the 1960s and 1970s; networked personal computers have only been a reality since the introduction of the IBM PC in 1983. And it is clear that the introduction of new technologies is not a mandatory result of their availability. Video conferencing, for instance, which is a reasonably well-developed technology that has been available for 10 years or more, has not been widely adopted, because it does not seem to meet a demand widely expressed by enterprises.

On the other hand, the networked desktop PC has over the past decade become pervasive throughout business and public sector organizations of many kinds, despite the fact that the management and diffusion of networked personal computers is an expensive and difficult business. The cost of maintaining and providing software (total cost of ownership, or TCO) for a single networked computer by a corporation was estimated in 1987 by the Gartner Group, a commercial consultancy, at US$9800.00 per annum, including depreciation on the machine itself. Although the full implications of the TCO analysis have only recently been understood, the high level of investment in ICTs by enterprises is expected to show a return for those enterprises. We have sought to show that the use of ICTs to effect cost-cutting through elimination of many job categories may have had the unexpected effect of empowering remaining workers, and although troubling issues of control, surveillance and personal civil rights remain, the alienation arising from the introduction of automated process control technologies into the factory has not largely been replicated in the office as a result of development of ICTs.

Jane finishes work later than she had hoped she would, and walks to the Docklands Light Railway station, where a computer-controlled train without a driver – an idea introduced with the Victoria Line in 1972, but not implemented because of fears about passenger reaction – whisks her home. Like many employees, she has a computer at home and can dial into her e-mail account at work. But tonight, she resolves, she won't.

REFERENCES

Adams-Webber, J. (1981) Empirical developments in personal construct theory, in Bonarius, H., Holland, R. and Rosenberg, S. (eds) *Personal Construct Theory*, Macmillan, London.

Argyle, M. and Cook, M. (1976) *Gaze and Mutual Gaze*, Cambridge University Press, Cambridge.

Blauner, R. (1964) *Alienation and Freedom*, University of Chicago Press, Chicago, IL.

Braverman, H. (1974) *Labor and Monopoly Capital: The Degradation of Work in the Twentieth Century*, Monthly Review Press, New York.

British Council (1997) *Information on Women in the UK*, Published on the Internet at http://www.britcoun.org/social/gadwomuk.htm

Buchanan, D. and Huczynski, A. (1997) *Organizational Behaviour: An Introductory Text* (3rd edn), Prentice Hall, Hemel Hempstead.

Dosi, G. *et al.* (eds) (1988) *Technical Change and Economic Theory*, Pinter Publishers, London.

Fincham, R. and Rhodes, P. (1992) *The Individual, Work and Organisation: Behavioural Studies for Business and Management Students* (2nd edn), Oxford University Press, Oxford.

Foucault, M. (1977) *Discipline and Punish: the Birth of the Prison*, trans Sherida, A., Vintage, New York.

Friedrichs, G. and Schaff, A. (1982) *Microelectronics and Society: for Better, for Worse*, Pergamon Press, Oxford.

Furche, A. and Wrightson, G. (1996) *Computer Money: A Systematic Overview of Electronic Payment Systems*, D-punkt Verlag, Frankfurt.

Goffman, E. (1971) *The Presentation of Self in Everyday Life*, Penguin, Harmondsworth.

Hackman, J. and Oldham, G. (1975) Development of the job diagnostic survey, *Journal of Applied Psychology*, 60, 159–70.

Kelly, G.A. (1955) *The Psychology of Personal Constructs*, Norton, New York.

Kling, R. (1996) *Computerization and Controversy: Value Conflicts and Social Choices* (2nd edn), Academic Press, San Diego.

Knights, D. and Willmott, H. (1988) *New Technology and the Labour Process*, Macmillan, Basingstoke.

Knights, D. and Willmott, H. (1990) *Labour Process Theory*, Macmillan, Basingstoke.

Kondratiev, N. (1925) The major economic cycles, *Voprosy Konjunktury*, 1, 28–79; English translation reprinted in *Lloyds Bank Review* 129 (1978).

McLoughlin, I. and Clark, J. (1988) *Technological Change at Work*, Open University Press, Milton Keynes.

Nichols, T. and Beynon, H. (1977) *Living with Capitalism*, London, Routledge.

Office of National Statistics (1998) *Annual Abstract of Statistics*, HMSO, London.

Perez, C. (1983) Structural Change and the Assimilation of New Technologies in the Economic and Social System, *Futures* 15 (5), 357–75.

Robbins, S. (1998) *Organizational Behavior: Concepts, Controversies, Applications* (8th edn), Prentice-Hall, Upper Saddle River, NJ.

Schumpeter, J. (1934) *The Theory of Economic Development*, Harvard University Press, Cambridge, MA.

Schumpeter, J. (1939) *Business Cycles*, McGraw-Hill, New York.

Schumpeter, J. (1943) *Capitalism, Socialism and Democracy*, Allen & Unwin, London.

Smith, A. (1776) *The Wealth of Nations* (Reprinted 1982) Penguin, Harmondsworth.

Section 3
The Limitations of
Management

The four chapters in this section deal with areas that are both topical and controversial, namely corporate culture, HRM, labour flexibility and the impact of the global economy on management. The theme which links these chapters is the extent to which the managements of individual firms are able to develop proactive strategy to alter the course of competitive advantage, or must merely react to forces outside their control. Whilst the issues of the global economy feature most clearly in the chapter by Adcroft and Willis, developments in globalization represent key influences in culture change at the level of the firm and in the emergence of HRM and recent approaches to flexibility.

Needle offers a broad review of organizational and corporate culture and is keen to differentiate between them. The concept of organizational culture is viewed as descriptive and analytical, where individual organizations are seen as the unique product of a complex interaction of variables. Corporate culture, on the other hand, is viewed as a management strategy to change the organization to achieve competitive advantage through people. He charts the historical development of these approaches and cites influences both of management ideas such as scientific management, human relations and organizational development, as well as the contextual influences of global competition, Japan and the New Right. The critical focus, understandably, is aimed at managerial attempts to change culture. He challenges the utility of corporate culture as a management tool, citing a number of difficulties. These arise from the complexity of the concept, the problems of changing employee values, employee resistance and a number of ethical problems. Ultimately, Needle argues, the effective introduction of culture change is hampered by a series of economic and labour market forces, which managers are unable to control. This is illustrated by a case study of the leading electronics firms in South Korea, where significant investments in the development of corporate cultures have been powerless in the face of economic and market changes in the late 1990s. Whereas corporate culture may be limited in its utility, the more analytical approaches associated with the 'organization culture' perspective may offer management greater insights into the workings of their own organizations.

Fenwick and Murton present a brief historical overview of industrial relations from post-war to the present day, including the emergence of HRM. The influences they acknowledge are similar to those presented by Needle, perhaps not surprisingly, given the close association between HRM and culture change. HRM is presented, not as a unified concept, but one which incorporates 'hard' and 'soft' elements as well as offering a number of approaches to industrial relations. A review of the evidence, both from the UK and elsewhere, concludes that the conduct of industrial relations has indeed changed in recent years. In the UK there has been a significant fall in union membership accompanied by moves by management to de-recognize unions for bargaining purposes and a trend away from collective bargaining towards individual performance-related pay. However, the authors argue that the evidence for management adopting strategic approaches to HRM, particularly in the UK, is weak. Fenwick and Murton view this lack of a strategic approach as typical of UK management and see it as part of the historic preference for short-termism. Instead of purposeful strategy, they argue that managers have been opportunistic in adopting reactive policies to fit the prevailing economic and political forces. Nonetheless, they concede that HRM is a popular concept and see that popularity deriving not so much from its impact on competitive advantage but from its promise of a rhetoric to legitimize management behaviour. Ultimately they conclude, as others have done, that, to a large extent, the HRM debate has been manufactured by academics and that the impact on organizations has been slight.

In the chapter which follows Murton argues that whilst flexibility became a dominant theme in the 1970s, authors have tended to ignore its relatively long history. He contends that the focus has been managerial and almost exclusively on labour flexibility and the needs of employers. He examines the role of key drivers, in particular the global economy, but also accepts the part played by governments, changes in manufacturing associated with just-in-time methods and the growth of the service industries. He offers a review of the various forms of labour flexibility using the traditional classifications of numerical, functional, temporal and financial, but locates these within an analytical framework offered by Beatson (1995a). The evidence of flexible practices taken from across Europe suggests a very mixed picture, with greater variation within sectors and countries than between them. Murton raises a number of key issues including job insecurity, social exclusion and (for those in full-time employment) stress and work intensification, issues raised elsewhere in this volume by Clark, Chandler and Barry. He notes the significant impact on the female labour force, citing Hakim's 1996 finding that the 'secondary' female work force in the UK accounts for some 40 per cent of the total employed, male and female. Whilst flexibility is seen clearly as a managerial response and hence the direct result of management decision-making, Murton makes some interesting observations. In most cases the introduction of more flexible forms of working is a reactive strategy, particularly in the UK as a short-term cost cutting response to shareholder pressure. He sees this as the easy option and questions whether the focus on labour flexibility is misguided when other forms of flexibility, as in operations and marketing, may offer more effective strategies. This is reinforced by the relatively weak link between labour flexibility and economic success criteria. Indeed, Murton argues that, in some cases, the drive for labour flexibility may be incompatible with other strategic goals, such as enhancing customer service levels.

Adcroft and Willis, in their chapter, are keen to open a new debate about the way organizations are managed. They acknowledge that the key factor facing modern managers is the working of the global economy. However, they view the analysis to date as somewhat unhelpful, hampered by differences in definition, focus and understanding and complicated by the sheer complexity of the forces at work. The consequence, they argue, is evident in the inability of writers to predict the impact on the individual firm and in the plethora of advice currently on offer to managers. The traditional approach in the literature and the traditional management response is characterized as optimization. Managers of different firms are encouraged to consider their environment in similar ways, and ultimately respond with similar strategies, inevitably involving an incremental response to external changes. The authors argue that such strategies are only successful where there is limited competition and where the external conditions of operation are broadly similar between competing firms. Such conditions are rare. They illustrate this perspective by reference to business process re-engineering and lean production. The latter forms the basis of a comparative analysis of the car manufacturing industry in Japan and the USA. Their conclusion is that the US firms could not hope to compete with the most economically successful firms in Japan in terms of 'lean production' due to the inherent differences in employment in the two countries. The illustrations confirm that the conditions under which firms operate are rarely the same, nor should there be an expectation that they will be, in an increasingly global economy. However, following optimization strategies, not only are managements trapped by forces outside their control, but they end up making similar types of decision. Adcroft and Willis conclude by offering management some hope. The way forward lies not in management accepting their position of relative powerlessness, but in adopting strategies of innovation and in competing by being different.

The chapters in this section deal with issues at the heart of current debates about the efficacy of management in an international context. They are concerned to look beyond the rhetoric of management gurus and the simplistic accounts of many texts. They place their analyses against a background of 'real-world' relationships and, in so doing, demonstrate the limitations of management.

Culture at the level of the firm: organizational and corporate perspectives

7

David Needle

INTRODUCTION

In this chapter a distinction is made between the use of the term *organizational culture* and that of *corporate culture*, as we attribute different meanings to each. In the literature the two labels are used interchangeably. However, in this chapter, organizational culture is viewed as a relatively descriptive concept that depicts culture at the level of the firm in terms of a collection of constituent variables. The organizational perspective acknowledges that members of organizations possess certain values and sets out to explore underlying assumptions. Corporate culture, on the other hand, is seen as both normative and prescriptive. It makes assumptions about employees that it does not explore and constitutes a set of beliefs and values that are deliberately created as part of management strategy, and which are used to guide behaviour and processes within the organization. This distinction is similar to that used by other writers. Smircich (1983) distinguished between analytical and managerial perspectives, a theme clearly taken up by Wilson and Rosenfeld (1990) in their identification of analytical and applicable schools of thought.

Although the terms organizational and corporate culture did not appear in common usage before the late 1970s, the origins, more especially of corporate culture, can be traced back to the early part of the century. Interest in the concept took off in the 1980s with the publication of the highly influential *In Search of Excellence* (Peters and Waterman 1982). This placed corporate culture firmly on the managerial agenda as managers across the globe embraced the concept of culture change as a turnaround strategy. The ensuing treatment of culture at the level of the firm varied considerably ranging across the banal, the simplistic, the misleading, the highly complex, the impenetrable academic and the highly critical. Many authors (for example, Hofstede 1986, Brown 1995) bemoan the lack of meaningful research. In its place we are faced with a stream of definitions, classifications and critiques, the last usually aimed at the so-called excellent companies. In some ways this chapter extends that tradition, but also attempts to offer a guide through the often confusing territory and concludes by questioning the utility of the concept itself.

This chapter will examine some of the historical and contextual factors which have influenced interest in culture at the level of the firm as well as a review of the various perspectives authors have used in analysis. The title of this chapter uses culture at the level of the firm to distinguish it from culture at the level of society, although the latter inevitably influences the former. The utility of the concept is brought into question by reviewing a range of critical literature and by a brief study of three major companies in South Korea. We begin with issues of definition.

THE TERMS DEFINED

Almost every writer on culture at the level of the firm attempts some kind of definition. A sample is provided below.

> The way we do things around here (Deal and Kennedy 1982: 4).

> An amalgam of beliefs, ideologies, language, ritual and myth (Pettigrew 1979: 572).

> Collective programming of the mind which distinguishes members of one organization from another (Hofstede 1991: 180).

> The pattern of beliefs, values and learned ways of coping with experience that have developed during the course of an organization's history and which tend to be manifested in its material arrangements and in the behaviour of its members (Brown 1995: 8).

> a) A pattern of basic assumptions, b) invented, discovered or developed by a particular group c) as it learns to cope with problems of external adaptation and internal integration, d) that has worked well enough to be considered valid, and e) is to be taught to new members as the f) correct way to perceive, think and feel in relation to those problems (Schein 1990: 111).

The quote from Deal and Kennedy is frequently used in both managerial and academic treatments of the subject. It is in fact not the authors' own, but a quote from Marvin Bower, the then managing director of McKinsey, for whom Deal and Kennedy were consultants. Their definition is typical of the language used in many of the managerial texts and is sufficiently broad to add little to our understanding of the concept. Despite the plethora of other definitions, the somewhat random sample offered above display a number of similarities. Whilst Pettigrew and Hofstede offer succinct definitions those of Brown and Schein attempt to detail the key elements. These would appear to be beliefs and values that are developed in an organization over time, are learned by its members, are used to guide their behaviour and solve their problems, and are manifested in the language used and in every aspect of organization life. Several writers (Schein 1990; Trompenaars 1993) see the culture in terms of a hierarchy of levels, with underlying assumptions at the base, working through values and beliefs, to be displayed as a series of artefacts, processes and procedures.

BACKGROUND AND HISTORY

The intellectual origins of many concepts in organizational behaviour will vary dependent upon the particular perspective used by the writer. Culture is no exception, with its antecedents being traced through anthropology, psychology, and sociology, as well as through various stages in the development of management thought. The language of all these can be observed in the literature. Schein (1990) goes further, viewing the treatment of culture as lying at the intersection of several social sciences.

He does however acknowledge that the biases of each particular discipline can be observed.

An early appearance of several key concepts can be found in the work of Durkheim, notably in *Suicide* (1952) and, more pertinently, in *The Division of Labour in Society* (1933). In much of his work Durkheim focuses on the bonds that tie individuals to society, in particular the part played by shared values. This was a key feature in explaining the phenomenon of suicide and was an important feature of work arrangements. The firm and more especially the division of labour within it were viewed as sources of integration and stability for the whole society. Ray (1986) offers an excellent analysis of the Durkheimian underpinning used by many authors concerned with culture at the level of the firm. One such writer was undoubtedly Mayo (1960, 1975). Whilst Ray (1986) sees Mayo as being less concerned with values than with mechanisms for group membership, many of the ideas developed by Mayo and later writers in the tradition of Human Relations are the forerunners of some central ideas of corporate culture. Like Durkheim, Mayo was concerned with the breakdown of social order in society. For Mayo this came from industrialization, rapid economic growth, labour mobility, associated migration from rural areas to the cities and from less developed parts of the world to the emerging industrialized economies, of which the USA was a prime example. The antidote to the problems caused by this dislocation of society was the need for individuals to have a focus and feel part of a wider social group. Mayo and later Human Relations theorists focused on the pivotal role played by the work group, and in particular group norms, both as a source of motivation and control in the workplace, and also as a source of integration in society. Most of these ideas have been embraced readily by the managerialist views of the corporate culture 'school'.

The unitary perspective prevalent in the Human Relations School continues the tradition of the earlier work of Taylor, with its pre-echoes of more contemporary corporate advocates of culture change.

> the really great problem involved in a change from the management of initiative and incentive to scientific management, consists in a complete revolution in the mental habits of all those engaged in management as well as the workmen (Taylor 1947: 131).

For Taylor this could only come about through 'the close, intimate, personal co-operation between management and men' (Taylor 1947: 26).

The antecedents of managerially inspired culture change can also be traced back to the Organization Development (OD) movement which emerged in the 1960s and became popular, especially with several multinationals in the 1970s, notably Shell, Exxon and IBM. OD was concerned with planned change in organizations to achieve greater effectiveness. The focus was invariably upon the management of culture and the use of a variety of techniques, referred to as intervention strategies to change the behaviour and ultimately the values of organization members. Change techniques in OD, notably those associated with the work of Lewin (1952) and Bennis (1966), re-emerge in later treatments of culture change. Similar approaches were also to be found in the development of the concept of organizational climate (Taguiri and Litwin 1968), which some see as the forerunner of more specific writings on corporate culture. The advocates of organizational climate emphasize the benefits of a 'healthy' organization, depicted by, for example, high levels of staff morale and commitment. An important strand in the OD literature is the importance of senior management in leading and supporting, but invariably devising the change agenda. These themes re-emerge in the seminal works of Schein in the 1980s (Schein 1983, 1985), with their focus on leadership as the central element in culture change.

Schein's work in the 1980s was just part of a stream of books and articles, establishing organizational and corporate culture as one of the key management themes of that time. Its status was reinforced through its central role in processes such as Total Quality Management (TQM) and Human Resource Management (HRM). Reference has already been drawn to the 'excellence movement', taking as its focal point the work of Peters and Waterman (1982). The key theme of their book was that, based on research into successful US firms, attributes could be identified, but more significantly be copied, by those firms aspiring to excellence. Key themes of corporate culture prevail throughout their book, notably the importance of committed leadership, the central part played by shared values and beliefs and the role of integration. In many ways ideas for the book came out of the author's connection with the international consultancy firm, McKinsey, from whose stable also came Pascale and Athos (1982) and Deal and Kennedy (1982). All these works were influenced by a specific consulting framework, referred to as the 7-S approach, which in essence was a framework for culture change.

By the late 1980s there were signs that the interest in culture at the level of the firm was running out of steam as the sheer volume of managerial literature had said virtually everything that could be said on the subject. There emerged instead a critical strand that raised questions not only about the utility of the concept, but also about the very nature of the concept itself. A representative sample of the more telling contributions in this genre would include Ray (1986), Meyerson and Martin (1987), Silver (1987) and Willmott (1993), whose main ideas are summarized later in this chapter.

The above account chronicles the development of the concept by reference to seminal influences and the key movers and shakers. As with most influential ideas in management, the context within which they arise is also of considerable importance. At least two such contexts lay behind the growth of interest in the 1980s. These were the focus on Japanese management and the emergence of the 'New Right' as a radical departure in political economy, particularly in the UK and USA, but also in other countries such as Germany.

The less critical explanations for the rise of the post-war Japanese economy and the world dominance of many of its sectors and firms highlight features of Japanese firms, management style and organizational processes that stress shared values, commitment and which see the firm as a family network. Many treatments of corporate culture either take this idealized view of the Japanese firm as a role model, or, more often, use it as a departure point for their own ideas on culture, notably Ouchi (1981).

In terms of political economy the 1980s, through the Thatcher administrations of Britain, with Reagan in the USA and, to a lesser extent, Kohl in Germany, the climate was supportive of the use of corporate culture, not only as a turnaround strategy, but also as an effective means of employee control. In short, corporate culture became a tool of the New Right. A series of recessions was met by exhortations to work harder, be more flexible, more responsive and more entrepreneurial. Phrases such as 'Victorian values' and the 'enterprise culture' became commonplace. In the UK, anti-union legislation and the growth of anti-union public opinion, fostered by a prevailing culture of entrepreneurialism, together with the impact of recession and increasing global competition, offered the ideal conditions of growth for not only the central ideas of corporate culture, but also those of HRM and TQM. In most treatments of HRM, corporate culture emerges as a key element, in that the application of the core ideas of HRM (communication, involvement, reward systems) lead to a changed culture that invariably includes commitment, goal congruence, improved quality and flexibility. This changed culture supposedly leads to improved performance.

PERSPECTIVES

In this chapter we have been careful to distinguish between organizational culture, representing a more academic approach to the subject, and corporate culture, representing a managerial perspective. In this section we explore these differences a little further.

Organizational culture sees culture comprising a number of variables, the combination of which leads to observable differences between organizations, including those operating in the same business. This approach is often used to aid our understanding of organizational behaviour issues and to explain differences between organizations. Models or metaphors are often used to cut through the complexities brought about by the large number of potential variables. Corporate culture on the other hand views culture as a clear managerial device to achieve strategic ends, especially those concerned with the management control of labour. We will deal with each of these perspectives in turn.

THE ORGANIZATIONAL CULTURE PERSPECTIVE

The organizational culture perspective sees organization in terms of a unique combination of variables. These include its history, technology, product market, type of employees, type of ownership, its leadership and its strategy. Other influences include the broader culture of the country or region, the prevailing political economy and the behaviour of the stakeholders.

Many attempts have been made to simplify this range of variables through the use of models attempting to draw distinctions between generic types of organization. An early and highly simplistic attempt was made by Harrison (1972) who classified the character or ideology of organizations under four categories; power, role, task and person. This same classification was popularized by Handy (1976), who referred specifically to these categories as cultures, to some extent denuding Harrison's work of its critical overtones. Since then, countless authors have attempted their own classification, ranging from the simplistic and managerial, such as Deal and Kennedy (1982), through the moderately complex and academic, such as Hofstede *et al.* (1990) to the more complex such as Scholz (1987), who attempts to combine both academic and managerial perspectives.

If we view organizational culture as comprising an almost infinite range of variables, then we may conclude that organizational culture is just another name for organization and as such is not a discrete variable that can be manipulated. Meyerson and Martin (1987) subscribe to the view that culture is not a discrete variable. They view culture as a socially constructed reality and thus the importance for them is how we perceive it. They offer three paradigms.

Paradigm one views the organization as typified by shared values, strong leadership and consensus. Although ambiguity is denied, change nevertheless can take place and is often associated with a change in leadership. They cite the case of the US Peace Corps, as it changed from an ideologically driven organization under the Kennedy administration, with a primary concern for social issues, to a more pragmatic organization under the Nixon regime with a focus on technical projects. Ambiguity was restricted by clear guidelines from the top and through the changing nature of the recruits.

Such a view of culture comes through more in the managerial treatments of the subject such as Deal and Kennedy (1982) and Peters and Waterman (1982), but it is also to be found in those stressing the importance of leadership, notably Schein (1985).

Paradigm two acknowledges the presence of sub-cultures within an organization, perhaps reflecting different values. Meyerson and Martin see these collections of values as the major source of difference between organizations in that their combination creates a unique environment for each. This perspective is also to be found in Whipp et al. (1989), where organizations are seen as multicultural entities. This paradigm acknowledges the presence of conflict, but Meyerson and Martin feel that, in most cases, ambiguity is channelled and conflict only arises when two or more sub-cultures overlap. In reality most organizations have procedures to ensure that potentially conflicting groups can co-exist effectively. This occurs through mechanisms for integration (as in Lawrence and Lorsch 1967) and, for example, in most procedures for industrial relations. Traditionally the treatment of sub-cultures in the literature tends to focus upon occupational groups, such as research versus production staff, or groups that are assumed to have different goals such as management and unions. By contrast, the literature is relatively devoid of references to sub-cultures based around differences of gender or ethnic background.

The third paradigm is one in which ambiguity is not only accepted but is an important tension that is part of the organization's *raison d'être*. Meyerson and Martin cite universities as the kind of organization that thrives on ambiguity and also see it as a feature of certain types of social services. Unfortunately the authors are unable to provide much evidence to support their third paradigm. The reality is probably that some organizations, whilst more tolerant of ambiguity than others, will ultimately prevent that ambiguity from becoming dysfunctional. In this case there would appear to be little difference between paradigms two and three. In the case of universities in the UK, there is evidence in the 1990s of a much clearer central management direction, born out of a context of successive financial squeezes. This suggests that there may be certain conditions for the tolerance of ambiguity. In the case of UK universities, and other public organizations, those conditions are heavily influenced by financial arrangements. A similar situation occurred in the National Health Service with the introduction of the Griffiths Report in 1986. This heralded a new culture of management control by non-medical staff and introduced greater measures of financial accountability. The power of the senior medical teams was challenged with the resulting clash of sub-cultures. Bourn and Ezzamel (1986) note that the reaction of the medical staff, in particular, was their polarization of the issues into the caring and humane medical teams versus the non-caring, bureaucratic management.

Whilst Meyerson and Martin regard culture as a discrete variable that cannot be manipulated, this is not the view of those who subscribe to a more managerial perspective, which we have dubbed corporate culture.

THE CORPORATE CULTURE PERSPECTIVE

This perspective focuses on the use of culture as a control device to enhance performance through the development of greater commitment and the integration of all employees at all levels in the organization. It is this perspective on culture at the level of the firm that attracts the greatest critical attention. Some writers, notably Willmott (1993), view the manipulation of culture in this way as highly questionable, referring to it as the 'dark side of the force' and likening it to an Orwellian 1984. He gives it the term 'corporate culturism'. Others, such as Thompson and McHugh (1990), whilst offering similar criticisms, also see some benefits to employees through the more paternalistic strategies of employers.

The corporate culture perspective views organizations in terms of a set of strong values passed down by management and reinforced by procedures and rituals which emphasize and reward appropriate behaviour, together with a cultural network, comprising a system of communication to spread the values and create corporate heroes. The classic example of this kind of organization is Hewlett Packard, with its twin hero figures, Bill Hewlett and Dave Packard.

The processes involved in creating such corporate cultures would appear to operate as follows. The senior management set goals and issue guidelines which promote strongly held shared values; common emphases are enthusiasm, diligence, loyalty and customer care. To ensure that the guidelines reach all employees there is a corresponding investment in various types of communication as well as procedures to develop integration. Some firms pay particular attention to the physical layout, and some like Hewlett Packard try to achieve a corporate style that is recognizable wherever they operate. The goals of the company are invariably written and tend to stress the value and contribution employees can make. Heroes and myths play an important role both in creating shared values and in integration. Rituals are important too and can take the place of formalized work-related activities, such as team meetings, or out-of-work social activities, where participation is the norm. The organization structure strengthens the culture by a common focus upon autonomous units to enhance group identity and loyalty. Recruitment and selection methods tend to be rigorous to screen out unsuitable candidates and ensure a fit between the recruit and the prevailing culture. Considerable emphasis is also given to induction and training as the primary vehicles for cultural socialization. All these processes can be found in companies such as Hewlett Packard, where great emphasis is placed upon the maintenance of a particular culture, and in the three Korean firms referred to later in the chapter.

Those who subscribe to this kind of vision of organizations, argue that companies displaying such characteristics are invariably more successful than those that do not (Peters and Waterman 1982; Deal and Kennedy 1982). We examine this claim by reference to a number of studies that have been carried out examining the impact of culture on strategy and on performance.

In the work of Peters and Waterman, culture becomes the strategy, and their one best way is both the culture and the strategy to achieve corporate success. The link between culture and strategy, albeit in a less prescriptive way can also be found in the work of others. Brown (1995) sees the link as inevitable, for he argues that the culture of an organization will determine key strategic elements, including how the environment is perceived and interpreted, how information is analysed, and how the main players react. This echoes the earlier work of Miles and Snow (1978). They identify three types of organization: defenders, prospectors and analysers. Each of these are culturally different and each pursue different strategies. A similar, but more prescriptive theme occurs with those who stress the importance of a fit between culture and strategy (Scholz 1987; Hofstede 1991). Where there is a mismatch between culture and strategy, performance suffers, a factor which may lie behind the failure of so many mergers and acquisitions.

The notion of a culture–strategy fit also underpins many studies on culture change, where culture is manipulated to achieve the desired strategic ends. At best, this represents an understanding by management that successful implementation of a strategy requires consideration of behavioural and culture change and a corresponding investment in training and other processes. The case of British Airways is a good illustration of this kind of change process (Bruce 1987; Goodstein and Burke 1991; Höpfl et al. 1992). At worst however, it represents a vague hope on the part of management that simple exhortations to culture–change will bring about the desired strategic change. There is some evidence to suggest that 'successful' culture change is dependent upon some kind of crisis (Schein 1985; Williams et al. 1989), although Schein (1985), argues strongly that different kinds of culture are needed at different stages in the organization's history, again supporting the importance of a culture-strategy fit.

The British Airways case mentioned above is often cited as an example of how culture, or more specifically culture change, can lead to improved performance. Goodstein and Burke (1991) attempted to provide links between culture change and the conversion of a $900 million loss into a $435 million profit. Even more measured accounts, such as those of Höpfl et al. (1991) point to some success factors and argue that the 'new' culture at British Airways enabled it to withstand subsequent pressures on business such as those associated with the Gulf War and the deregulation of transatlantic routes. Links between culture and performance were also postulated by Gordan and Ditomaso (1992) who found some correlation between the strength of a widely shared culture and short-term financial performance. In Whipp et al. (1989) an analysis was made of Jaguar, a blue-chip car producer with a sought after product and strong export market. The placing of Jaguar under BL management in the 1970s resulted in a performance decline, explained as a clash of cultures between Jaguar employees and BL management. It was a case of a specialist versus volume car manufacturer, where energies were diverted as Jaguar management engaged in political battles to retain a distinctive corporate identity. Performance at Jaguar improved dramatically in the 1980s, when free from the restrictions of BL, a new management team attempted to recreate the values of the company's most successful era through a focus on costs, quality and incremental quality improvements.

Yet the studies by Gordan and Ditomaso and by Whipp et al. also point out the dangers of linking culture and performance too directly. Both acknowledge the likely interference factor of a whole range of variables. In the case of Jaguar, the performance of the company, especially in its main export market, the USA, was aided significantly by a favourable sterling–dollar exchange rate. Limitations on the research findings such as those mentioned together with the inadequate and inconclusive nature of much of the research into culture at the level of the firm have led many to question its utility as a concept. It is to these issues we now turn.

CRITIQUE

In some ways it might be argued that this entire chapter is a critique of the concept of culture at the level of the firm, and the above sections are liberally sprinkled with a fair amount of critical comment. None the less, given the focus of much of the work about culture, it is useful to gather together a number of perspectives and research findings which challenge the central concept in a variety of ways. We can break these down into five areas; questions about the meaning of the concept, issues of complexity, questions of feasibility, desirability and, finally, comments offering a more 'positive' viewpoint. The first two of these areas relate to both organizational and corporate culture, whilst the others focus more specifically on the managerial and strategic bias of corporate culture.

Does the concept have any meaning?

This is an issue that has already been introduced in our examination of perspectives. The question arises from the issue of whether or not culture can be seen as a discrete variable within organizations. If it cannot, as some maintain (Meyerson and Martin 1987), then it raises the question as to whether the concept, certainly of organizational culture can be differentiated from the concept of organization itself, and as such has any meaning. Also in early attempts to devise classifications of cultures, notably those of Harrison (1972) and Handy (1976) the work would not be out of place in a treatment of organization structures rather than cultures.

The concept is too complex

The major concern here relates to problems caused by the existence of a large number of variables. If culture does exist, then we have a problem of isolating and measuring it. This in turn leads to serious criticisms of the research that has been carried out. Whilst much of this criticism is aimed at the methodologies of Peters and Waterman and the identification of their 'excellent companies' (Hitt and Ireland 1987; Silver 1987), any research into culture contains such difficulties and may explain why so many articles and books are dependent upon anecdotes from key participants as the major form of data. Hitt and Ireland (1987) challenge the rigour of much of the research. They cite as part of their evidence the analysis that the so-called excellent companies of the Peters and Waterman study performed no better on stock market valuation than other 'non-excellent' companies appearing in the *Fortune 1000* listing. Silver (1987) attacks the methodology of Peters and Waterman and questions both the basis of their sample and its manipulation to present detailed accounts of some firms, but not of others. Overall he likens the research problems of *In Search of Excellence* to the methodologically flawed Hawthorne Studies, except that he acknowledges the superior science of the latter over the former.

There are other elements that contribute to this complexity. The exhortations of corporate literature and of top management can appear markedly different from the realities of organizational life. In this vein, Watson (1994) makes a clear distinction between official and unofficial cultures existing within organizations at the same time. He argues that each has its own particular discourse, in that whilst the official culture talks about 'empowerment, skills and growth', the unofficial reflects upon 'control, jobs and costs' (Watson 1994: 112). This perspective accords with that of others who see the organization comprising a number of different sub-cultures (Meyerson and Martin 1987; Whipp *et al.* 1989). A further complexity occurs in that organizations are dynamic and the culture will change at different stages of their development (Schein 1985; Whipp *et al.* 1989).

The use of corporate culture as a management tool is not feasible

A number of limitations in the management use of culture have been identified. Some authors believe that the significance of culture is overstated, and that variables such as product/market, size and monopoly power are more important (Carroll 1983). The case of IBM frequently crops up in the literature where it is questioned whether their dominance of the market was a function of culture or monopoly power. The excellence guru himself, in a later book, used market changes to explain the fall from grace of some of his original sample (Peters 1987). Willmott (1993) argues that changing economic conditions have much more impact on a firm's performance than does culture, a point supported by the review of Korean firms in the next section.

Several authors maintain that the kind of culture seen in firms such as Hewlett Packard and IBM may simply not be appropriate in certain types of organization. As Dawson writes,

> Their 'slim, consensual organizations' of the future are probably applicable to firms employing professionals and technicians from the primary labour market in the development and operation of new technology or highly fashionable products and processes. They may however be less successful in other technological, product or labour market conditions (Dawson 1986: 137).

One may conclude from this that certain types of culture, notably that associated with the 'excellent' companies, is incompatible with certain types of company, specific types of work, and, almost certainly, the presence of an active trades union movement. There is clearly conflict here with the concept of the flexible firm. It may be difficult to establish corporate values and gain commitment amongst a growing number of part-time and contract employees. Similar findings were made by Ogbonna and Wilkinson (1990) who found that culture change in a supermarket was thwarted by a high number of part-time, low skilled and uncommitted employees at all levels of the organization.

Labour market issues are clearly important here, particularly when combined with employee characteristics related to job mobility. In the case of Korean companies, we may see in the later section that considerable investment is placed in corporate culture. The supporting factor here is the absence of inter-firm mobility. Where the larger corporations are concerned, Koreans tend to stay with the same company for their entire working life and rarely switch firms. A marked contrast can be found in Singapore. Here, job changing is frequent and an accepted route to career and salary enhancement. As a consequence, firms have difficulty sustaining a particular culture.

The imposition of a management-led corporate culture may be difficult in that members of an organization have allegiances to other groups, and in some cases this may be greater than their allegiance to their employer (Meyerson and Martin 1987; Whipp *et al.* 1989). Even where there appears to be consensus there may be an alternative explanation. Anthony (1990) argued that the apparent committed teamwork in some Japanese firms could be explained not in terms of the members' commitment to the organization but rather as an expression of group solidarity in a hostile environment.

Even where conditions are 'favourable', cultures may be very difficult to change. Scholz (1987) maintains that culture change can take anything from 6 to 15 years, whilst Hofstede (1991) argues that the values of the founders may shape the practices of employees in a firm, but not their values. For Anthony (1990), culture change was often mistaken for resigned behavioural compliance under the threat of sanctions. However a counterpoint to this view is put forward by Höpfl *et al.* (1992). Whilst agreeing with the main point that cultures are difficult to change, she argues, from the study of British Airways, that behaviour change can be made through training. She goes on to challenge the such notions as 'resigned behavioural compliance':

> employees are not infinitely gullible, pacified by corporate bromides lacking in a realistic appreciation of their own commitment (Höpfl *et al.* 1992: 34).

Further difficulties arise in that attempts by senior management to bring about culture change by imposing their values on the rest of the organization can often leave them isolated, and therefore cut off from the realities of everyday life at work (Anthony 1990; Ogbonna and Wilkinson 1990; Watson 1994).

Ultimately, as we have already shown, the utility of the concept is brought into question by the continued difficulty in establishing any meaningful links between culture, strategy and performance. Dawson (1986) raises the fundamental question as to whether culture is a cause or a consequence of a firm's success. In other words, do successful firms display certain cultural characteristics, which result from their success rather than contributing to it. She maintains that less successful companies tend to have more controls and give their employees less autonomy. Proponents of the link between culture and performance, such as Kotter and Heskett (1992) can find little more to say beyond that successful firms tend to be adaptive to changing conditions, have effective leadership and satisfy their stakeholders; hardly revolutionary management advice. Even they uncover cases where firms with 'strong cultures' also have relatively poor performance.

The use of corporate culture as a management tool is not desirable

The key issue here is one of ethics (see the chapter by Pirie in this volume). If we take such positions as that of Willmott (1993), then employees of companies displaying 'strong' cultures are likened to the brainwashed inhabitants of Orwell's *1984*. Willmott goes on to argue that corporate culturism, as he refers to it, is redolent with the 'doublethink' of Orwell's world. There would appear to be clear contradictions. It is true that in companies such as Hewlett Packard, employees are encouraged to be creative, yet are expected to conform; to be individualistic within a corporate image of a vast collective; to exhibit freedom, yet be subject to considerable expectations as to appropriate behaviour. The whole issue is probably best summed up by Peters and

Waterman's notion of 'simultaneous loose–tight properties'. Under such conditions individuals were encouraged to operate as free, creative individuals, within a cloak of tight collective corporate control. For Willmott the contradictions are part of the use of corporate culture as a control mechanism.

> That is the seductive doublethink of corporate culture; the simultaneous affirmation and negation of the conditions of autonomy (Willmott 1993: 526).

A number of writers, notably Silver (1987), are concerned about the exploitative potential of corporate culture. The essence of such criticism is that the emphasis on the moral commitment of the workforce is simply a means of achieving high productivity on the cheap. Silver singles out McDonald's for particularly harsh criticism.

> The lively, people-oriented culture is but a complement to the speeded up, Taylorized assembly line production of food . . . grease burns, irregular hours, autocratic bosses, sexual harassment and low wages all come with the quarter pounder (Silver 1987: 109–10).

Ethical or exploitative, corporate culture may be undesirable simply because it mitigates against change (Soeters 1986). In Rank Xerox, middle management were so cast in an identical mould of strong corporate values, that they were dubbed 'xeroids'. Their programmed thinking and a successful company, built on the patent protection of the photocopying machine, rendered them impervious to a changing business climate and, ultimately, unable to respond to increased competition (Williams *et al.* 1989).

Culture as a useful concept

Thus far in the critique we have focused on the problematic aspects of organizational and corporate culture, yet even some of the more critical writers have identified some benefits. Of course, one must always add the rider, benefits for whom and at what cost? For Ray (1986), following a strand from Durkheim through Mayo, corporate culture offers management co-ordination and control via a moral involvement of the workforce. It is also claimed to reduce conflict and uncertainty, particularly through the emphasis on clear guidelines and effective training (Deal and Kennedy 1982). Peters and Waterman (1982) stress the benefits to employees, notably a sense of belonging and good pay, through their participation in benevolently parternalistic, successful organizations. Culture has also been viewed as a vital link between the rational and the subjective aspects of determining strategy and is seen as the element that turns strategy into a reality (Whipp *et al.* 1989). A similar position is taken up by Schein (1990). The value of corporate culture for him is its contribution in helping organizations guide their evolution,

> to enhance cultural elements that are viewed as critical to maintaining identity and to promote the unlearning of cultural elements that are increasingly dysfunctional (Schein 1990: 117).

In this way, several public sector organizations in the 1980s and early 1990s embraced notions of culture change as an attempt to shift the focus of their organization towards such goals as service to the community. Paradoxically such cultural focus was seen as a solution to the problems of the public sector by more radical commentators who embraced the rhetoric of corporate culture at the very time it was being questioned elsewhere.

If for nothing else, an analysis of culture at the level of the organization may assist us in gaining fresh insights into the realities of organizational life and obtain a richer picture. For example, a focus on culture and, in particular, sub-cultures, as large public organizations such as universities and hospitals undergo change, may lead to a greater understanding of the underlying issues. In hospitals, we have already referred to the tensions between the medical staff and budget-conscious administrators. In universities similar tensions exist between academics and senior management. Academics see traditional freedoms being eroded by management initiatives responding to a harsh financial climate and government funding, increasingly tied to performance indicators. Such external pressures are challenging the traditional values that underpin the culture.

In the next section we continue some of the themes outlined above through the examination of three firms in South Korea. The cases explore the relationship between culture and performance, and, in particular, speculate on the relative impact of culture versus economy.

CORPORATE CULTURE, THE KOREAN FIRM AND THE IMPACT OF ECONOMIC CHANGE

The information presented in this section is based on research carried out at the end of 1995 in three electronics firms in Seoul and from reviews of the South Korean economy at the end of 1997 and the beginning of 1998. The three major firms, LG, Samsung and Hyundai are all part of larger industrial groups. In the electronics field they are the country's three leading firms, all with extensive global operations. Data were collected from their own corporate literature and, in each case, from structured interviews with representatives of senior management.

By the end of 1995 the growth of the South Korean economy was well documented, and companies such as Hyundai, Samsung and Daewoo had entered the household vocabulary of the western world. There are clear parallels with Japan in that economic growth was based, amongst other factors, upon long working hours and low wages within the context of a close relationship between the business community and the state. By the end of 1995 economic growth had slowed as the new generation of Koreans placed a higher value on leisure time. Wages rose considerably and the working week fell to less than 50 hours, although Saturday morning working was invariably the norm. Until the economic crisis of 1997 the larger corporations managed to survive the changes, partly because they were so cash-rich from earlier times, partly through borrowing, partly because of the security of government backing and partly because they were in the process of shifting labour costs overseas to cheaper locations such as China and India. Throughout the economic changes, the one constant has been the importance the three companies give to corporate culture, and their efforts to maintain it. The findings below relate to all three companies unless specifically stated otherwise.

The interviews with representatives of the major companies took place at their corporate headquarters in Seoul. These large buildings, in common with the offices of many large Korean firms, are notable for the range of concessionary shops and services to be found in the basement. As well as the statutory pub there are usually a number of different types of restaurant, invariably a bank if not two, and shops including a pharmacy. In Samsung there were clothes concessions arranged as a street market, selling cut-price suits to employees. It is important to remember that these are shops and services are dedicated to the employees of one company and are not normally for general use, since they lie within the company security system. The image was that of the firm as a village.

All the managers interviewed were familiar with the latest buzzwords. The concept of corporate culture was well-known and, there being no equivalent phrase in Korean, the English form was used both in conversation and corporate literature.

Corporate values were both well publicized and seen as an important part of management strategy. Recurring themes were creating value for customers, the importance of the dignity of the individual, the importance attached to the life of employees outside work and the aim of creating a better world for all. All focus on the goal of becoming a world class company in the twenty-first century. Both corporate literature and management conversation featured such value statements, as well as the usual exhortations towards corporate excellence. The following example is from the Hyundai brochure.

> The Hyundai Group has cultivated a corporate environment the reinforces and fosters four main attributes . . . self motivation, perseverance, creative thinking and diligence . . . create the very foundation of the Hyundai Group.

The corporate values are often reinforced by symbols. In the case of Samsung, the importance of family life is emphasized by the symbolic switching off of the lights in the head office building at 16.00 hours. As a senior manager stated,

> let's go out and do something valuable for yourself and your family, for when you create value for yourself and your family you come in the following morning fresher than ever.

The reality is that lights can be turned on again for those with urgent work to finish, but the gesture is made.

In all cases it would appear that there has been a comparatively recent attempt to re-launch their corporate cultures. For LG the key task was to change its management style from traditional authoritarian, with an emphasis on volume production, to greater involvement and an emphasis on quality and new product development. In keeping with other major Korean firms, the company used the international consultants, McKinseys. In Samsung's case a new corporate philosophy was developed three years earlier as part of a top-down initiative to face what management saw as a critical situation resulting from an increasingly competitive world market. In LG's case the catalyst for change was a major strike and the need for a closer relationship with the trade unions, including much greater disclosure of information. In contrast with the strong cultures of US firms, which are invariably associated with non-union firms, most Korean firms emphasizing corporate culture are highly unionized.

The key mechanism for cultural induction, change and maintenance was training. All companies possess a separate training centre at which new employees spend anything from an initial two to four weeks. The sole focus of initial training is socialization into the corporate culture. Further 'cultural' training at these centres follows promotion and, in LG's case, all employees spend a few days each year at the centre for periods of reinforcement. Samsung reinforces the formal training by placing the employees in teams and by using games and competitions. Invariably this initial training period will include a visit to the mountains for a couple of days when teams are encouraged to engage in collective activities such as hill walking and more sedentary pursuits such as writing songs.

In two of the firms, corporate culture has been institutionalized within the organization structure. LG has created a special unit whose main task is to study the LG corporate culture and determine how it should develop and how it should be portrayed, particularly the kind of images that should be used. In Hyundai there is the Hyundai Institute for Human Resource Development, an off-site education and training centre with its own accommodation. Other processes reinforce the structure. In LG a recent programme at Head Office encouraged all employees, irrespective of rank, from a particular area to meet once a month in the pub located in the basement. Beer is provided by the company and employees are encouraged to talk about such matters as company performance, department performance and working conditions. In Hyundai each department holds regular monthly meetings.

In addition to training, the companies use a variety of employee welfare provisions to transmit core values through. These include programmes of education, with opportunities to learn languages and develop skills in leisure activities such as golf. All make accommodation available, especially for single employees. In Hyundai's case these are corporate flats, courtesy of Hyundai Construction. All have extensive leisure facilities in a number of locations and sponsor both amateur and professional sports teams across a wide range of sports.

In keeping with other major Korean firms, the three firms pride themselves on their work in the community. The LG Yonam Foundation awards student scholarships and funds libraries whilst LG Welfare provides aid to the disabled and has established community centres in low income areas. Samsung has an established global assistance programme, which includes relief aid both domestically and internationally, as in the case of the Kobe earthquake. Samsung is active in sponsorship, being behind activities as diverse as the Korean Cultural Centre at the Victoria and Albert Museum in London and Romanian soccer teams. Hyundai provides medical services, subsidizes social welfare organizations and offers scholarships, particularly to individuals displaying 'extraordinarily high morals and values'. All are keen to publicize their environmental protection programmes.

The three companies stress the importance of the founding fathers in establishing the company and its core values, but all are keen to stress their declining influence. None the less members of the founders' family can still be found in certain key positions, although the companies are keen to assert that such appointments are based strictly on merit. The founding families, certainly as far as Samsung and Hyundai are concerned, provide the key link between the company and the state via political parties. Whilst the direct activity in the firm of the founding fathers may have declined, the political activity has not. The reality is probably that their influence is still highly significant.

ECONOMIC CHANGE IN SOUTH KOREA 1997–98

When the interviews were carried out in late 1995, the Korean economy was still in its growth phase and managers were confident. The companies involved were expanding and planning acquisitions in the west. Within a year the signs were less encouraging, initially as a result of market changes and more recently due to a currency collapse which exposed the fragile side of the South Korean economy.

In 1996 there was a sharp fall of around 80 per cent in the price of the 16 megabit D-ram microchip, the leading product for all three companies and one of the mainstays of their prosperity. The companies were partly to blame for this turnaround, since over-investment and rapid expansion resulted in over-capacity. The market was flooded, so killing the goose that had laid the golden egg. The 1996 accounts for all three firms showed sharp falls in profit: Samsung 93 per cent, Hyundai 92 per cent, and for LG an 88 per cent fall. The figures would have been even worse, were it not for changed accounting practices which reduced costs by lengthening the period for depreciation. Overseas expansion plans were delayed and there was a switch to produce higher value products, particularly the 64 megabit chip. The impact of these losses was critical to the Korean economy, given that Korea made up 30 per cent of the world market in the 16 megabit chip.

Faced with such market decline and still rising wages, the government responded at the end of 1996 with the establishment of new labour laws to give employers greater flexibility in the hiring and firing of labour. Workers were shocked by the speed of this response and, although the new laws gave some increased freedoms to trade unions, the introduction of the new freedoms were to be delayed by several years. The unions focused on the immediate threat to job security across the economy and there followed four weeks of widespread strikes.

In 1997 and into 1998, there were further major setbacks for the Korean economy and its leading firms. Following problems in Thailand, Indonesia and Malaysia, South Korea, along with many countries in the region, suffered a major currency and stock market collapse. In one year the value of the Korean won to the US dollar fell 51 per cent and the value of the stock market fell by 42 per cent. By the end of 1997 the external debt had reached record proportions at £122 billion and a country that was the world's eleventh largest in GDP terms, had its credit status downgraded to place it on a par with Pakistan and the Dominican Republic. Several major companies were placed at risk; some such as the Jinro Drinks group went out of business, whilst others, like the car firm Kia, only survived through government intervention. It emerged that the three companies had massive debt/equity ratios, with Hyundai at 437 per cent, LG at 347 per cent and Samsung at 267 per cent. The International Monetary Fund stepped in with a rescue package of US$55 billion dollars with severe measures limiting the growth of the economy and restructuring financial markets.

A number of related factors were responsible for this financial crisis. The economy of the region had been destabilized by the strength of the US dollar, with the subsequent devaluation of local currencies. Firms that had borrowed heavily to expand were now faced with rapidly escalating debts and increased pressure as foreign banks sought to recoup their loans. Lying behind this were allegations of over-investment without proper project evaluation, inexperienced management, nepotism and the inappropriate mix of political and business decisions. The economic crisis, worsened by the continued decline in the world electronics market, served to expose the shaky fundamentals of the South Korean economy and the crippling effects of bad debt at both national and company level.

CORPORATE CULTURE AND ECONOMIC FACTORS

The case of the rapid decline in the fortunes of Hyundai, LG and Samsung as well as the economy as a whole raises a number of questions pertinent to our discussion of corporate culture. It is clear from the events in Korea since 1996 that management in the three companies were powerless in the face of market changes and economic collapse. However large the investment in the creation and maintenance of a strong corporate culture, the forces at work were too great and were beyond the influence of cultural arrangements. One might speculate that were it not for the investment in the development of a particular culture then the problems for the three firms would be even worse. An evaluation of this would entail the correlation of comparative data on the performance of a whole range of firms and even then, as we have seen earlier in this chapter, links between culture and performance are notoriously difficult to prove. In any case, the investment in the development of a corporate culture by these companies can be found in other large, and some much smaller, firms in South Korea. Furthermore we should not forget that a key factor was also the over-supply in the major product market for all three firms.

CONCLUDING REMARKS

In this chapter we have been careful to make the distinction between organizational culture and corporate culture. Organizational culture represents an academic approach which attempts to make sense of the workings of a particular organization by reference to the combination of its constituent variables. Corporate culture, on the other hand, sees culture as a variable in its own right to be manipulated for specific strategic ends.

The experience of Korean firms since 1996 would seem to suggest that product markets, financial markets, politics and trade unions have more influence upon company performance than culture. As a consequence there would appear to be severe limits upon management action to create or change a culture. This reinforces the position taken in the critique, that corporate culture as a strategic tool and control device has limited utility. As a consequence, management investment in the creation and maintenance of a particular culture may be a fashion that is already past its time. Paradoxically, the more academically-oriented perspective of organizational culture may well offer more value to managers in the longer term by enabling them to determine the practicalities of specific strategic directives given a particular culture. The dramatic changes in the South Korean economy may be a worst-case scenario and we may need to focus on the extent to which the culture of those three firms emerges from the economic collapse largely intact or whether it has been changed. These questions inevitably cross the border between national and corporate value systems and the extent to which corporate values reflect much broader cultural values operating at national and regional levels.

REFERENCES

Anthony, P.D. (1990) The paradox of the management of culture or 'He Who Leads is Lost', *Personnel Review*, 19 (4), 3–8.
Bennis, W. (1966) *Changing Organizations*, McGraw Hill, New York.
Bourn, M. and Ezzamel, M. (1986) Organizational culture in hospitals in the National Health Service, *Financial Accountability and Management*, 2 (3), 203–5.

Brown, A. (1995) *Organisational Culture*, Pitman, London.

Bruce, M. (1987) Managing people first: bringing the service concept into British Airways, *Industrial and Commercial Training*, 19 (2), 21–7.

Carroll, D.T. (1983), A disappointing search for Excellence, *Harvard Business Review*, 63, Nov–Dec, 78–88.

Dawson, S. (1986) *Analysing Organizations,* Macmillan, London.

Deal, T.E. and Kennedy, A.A. (1982) *Corporate Cultures*, Penguin, Harmondsworth.

Durkheim, E. (1933) *The Division of Labour in Society*, Free Press, New York.

Durkheim, E. (1952) *Suicide: A Study in Sociology*, Routledge and Kegan Paul, London.

Goodstein, L.D. and Burke, W.W. (1991) Creating successful orgainization change, *Organizational Dynamics*, 19 (4), 5–19.

Gordan, G.G. and Ditomaso, N. (1992) Predicting corporate performance from organizational culture, *Journal of Management Studies*, 29 (6), 783–98.

Handy, C. (1976) *Understanding Organizations*, Penguin, Harmondsworth.

Harrison, C.R. (1972) Understanding your organization's character, *Harvard Business Review*, 50 (3), 119–28.

Hitt, M. and Ireland, D. (1987) Peters and Waterman revisited: the unending quest for excellence, *Academy of Management Executive*, 1 (2), 91–8.

Hofstede, G. (1986) Editorial: the usefulness of the organizational culture concept, *Journal of Management Studies*, 23 (3), May, 253–7.

Hofstede, G. (1991) *Cultures and Organizations: The Software of the Mind*, McGraw Hill, London.

Hofstede, G., Neuijen, B.N., Ohayv, D.D. and Sanders, G. (1990) Measuring organizational cultures, *Administrative Science Quarterly*, 35, 286–316.

Höpfl, H., Smith, S. and Spencer, S. (1992) Values and valuations: the conflict between culture change and job cuts, *Personnel Review*, 21 (1), 24–37.

Kotter, J.P. and Heskett, J.L. (1992) *Corporate Culture and Performance,* The Free Press, New York.

Lawrence, P.R. and Lorsch, J. (1967) *Organization and Environment*, Harvard University Press, Cambridge, MA.

Lewin, K. (1952) *Field Theory in Social Science,* Tavistock, London.

Mayo, E. (1960) *The Human Problems of Industrial Civilization*, The Viking Press, New York.

Mayo, E. (1975) *The Social Problems of Industrial Civilization*, Routledge and Kegan Paul, London.

Meyerson, D. and Martin, J. (1987) Culture change: an integration of three different views, *Journal of Management Studies*, 24 (6), 623–47.

Miles, R.E. and Snow, C.C. (1978) *Organizational Strategy, Structure and Process*, McGraw Hill, London.

Ogbonna, E. and Wilkinson, B. (1990) Corporate strategy and corporate culture: the view from the checkout, *Personnel Review*, 19 (4), 9–15.

Ouchi, W.G. (1981) *Theory Z,* Addison Wesley, Reading, MA.

Pascale, R.T. and Athos, A.G. (1982) *The Art of Japanese Management*, Penguin, Harmondsworth.

Peters, T.J. (1987) *Thriving on Chaos,* Macmillan, London.

Peters, T.J. and Waterman, R.H. (1982) *In Search of Excellence: Lessons from America's Best Run Companies,* Harper and Row, London.

Pettigrew, A. (1979) On studying organizational cultures, *Administrative Science Quarterly*, 24 (2), 570–81.

Ray, C.A. (1986) Corporate culture: the last frontier of control, *Journal of Management Studies*, 23 (3), 287–97.

Schein, E.H. (1983) The role of the founder in creating organization culture, *Organizational Dynamics*, (12), 13–18.

Schein, E.H. (1985) *Organization Culture and Leadership,* Jossey-Bass, San Fransisco.

Schein, E.H. (1990) Organizational culture, *American Psychologist*, 45 (2),109–19.

Scholz, C. (1987) Corporate culture, *Long Range Planning*, 20 (4), 78–87.

Silver, J. (1987) The ideology of excellence: management and neo-conservatism, *Studies in Political Economy*, 24, 5–29.

Smircich, L. (1983) Concepts of culture and organizational analysis, *Administrative Science Quarterly*, 28, 339–58.

Soeters, J.L. (1986) Excellent companies as social movements, *Journal of Management Studies*, 23 (3), 299–312.

Taguiri, R. and Litwin, G.H. (eds) (1968) *Organizational Climate: Exploration of a Concept,* Harvard Business School, Boston, MA.

Taylor, F.W. (1947) *The Principles of Scientific Management,* Harper and Row, New York.

Thompson, P. and McHugh, D. (1990) *Work Organizations: A Critical Perspective,* Macmillan, London.

Trompenaars, F. (1993) *Riding the Waves of Culture,* Economist Books, London.

Watson, T.J. (1994) *In Search of Management: Culture, Chaos and Control in Management Work,* Routledge, London.

Whipp, R., Rosenfeld, R. and Pettigrew, A. (1989) Culture and competitiveness: evidence from two mature UK industries, *Journal of Management Studies*, 26, (6), 561–85.

Williams, A., Dobson, P. and Walters, M. (1989) *Changing Culture: New Organizational Approaches*, Institute of Personnel Management, London.

Willmott, H. (1993) Strength is ignorance; slavery is freedom: managing culture in modern organizations, *Journal of Management Studies*, 30,(4), 515–52.

Wilson, D.C. and Rosenfeld R.H. (1990) *Managing Organizations,* McGraw-Hill, London.

Human resource management and industrial relations

8

Peter Fenwick and Adrian Murton

INTRODUCTION

This chapter considers the significant changes that have occurred in British industrial relations in the last two decades and assesses the role in them of a projected 'new' approach to the management of employees, the 'Human Resource Management' or 'HRM' model. To do so, the established practices of industrial relations (IR) in the UK of the immediately preceding period are described and contrasted with the inimical structural and cultural conditions of the 1980s and 1990s. These pressures have been interpreted as a fertile growing medium, or 'compost' in the case of radical analyses (Legge 1995: 80), for HRM. Consequently, the dimensions of the model are explored, along with its two major versions of 'soft' and 'hard' HRM and their implications for the management of IR. This is then examined in the light of the empirical evidence of change, which suggests that HRM's importance resides more in its rhetorical role than as a guide to actual developments in labour issues. This leads into a critical discussion of the postmodernist concept of a 'discourse', or how the supposedly ubiquitous language of HRM may inform and seek to justify managerial action in IR. The chapter concludes that no one model or framework is adequate to an analysis of the variety and complexity of 'modern' industrial relations.

CONTEXT

When John Dunlop developed the concept of an industrial relations system in the 1950s he established industrial relations as a separate and distinct area of study. At the centre of his system was an emphasis upon rule-making processes, with employment rules the main outcome of the system. Subsequent definitions of the subject have emphasized these outcomes together with the ways in which the rules are made and administered (see Clegg 1979; Flanders 1970). However, whilst the concept of an industrial relations system and the definition of the subject have proved contentious (see Hyman 1975) there is general agreement that the form of industrial relations that emerged in Britain in the late nineteenth century – and which continues to influence aspects of industrial relations to the present day (Edwards 1995) had a number of distinct characteristics which are described below.

First has been the emphasis placed upon 'voluntarism' – that voluntary agreement between the parties to industrial relations was preferable to compulsion through the law. This involved the state in an approach characterized by non-intervention in issues between employers and employees, so that legislation enacted was designed to keep the state, and particularly the courts, away from direct involvement in industrial relations.

A second feature has been the tradition of management preferring to deal with trade unions through associations of employers rather than directly themselves. This meant that negotiations occurred away from the point of production, kept wages out of competition and provided a countervailing force to the power of trades unions (Palmer 1983). As well as ensuring that collective bargaining became the 'fulcrum' of industrial relations in Britain, it also meant that, outside of the largest organizations, the personnel function remained under-developed or non-existent.

The final characteristic has been the nature and complexity of trade unionism. For many unions, craft traditions have remained important, influencing the often sectionalist and economistic concerns of unions and their development on occupational and industrial lines, and has meant that union structure has been both complicated and competitive.

In summary, the industrial relations arrangements which characterized Britain for much of this century were collectivist, based around industry-wide collective bargaining underpinned by a loose framework of law founded upon statutory immunities.[1] For the most part, industrial relations concerns were kept away from the individual firm, and where employers had to consider industrial relations issues in any strategic sense, these were confined largely to the areas of trade union recognition and collective bargaining.

These arrangements appeared to work satisfactorily until the late 1950s when pressures from full employment and sustained product demand began to undermine their effectiveness, pressures which became more acute in the late 1960s as the 'post-war boom' slowed and worker expectations became more difficult to meet. Concerns were raised about the alleged 'power without responsibility' of trades unions, the rising incidence of strikes, relatively low productivity and inflation (Inns of Court Conservative and Unionist Society 1958; Shanks 1961) and, at the organizational level, the rise of shop stewards, wage drift and 'restrictive practices'. In 1965, in response to these concerns, the then Labour government established a Royal Commission (see Donovan 1968) to examine relations between trades unions and employers; its subsequent report was published in 1968.

Whilst it has been the subject of much criticism and revision, both at the time and since (Turner 1968; Dunn 1993; Metcalf 1993) the Report of the Donovan Commission is regarded as one of the most significant documents on British industrial relations this century, both in terms of its diagnosis of the 'problems' of industrial relations and in its prescriptions for change. For the Commission, the root problem of British industrial relations lay in its informality, and argued that the changes necessary to the system required voluntary reform of collective bargaining institutions rather than legal regulation.[2] Within this, the reform of procedures was seen as particularly necessary to reflect local, company or plant level concerns rather than considerations at the industry level (e.g. Fox and Flanders 1969).

Significantly, Donovan stressed that the responsibility for change lay with management. In practice, wage drift,[3] poor utilization of employees and rising stoppages were issues taking place within organizations for which management had direct responsibility (Donovan 1968). For the Commission, the need to professionalize the management of employees and for management to deal effectively with industrial relations matters was critical if these issues were to be dealt with and improvements made. However, as writers such as Flanders and others made clear, management could only regain control of industrial relations by sharing it with trades unions and their representatives (Flanders 1970; McCarthy and Ellis 1973).

THE 1970S AND REFORMISM

The decade following the Donovan report represented the high point of 'reformism' and the emphasis upon formalization, proceduralism and collectivism in Britain[4] (Storey 1992). By the middle of the decade, significant steps had been taken within industries and organizations to professionalize industrial relations, introduce or improve jointly agreed procedures and reform payments systems and collective bargaining (Brown 1981). These initiatives were encouraged by government, which supported collective bargaining and trade union membership through legislation, and the newly established Advisory Conciliation and Arbitration Service (ACAS). The latter was formally charged with the promotion of 'good industrial relations' (Purcell 1981), interpreted as a commitment to collective bargaining, trade unionism, and formal procedures. Furthermore, developments in joint agreements at the organizational level were mirrored at the political. From the early 1960s governments had sought trade union involvement in certain areas of policy and this 'bargained corporatism'[5] as Crouch (1982, 1995) described it, reached its zenith between 1974 and 1979 with the Labour government's Social Contract. Under this arrangement unions agreed to wage restraint in return for substantial changes in taxation and redistribution of income.

The consequences of this period of reformism were particularly significant for those directly involved in industrial relations. Trades unions, which had experienced modest membership growth in the 1950s and early 1960s, saw rapid gains during the 1970s. From 1970 to 1979, membership increased by two million, reaching 13.2 million by the end of the decade, representing over 58 per cent of the working population. These gains in membership were often mirrored in the extent of trade union involvement in decision-making at both political and company levels. Although rarely involved in higher-level consultation or negotiation of strategic decisions within companies, unions had achieved considerable involvement in political decision-making and in many sectors at the workplace level (Brown 1981).

Personnel management witnessed a similar growth in this period. The Donovan prescription for greater professionalization in personnel management was aided by a number of developments. The organizational changes and increasing size and complexity of organizations required specialist staff to manage industrial relations issues (Batstone 1984). These were reinforced by the support and encouragement given to trades unions and collective bargaining, and by the increasing importance of individual employment legislation associated with Britain's membership of the European Community. Within organizations, the development of structured internal labour markets and career planning gave an impetus to personnel as 'advisors' and 'regulators' (Storey 1992), whilst the formalization and proceduralization of industrial relations gave scope to a growth in 'contracts managers' (Tyson and Fell 1986), servicing and negotiating agreements with trades unions.

The extent of change and the 'proceduralization' of industrial relations in the 1970s is supported by survey data evidence from manufacturing conducted by Brown

(1981) and to a limited extent from the more comprehensive work by Daniel and Millward (1983). This evidence points to a trend to formalize industrial relations arrangements with trades unions and their representatives, to a spread of jointly-agreed procedures as well as to wholesale reform of collective bargaining and systems of reward. These developments have been described as representing a particular organizational approach or style of managing industrial relations, a shift to what has been termed a 'bargained constitutionalist' style (Purcell and Sisson 1983) associated with operating in mass markets and producing largely standardized products or services within 'Fordist' production systems.[6] Such an approach is characterized by recognition of trades unions, highly specific collective agreements and an emphasis on joint decision-making on a wide range of issues, but one regarded as poor at managing change (Purcell and Ahlstrand 1994). Whilst many organizations were moving to embrace this style, the changes need to be placed in perspective. Brown (1981) has argued that many of these initiatives were introduced without a coherent strategy and that many companies were managing industrial relations opportunistically, treating industrial relations largely as a 'fire-fighting' activity (Purcell and Sisson 1983). In consequence 'traditional personnel management' may have received a boost from the post-Donovan reforms but it was still lacking coherent strategies and was largely absent from boardrooms.

CHANGING CONTEXTS: DEVELOPMENTS SINCE 1979

In the period since 1979, the styles of managing industrial relations that had emerged in the post-war period were faced with a series of inter-related developments which cumulatively argued for radical change. The extent to which this has occurred is still a matter of some debate, as will be more fully considered below, but there can be little doubt that all the parties to industrial relations have experienced major shifts in the structural and cultural conditions (in the sense of assumptions and beliefs about appropriate practices) in which their decisions are made. In this section, we consider these major contextual changes, most accounts of which have given primacy to an intensification of competition in markets for goods and services (e.g. IPD 1997; Legge 1995; Blyton and Turnbull 1994). This, it is argued in turn, has required a 'sharpening up' (Hendry 1995) of established forms of labour management in order that organizations can react more effectively to the qualitatively different environment which they are perceived to inhabit.

Any account of the intensification of competition must include the contribution of globalization, which essentially involves an increasing interconnectedness of national economies. This has been enabled by the diffusion of information technology, for example in the networking of financial markets, and by the lowering or elimination of barriers to trade through a series of international agreements. Allied to this has been the growth in the size and power of multinational companies, which can encourage competition between subsidiaries and even countries for resources, and the spectacular growth (until recently) of the economies of Japan and the Pacific Rim. As a consequence, the performance of the UK economy is in large measure dependent on decisions made across the world, and its firms have been exposed to growing competition both in domestic and export markets.

Global competition also informs the expectations of consumers about acceptable levels of quality and has compounded an established trend in the UK and other developed economies towards increasingly customized tastes, which reject standardized output in favour of differentiated products. Rapid changes in technology which lead to innovation in products and the processes by which they are made, together with its ability to lower entry barriers to previously stable markets, have also added to the turbulence faced by British firms. Moreover, the economy has been afflicted by periodic and severe recessions, generally worse than those of its major competitors (Oulton 1994), which have forced companies to compete more aggressively in declining domestic markets. Such developments had clear implications for the particular form and content of industrial relations arrangements that had been encouraged and established themselves in Britain in the 1970s.

It is also important to recognize that since 1979 UK government policy has altered radically, emphasizing the value of competitive intensity to the objective of increased corporate efficiency. Keynesian demand-management by government, whose attempts to control the level of unemployment and wage inflation had provided a vital underpinning to the development of industrial relations in the UK, was rejected by the presiding analysis of monetarist and 'supply-side' economics of the 1980s. This rejected Keynesianism as inherently inflationary, for its failure to manage unemployment and its encouragement of a progressive encroachment by the state into economic decision-making, which produced punitive levels of taxation together with unacceptable constraints on individual and commercial freedom. More particularly, government intervention discouraged competition between firms (and workers) in 'free' markets, whose operation was seen to be a guarantor of economic efficiency. In brief, the exposure of organizations, both in the private and public sectors, to new sources of competition would provide the 'discipline' of either producing efficiently and in response to consumer demand or losing market share.

Consequently, a raft of measures was introduced in the 1980s and 1990s to make the economy more subject to market forces. These included the liberalization of markets by the reduction or elimination of barriers to entry to, for example, the financial services industry and the subjection of previously public monopolies such as refuse collection to 'Compulsory Competitive Tendering'. The public sector was deregulated, through privatization and the removal of direct government controls in, for example, the creation of 'agencies' within the civil service. It was also 'marketized' by the introduction of market or quasi-market forces where the prospect of private sector competition was limited, such as the establishment of the internal market within the National Health Service (NHS). Crucially, these reforms were to occur within the constraints of a 'tight' monetary policy, involving the control of the growth of the money supply and, more significantly over time as the latter became increasingly difficult to manage, the target of a high and stable exchange rate. In consequence, the discipline of market forces would be complemented by the rigours of monetarism to achieve the non-inflationary growth of output.

However, the 'Thatcherite' reforms of the economy were not simply disciplinary in nature. At the same time, government would 'remove impediments which prevent people and firms responding quickly to changing conditions and market demand' (Treasury 1984) in order to allow businesses to make the transition to a more competitive environment. Crudely, the 'stick' of increased competition within tight monetary conditions would be wielded with the 'carrot' of reforms which allowed entrepreneurs and managers more scope for decision-making about entry to markets and the use of resources. Both were designed to increase employers' relative bargaining power. In particular, successive administrations from 1979 were to introduce changes in the operation of labour markets which, in their cumulative effects, have had far-reaching implications for industrial relations.

In a clear rejection of the prior Keynesian consensus, the Conservative government was prepared to allow unemployment to rise. In its analysis, joblessness to a significant extent flowed from the excessive bargaining power of trades unions. As 'market imperfections' given their monopoly supply of labour, unions prevented (real) wages from falling to 'market-clearing' levels at which unemployment could be removed. Rather than acting as 'sword of justice',[7] they disenfranchised the unemployed by preventing them from competing for jobs (e.g. Hanson and Mather 1988). Furthermore, unions were seen as barriers to the introduction of more efficient working practices, vital if organizations were to succeed in the face of heightened competition. Indeed, for the ideologues of the 'New Right', trades unions did not even provide a means for the resolution of conflict, but were an important source of it, as exemplified by Britain's comparative incidence of industrial disputes.

The policies pursued by successive Conservative administrations also drew sustenance from and helped to sustain the values of the 'enterprise culture' (Legge 1995: 80f.). The idea of 'enterprise' is founded on a vision of bold, risk-taking, energetic and self-reliant individuals driving commercial decision-making in 'free' markets. Thus, the 'strong' are released from the constraints of punitive personal taxation, the dead-hand of union restrictions and stultifying monopolies, so that organizations are led by individuals who are motivated and empowered to respond to the challenge of unbridled market conditions. Such rhetoric was not limited to 'captains of industry', however, but also embraced the role of line managers and even the unemployed, who were to be weaned off the attitudes of passivity and dependency engendered by the welfare state in order that they could become active participants in the labour market. This 'can do' orientation necessarily responded with hostility to institutions like trades unions and the social security system for being supposedly hostile to the spirit of enterprise (Legge 1995: 81).

Whether such assumptions are correct is not at issue here (but see e.g. Freeman and Medoff 1984; and Nolan and O'Donnell 1995 for alternative perspectives). Rather, they were a justification for the use of rising levels of unemployment to reduce union bargaining power, in that 'excessive' wage settlements or continued 'restrictive practices' would result in the loss of union members' jobs. This policy was reinforced by a series of legislative initiatives which were introduced on a step-by-step basis by the Thatcher and Major administrations (for a full discussion of these see Dickens and Hall and also Crouch, both in Edwards 1995).

In essence the reforms significantly altered the relationship between trades unions and employers by restricting the latter's immunity from legal redress against industrial disputes, rendering unlawful actions such as sympathy strikes or disputes pursued in the absence of a majority of affected members voting for it in a secret ballot. The conduct of a lawful strike was also hampered by the ruling that unions could not discipline individual members for failing to participate in them. Further, the winning of recognition from new employers was made more difficult, as well as the retention of existing membership by, for example, the outlawing of the closed shop. Indeed, the assault on their bargaining power would make unions less attractive to prospective members, compounded by the dilution of individual employment rights (such as protection against unfair dismissal), which had hitherto made unions attractive in their ability to defend them.

Other government policies also sought to marginalize trades unions. As an employer it was prepared to confront unions in or even provoke them to lengthy strikes, as in the steel and coal industries and in the civil service. Cuts in unemployment benefits and in the level of direct taxation were designed to encourage the unemployed to compete more actively for available jobs, and further measures were introduced to make labour markets more competitive and flexible. For instance, changes in the housing market, such as the sale of council houses, and the introduction of 'portable' pensions that could be easily transferred between employers, allied to educational reforms such as the accreditation of prior work experience and the provision of a wider range of vocational qualifications, would all contribute to the increased geographical and occupational mobility of labour. In short, these measures, supported by the encouragement of savings funds, including privatized share issues, would enable individual employees to exercise their 'exit options' in the face of poor or tyrannical employers (Hanson and Mather 1988). Collective representation would become unnecessary.

Finally, to this litany of policy reforms of the labour market, one must add the major structural changes that have occurred largely independently of them. The shift of employment out of the secondary sector has seen the loss of around four million jobs since the mid-1960s, many of them unionized. Combined with the large increase in the participation of females in the labour force and its ageing, this has brought about a major change away from the young, male, manual worker in unionized firms characteristic of the 1960s and 1970s to a composition perhaps inimical to 'traditional' industrial relations (Legge 1995: 78).

ASSESSMENT

Overall, the consequence of these changes for many of the established institutions of British industrial relations has been considerable. For trades unions, the gains of the 1970–79 period were eliminated in the subsequent four years and membership has fallen continuously since then. In 1997 there were estimated to be fewer than eight million people in trade union membership, a fall of over 5 million since 1979 (see Table 8.1). This decline has been concentrated disproportionately amongst male manual workers in manufacturing and the extractive industries (Waddington and Whitston 1995), and is closely linked to structural shifts in the economy, associated changes in workforce composition, as well as to the cyclical impact of unemployment and the political complexion of the government in power (Metcalf 1989; Disney 1990; Kelly 1990). However, it is also clear that during the decade employer perceptions of the utility of unions changed. This is reflected in their increasing reluctance to recognize unions in newly established plants, and the development from the late 1980s to de-recognize established trades unions. The decline in trade union membership and density has contributed to a decline in the importance and influence of collective bargaining, and particularly a demise of multi-employer bargaining arrangements (Purcell 1991).

The overall impact of the changes in the wider context of industrial relations in Britain has been to enhance the ability of managers to effect significant changes in the management of labour. This, coupled with the decline in trade union influence and

Table 8.1 Trade Union Membership and Strike Activity 1960–1997

Year	TU M'ship (millions)	TUD (%)	Strikes	WDL
1960	9.84	44.2	2832	3 024
1965	10.33	44.2	2354	2 925
1970	11.18	48.6	3970	10 980
1975	12.03	50.7	2282	6 012
1979	13.29	54.2	2080	29 474
1980	12.95	52.8	1348	11 964
1985	10.82	44.1	903	6 402
1986	10.54	43.0	1074	6 920
1987	10.48	42.7	101	3 546
1988	10.38	41.7	781	3 702
1989	10.20	41.2	701	4 128
1990	9.95	41.6	630	1 903
1991	9.59	39.3	369	761
1992	9.05	37.2	253	528
1993	8.70	35.6	211	649
1994	8.28	34.1	205	278
1995	8.03	32.9	235	415
1996	(7.22)	(31.3)	244	1 303
1997	(7.12)	(30.2)	216	235

Sources: TUD [= trade union density], Strikes and WDL; working days lost through strikes in thousands: *Employment Gazette* selected issues. Trade union membership: Certification Officer: Labour Market Trends February 1996 except 1996 and 1997 from LFS; Cully and Woodland 1998.

collective bargaining as a regulatory mechanism, requires us to: 'Move beyond the exclusive preoccupation with the collective aspects of the employment relationship' (Sisson 1993: 209).

This involves a re-conceptualization of the nature and form of the employment relationship, one which places a greater emphasis upon individualized relations between employers and employees and to the role of managers in shaping that relationship. These developments have led commentators to talk increasingly of 'employee relations' rather than industrial relations, and of HRM, and it is the latter that has been perhaps the most influential conceptual framework in the re-envisioning of industrial relations. It is to that which we now turn.

CONCEPTS – HUMAN RESOURCE MANAGEMENT

The period since the late 1970s could, therefore, be interpreted as the conjunction of a series of contextual changes that rendered the Donovan tradition of pluralism and institutional regulation outdated, ineffectual and largely superfluous. Its rigidities, founded on extensive rules and proceduralism, made the management of staff in organizations unresponsive to shifting market conditions, inadequately concerned with the achievement of competitive advantage and inappropriate to the redistribution of bargaining power that had occurred towards employers. Such developments, allied with the ideological assumptions of the 'enterprise culture' and associated, popular managerial nostrums, both required and enabled qualitative change in people management.

Consequently, a fertile soil has been produced for the growth of a 'new orthodoxy' (Guest 1991) that represents a break with the past and is sufficiently robust to constitute a viable policy framework. The key significance of HRM is that it has been presented as such a model, in the sense of both a guide for managerial (and trade union) action and a primary explanation of the radical changes that have been observed or adduced in the last two decades. What is less clear is the precise meaning of HRM, although Legge (1995) observes several common themes or key features which are discussed below.

Key characteristics of HRM

Chiefly, rather than the management of employees being marginal to business strategy, HRM emphasizes its contribution to the achievement of sustained competitive advantage. Integration with strategic planning, or an 'external fit', enhances the value of human resources. This is complemented by a set of employment policies that are consistent with one another or mutually supportive, e.g. the linking of developments in job design with selection methods, training interventions and novel forms of reward. Such initiatives demonstrate an 'internal fit' or integration to maximize their impact on employee flexibility, productivity and the quality of their work.

Moreover, they may consolidate and extend an appropriate corporate culture which, in essence, expresses the assumptions of senior management about the behaviours that make the organization a success (e.g. Schein 1985; Johnson and Scholes 1993). Also, human resource decisions, by being pivotal to the core performance of the business (Storey 1992: 27), are a central concern of line management, encouraging them to take more responsibility for their staff, as opposed to relying on the expertise of a specialist personnel function. People management is thus integrated with the organization's operational decision-making, rather than merely espoused in official policies that may fail to meet operational needs.

'Soft' and 'Hard' HRM

However, HRM is not a unified concept. Two broad versions of it have been discerned (Storey, 1989, 1992): 'hard' HRM and 'soft' HRM. Common to each is the notion of strategic integration, both external and internal, but there are important differences of emphasis. 'Hard' models view employees as principally a passive resource to be acquired and deployed, with a rational, quantitative and calculative (Legge 1995) approach to the full utilization of the workforce in order to achieve competitive advantage. Some autonomy may be afforded to staff, especially in dealings with customers in view of the productivity gains of dealing with problems at their source, but workers will simultaneously be controlled through detailed performance targets and sophisticated monitoring (Guest 1995: 117). Exemplar organizations may include many in the fast food industry, call centres or new factories staffed with a young and compliant workforce (Guest 1995).

'Soft' HRM sees employees in more proactive terms and as a valuable resource whose competencies, skills and attitudes are to be appropriately nurtured. People 'make the difference' competitively by their ability and willingness to develop a range of skills and perform a variety of tasks, to make an active contribution to continuous improvement in quality standards and to continue learning in their work. Consequently, the 'soft' version draws upon the traditions of human relations' and neo-human relations' thought (Storey 1992: 28), through its emphasis on the role of managerial leadership in the release of workers' potential, its advocacy of increased employee discretion and participation in job-related decision-making, its encouragement of trust and co-operation and its focus on the individual or small group as the primary site for management attention.

However, while these antecedents to HRM were concerned to improve employees' job satisfaction or 'quality of working life' in order to improve productivity or reduce levels of industrial conflict, 'soft' HRM goes beyond this in its concern with business strategy and its objective of worker 'commitment'. This is reflected in recent discussion of 'high commitment' or 'high involvement' management rather than HRM (Lawler 1994; Wood and Albanese 1995). Such an emphasis embraces employee identification with the goals and values of the business, a desire to belong to the organization and to make efforts on its behalf (Guest 1995: 113), thereby reinforcing the significance of managing corporate culture through the dissemination of beliefs, assumptions and values expressing the needs of the business. The issue of commitment is critical and has produced much academic debate. Essentially, it is functional, in that it generates employees' self-directed rather than rigidly channelled behaviour, encouraging flexibility and adaptability in the face of complex and ever-present change. Workers are thus seen as proactive and resourceful, not passive and malleable, with employee relations founded on 'high trust' in contrast to endemic suspicion and 'zero-sum' bargaining:

> The new HRM model is composed of policies that promote mutuality – mutual goals, mutual respect, mutual responsibility. The theory is that policies of mutuality will elicit commitment which will in turn yield both better economic performance and greater human development (Walton 1985: 64).

Indeed, the 'soft' model may be interpreted as the dominant representation of HRM (e.g. Keenoy 1997), encouraging considerable speculation about its implications for industrial relations.

Developing the 'Soft' HRM Model

Storey's work (1992, 1995) provides a useful and influential exploration of the meaning of 'soft' HRM and its principal dimensions. Certainly, its assumptions are perceived as diametrically opposed to those of 'hard' HRM. Both are clear departures from the Donovan tradition, but in its pursuit of commitment, the 'soft' model represents a 'truly distinctive' break and a 'more severe test' (Storey 1992: 25) of the extent to which there has been qualitative change in the management of workforces. Storey summarizes the model as follows and it is represented in more detail in Figure 8.1:

> Human resource management is a distinctive approach to employment management which seeks to achieve competitive advantage through the strategic deployment of a highly committed and capable workforce, using an array of cultural, structural and personnel techniques (Storey 1995: 5).

Storey is at pains to argue that the model is not an academic construction or simply asserted, but is built around his managerial respondents' depictions of the 'was' and

1 Beliefs and assumptions
   That it is the human resource which gives competitive edge.
   That the aim should not be mere compliance with rules but employee commitment.
   That therefore employees should be carefully selected and developed.

2 Strategic qualities
   Because of the above factors, HR decisions are of strategic importance.
   Top management involvement is necessary.
   HR policies should be integrated into the business strategy – stemming from it and contributing to it.

3 Critical role of managers
   HR practice is critical to the core activities of the business, it is too important to be left to personnel specialists alone.
   Line managers need to be closely involved as deliverers and drivers of HR policies.
   Greater attention paid to the management of managers themselves.

4 Key levers
   Managing culture is more important than managing procedures and systems.
   Integrated action on selection, communication, training, reward and development.
   Restructuring and job design to allow devolved responsibility and empowerment.

Figure 8.1 The HRM model
Source: Storey 1995: 6.

their preferred path for the development of labour management. The framework was, therefore, formulated and reformulated inductively, using the stream of data derived from his research undertaken in the mid-1980s across a range of industries and sectors in 15 'core case companies', which were studied in depth, and 25 'panel companies' (Storey 1992: xiii). Crucially, then, the model is not intended to be either an exhaustive description of current practices or a prescription of the direction and nature of change. Instead, 'it is a representation made by reconstructing the implicit models of the managers interviewed' (Storey 1992: 34).

In other words, Storey produces a 'conceptual framework' (Storey 1992: 34) that seeks to capture the generic 'recipe' of his respondents, or their beliefs and assumptions about 'the path to follow' towards desired 'achievable states' (Storey 1992: 34) in people management. Therefore, using a social action perspective, he seeks to demonstrate a fundamental change in managerial frames of reference from those associated with 'Personnel and Industrial Relations' (Storey 1992: 35). This is not simply a reversion to unitarism from pluralism, but a radical shift in managerial understandings that guide action, intimated by certain key phrases that were extremely 'rare' (Storey 1992: 35) in any discussion of employment relations in the 1970s, such as 'business need', 'markets' and 'customers'.

A key purpose of the model is to act as a classificatory device for determining what is and what is not HRM (Storey 1992: 34), but it also generates two central issues. Firstly, to what degree is the framework a valid representation of a generalizable managerial formula and, secondly, what is its relationship with concrete initiatives, including their depth, durability and the extent to which they have replaced past practice? Storey is careful to enter certain caveats about the model's expression in managerial action, distinguishing between HRM as a style of approach and as a realized pattern of relations (Storey 1992: 46). Espoused or desired practices may be difficult to implement, as they are subject to intra-managerial contestation or confronted by conditions inimical to HRM. The latter may include product market or financial pressures restricting management's strategic choice; technology offering only limited scope for employee discretion, and adversarial, multi-union industrial relations, characteristic of much of the public sector. The 'soft' recipe will inform action, but must not be used to reify its often 'incomplete and amorphous nature by attributing to it a spurious coherence' (Storey 1992: 17). None the less, the model can be used as a yardstick against which to interpret data and to analyse the phenomenon of an apparently widespread introduction of HRM-style initiatives in British organizations, one pivotally informed by the key beliefs and assumptions of the model.

Despite the apparent clarity of Storey's distinction between 'hard' and 'soft' models, in practice HRM has been burdened or possibly strengthened by its 'brilliant ambiguity' (Keenoy and Anthony 1992). Yet, the emphasis upon commitment and involvement focuses attention on Storey's 'soft', and 'best practice' elements within HRM and provides a clear template against which to assess what organizations are actually doing in their management of people.

HRM AND INDUSTRIAL RELATIONS

Clearly, as a schema informing managers' actions and their interpretations of contextual change, HRM in both its versions has provided a starting point for any recent discussion about British industrial relations (Guest 1998: 38) and has implied a profound change in its nature. Despite this: 'The discussion of HRM is one of the less well-developed areas in the wider considerations of the HRM debate' (Beardwell 1998: 203).

For Storey (1992: 36), also, the role of unions 'is by no means clear' , although the unitarist label is seen to broadly express managers' views. Indeed, 'Those few industrial relations academics who have actually passed comment on the relationship between industrial relations and HRM have typically viewed the latter as a threat to the former' (Storey 1992: 243).

This negative view has been explored by Guest, who sees the pursuit of organizational commitment as potentially rendering trades unions irrelevant, while the goal of cost advantage may discourage management from carrying the possibly high costs of union recognition (Guest 1995: 111–12), such as a 'mark-up' on wages. Similarly, Legge (1995) considers both the 'hard' and 'soft' models to be seriously at odds with the traditional industrial relations of voluntaristic collective bargaining, joint regulation of a range of issues, including the utilization and deployment of labour, and procedures for the defence of workers' rights.

'Soft' HRM envisages employees demonstrating commitment, working flexibly and 'beyond contract' and involves individualistic managerial practices, such as the careful selection of the 'right' employees, performance-related pay, direct communication and the use of employee involvement in task-related decision-making. All bypass and marginalize trades unions or offer an alternative policy framework for non-union organizations. 'Hard' HRM seeks to use employees at management's discretion and is necessarily hostile to any narrowing of its scope by collective bargaining.

Nevertheless, there is an alternative scenario, which has been variously described, whereby 'soft' initiatives could be wedded to an acceptance of the legitimacy of pluralism. Guest sees a 'high priority' for (soft) HRM and industrial relations as a viable option for both firms and unions where there is a co-operative environment, principally given its production of a 'dual commitment', i.e. to the organization and the union (Guest 1995: 134). Such a 'new realism' is cited as evident in Nissan, Rover and other motor manufacturers and, although the role of the trades unions may be ambiguous in practice, the policies inherent in the 'soft', high utilization approach could realistically even be championed and defended by them. For instance, unions would support, fair selection, the development of their members' skills, 'high basic pay, high trust, autonomous work groups [. . .] and many more elements. Above all, unions would welcome single status and guarantees of job security' (Guest 1995: 134). Writing about the USA, Kochan and Dyer (1995) have advocated the acceptance of an intrinsic conflict of interests between the parties to industrial relations, but also their mutual recognition of the need to resolve differences efficiently and in a fashion that maintains their commitment and capacities for pursuing joint gains. For Guest, and Kochan and Dyer, such outcomes are preferable to an alternative of employment relations founded on the principles of the free market and the values of 'hard' HRM.

Such views have crystallized in the UK into the concept of 'partnership', as advocated by the Involvement and Participation Association (1997) and supported in publications by both employers' and professional bodies, e.g. the Institute of Personnel and Development (IPD 1997) and the Trades Union Congress (TUC 1997; Monks 1998). The central features of this still embryonic term comprise a stress on management–union co-operation as vital for business survival and success, signalling a consequent break from adversarial industrial relations, but also a continued role for collective bargaining and a wider scope for consultation with employees and their representatives. For the TUC's General Secretary, John Monks (1998), partnership is founded on the 'four prongs' of employment security in return for an acceptance of new working practices; the consolidation and extension of 'employee voice'; fair financial rewards, and investment in training.

These and other features of the terminology of 'partnership' have been more fully explored in the academic literature (e.g. Marchington 1998; Claydon 1998, and Coupar and Stevens 1998), which emphasizes the reciprocal obligations of management and trades unions. That is, continued collective representation and the realization of the benefits sought for members is dependent on unions' acceptance and encouragement of employees' flexibility, of their readiness to train and learn new skills and their pursuit of continuous improvement in work standards. In addition, unions are expected to embrace managerially sponsored forms of employee involvement, such as direct management communication, teamwork and financial participation, and even to support an agenda for negotiation and consultation that is 'strategic and business-focused' (Coupar and Stevens 1998: 145). The return for employers is increased productivity and organizational performance, which is further enhanced by staff's improved understanding of the business and contribution to management's decision-making.

This set of mutually determined operational practices and processes is underpinned by certain values and behaviours and a set of complementary practices in employment management (Marchington 1998). Thus, managers recognize that employees have the legitimate right to a collective voice and 'an influence over (some) managerial decisions' (Marchington 1998), while unions accept management's right to expect certain levels of employee performance. The tenor of employee relations is one of 'mutual obligation, trust and openness' and a commitment to organizational success (Coupar and Stevens 1998), which is supported by harmonization, a commitment to employment security and a willingness to invest in employees' development and life-long learning (Marchington 1998).

> Consequently, an examination of 'partnership' reveals the potential at least for 'a new fusion of human resource management and industrial relations built around a greater reciprocity of interests' (Coupar and Stevens 1998: 145).

Certainly, we can discern in the concept many echoes of 'soft' HRM, both in terms of values, such as the importance of employees' organizational commitment, and of 'key levers' or employment practices, including harmonization of terms and conditions, teamwork and increased managerial communication. However, what evidence is there for it or, indeed, for any of the other paths of change in industrial relations implied by HRM?

EMPIRICAL EVIDENCE

In examining trends in industrial relations and their relationship with HRM, a number of questions are posed by the foregoing analysis. For example, does research suggest a fundamental change in frames of reference for the management of labour across significant parts of British industry? More especially, does it reveal a qualitative shift in the direction of 'soft' HRM? If so, has this meant a marginalization of trades unions by individualistic human resource policies or the emergence of 'partnership' approaches? Alternatively, have diminished trade union presence and power meant tighter managerial control and deployment of workforces characteristic of 'hard' HRM? Also, and regardless of which version of HRM has proved paramount, do the data reveal 'strategic' management of HRM and industrial relations, in the sense of their integration with the development and delivery of competitive strategy, the choice of mutually supportive employment practices and their consolidation in the decision-making of line managers?

Turning to research, it is apparent that in order to identify qualitative changes in the management of people we require a case study rather than a survey method. This is particularly important when it is borne in mind that much of the material relating to the take-up of HRM and changes in industrial relations is derived from survey data. With these important caveats in mind, we discuss some of the main findings and raise some questions concerning omissions in the research conducted thus far. Early survey-based evidence for the USA reviewed by Guest (1991) suggested that, although there was evidence of the use of the 'new' techniques, they provided no indication that organizations were using a combination of techniques which would have suggested a planned and integrated HR strategy. Furthermore, the changes which were taking place were largely confined to non-union companies, and as Kochan et al. (1986) noted, moves towards participative management and sophisticated HRM policies were not the dominant pattern in US companies.

Survey evidence from the UK (Daniel and Millward 1983; Millward and Stevens 1986; Millward et al. 1992; Marginson et al. 1988, 1993) suggests that whilst significant changes have been taking place in the management of labour it would be wrong to interpret these as representing a move towards human resource management in any distinctive sense. Significantly such evidence points to two important developments. First, that where HRM initiatives are found these are more often in unionized rather than non-unionized workplaces (Sisson 1993; Storey 1992; Wood 1995). Second, that there are important differences between UK and foreign-owned companies in their adoption of HRM-related techniques, with the latter far more advanced in terms of take-up (Millward *et al.* 1992; Marginson *et al.* 1993).

Subsequent work by Millward (1994) on the take-up of HRM suggests little evidence of policies to increase employee commitment. Indeed, Guest argues that 'There are virtually no published studies showing that any kind of intervention has any kind of impact on levels of commitment to the organization' (Guest 1998: 42). Similarly, Millward has observed that:

> High trust practices associated with HRM had become less common not more common during the 1980s (and overall) . . . we could find little evidence that the very substantial growth in non-unionism was accompanied by a growth in HRM or more progressive management practices (Millward 1994: 127–30).

The extent to which these observations are applicable to the 1990s is evidenced from official statistics, case study and survey data. The 1990s have witnessed an increasing number of unfair dismissal and discrimination cases going to Industrial (now Employment) Tribunals and Citizens Advice Bureaux (Edwards 1992; Blyton and Turnbull 1994; Abbott 1998), with small firms accounting for the majority of cases. Furthermore, individual conciliation cases dealt with by ACAS reached record levels in 1997 for the sixth year in succession, with the majority of these concerned with unfair dismissal (ACAS 1998). However, for a more illuminating insight into what is actually taking place in British workplaces, we need to examine case study and survey work, in particular the work of Storey (1992) and that of Pettigrew and his colleagues (Sparrow and Pettigrew 1988a, 1988b; Hendry and Pettigrew 1988; Pettigrew and Whipp 1991). In view of its particular links with industrial relations, our discussion concentrates on the work of Storey, drawing upon later studies to indicate the extent to which further changes are taking place in the management of employees.

Storey's main research (1992, 1993), informed by the 'soft' model presented in Figure 8.1, examined the extent to which his 'key' companies were moving towards HRM. His principle conclusion is worth quoting for the nature of the wording used. He argued that there had been a 'remarkable take-up by large British companies of initiatives which are in the *style* of the human resource management model' (1992: 28, emphasis added).

This conclusion is made in spite of the fact that only two of his main companies were adopting a majority of techniques, many were no longer using techniques they had introduced, less than half the companies were introducing initiatives strategically, and fewer than 15 per cent were using the key levers to shape employment relations. As he conceded in a later work it was 'Often difficult to ascertain that there was in fact any "strategic" approach to the management of labour' (Storey 1993: 538).

Furthermore, there is little evidence that the initiatives introduced were part of an integrated approach in these companies (see also Wood 1995; Wood and Albanese 1995). As Pendleton (1991) has shown in BR (one of Storey's 'key' companies), policy shifted between 'soft' and 'hard' versions of HRM depending on the vagaries of political pressure and the perceptions of trade union power at particular points in time. Furthermore, many of the initiatives pursued by these companies did not cover all employees, schemes such as PRP were often targeted at specific groups, and not always with desired results (Pendleton 1991).

Despite its importance and influence Storey's (1992) work provides a picture which confirms much of the earlier survey-based research, suggesting that initiatives developed were often not firmly grounded and represented largely opportunistic moves to meet certain short-term concerns of specific interests within organizations. It is also notable that Storey's sample companies were large, often multi-divisional, with a degree of market power and where the potential for strategic choice was greatest. In his later work (Storey 1994), this point is acknowledged, and although the evidence for take-up of initiatives is again superficially impressive, many of the small companies surveyed had not taken up any of the initiatives and in those that had there was again little evidence to suggest strategic integration.

A further issue is that the changes in the management of human resources appear to have done little to enhance the status and influence of the personnel function (Guest 1993; Sisson 1995) and that overall, it is hard to disagree with Sisson's observation that:

> The likelihood is that, for the average UK employee, the experience of personnel management in Britain in the mid 1990s is less like the HRM organisation than it was a decade ago (and that) it is difficult to envisage, when the recession ends, the widespread take-up of the HRM organisation in Britain (Sisson 1994: 41).

INDUSTRIAL RELATIONS AND EMPLOYMENT PRACTICES

The debate on the emergence of a new industrial relations in Britain has focused on two approaches (Beardwell 1992). The first has emphasized changes in the institutional framework, particularly collective bargaining, together with the reassertion of a more managerially determined industrial relations agenda (Batstone 1987; Purcell 1991). The second approach has concentrated upon a perceived philosophical shift towards individualism, the emergence of HRM and non-unionism.

In practice the evidence for the first approach is mixed. Many of the 'new' initiatives are not as novel as they appear (e.g. single union deals, Gall 1993) and many are atypical of much of the contemporary industrial relations scene. However, the period from the late 1970s supports the view that in many workplaces a de-collectivization of industrial relations has been taking place (Smith and Morton 1993; Martin et al. 1991; McLaughlin and Gourlay 1994). Results from the Workplace Employee Relations Survey 1998 indicates that over half of all workplaces in the public and private sectors had no recognized trade union, and the percentage of workplaces with no union members at all rose from 36 per cent in 1990 to 47 per cent in 1998 (Cully et al. 1998).

Further evidence in support of change comes from coverage of collective bargaining arrangements. Work by Brown and Walsh (1994) indicates that in the private sector the percentage of employees covered by multi-employer (industry-wide) bargaining fell from 60 per cent in 1950 to 10 per cent in 1990, whilst those covered by single employer bargaining over the same period increased from 20 per cent to 40 per cent. Overall, the proportion of private sector employees covered by collective bargaining fell throughout this period from 80 per cent to 50 per cent, and that by 1997 this had fallen to around 40 per cent in manufacturing alone (Cully and Woodland 1998). Thus, whilst the dismantling of multi-employer arrangements, the push to decentralize in the 1980s and the marginalizing of trade unions have been significant (3) (see Brown and Walsh 1991; Purcell 1991; Jackson *et al.* 1992; Avis 1990), the moves towards non-unionism and de-recognition have perhaps overshadowed these developments (Millward *et al.* 1992; Marginson *et al.* 1993).

Other recent trends in collective bargaining include a reduction in the frequency of negotiations with moves to two-year and three-year deals, and a contraction in bargaining scope, with fewer issues subject to joint regulation (Millward *et al.* 1992). Additionally, there has been an increase in the linkage of issues to pay (Marsden and Thompson 1990) with 'something for something' bargaining much more commonplace, particularly requirements for more flexible working. Thus, tighter management control over collective bargaining has led to pay rises increasingly conditional upon productivity improvements (Brown *et al.* 1995).

Similar evidence on declining bargaining scope comes from the second Company Level Industrial Relations Survey (CLIRS) (Marginson *et al.* 1993), where 60 per cent of large companies reported a decline in the range of matters subject to negotiation. This is further confirmed by case study evidence from the motor industry (Marsden *et al.* 1985, Williams *et al.* 1994), coal-mining (Edwards and Heery 1989; Richardson and Wood 1989; Metcalf 1989), steel (Blyton 1992) and the docks (Turnbull and Weston 1992; Turnbull 1993).

A further development has been a continued shift towards individual negotiation, particularly individualized pay through performance related pay (PRP). The spread of such schemes has been significant (Millward *et al.* 1992; Kessler and Purcell 1992; Kessler 1994), often targeted at management grades (as in British Rail, the Post Office and local authorities), although frequently with limited success (e.g. BR, Pendleton 1991, and BT). The general view is that such schemes do not have the motivational qualities claimed for them, and for average performers in particular there may be de-motivational consequences (Thompson 1992; Marsden and Richardson 1994).

It is significant that many of the best publicized examples of attempts to place industrial relations on a different footing in the 1980s and 1990s have been in organizations where established styles of managing industrial relations were founded on detailed collective agreements and characterized by adversarial bargaining relationships (e.g. Purcell and Ahlstrand 1994). In addition to the examples cited in this section companies such as Rover, Shell, Mobil and ICI have all tried in different ways to move to arrangements more conducive to handling change, some of which have embraced the more philosophical variant of 'New Industrial Relations'.

Turning to the second interpretation of the 'New Industrial Relations' evidence, trends towards a non-union industrial relations are increasingly in evidence. The results from WIRS3 (Workplace Industrial Relations Survey) show that establishments set up in the 1980s have been much less willing to grant union recognition than those founded in the 1960s and 1970s (see also Disney *et al.* 1995). This reflects a reduced willingness by employers to recognize unions, illustrated by an increase in de-recognition of one or more unions in the late 1980s (Claydon 1989; Gregg and Yates 1991; Millward *et al.* 1992; Marginson *et al.* 1993; but cf. Gall and McKay 1998), but possibly also, a reduced willingness by employees to join trade unions

(McLaughlin and Gourlay 1994). However, in the 1990s, the picture has changed, new recognitions have exceeded the number of derecognitions, and since 1994 more employees have been affected by the former than the latter (Claydon 1998; Gall and McKay 1998). This development could partly reflect the belief that the government would change and more recently the effects of the new government's 'Fairness at Work' White Paper (published in May 1998) on statutory recognition of trades unions by employers, where it is desired by a sufficiently large proportion of the workforce.

The trend away from recognition began prior to the 1980s, but clearly accelerated during this decade (Claydon 1989; Guest 1995). However, where a union is not recognized there is little evidence that management replaces it with an HRM strategy to obtain workforce commitment (Millward 1994; Marginson *et al.* 1993). Indeed, the evidence suggests that it is unionized companies where HRM-type initiatives appear to be much more prevalent (Millward *et al.* 1992; Storey 1992; Wood and Albanese 1995) and that only US owned companies are promoting 'individualised HRM' – a high HRM, non-union approach (Guest 1995). This said, recent evidence from WERS 98 (Workplace Employee Relations Survey) suggests that the picture is more complex, with a large number of organizations operating with a package of employee involvement initiatives. What is currently unclear, is the extent to which these are clustered amongst firms with particular characteristics, and the quality of the initiatives themselves. What has emerged is that managers and employees often hold very different views about the existence of such initiatives and their efficacy where present (Cully *et al.* 1998).

The previous WIRS3 results highlight other characteristics of non-union industrial relations which led one commentator to talk of them in terms of a 'Bleak House' (Sisson 1993). That report concluded that:

> Employee relations in non-union industrial and commercial workplaces had relatively few formal medium through which employees could contribute to the operation of their workplaces in a broader context than that of the specific job. Nor were they as likely to have opportunities to air grievances or resolve problems in ways that were systematic and designed to ensure fairness of treatment (Millward *et al.* 1992).

In light of these observations Guest's statement that workers in non-union plants are two-and-a-half times more likely to be dismissed than those in unionized plants should not be surprising. The evidence on non-unionism is none the less sparse despite the fact that in numerical terms the small-firm sector, where non-unionism is most common, is so large. Data which is available suggests many owner-managed firms adopt a 'traditionalist' approach viewing unions as an unwarranted intrusion into their 'right' to manage their enterprise as they see fit (Rainnie 1989). More generally, there appears to be increased management by stress, surveillance and control (Keenoy 1997; Legge 1995), possibly reinforced by the employment of techniques associated with TQM and Business Process Engineering. Nevertheless, other commentators would argue that the 'victims' of the 'black hole/Bleak House' firm must be set in the 'wider context of high commitment and its "accomplices" which may appear doubly attractive by comparison' (Beardwell 1998).

Overall the evidence on HRM and industrial relations suggests that employers appear to have followed Conservative administrations' example as an employer in slowly withdrawing support from institutional industrial relations (Guest 1995) and, as Edwards (1995) has suggested, the trends in the 1980s and 1990s have made the connection between worker and employer more direct: the increasing market-based pressures to perform have often meant a more highly regulated regime within companies. However, such a pragmatic or opportunistic reaction to competitive conditions, as opposed to a planned, considered approach to staff, has cast doubt on management as a strategic actor, as Sisson and Marginson (1995) have argued.

> It has rarely been recognised . . . that a strategic approach sits very uneasily with the reality of management decision-making in a context where business considerations are impacting ever more sharply on industrial relations practice and the institutional context serves to emphasise short-run returns (Sisson and Marginson 1995: 117).

This issue of the wider context in which management decision-making takes place is an area taken up in the final section. The general conclusion from the evidence is that whilst significant changes have and are taking place in the institutional framework of industrial relations, these are driven by essentially opportunistic concerns, often relating to flexibility, rather than a clear coherent strategy. In Guest's terms, outside of larger organizations, the 'black hole' option appears to be becoming more prevalent with a trend towards traditional and paternalistic management styles (Purcell and Ahlstrand 1994), as the companies most associated with the sophisticated human relations approach – such as IBM – appear to falter.

A SUMMARY AND CRITIQUE

Our review of the evidence produced by recent research suggests that 'soft' HRM in a developed form remains limited to a handful of exemplar organizations, and even there it may be under threat. Consequently, whilst there is some support for the marginalization of trades unions by individualistic practices, there is currently limited evidence for the scenario of 'partnership', although this a relatively recent idea. More generally, 'partnership' is potentially undermined by an absence of managerial commitment to such agreements and entrenched obstacles to co-operative bargaining behaviour where there remain serious conflicts of interest (Claydon 1998). Further, the related continuance of 'us and them' attitudes among both parties and the limited concessions available to unions pursuing policies of incorporation or partnership may undermine the recruitment and retention of membership (Claydon 1998).

The lack of empirical support for the take-up of HRM and high commitment practices in Britain is significant but needs to be seen in the wider context of management decision-making in organizations. Following Storey and Sisson (1989), the key structural impediments to HRM can be identified together with some of the consequences for HRM-type practices. The main contextual factors are listed below.

First, the central issue in the take-up of HRM relates to systems of corporate governance and associated patterns of ownership and control (Sisson 1994, 1995), with a domination of outsider systems of control through shareholders (Franks and Meyer 1992) and pressure through this system for organizations to deliver short-term results. The fact that evidence for the take-up of HRM initiatives appears to be concentrated amongst foreign-owned companies also reflects differences in systems of corporate ownership and control. In the UK many companies operate under a constant threat of takeover if short-term results fail to meet largely financial criteria of appropriateness.

Second, much of the UK manufacturing sector and increasing parts of services are dominated by the activities of large multi-national companies (Marginson 1994). UK multinationals in particular, where they remain in the UK, tend, at least in manufacturing, to opt for low skill, low value added production (Williams *et al.* 1990). The emphasis on training, arguably a key element in HRM, is a relatively minor consideration.

Third, in light of the above, many organizations require low-skill and discretion from their employees, and as a result conventional methods of controlling employees may be more cost-effective than HRM (Guest 1989; Claydon 1996). Furthermore, the rise in unemployment may also have meant that managers have been able to secure compliance from skilled workers without having to pursue HRM policies.

Fourth, there are the historical traditions of British management, exhibiting a preference for pragmatism associated with a general lack of training and education (Constable and McCormick 1987; Handy 1987) and an anti-intellectualism. Within managerial ranks the traditional importance of the accounting function has also served to reinforce this tendency (Armstrong 1989, 1995). Given the financial pressures operating on organizations, the numerical and symbolic importance of accountants should not be surprising, but none the less helps to reinforce short-term decision-making within organizations.

Fifth, is the reduction in size of employing establishments in the 1980s and 1990s. This may have eased monitoring and control issues for management and reduced the incentive for HRM style practices.

Sixth, and the corollary of the earlier point is the continued low status and influence of the personnel function and the lack of personnel representation on boards of directors (Legge 1978; Watson 1977; Tyson and Fell 1986; Sisson 1994, 1995).

An important consequence of these factors is the constraints they place on the 'strategic' management of people, which is central to both 'soft' and 'hard' HRM. The environmental stimulus to short-term profitability, pragmatism and a reaction to shifting market pressures militates against a planned and integrated approach to employment, accentuated by the limits to managerial voluntarism in increasingly turbulent environments. However, where pressures for short-term results are less immediate, skilled workers at a premium and employee development a key factor in competitiveness, HRM policies may be more in evidence. Foreign-owned companies such as Bosch, AEG, Honda, and Nestlé and UK companies such as the Virgin Group would be examples here.

These examples notwithstanding, the structural and historical constraints on the emergence of a distinctive, long-term approach to the development and multiskilling of individuals suggests a continuation of reactive and opportunistic management. With intensifying competition, such a practice may lead to more autocratic styles with less concern for people-related issues (see, for example, Colling 1995, on British Airways). This, allied to a more de-regulated labour market and a greater emphasis on managerial prerogative stressing market-based responses rather than developed internal labour markets, suggests the likelihood of greater employment insecurity for workers in the future.

Yet HRM models are not simply faced with external constraints: they are seriously impaired as guides of the 'path to follow' by a clutch of internal weaknesses and contradictions. Their simplistic conceptualization of employment strategy as unproblematically flowing from, whilst also contributing to business strategy does not sit easily with observable practice. First, this reveals that employment intitiatives are not 'matched' to some strategic position designated in advance by senior management, but that both tend to emerge over time out of a complex blend of multi-level decision-making, resistance, politicking, etc. in organizations (e.g. Mintzberg 1990; Whittington 1993; Boxall 1996). In any case, it is not clear what definition of strategic position is being used in HRM approaches (Guest 1998): is it for example, 'competitive strategy' (Porter 1985) or 'strategic management styles' (Goold and Campbell 1987)? Secondly, employment decisions have been characterized as 'third order' (Purcell and Ahlstrand 1994), in that they follow in the train of higher priority management decisions about market entry and the design of organizational structures or control systems. As such, 'strategic choice' in human resource decisions is minimal, as its contribution to the formation of business strategy.

A related criticism of HRM is that it advocates an alignment between such human resource initiatives and business strategy, even though the latter must respond to market pressures. These may require cost minimization and 'hard' initiatives in people management, conflicting with the 'absolutist' prescriptions of 'soft' HRM (Legge 1995). Moreover, there is no consensus about what the latter's 'key levers' or critical content may be (Guest 1998; Storey 1992) or about whether HRM is unitarist or pluralist in its assumptions (Storey 1992). (Compare, for example, Beer *et al.*'s (1984) emphasis on different 'stakeholder' interests with the 'broadly unitarist' thrust of Storey's model (1992).) Further contradictions exist in the simultaneous advocacy of individualism and teamwork, and of a 'strong' culture of deeply held and widely shared beliefs, but also employee flexibility. Organizational culture and flexibility are, like strategy and commitment, also very difficult to define and, therefore, manage on a practical level.

In fact, a leading and early proponent of HRM has conceded that:

> after all this time, we still cannot agree what we mean by HRM. I used to think that after the initial debates that this did not matter. Now I am not so sure. If we wish to debate on common ground and to find out whether HRM works, we do need to know what 'it' is (Guest 1998: 40).

If HRM lacks conceptual and definitional coherence, together with a grounding in organizational practice, why, then, has it been a starting point for debates about industrial relations? Why has it been so 'hyped'? To understand this, HRM must be understood as primarily a cultural and linguistic construction, as opposed to one realized in material practices. This leads us to consider an analysis of the phenomenon from a 'postmodern' perspective. We can only touch on this school of thought here, but for an excellent and thorough review of its implications for labour management see Legge (1995: ch 9).

HRM AS A MANAGERIAL RHETORIC AND 'DISCOURSE'

The language of HRM may be viewed 'as an essential component of whatever HRM is' (Keenoy 1997: 838) because it functions as a rhetoric to legitimize managerial actions by the production of images of 'reality'. For example, 'the presumed and projected demands of the global market' render change in industrial relations as 'normal' or inevitable (Keenoy 1997), even though such justifications may 'mask' (Keenoy and Anthony, 1992) employment practices which singularly fail to demonstrate the features of 'soft' HRM or 'strategic' action.

However, HRM can be analysed as going beyond mere legitimation or mystification to functioning as a managerial 'discourse'. This concept may be defined as the use of language and argumentation not simply to reflect or justify what is being talked about, but actually to construct and even constitute that area of organizational life. In other words, the rhetoric of human resource management informs the 'reality' of its practices. The language of management and others subscribing to the discourse of HRM shapes the way employees make sense of their work and how they participate in it (Alvesson and Willmott 1996: 100). Thus, for Keenoy and Anthony, HRM:

> embraces the uncertainties of employee existence, imposes order and meaning on them and provides the employee with a predictable, secure and carefully projected and rewarded understanding of organizational life (Keenoy and Anthony 1992: 243).

This discursive role of HRM is visible in its 'ideological onslaught on the 'normal science' linguistic images of industrial relations' (Keenoy 1997: 836). In other words, traditional notions such as 'unions', 'collective bargaining', 'conflict' and 'personnel management' are countered by a new set of images: 'flexibility', 'quality', 'deregulation', 'non-union' etc. (Keenoy 1997). In this way, industrial relations is 're-imagined' as a 'co-operative, perilous journey' in an external business environment characterized by endemic competition, rather than as an internal power relationship typified by endemic conflict (Keenoy 1997). Therefore, central to the discourse of HRM is a projected or argued-for 'logic' of the market which necessitates a radical overhaul of industrial relations. It also generates an alternative vision of IR that embraces an identity of manager and worker interests, facilitating a reconstitution of perceptions about the nature of the employment relationship, which, in turn, informs permissable managerial action. Thus, unitarist/individualistic initiatives, such as empowerment, teamwork and task-related employee involvement, are privileged over those associated with 'old' IR.

The discursive role of HRM is aptly summarized by one of its proponents:

> it is a construct about which we have little firm [empirical] information which yet has the capacity to exert a profound influence on the environment about it . . . the compelling image of HRM, with its ability to reconfigure the employment relationship in ways that can be attractive to both employers and employees. Indeed, within this imagery, it is HRM which is the vibrant influence on this relationship, not our former reliance on public policy and procedural reform (Beardwell 1998: 207).

Furthermore, by propagating a representation of the market as dynamic and always in flux, HRM acts as a discursive resource to engender continuous change in employment management. It is a 'phenomenal form that is always in the process of "becoming"' (Chia, quoted in Keenoy 1997: 839), thereby confronting the perceived rigidities of collective agreements.

A key conclusion to be drawn from a postmodernist analysis of HRM is that it is not the empirical presence or absence of HRM-style initiatives that is the measure of its significance, but a continuing discursive clout. HRM evinces a 'disciplinary' role by calling into being through language a rationale and framework for major reform in industrial relations. The 'reality' of intensifying competition also implicates a range of practices in the management of staff. As such, 'hard' and 'soft' practices are not 'diametrically opposed' (Storey 1992: 26) but complementary in organizational struggles to win competitive advantage. Consequently, 'hard' resourcing issues such as mass redundancies can be portrayed as 'tough love', necessary to preserve the 'healthy body' of the organization (Keenoy and Anthony 1992) and maintain the employment benefits of the 'core' workforce. Thus, HRM demonstrates a 'brilliant' (Keenoy and Anthony 1992) and 'intrinsic ambiguity' (Keenoy 1997) as a symbolic label that is able to accommodate a variety of apparently contradictory employment policies, rather than be disconfirmed by their revelation through research in organizations.

HRM, INDUSTRIAL RELATIONS AND POWER

Postmodernist thought can, therefore, amplify our understanding of the phenomenon of HRM. However, a problem with its analysis is the abstraction of discourse from power relations. Who manufactures HRM and whose interests are best served by it? Also, should we not try to explain the gap between the projected realities of HRM and 'the real and present facts of experience – inequality, . . . unemployment, massive and increasing differentials of wealth and power' (Norris, quoted in Thompson 1993:196), not to mention markets that are dominated by monopolists or oligopolies rather than epitomized by the icon of entrepreneurial competition?

Of course, a postmodernist retort to the latter view would be to argue that such 'facts' are the product of the competing voice or language of the political left (or 'critical modernity'), and that an objective truth is *not* 'out there' to be revealed by the neutral methodology of social science. Nevertheless, the self-enclosed discourse (Thompson 1993) of HRM must be set against the impact on business performance and the social outcomes of actual choices in the management of employees. It may be argued that the experience of success or failure with specific initiatives is as or more important in the formation of a pattern of employment practices than the vehicle of HRM rhetoric. 'What works' is also informed by management's power to act. While the discourse of HRM is a useful resource, managerial power does not reside solely in language, but also in the possession of material sanctions and rewards that are founded on the privileged position of employers in society. In the same vein, employees are not the passive recipients of 'cultural doping' (Alvesson and Willmott 1996: 103); they have their own interpretations of reality and conceptions of fairness and justice. Management cannot unproblematically 'colonize' (Alvesson and Willmott 1996) their workforce's understandings and values – they are still faced with resistance and the winning of consent.

As to which groups are served by the discourse of HRM, Storey readily acknowledges the role of 'professional vested interests' in the creation of its 'evocative rhetoric' (Storey 1992: 24). Legge (1995) explores this more fully in her consideration of 'actor-network' theory, which argues that a range of social actors, including Conservative governments, personnel and line managers, together with academics, has an interest in constructing and purveying the discourse of HRM. Yet the 'language of HRM is that of managerial triumphalism without doubt' (Legge

1995: 325) and HRM may be construed as a project of 'organised persuasion' (Legge 1995: 318 quoting Latour) that makes familiarity with, at least, its rhetoric an 'obligatory point of passage for 'progressive' management, consultants and so on' (Legge 1995).

However, Guest argues that: 'it seems that academics have bought the rhetoric more readily than the rather more sceptical practitioners. This suggests that even the rhetoric of HRM has failed' (1998: 43).

The idea that HRM is an academic manufacture is, perhaps, a more valid (if also more mundane) explanation of the lack of empirical evidence for it than its role as a legitmatory language 'masking' labour commodification and intensification. In any case, the research on developments in industrial relations shows a complex picture of a varied set of practices across organizations, industries and sectors in the 'modern' economy. This is not to deny that there are arguably important and real underlying features to the management of employment relations, such as the asymmetrical distribution of power and inherent conflict between employers and employees, but also their interdependent interests in the pursuit of employment practices that contribute to organizational success. Yet, the extensive differentiation in the management of industrial relations requires, at the very least, something more than the HRM model alone can offer.

Notes

1 The legal framework has traditionally relied upon what Wedderburn (1986) termed the 'golden formula'. That is, that certain acts, such as 'peacefully persuading a person from entering a place of employment' was immune from prosecution though the courts as long as that act was 'undertaken in contemplation or furtherance of a trade dispute'. What constituted a trade dispute was also set down in law, but like the immunities, has been subject to statutory and judicial review, most notably under the Employment Act 1982.

2 Given the tradition of pluralism underpinning the Commission and many of its members, the voluntarism v legalism issue was a critical issue (see Shonfield's note of dissent at the end of the report). However, for the main report, voluntary reform was seen as preferable to legal compulsion, in part because of the Commission's emphasis on procedural reform, and because of the general concern that greater legal regulation of employment relations might create more problems than it solved.

3 Wage drift is defined here as the gap between wage rates and earnings, with the latter including overtime, bonuses, shiftwork premia, etc.

4 Formalization involved a move towards formal, written procedures, clearly communicated and away from informal understanding and custom and practice. This links with a greater emphasis on procedures generally and the involvement in developing and operating them of trades unions or their representatives.

5 Essentially a form of formalized negotiated compromises between the main parties at national level. Involvement in national decision-making in return for agreements on wage restraint for example.

6 For more detail on this see Purcell and Ahlstrand (1994) on management styles and Wood (1989) on developments in the nature of work.

7 The 'Sword of Justice' argument is in part about equity and fairness but also about encouraging employers to be more efficient and effective in their utilization of staff.

REFERENCES

Abbott, B. (1998) The Citizens Advice Bureaux – a new actor in industrial relations?, *Industrial Relations Journal*, 29 (4).

ACAS (1998) *Annual Report, 1997*, ACAS (Advisory, Conciliation and Arbitration Service), London.

Alvesson, A. and Willmott, H. (1996) *Making Sense of Management: A Critical Introduction*, Sage, London.

Armstrong, P. (1989) Limits and possibilities for HRM in an age of management accounting, in Storey, J. (ed.) *New Perspectives in Human Resource Management*, Routledge and Kegan Paul, London.

Armstrong, P. (1995) Accountancy and HRM, in Storey, J. (ed.) *Human Resource Management A Critical Text*, Routledge, London.

Avis, B. (1990) British Steel: A case of the decentralisation of collective bargaining, *Human Resource Management Journal*, (1): 90–99.

Batstone, E. (1984) *Working Order*, Blackwell, Oxford.

Batstone, E. (1987) *The Reform of Workplace Industrial Relations: Theory, Myth and Evidence*, Clarendon Press, Oxford.

Beardwell, I. (1992) The new industrial relations – a review of the debate, *Human Resource Management Journal*, 2 (2).

Beardwell, I. (1998) Bridging the gap? employee voice, representation and HRM, in Sparrow, P. and Marchington, M. (eds), *Human Resource Management: The New Agenda*, Pitman, London.

Beer, M., Spector, B., Lawrence, P., Mills, Q., and Walton, R. (1984) *Managing Human Assets*, Free Press, New York.

Beer, M., Spector, B., Lawrence, P., Quinn Mills, D. and Walton, R. (1985) *Human Resource Management: A General Managers Perspective*, Glencoe, Il, Free Press.

Blyton, P. (1992) Steel: a classic case of industrial relations change in Britain, *Journal of Management Studies*, 29 (5).

Blyton, P. and Turnbull, P. (1994) *The Dynamics of Employee Relations*, Macmillan, London.

Boxall, P. (1996) The strategic HRM debate and the resource-based view of the firm, *Human Resource Management Journal*, 6 (3).

Brown, W. (ed.) (1981) *The Changing Contours of British Industrial Relations*, Blackwell, Oxford.

Brown, W. and Walsh J. (1991) Pay determination in Britain in the 1990's: the anatomy of decentralisation, *Oxford Review of Economic Policy*, 7 (1).

Brown, W. and Walsh, J. (1994) Managing pay in Britain, in Sisson, K. (ed.), *Personnel Management: A Comprehensive Guide to Theory and Practice in Britain*, Blackwell, Oxford.

Brown, W., Marginson, P., and Walsh, J. (1995) Management: pay determination and collective bargaining, in Edwards, P. (ed.), *Industrial Relations: Theory and Practice in Britain*, Blackwell, Oxford.

Claydon, T. (1989) Union derecognition in Britain in the 1980s, *British Journal of Industrial Relations*, 27 (2).

Claydon, T. (1994) Human resource management and the labour market, in Beardwell, I. and Holden, L. (eds) *Human Resource Management: A Contemporary Perspective*, Pitman, London.

Claydon, T. (1996) Union derecognition: a re-examination, in Beardwell, I. (ed.), *Contemporary Industrial Relations: A Critical Analysis*, Oxford University Press, Oxford.

Claydon, T. (1998) Problematising partnership: the proposals for a co-operative bargaining agenda, in Sparrow, P. and Marchington, M. (eds), *Human Resource Management: The New Agenda*, Pitman, London.

Clegg, H.A. (1979) *The Changing System of Industrial Relations in Great Britain*, Blackwell, Oxford.

Colling, T. (1995) Experiencing turbulence: competition, strategic choice and the management of human relations in British Airways, *Human Resource Management Journal*, 5 (5).

Constable, R. and McCormick, R.J. (1987) *The Making of British Managers: A Report of the BIM and CBI into Management Training, Education and Development*, London, British Institute of Management.

Constable, R., and McCormick, R.J. (1987) *The Making of British Managers: A Report of The BIM and CBI into Management Training Education and Development*, British Institute of Management, London.

Coupar, W. and Stevens, B. (1998) Towards a new model of industrial partnership: beyond the HRM versus industrial relations debate, in Sparrow, P. and Marchington, M. (eds), *Human Resource Management: The New Agenda*, Pitman, London.

Crouch, C. (1982) *Trade Unions: The Logic of Collective Action*, Fontana, London.

Crouch, C. (1995) The state: economic management and incomes policy, in Edwards, P. (ed.), *Industrial Relations: Theory and Practice in Britain*, Blackwell, Oxford.

Cully, M. and Woodland, S. (1998) Trade union membership and recognition 1996–97: an analysis of data from the certification officer and the LFS, *Labour Market Trends*, July.

Cully, M., Woodland, S., O'Reilly, A., Dix, G., Millward, N., Bryson, A., and Forth, J. (1998) *The 1998 Workplace Employee Relations Survey: First Findings*, DTI, London.

Daniel, W.W. and Millward, N. (1983) *Workplace Industrial Relations in Britain: The DE/PSI/SSRC Survey*, Heinemann, London.

Dickens, L. and Hall, M. (1995) The state: labour law and industrial relations, in Edwards, P. (ed.), *Industrial Relations: Theory and Practice in Britain*, Blackwell, Oxford.

Disney, R. (1990) Explanations for the decline in trade union density in Britain: an appraisal, *British Journal of Industrial Relations*, 28 (2).

Disney, R., Gosling, A. and Machin, S. (1995) British unions in decline: an examination of the 1980s fall in trade union recognition, *Industrial and Labour Relations Review*, 48: 403–19.

Donovan, Lord (Chairman) (1968) *Report of the Royal Commission on Trade Unions and Employer's Associations 1965–68*, HMSO, Cmnd 3623, London.

Dunn, S. (1993) From Donovan to . . . Wherever, *British Journal of Industrial Relations*, 31 (2).

Durey, R., Gosling, A. and Machin, S. (1993) What has happened to trade union recognition in Britain, CEP P Paper No. 130. London, LSE.

Edwards, P.K. (1992) Industrial conflict, *British Journal of Industrial Relations*, 30 (3).

Edwards, P.K. (1995) The employment relationship, in Edwards, P.K. (ed.), *Industrial Relations: Theory and Practice in Britain*, Blackwell, Oxford.

Edwards, C. and Heery, E. (1989) *Management Control and Union Power, A Study of Labour Relations in Coal Mining*, Clarendon Press, Oxford.

Flanders, A. (1970) *Management and Unions: The Theory and Reform of Industrial Relations*, Faber, London.

Fox, A. and Flanders, A. (1969) The reform of collective bargaining: from Donovan to Durkheim, *British Journal of Industrial Relations*, 7 (2).

Franks, J. and Mayer, C. (1992) Corporate control: a synthesis of international evidence, unpublished paper, London Business School/University of Warwick.

Freeman, R. and Medoff, J. (1984) *What Do Unions Do?* Basic Books, New York.

Gall, G. (1993) What happened to single union deals: a research note, *Industrial Relations Journal,* 24 (1).

Gall, G. and McKay, S. (1998) Developments in union recognition and de-recognition in Britain, paper presented at British Universities Industrial Relations Conference, July.

Goold, M. and Campbell, A. (1987) *Strategies and Styles: The Role of the Centre in Managing Diversified Corporations*, Blackwells, London.

Gregg, P. and Yates, A. (1991) Changes in trade union and wage setting arrangements in the 1980s, *British Journal of Industrial Relations*, 29 (3).

Guest, D. (1989) Human resource management: its implications for industrial relations and trade unions, in Storey, J. (ed.) *New Perspectives on Human Resource Management*, Thomson Learning, London.

Guest, D. (1990) Human resource management and the American dream, *Journal of Management Studies*, 27 (4).

Guest, D. (1991) Personnel management: the end of orthodoxy? *British Journal of Industrial Relations*, 29 (2).

Guest, D. (1993) Current perspectives on HRM in the UK, in Brewster, C. (ed.) *Current Trends in HRM in Europe,* Kogan Page, London.

Guest, D. (1995) Human resource management, trade unions and industrial relations, in Storey, J. (ed.), *Human Resource Management: A Critical Text*, Routledge, London.

Guest, D. (1998) Beyond HRM: commitment and the contract culture, in Sparrow, P. and Marchington, M. (eds), *Human Resource Management: The New Agenda*, Pitman, London.

Hall, G. and McKays, S. (1998) Union recognition and derecongition in britain, Payer Pewed & BUIRA Conference at Keele University, July.

Hanson, C. and Mather, G. (1988) *Striking out Strikes: Changing Employment Relations in the British Labour Market*, Hobart Paper No. 10, Institute of Economic Affairs, London.

Handy, C. (ed.) (1987) *The Making of Managers: A Report on Management Education, Training and Development in the United States, West Germany, France, Japan and the UK*, National Economic Development Office.

Handy, C.B. (1987) *The Making of Managers,* NEDO, London.

Hendry, C. (1995) *Human Resource Management: A Strategic Approach to Employment*, Butterworth-Heinemann, Oxford.

Hendry, C. and Pettigrew, A. (1988) Banking on HRM to respond to change, *Personnel Management*, 19 (11).

Hyman, R. (1975) *Industrial Relations: A Marxist Introduction*, Macmillan, London.

Inns of Court Conservative and Unionist Society (1958) *A Giant's Strength: Some Thoughts on the Constitutional and Legal Position of Trade Unions in England*, The Society, Johnson, 315.

Involvement and Participation Association (1997) *Towards Industrial Partnership: New Ways of Working in British Companies*, IPA, London.

IPD (1997) Employer Relations into the 21st Century, an IPD, P Paper: IPD, London.

Jackson, M., Leopold, J.W. and Tuck, K. (1992) Decentralisation of collective bargaining: the case of the retail food industry, *Human Resource Management Journal* 2 (2).

Johnson, G. and Scholes, K. (1993) *Exploring Corporate Strategy: Text and Cases*, Prentice-Hall, London.

Keenoy, T. (1990) HRM: a case of the wolf in sheep's clothing?, *Personnel Review*, 19 (2).

Keenoy, T. (1997) Review article: HRMism and the languages of re-presentation, *Journal of Management Studies*, 35 (5).

Keenoy, T. and Anthony, A. (1992) HRM, metaphor, meaning and morality, in Blyton, P. and Turnbull, P. (eds), *Reassessing Human Resource Management*, Sage, London.

Kelly, J. (1990) British Trade Unionism 1979–1989: change, continuity and contradictions, *Work, Employment and Society* (special issue).

Kessler, I. (1994) Performance pay, in Sisson, K. (ed.), *Personnel Management: A Comprehensive Guide to Theory and Practice in Britain*, Blackwell, Oxford.

Kessler, I. and Purcell, J. (1992) Performance related pay – objectives and application, *Human Resource Management Journal*, 2 (3).

Kochan, T., McKersie, B. and Katz, H. (1986) *The Transformation of American Industrial Relations*, Basic Books, New York.

Kochan, T. and Osterman, P. (1994) *The Mutual Gains Enterprise: Forging Partnership Among Labour, Management and Government*, Harvard Business School Press, Boston, MA.

Kochan, T., and Dyer, L. (1995) HRM: an American view, in Storey, J. (ed.) (1995) *Human Resource Management: A Critical Text,* Thomson Learning, London.

Kochan, T., McKersie, B. and Katz, H. (1997) *Partners for Progress: Next Steps of the New Unionism*, London, TUC.

Lawler, E.E. (1992) *The Ultimate Advantage: Creating the High Involvement Organisation*, Jossey-Bass, San Francisco.

Lawler, E.E. (1994) From job-based to competency-based organisations, *Journal of Organisational Behaviour*, 15: 3–15.

Legge, K. (1978) *Power, Innovation and Problem-Solving in Personnel Management*, McGraw Hill, London.

Legge, K. (1995) *Human Resource Management: Rhetorics and Realities*, Macmillan, London.

Legge, K. (1998) Flexibility: the gift wrapping of employment degradation in Sparrow, P. and Marchington, M. (eds), *Human Resource Management: The New Agenda*, Pitman, London.

McCarthy, W.E.J and Ellis, N. (1973 *Management by Agreement: An Alternative to the Industrial Relations Act*, Hutchinson, London.

McLoughlin, I. and Gourlay, S. (1994) *Enterprise Within Unions: Industrial Relations in the Non-Union Firm*, Buckingham, Open University Press.

Marchington, M. (1998) Partnership in context: towards a European model, in Sparrow, P. and Marchington, M. (eds), *Human Resource Management: A New Agenda*, Pitman, London.

Marginson, P. (1994) Multinational Britain: employers and work in an international economy, *Human Resource Management Journal*, 4 (4).

Marginson, P., Edwards, P.K., Martin, R., Purcell, J. and Sisson, K. (1988) *Beyond the Workplace: Managing Industrial Relations in the Multi-Establishment Enterprise*, Blackwell, Oxford.

Marginson, P., Armstrong, P., Edwards, P.K., Purcell, J. and Hubbard, N. (1993) *The Control of Industrial Relations in Large Companies*, Warwick Papers in Industrial Relations, No. 45.

Marsden, D. and Thompson, M. (1990). Flexibility agreements – their significance in the increases in productivity in British manufacturing since 1980, *Work, Employment and Society*, 4 (1).

Marsden, D. and Richardson, R. (1994) Performing for pay? The effects of 'merit pay' on motivation in a public service, *British Journal of Industrial Relations*, 32: 243–62.

Marsden, D., Morris, T., Willman, P., and Wood, S. (1985) *The Car Industry: Labour Relations and Individual Adjustment*. London, Tavistock.

Martin, R., Fosh, P., Morris, H., Smith, P. and Undy, R. (1991) The decollectivisation of trade unions? Ballots and collective bargaining in the 1980s, *Industrial Relations Journal*, 22: 197–208.

Metcalf, D. (1989) Water notes dry up: the impact of the Donovan reform proposals and Thatcherism at work on labour productivity in British manufacturing, *British Journal of Industrial Relations*, 28 (1).

Metcalf, D. (1993) Industrial relations and economic performance, *British Journal of Industrial Relations*, 32 (2).

Millward, N. (1994) *The New Industrial Relations?* PSI, London.

Millward, N. and Stevens, M. (1986) *British Workplace Industrial Relations 1980–1984: The ED/ESRC/PSI/ACAS Surveys*, Gower, London.

Millward, N., Stevens, M., Smart, D. and Hawes, W.R. (1992) *Workplace Industrial Relations in Transition: The ED/ESRC/PSI/ACAS Surveys*, Dartmouth, Aldershot.

Mintzberg, H.A. (1990) Strategy formation: schools of thought, in Frederickson, J. (ed.) *Perspectives on Strategic Managemen*, Balfer, Boston.

Mintzberg, H. and Quinn, B. (1992) *The Strategy Process: Concepts, Contexts, Cases*, Prentice-Hall, London

Monks, J. (1998) Trade unions: enterprise and the future, in Sparrow, P. and Marchington, M. (eds), *Human Resource Management: The New Agenda*, Pitman, London.

Nolan, P. and O'Donnell, K. (1995) Industrial relations and productivity, in Edwards, P.K. (ed.), *Industrial Relations: Theory and Practice in Britain*, Blackwell, Oxford.

Oulton, N. (1994) *Productivity and Growth: A Study of British Industry, 1954–1986*, Cambridge University Press, Cambridge.

Palmer, G. (1983) *British Industrial Relations*, Allen and Unwin, London.

Pendleton, A. (1991) The barriers to flexibility – flexible rostering on the railways, *Work, Employment and Society*, 5.

Pettigrew, A. and Whipp, R. (1991) *Managing Change for Competitive Success,* Blackwell, Oxford.

Porter, M. (1985) *Competitive Advantage: Creating and Sustaining Superior Performance*, Free Press, New York.

Purcell, J. (1981) *Good Industrial Relations: Theory and Practice*, Macmillan, London.

Purcell, J. (1991) The rediscovery of the managerial prerogative, *Oxford Review of Economic Policy*, 7 (1).

Purcell, J. and Sisson, K. (1983) Strategies and practice in the management of industrial relations, in Bain, G.S. (ed.), *Industrial Relations in Britain*, Blackwell, Oxford.

Purcell, J. and Ahlstrand, B. (1994) *Human Resource Management in the Multi-Divisional Company*, Dartmouth, Aldershot.

Rainnie, A. (1989) *Industrial Relations in Small Firms*, Routledge, London.

Richardson, R. and Wood S. (1989) Productivity Change in the Coal Industry and the New Industrial Relations, *British Journal of Industrial Relations*, 27.

Schein, E.H. (1985) *Organisational Culture and Leadership*, Jossey-Bass, San Francisco.

Shanks, M. (1961) *The Stagnant Society*, Pelican, London.

Sisson, K. (1993) In Search of HRM, *British Journal of Industrial Relations*, 31 (2).

Sisson, K. (1993) *Managing Human Resources and Industrial Relations*, Blackwell, Oxford.

Sisson, K. (1994) Personnel management, paradigms, practice and prospects, in Sisson, K. (ed.), *Personnel Management: A Comprehensive Guide to Theory and Practice in Britain*, Blackwell, Oxford.

Sisson, K. and Marginson, P. (1995) Managerial systems, structure and strategy, in Edwards, P. (ed), *Individual Relations Theory and Practice in Britain*, Blackwell, Oxford.

Sisson, K. (1995) Human resource management and the personnel function, in Storey, J. (ed.) *Human Resource Management: A Critical Text*, Thomson Learning, London.

Smith, P. and Morton, G. (1993) Union exclusion and the decentralisation of industrial relations in contemporary Britain, *British Journal of Industrial Relations*, 31 (1).

Smith, P. and Morton, G. (1993) Union exclusion and decollectivisation of industrial relations in contemporary Britain, *British Journal of Industrial Relations*, 3 (1).

Sparrow, P. and Pettigrew, A. (1988a) Strategic human resource management in the computer supply industry, *Journal of Occupational Psychology*, 61 (1).

Sparrow, P. and Pettigrew, A. (1988b) Contrasting HRM responses in the changing world of computing, *Personnel Management*, 20 (2).

Storey, J. (ed.) (1989) *New Perspectives in Human Resource Management*, Routledge, London.

Storey, J. (1992) Developments in the Management of Human Resources, Blackwell, Oxford.

Storey, J. (1993) *The Take-Up of New Management Practices. A Leicestershire Survey*, Loughborough University Business School and Leicestershire Training and Enterprise Council.

Storey, J. (1994) How new style management is taking hold, *Personnel Management*, January: 32–34.

Storey, J. (1995) Human resource management: still marching on and marching out?, in Storey, J. (ed.), *Human Resource Management: A Critical Text*, London, Routledge.

Storey, J. and Sisson, K. (1989) The limit to transformation: human resource management in the British context, *Industrial Relations Journal*, 21 (1).

Thompson, M. (1991) *Pay for Performance in the Employer Experience*, Institute of Management Studies, Sussex.

Thompson, M. (1992) *Pay for Performance in the Employer Experience*, Institute for Manpower Studies, Sussex.

Thompson, P. (1993) Postmodernism: fatal distraction, in Hassard, J. and Parker, M. (eds) *Postmodernism and Organisation*, Sage, London: 183–203.

Trades Union Congress (1997) *Parties for Progress: Next Steps for the New Unionism*, TUC, London.

Turnbull, P. (1993) Docks, in Pendleton, A. and Winterton, J. (eds), *Public Enterprise in Transition: Industrial Relations in State and Privatised Corporations*, Routledge, London.

Turnbull, P. and Weston, S. (1992) Co-operation or control: capital restructuring and labour relations in the docks, *British Journal of Industrial Relations*, 31 (1).

Turner, H.A. (1968) The Royal Commission's Research Papers, *British Journal of Industrial Relations*, 6 (3).

Tyson, S. and Fell, A. (1986) *Evaluating the Personnel Function*, Hutchinson, London.

Waddington, J. and Whitton, C. (1995) Trade unions: growth, structure and policy, in Edwards, P. (ed.), *Industrial Relations: Theory and Practice in Britain*, Blackwell, Oxford.

Walton, R.E. (1985) From control to commitment in the workplace, *Harvard Business Review*, 63 (2).

Watson, T. (1997) *The Personnel Managers: A Study in the Strategy of Work and Employees*, Routlede and Kegan Paul, London.

Watson, T. J. (1977) *The Personnel Managers*, RKP, London.

Wedderburn, K.W. (1986) *The Worker and the Law* (3rd edn) Penguin, Harmondsworth.

Whittington, R. (1993) *What is Strategy – and Does it Matter?* Routledge, London.

Williams, K., Williams, J. and Haslam, C. (1990) The hollowing out of British manufacturing, *Economy and Society*, 19 (4).

Williams, K., Haslam, C., Johal, S. and Williams, J. (1994). *Cars: Analysis, History, Cases*, Berghahn, Providence.

Wood, S. (1989) *The Transformation of Work? Skill Flexibility and the Labour Process*, Unwin, London.

Wood, S. (1995) The four pillars of HRM: are they connected?, *Human Resource Management Journal*, 5 (5).

Wood, S. and Albanese, M.T. (1995) Can we speak of a high commitment management on the shop floor?, *Journal of Management Studies*, 32 (2).

Labour markets and flexibility – current debates and the European dimension

9

Adrian Murton

INTRODUCTION

For much of the period since the late 1970s, contemporary discussion of employment has been dominated by the theme of flexibility, even if that term has not always been particularly well-defined, nor its link with business performance well-established. It is also a concept with a long history, with much of nineteenth-century industrial organization in the UK relying on contract workers and the flexibility of skilled employees for its effective functioning (Littler 1982; Hyman 1995). Recent evidence has also shown that examples of currently fashionable forms of flexibility were establishing themselves in some sectors of employment in the UK in the 1950s (Pollert 1991; Hakim 1987), and some long before this.

The interest in flexibility in the 1980s and 1990s has partly stemmed from the fact that it has been largely 'driven' by employer and business 'needs'(Atkinson and Meager 1986; Elger 1991). Much of the most influential work in this area in the UK has been distinctively managerialist in tone with flexibility constituting a significant element in 'New managerialism's' project to establish new organizations and ways of working (Peters and Waterman 1982; Drucker 1988; Kanter 1989). Such ideas have not been without influence in the wider political arena, particularly in the UK and the Netherlands where governments committed to privatization of state utilities and cost-reduction have actively encouraged moves towards non-standard employment.

For academics, the treatment of flexibility has often tended to play down the extent of flexibility in previous production systems, and to over-emphasize the extent to which the current period marks a dramatic break with past practice. This has been particularly notable in the debates over 'flexible specialization' and 'post-Fordism' (Piore and Sabel 1984; Wood 1989). Yet it is clear that, in terms of work organization and new approaches to managing staff, the 1980s and 1990s have been characterized as much by continuity as by change (Cross 1988; Edwards 1995; Nolan and Walsh 1995).

Furthermore, academic discussion has at times portrayed flexibility as an end in itself for organizations, rather than as one element of managerial concern, seen as necessary to secure other goals (Pollert 1988; Wood 1989). The emphasis in this chapter is on attempting to contextualize flexibility and flexible work patterns more effectively and to locate discussion of them and management behaviour generally in the wider context of economic factors and the changing international division of labour (Nolan and Walsh 1995). Such an approach should allow for 'the conditioning effects of structural relations over management behaviour' to be more effectively explored. To embrace such an approach requires a focus on a number of countries to appreciate the diversity of contexts. It is such a perspective that informs the discussion of flexibility in this chapter.

The current interest in various forms of flexibility derives from a combination of factors of which the most influential has been the impact of the globalization of capital and how the pressures generated by this are interpreted and acted upon by managers at the enterprise and establishment levels. It is argued that the globalization issue, the industrialization of so called 'third world' economies and the associated complexity and fragmentation of markets (Piore and Sabel 1984; Wood 1989) have all placed a premium upon an organization's responsiveness and adaptability to unpredictable and unforeseen market conditions (Atkinson and Meager 1986). These pressures have reduced the scope for 'X-inefficiencies' (Liebenstein 1966) and monopoly rent extraction at the organization level and may have increased the pressure for cost cutting and changes to industrial relations practices (Beatson 1995).

An additional impetus for greater flexibility within Europe has been concerns over the non-wage costs of labour (Atkinson and Meager 1986; European Commission 1995). Within the European Union (EU) the high level of such costs, and the associated concept of the *social wage* (that is money wage plus social benefits) continues to be a particular issue in Spain, France and Germany. As Standing (1997) has argued;

> globalisation means trade and investment are increasingly linked to differential costs . . . among which differential labour costs have reflected differences in the social wage (Standing 1997).

In consequence, pressures have built up on governments to diminish the 'burden' of the social wage on employers, a stance which has often entailed an assault on broader social settlements. Such an approach is typified by the policies of the Thatcher governments in the UK in the 1980s, and to a lesser extent in other parts of the EU and what was Eastern Europe. Furthermore, the attempts to dismantle aspects of social settlements have increasingly brought the state into conflict with its own citizens and led to active resistance, most notably in France, Germany and Denmark.

A further pressure towards greater flexibility has been the impact of process technology, and associated techniques such as just-in-Time production, placing a premium on the acquisition of new and specific skills and the upskilling of certain categories of worker (Beatson 1995a). Additionally, there is the well-documented 'retreat' into 'core business' by a large number of organizations and the contracting out of areas of work not deemed to be 'core' or to dispose of areas perceived to be a 'problem' (Atkinson and Meager 1986). Perhaps ironically in view of the source of the pressures for change, it has been the public sector in much of the expanded EU and in Eastern Europe which has been at the forefront of developments in this area, with considerations of cost and political ideology influencing these initiatives in the UK and the Netherlands in particular (European Commission 1995).

Within the EU, the changing structure of employment has been an additional factor affecting the spread of certain forms of flexible working, associated with the decline in manufacturing and manufacturing employment, and the rise of the services sector. However, the extent of this trend differs between countries, with agriculture continuing to be important in a number of European states.

More recently, pressure has been mounting from the EU itself and from international bodies such as the OECD to embrace flexibility in labour markets and working practices. Prompted by high levels of unemployment, high social costs and long working hours in some parts of the EU there has been encouragement to adopt work-sharing initiatives, part-time working and a reassessment of the balance between work and non-work and the gender division of labour within the household (European Commission 1995). Recent EU directives in the areas of working time, part-time working and parental leave are all indicative of these concerns.

The remainder of the chapter is structured as follows. We begin by outlining the framework for distinguishing forms of flexibility developed by Beatson (1995), and employ this to distinguish the dominant forms of flexibility prevailing in individual EU countries. This is followed by an analysis of particular forms of flexible working in the UK, and of differences in the use of flexibility between individual nation states. This emphasizes the role of national systems of labour market regulation, corporate governance and enterprise calculation in accounting for such differences, together with variations in industry mix and structure. In the final section we focus on a number of critical and more macro concerns with labour market flexibility, in particular the continued gender segregation of work and the feminization of employment. This is followed by consideration of the potentially damaging consequences of greater segregation between 'good' jobs, 'bad' jobs and no jobs and associated concerns with 'inclusion' and 'exclusion' in the wider society (Hutton 1995). The chapter concludes by exploring the wider public policy implications of greater casualization of employment for issues such as skills acquisition and development, and questions the increasing attention paid by policy makers to labour market flexibility to the apparent neglect of other forms of flexibility.

Before proceeding it is appropriate to introduce a cautionary note in the discussion of the statistics used in this chapter. In practice, comparison of statistics on flexible working across EU countries is complicated by differences in definition. This applies particularly to part-time working where considerable variation exists in terms of the hours thresholds used by member states. Although this may have little impact on the status and statutory rights accorded to those working part-time, it reminds us that different categories of part-time working exist (De Grip *et al.* 1997), and to exercise caution in interpreting some of the data on the extent of forms of flexible working.

FLEXIBILITY DEFINED

In his work for the UK Department of Employment, Beatson (1995a) developed a typological framework for analysing the different forms of labour market flexibility found in individual countries. Starting from the premise that flexibility was:

> about the ability of markets (and the agents that operate in them) to respond to changing economic conditions (Beatson 1995a: 1).

He went on to distinguish between micro-flexibility – that which operates at the level of the firm or establishment – and macro – flexibility which is seen to operate at the aggregate economy-wide level and concerns real wage flexibility and aggregate employment and hours worked. His model is shown diagrammatically in Figure 9.1. The principle focus in this chapter is on flexibility at the micro-level although reference will be made to the broader level where this is appropriate.

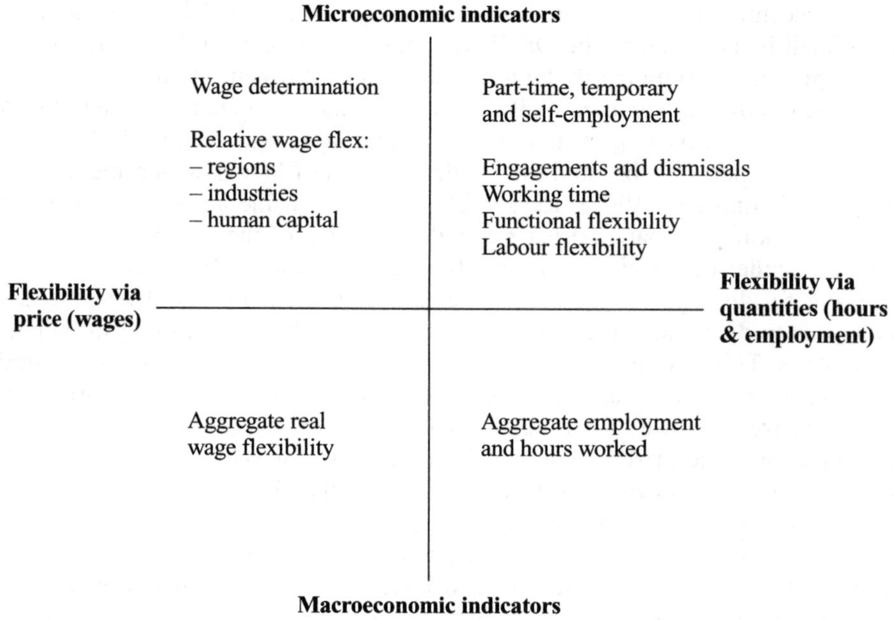

Microeconomic indicators

Wage determination

Relative wage flex:
– regions
– industries
– human capital

Part-time, temporary
and self-employment

Engagements and dismissals
Working time
Functional flexibility
Labour flexibility

**Flexibility via
price (wages)**

**Flexibility via
quantities (hours
& employment)**

Aggregate real
wage flexibility

Aggregate employment
and hours worked

Macroeconomic indicators

Figure 9.1 Indicators of Labour Market Flexibility
Source: Beatson 1995

At the firm or establishment level Beatson makes a further division into three areas: flexibility on the extensive margin, flexibility on the intensive margin and wage or reward flexibility. The first of these refers to what is more commonly described as *numerical flexibility*, the use of part-timers, and temporary workers whose numbers and hours can be varied relatively easily and cheaply to meet organizational requirements. Additionally this category includes a form of *distancing flexibility* (Atkinson and Meager 1986), the use of contract staff or self-employed freelancers who may provide a contract for service but are not employees of the organization. The second, flexibility on the intensive margin, relates to *functional flexibility* and to *temporal or working time flexibility*. The former is concerned with flexibility across functional areas within an organization and implies an emphasis on the acquisition and updating of appropriate skills via on-the-job training. The second category relates to the more intensive use of labour, or the closer matching of organizational requirements with staffing levels. Moves to seven-day working, shiftworking and overtime would all be examples of this form of flexibility. The use of wage or reward flexibility, often referred to as *financial flexibility* relates to the linking of reward more closely with organizational or individual performance and includes such initiatives as performance related pay, share option and share ownership schemes. Additionally, Beatson notes that organizations may also be concerned with other forms of flexibility, such as relative wage flexibility and labour mobility.

It has recently been suggested that some of these forms of flexibility may be substitutes rather than complements for one another. Work by Boyer (1989) has argued that intensive flexibility in internal labour markets may not be compatible with certain forms of pay or numerical flexibility. Similarly, Tuselmann (1996) has stated that:

The type of flexibility a company may seek in a particular country, and the extent to which this can be achieved, is largely influenced by the system of industrial relations, labour market regulations, vocational education and training systems (VET) and the characteristics of labour markets. *The particular configuration of these factors makes it unlikely that companies can achieve a high level of all types of labour flexibility simultaneously* (Tuselmann 1996: 2–3 emphasis added).

The argument of this chapter is generally in support of this position but with the qualification that whilst forms of flexibility may operate as substitutes – in that it may not be possible to get these forms of flexibility *from the same individuals* – the range of forms of flexibility may be available to an organization from other individuals. The situation in the (old) western *Lander* of Germany is particularly illustrative. Those skilled workers in 'good jobs' in large corporations provided functional flexibility and increasingly temporal flexibility (Lane 1989), but it would be wrong to assume that such employers were unable to secure numerical flexibility; they simply obtained it from a different group, the large numbers of *gastarbeiter* or 'guest workers'. This said, factors both internal and external to an organization will tend to favour certain forms of flexibility over others and Beatson's (1995a) more general point – that there is more than one route to a flexible labour market, and more than one destination – is a critical observation and one to which we return later in this chapter.

LABOUR MARKET FLEXIBILITY: THE EUROPEAN EXPERIENCE

In this section an overview of developments in the forms of 'flexibility via quantity' at the micro-economic level within the countries of the EU is presented for the period since the early 1970s. The focus is in contrasting the experience of flexible working in the UK with other EU countries and to use this to facilitate a more detailed analysis of the factors which account for differences within the EU in the take-up of various forms of flexibility.

The experience of employment change in the EU since the 1970s exhibits a number of distinct characteristics. Against a background of high, and in many countries, rising unemployment there has been a declining number of jobs in the manufacturing sector, most marked in Finland, Sweden, the UK and Spain. This development has impacted mostly on the jobs market for men – particularly full-time jobs – which saw a decline of 4 per cent between 1975 and 1985, and a further decline in the early 1990s. In contrast, in the last 20 years participation rates of women have increased in all countries of the EU so that in the early 1990s 'women have accounted for the entire growth of the EU's workforce and are likely to continue to do so' (European Commission 1995). This changing composition of the EU workforce is an important component in the flexibility debate, even if its impact differs between member states. An overview of the forms of labour market flexibility within the European Union is contained in Table 9.1.

Flexibility on the extensive margin

Numerical flexibility: part-time work
Table 9.1 reveals that non-standard work patterns are an increasing feature in every European country 'despite differing legal, cultural and labour traditions' (Brewster 1995).

Table 9.1 Flexible work patterns within the EU

	Part-time work (%)			Temp. work (%)			Self-employed (%)		Shift (%)
	1973	1986	1995	1983	1993	1995	1973	1993	1995
Belgium	3.8	9.4	12.8	5.4	4.7	5.0	11.2	13.3	32.9
Denmark	22.0	23.7	21.2	12.5	10.7	12.0	9.3	7.0	39.5
Finland	6.7	–	8.3	11.3	13.5	16.0	6.5	9.5	–
France	5.9	11.7	14.9	3.3	10.2	12.0	11.4	8.8	23.6
Germany	10.1	12.9	15.8	9.9	10.2	10.0	9.1	7.9	21.8
Greece	–	–	4.8	–	–	10.0	–	–	–
Ireland	5.1	6.1	10.8	6.1	9.0	10.0	10.1	13.0	32.6
Italy	6.4	5.0	6.2	6.6	5.8	7.0	23.1	24.2	32.2
Netherlands	16.6	–	36.4	5.8	10.0	11.0	9.2	8.7	23.9
Portugal	7.8	6.0	8.0	13.1	8.6	10.0	12.7	18.2	10.1
Spain	–	–	6.9	15.6	32.0	35.0	16.3	18.7	12.5
Sweden	23.6	–	25.3	12.0	11.9	12.0	4.8	8.7	–
UK	16.0	–	23.8	5.5	5.7	7.0	7.3	11.9	51.8

Sources: 1973 and 1993 data from Standing (1997), 1986 data and 1995 data on temps from *Social Trends* 1997, 1998. Other 1995 data from Eurostat Community Labour Force Survey 1996.
*Shiftwork data relate to the percentage of employees working shifts, evenings or night-work.

This can be seen in the contrasts between 1973 and the early 1990s so that by 1993 'non-standard' employment accounted for over 30 per cent of total employment in every EU country (Standing 1997). Within this, the most common practices are those associated with variations in arrangements of working time, and of these part-time working emerges as the most marked feature of employment growth, with one in seven working in part-time jobs in the early 1990s (European Commission 1995; Brewster *et al.*1994; Rubery *et al.* 1998). By the mid-1990s over 90 per cent of organizations in Denmark, Netherlands, Norway, Sweden and Germany made use of part-timers, compared with over 60 per cent for the EU as a whole (Brewster *et al.* 1994). This growth in part-time working has also been essentially a female phenomenon with 95 per cent of the growth in jobs in the EU in the 1980s filled by women (European Commission 1995). In the Netherlands, two-thirds of all working women work part-time and it has been more recently suggested that the growth in part-time working constitutes a new type of labour market, concentrated mainly in the public sector within northern Europe (Meulders 1993).

In the UK there has been a fall in the number of full-time employees from 18 million in the late 1970s to less than 15 million today, with almost 2 million standard (F/T) jobs lost between 1989 and 1994 (Nolan and Walsh 1995). In contrast non-standard forms of employment have shown a marked increase, with half of all employers using flexible forms of work of some kind (Rajan *et al.* 1998). Significantly, part-time working has been on a trend increase in the UK since the 1950s (Hakim 1987), but it is the growth since the early 1970s that has been dramatic. Driven by the expanding service sector, the one in six individuals working part-time in 1971, had risen to almost one in three by 1993, representing over 6 million workers (Nolan and Walsh 1995; Beatson 1995a, 1995b). Again, this growth has been almost exclusively a growth of jobs for women, even though part-time working for men doubled between 1984 and 1995 (Legge 1998). Significantly, many of these jobs are also 'small', in the sense of involving fewer than 16 hours per week (Casey 1991), a factor also common to part-time jobs in the Netherlands (Marullo 1995).

Numerical flexibility: temporary working

In contrast to developments in part-time working the period since 1980 has witnessed a more modest growth in temporary working, although this appears to be changing in the 1990s. Despite lower absolute levels of use within the EU, research suggests that between 80 and 90 per cent of employers in all EU countries with the exception of Denmark and Turkey make some use of temporary workers (Brewster *et al.* 1994). Unlike part-time working, this area is tightly regulated by national legislation, with temporary employment agencies regulated in every EU country with the exception of Italy (Marullo 1995).

The growth in temporary work displays some interesting characteristics. Between 1987 and 1990, a third of all new jobs in the EU were temporary or fixed-term, representing 40 per cent of all additional jobs for men (European Commission 1995). Indeed, in the 1990s this area has provided virtually all of the increase in jobs for men within the European Union (European Commission 1996), even though the increase has been heavily concentrated in particular countries. Three quarters of the growth in temporary working has been in Spain, with over a third of men and women in Spain in temporary employment (Marullo 1995; Morgan 1996). However, in the 1990s, as Table 9.1 reveals, the growth of temporary work has become more general, with significant increases in Greece, Portugal and Germany's eastern *Lander* (Marullo 1995), as well as in France, Ireland and the Netherlands. This growth has not only varied between countries but significantly within them. In general within the EU, young (generally male) workers (under 25 years), have the highest incidence of temporary working, and those employed as production or service workers (De Grip *et al.* 1997).

In the UK the level of temporary working in the 1980s accounted for between 5 and 6 per cent of employment (Casey 1991), but consistent with trends in the rest of the EU, there has been an increase in its use in the mid-1990s (Sly and Stillwell 1997). Conventionally it has been assumed that temporary working is used essentially as a device by private sector employers to meet cyclical fluctuations in demand. Whilst this appears to remain the case (Casey *et al.* 1997) it has been the growing use of fixed-term contracts in the public sector (Millward *et al.* 1992) and to an extent the professions, which has accounted for much of the increase in the 1990s (Sly and Stillwell 1997).

Overall, temporary employment appears to be a characteristic of the more regulated labour markets of Spain and the Scandinavian countries. However, since the late 1980s the greatest increase in temporary working has taken place in France, Germany, and outside of the EU in Australia, where in the early 1990s almost a quarter of all employees were in temporary work (Standing 1997).

In contrast, self-employment has tended to dominate in economies where agriculture remains a sizeable activity – Ireland, and the southern states of Spain, Portugal, Italy and Greece (Beatson 1995a; Marullo 1995). Recent work for the UK, where this area has been subject to active political encouragement indicates first, that it is an activity largely confined to men, who constitute three-quarters of the total and that from a stable level in the 1970s numbers peaked in 1990 but have since declined slightly (Moralee 1998).

Distancing flexibility

Sub-contracting also exhibits significant contrasts in take-up. Information is limited, but recent work has suggested that in all major EU countries under pressure to cut costs and concentrate on core business activities this area has increased significantly (Brewster 1998). According to this research, half of all organizations surveyed in Germany's western *Lander* and the Netherlands, and a third of organizations surveyed in Spain, France, Finland, Eire and the UK indicated that they had increased their use of sub-contracting in the 1990s. The take-up of sub-contracting again appears to be significantly less in the Nordic countries than in other areas of the EU.

Flexibility on the intensive margin

Functional flexibility: multiskilling

In terms of flexibility on the intensive margin the limited survey evidence suggests that job boundaries across Europe have been broken down, particularly at lower levels within organizations (Boyer 1990; Beatson 1995a). The widening of jobs appears to have taken place in all areas in the UK, Sweden and Germany, and in all areas except management in Finland and Norway (Beatson 1995a) but care is needed in interpreting these developments. As we note in the discussion of the UK below, movement into horizontal job categories, or enlargement in the form of multi-tasking is much more common than genuine multiskilling, and such developments may also be characterizing functional flexibility in mainland Europe. However there are good reasons for believing that the experience of at least some EU countries may be different from that of the UK. Work on the French economy suggests that substantial moves to reorganize work in innovative ways has taken place, and with it the upskilling of staff (Jenkins 1998). Likewise, the experience of Germany has long testified to the importance that country has placed on skills development and upgrading (Lane 1989, 1995; Tuselmann 1996; Elger and Smith 1997), despite recent pressures to embrace areas of numerical flexibility particularly from small and medium sized enterprises (Tuselmann 1996).

In the UK the changed economic and political context in the 1980s and 1990s provided opportunities for both the state and employers to attempt significant changes to the employment relationship with the potential for greater functional flexibility, multiskilling and the more intensive use of staff. Perhaps the most important development has been the decline in trade union membership and influence and the collapse of large areas of institutional regulation of terms and conditions via (industry-wide) collective bargaining (Purcell 1991, 1993; Millward *et al.* 1992; Brown 1993; Brown *et al.* 1995). This re-shaped context has led to significant changes in work organization and the nature of jobs undertaken by workers (Cross 1988; ACAS 1988; Gallie *et al.* 1998). However, within UK manufacturing, the changes have tended to emphasize multitasking via job enlargement and rotation, rather than multiskilling through job enrichment (Cross 1988; Geary 1994, 1995). Such an approach is evident in developments in cellular manufacturing and the 'new flexible firm' in British owned manufacturing companies which have led to the introduction of 'forms of functional flexibility that allow the employment of essentially semi-skilled and unskilled labour' (Ackroyd and Proctor 1998: 174). Indeed, achieving flexibility across skills groupings appears to have been difficult with a limited commitment by management to increasing employee skills levels (Daniel 1987; ACAS 1988; Cross 1988), although recent evidence does suggest that some upskilling of the workforce has taken place since the early 1980s (Gallie *et al.* 1998).

A related area under attack in the 1980s and 1990s has been that of internal labour markets. In the mid-1980s it was estimated that over half of the employed workforce in the UK were covered by an internal labour market of some kind (Siebert and Addison 1991), but that through political pressures, the managerial vogue for 'downsizing', 'lean production' and contracting out, these have come under threat (Claydon 1994). The consequences of this development have been well documented in areas such as financial services (Herriot and Pemberton 1995).

Temporal flexibility

Finally, the evidence for temporal or working time flexibility indicates the continuing importance of shiftworking and overtime working. The former is widespread within the EU (Brewster *et al.* 1994; Brewster 1998), although it is considerably less important in the Nordic countries than in the UK and Spain. However, it does appear to be spreading more generally to new areas such as telephone sales and banking (Brewster 1998), suggesting a widening as well as a deepening in its use. In contrast, overtime working remains the most common form of flexibility in the UK despite its lack of cost effectiveness (Brewster *et al.* 1994),[1] but its use has declined in other countries such as Germany (Tuselmann 1996).

Significantly it is Germany where many of the recent and more innovative developments in temporal flexibility have taken place. Changes to the pattern of working time, reductions in standard full-time hours and work-sharing have been agreed at sector and company level (Tuselmann 1996) with well-publicized initiatives at VW and at BMW's Regensburg plant. However, the take-up of such schemes outside of these companies appears to have been limited (Blyton and Trinczak 1997). Evidence from Italy and France also suggests that moves to short-time working have been limited despite legislation on work-sharing having been introduced in France in 1993. Furthermore, annual hours schemes, long-established in the Nordic countries, and the Netherlands have increased in importance in Germany's western *Lander*, and the UK (Brewster *et al.* 1994).

In the UK, as more generally, temporal flexibility has been the result of management concerns to make optimal use of technologies, and to more effectively utilize space and equipment (Beatson 1995a, 1995b) as well as to provide a more comprehensive service to customers. Well-publicized examples of moves to seven-day working (as in coal-mining, and sections of the petrochemicals industry) and Sunday working (in retail) have attracted attention but have also tended to detract from more established forms of flexibility such as overtime and shiftworking which remain commonplace (Casey *et al.* 1997). Indeed, the substantial growth of (largely unpaid) overtime has been a notable feature of employment practices since the mid-1980s (Legge 1998). Furthermore, recent work on annualized hours in the UK suggests that government estimates of its take-up are probably overstated (Gall 1996) and that, outside of the public sector, the number of employees affected remains relatively small.

Flexibility in the UK: a disaggregated study

In this section the development of a particular mix of flexible working patterns is examined by means of a more disaggregated analysis, which illustrates the heavily skewed concentration of certain practices in certain industries and sectors within the

Table 9.2 Changes in flexible work patterns in UK 1984–1997

	Part-time(%)		Temporary employees (%)			Variable hours (%)	
	1984	1994	1984	1994	1997	1984	1994
Agriculture	19.4	20.7	9.8	7.6	11.0	44.7	68.7
Manufacturing:							
Food, drink	14.5	12.7	3.2	3.1	–	21.9	58.0
Textiles	16.4	11.2	2.2	2.3	–	22.1	42.0
Leather	19.8	16.1	4.9	1.6	–	25.7	38.3
Oil refining	4.2	3.8	3.7	6.5	–	35.1	53.3
Chemicals	6.8	5.0	2.6	6.1	–	28.6	59.1
Metals	5.2	5.5	1.7	2.3	–	30.3	58.8
Elec, gas, water	5.8	5.9	2.4	5.6	9.0	28.8	65.8
Construction	6.7	7.9	2.4	5.6	7.0	25.6	58.2
Services:							
Distribution	29.2	39.9	3.0	3.9	} 6.7	27.1	48.6
Hotels, etc.	57.2	54.2	9.7	10.2		46.4	57.4
Financial serv.	11.2	14.5	1.6	3.4	7.6	34.0	56.6
Business serv.	16.9	22.6	5.4	7.2	–	36.0	57.9
Other services	44.0	39.3	7.6	11.5	11.7	26.7	56.1
Public sector:							
Public admin.	10.6	14.0	3.5	5.8	} 10.0	29.4	62.2
Education	35.3	36.9	10.1	15.9		29.3	55.9
Health, etc.	39.8	46.2	4.4	7.3		24.6	52.2
All industries	20.4	25.4	4.3	5.6	7.6	30.2	56.4

Source: Casey *et al.* 1997, Labour Market Trends Selected issues 1997.
*Variable hours workers defined as those whose hours vary week to week as a result of overtime or because basic work hours are flexible.

UK and as a result, of their disproportionate impact on particular groups of individuals. The growth in practices and their variation across industries is detailed in Table 9.2, which draws upon Labour Force Survey Data for 1984, 1994 and 1997[2] (Casey *et al.* 1997).

Table 9.2 reveals that whilst the most common form of flexibility in the UK is that of variations in hours worked, this is largely accounted for by staff on standard working time arrangements who work overtime and/or shiftwork (Casey *et al.* 1997).[3] As was noted above, overtime working dominates variable working time practices, whilst recent estimates of shiftworking suggest that it affects around 16 per cent of men and 13 per cent of women, but is concentrated in certain industries and occupations (Casey *et al.* 1997). In contrast, the incidence of part-time working varies from 3 per cent of employees in 'oil and gas' to over half of those employed in 'hotels and restaurants'. Significantly, manufacturing firms not only make less use of part-timers than services, but their use actually declined over the period 1984–94. The growing use of part-timers is therefore a phenomenon heavily specific to the services sector, and within this to 'business services' and the public services sector. It is also a phenomenon heavily concentrated amongst certain occupational groups. Evidence for the early 1990s shows the practices concentrated amongst clerical workers, service workers (where over half of such staff were part-time) and amongst those working in sales (De Grip *et al.* 1997). Subsequent work has confirmed this with a concentration amongst more junior and less skilled staff and particularly personal service workers (Casey *et al.* 1997). Furthermore, evidence also points to significant variation between employers within the same industry in the degree to which use is made of part-timers (Walsh 1991; Horrell and Rubery 1991).

Many of these points also apply to temporary working. Whilst recent survey evidence suggests that over half of establishments make use of temporary staff (Heather *et al.* 1996), within manufacturing the extent of such practices remains limited and relatively stable (Sly and Stillwell 1997). However since the late 1980s the practice has been growing, particularly in the energy and finance sectors, and again in the public services sector. The latter accounted for 38 per cent of all temporary workers in Britain in 1996, with a concentration in the use of fixed-term contracts, in contrast to financial services where the use of agency temps predominated (Millward *et al.* 1992; Sly and Stillwell 1997). It is notable that professionals (such as accountants and IT professionals) account for the largest proportion of temporary workers of any occupational group, with 14 per cent of this group employed on a temporary basis and, in addition, they are amongst those working some of the longest hours in the UK (Sly and Stillwell 1997).

In the coverage of the EU and the UK it was noted that survey research on multiskilling was generally limited and evidence has tended to rely on case studies. Notwithstanding the criticisms of the extent to which genuine multiskilling has taken place, where changes have occurred they seem to have been particularly significant in manufacturing (ACAS 1988; Cross 1988). In contrast, flexibility on the extensive margin has been heavily concentrated in the public sector and private services. These developments merit attention because the services sectors in general are more insulated than most from the impact of globalization and that whilst they mark a significant break with employment practices in parts of the public sector, they provide a continuation of fairly long-established trends in private services. It is also notable that the growth of self-employment is closely linked to sectoral shifts with the rise of the private service sector, and to sub-contracting.

Overall, the data confirm considerable variation in flexible working practices within and between industries and also indicate a concentration of practices in specific sectors. In this chapter, we have drawn attention to the often significant differences between the private and public sectors in their take-up of particular forms of flexibility. Recent work has also highlighted the differences in flexible working practices between British owned manufacturing firms, and large private sector companies (Ackroyd and Lawrenson 1995, Ackroyd and Proctor 1998), and between these and foreign-owned companies (Millward *et al.* 1992). Thus, whilst considerable variation in the spread and take-up of flexible working practices is evident between individual EU countries, the UK evidence suggests that the differences within countries, and within industries and firms may be as, or more significant than those between countries. This is consistent with the results of work on employee relations within the EU (Marchington 1995), and suggests that variables such as industry, sector, firm size and ownership may be exerting a particularly powerful influence on patterns of flexibility. This point is returned to in the following section.

The results also indicate that in the UK changes in the pattern and mix of flexible working practices have been linked to deeper structural changes in the economy accelerated by historical practices, political influence and changed managerial preferences. Data limitations prevent further detailed analysis of developments but it is likely that the statistics are pointing to the emergence, or acceleration of, a more marked division between primary and secondary labour markets in some industries and occupations in the UK. This can be alternatively constructed in core and peripheral terms, in some cases within firms and establishments, and in others within different segments of the same industry, as for example between large and small firm sectors. These points are also developed further in the final section but it can be argued that such developments have served to further accentuate divisions within the workforce so that these changes have tended both to reinforce established forms of flexibility and the segmentation of the workforce, and to produce a more general and growing casualization of employment (Pollert 1991; Beynon 1997).

EXPLANATIONS FOR DIFFERENCES

From the analysis of the previous sections it is clear that the main forms of flexibility that predominate in a particular country at a given time are the result of a complex of factors operating at a variety of levels. If the main background factor behind change in all EU countries has been globalization and increased international competition, its impact has been uneven. Even where these pressures have been similar the responses in terms of flexible working practices have often differed markedly between countries, sectors and organizations. Distilling the work of a number of writers, the reasons for such differences are identified and explored with particular emphasis being placed on factors that condition and mediate organizational responses. In Figure 9.2, the main factors at each level are identified and in the following discussion their relationship with flexibility explored.

The factors identified in Figure 9.2 are not exhaustive but highlight the major influences on forms of flexible working. These tend to interact as in the case of part-time working, where sectoral and structural factors combine with organizational specific factors – competitive position, culture, organizational structure and size – to determine the extent of such flexibility (Clifford et al. 1997). For flexible working practices generally, the organizational level tends to be more important in less regulated employment systems such as the UK and the Netherlands, whereas the macro-level exerts more of an influence in the more centralized and regulated systems of Germany and the Nordic countries.

Macro-level variables

An illustration of the role of these broader macro-level variables is provided by the contrast of Germany and the UK. In Germany there exists a tightly integrated system of industrial order with a high degree of legal regulation, and through the legally established system of co-determination – clear rights and responsibilities of stakeholders (Lane 1989, 1995; Dore 1997). A longer term approach to business and profitability is facilitated by a credit-based financial system and weakly developed stock market which encourages a long-term perspective in investment, not just in plant and equipment, but also in people (Lane 1995; Elger and Smith 1997). This framework for operating has produced its own rigidities, but has forced companies to orientate themselves towards non-price competitive markets by

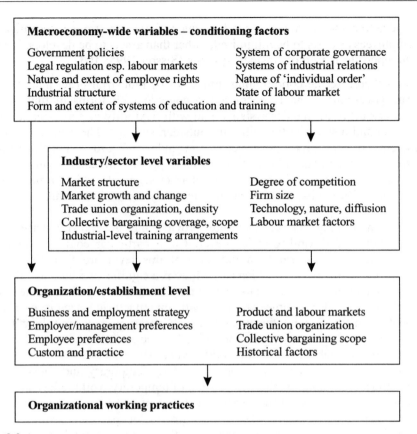

Macroeconomy-wide variables – conditioning factors

Government policies   System of corporate governance
Legal regulation esp. labour markets   Systems of industrial relations
Nature and extent of employee rights   Nature of 'individual order'
Industrial structure   State of labour market
Form and extent of systems of education and training

Industry/sector level variables

Market structure   Degree of competition
Market growth and change   Firm size
Trade union organization, density   Technology, nature, diffusion
Collective bargaining coverage, scope   Labour market factors
Industrial-level training arrangements

Organization/establishment level

Business and employment strategy   Product and labour markets
Employer/management preferences   Trade union organization
Employee preferences   Collective bargaining scope
Custom and practice   Historical factors

Organizational working practices

Figure 9.2

adopting what Streeck (1992) has termed a Diversified Quality Production (DQP) strategy, producing high value-added products, underpinned by largely consensual industrial relations (Tuselmann 1996).

In contrast the UK, and to an extent the USA, operates with highly fragmented institutional structures, weak links between the elements of the industrial order and a financial system which maintains an 'arms length' relationship with business generating pressure for high, short-term returns on capital (Lane 1989, 1995). It follows that management tends towards a preoccupation with financial affairs, with particular importance accorded to accountants within the higher echelons of management (Armstrong 1995; Sisson 1995). This in turn produces a relative under-investment in capital equipment and human resources and a tendency to operate in price-competitive, low value-added markets (Lane 1995; Sisson 1995; Nolan and Walsh 1995).

The contrast between the two approaches has been usefully summarized by Franks and Mayer (1992) in their discussion of 'insider' and 'outsider' systems of corporate governance. The former, associated with wider stakeholder control and characterizing Germany and the Nordic countries, and the latter, with external shareholder control, the UK and the USA. The implications of which for employees have been summarized by Sisson (1995):

Under 'outsider' systems, it can be argued, there is a stronger incentive to see employees as costs to be minimised, rather than assets to be developed, whereas the opposite is true of 'insider' systems (Sisson 1995: 103).

In general therefore the conditioning influences of industrial order and systems of corporate governance tend to encourage a concern with forms of functional and temporal flexibility in 'insider systems' and with flexibility on the external margins – numerical and distancing flexibility in 'outsider' systems. The critical point is that the systems of corporate governance and industrial order, the 'institutional-regulatory arrangements' (Dore 1997) which prevail in each country, help to encourage a focus on certain markets and market segments which in turn facilitate certain forms of flexibility and operate to effectively constrain or limit the take-up of others.

These conditioning factors therefore provide the general influences on the particular forms of flexibility which develop in a particular country. Additionally, factors which appear to exert an influence at this level are first, the industrial structure, notably the extent to which agriculture is a significant sector, and the size of the private and public services sector. These have been seen to influence the extent of self-employment and part-time working, with manufacturing sectors emphasizing functional flexibility. Second, the extent to which labour markets are subject to a high degree of legal and voluntary regulation. Whilst the degree of regulation in itself does not appear to affect labour market flexibility overall (Brewster 1998), it clearly has an effect on the take-up of certain forms, particularly temporary and agency working (Marullo 1995). In Spain, the rapid expansion of temporary working has largely been a response to restrictions on the hiring and firing of full-time employees (Marullo 1995; Morgan 1996). Whilst the recent growth of part-time working in the Netherlands has been due to employment legislation which has made redundancy and dismissal difficult (Hoogendoorn et al. 1992).

In the UK, it has been the prevailing view that temporary employment has tended to be cyclical (Sly and Stillwell 1997; Casey et al. 1997; Heather et al. 1996), a point confirmed by the experience of countries such as Portugal and Denmark. However, a number of governments in the EU relaxed legal constraints on temporary work in the 1980s[4] which was instrumental in the growth of new recruits on fixed-term contracts particularly in France and Germany in the 1990s. It is notable how many young workers are employed on such contracts in Spain, (60 per cent), Ireland (over 50 per cent) and Portugal (over a third) and reflects the characteristic labour market entry for young workers in these countries (De Grip et al. 1997). More generally the cross country variation in the use of fixed-term contracts reflects differences in labour market regulations and customs (European Commission 1995), together with prevailing levels of unemployment (European Commission 1995), and the relative importance of the agriculture and tourism sectors in a country's industry mix (Marullo 1995; European Commission 1995).

The experience of the UK and the Netherlands in the spread of fixed-term contracts also emphasizes the importance of political factors. In the UK political encouragement has been critical to both self-employment and the incidence of part-time working. The moves to privatize some areas of state activity and contract out parts of the public service sector have clearly influenced the take-up of both part-time and temporary working in the UK and the Netherlands.

Industry/sector level

The diversity between sectors in the use of flexibility has been noted above, but diversity within sectors is a characteristic of all EU countries. These differences appear to be closely linked to industrial structure and firm size. It is notable that in Germany where the sector level continues to exert a significant influence on employment practice by virtue of collective bargaining at this level, small and medium-sized employers have been seeking flexibility in different ways. Despite recent framework agreements on working time flexibility across 21 sectors, moves towards numerical flexibility are gathering pace, driven largely by these smaller firms (Tuselmann 1996).

These moves arise in part from the high wage and non-wage costs of the German economy, but may also be the result of a focus on different market segments. Whilst the German economy has created an environment in which companies can operate effectively in certain markets (and perhaps only in these), it provides less well for those that may be trying to compete in more price competitive markets. Recent concerns in the metalworking sector also raise doubts about how far the model is sustainable in the longer term, as leading firms are exposed to greater competition on both price and quality. An interesting example of this is the response of the German auto industry to both the 35 hour week and the arrival of greater Japanese competition.

The role of both technology and labour markets also appear to be important. Developments in technology have in some countries led to a focus on functional and temporal flexibility as organizations seek to make optimal use of expensive equipment. In contrast, the labour market issue has much to do with skills availability, the levels and types of training provided externally, pay levels and the extent to which there are 'pools' of appropriately qualified people available. These factors will have an impact on both internal and external flexibility.

Organization/enterprise levels

At this level the role of employer and management preferences reflected in business and employment strategies assume critical importance, particularly in decentralized structures where organization-based employment systems dominate (Purcell 1991). Within these the role of historical factors in guiding action remain significant as the continuing importance of part-time work in parts of the UK service sector testifies.

However, despite recent interest in resource-based approaches to business strategy, in practice where a strategic approach exists in the UK it is often based upon low-cost. Such a strategy tends towards a treatment of labour as a cost to be minimized and to encourage greater use of flexibility on the external margins. This said, managers often have to modify approaches to labour in light of particular factors and the role of trade unions in supporting some forms of flexible working and constraining others is in some situations considerable. It is significant that, at least in the UK, the areas where forms of numerical flexibility have been most widespread, and penetrated furthest, is where trade union organization is weak (private services), largely non-existent (hotels and restaurants), or has been the subject of a concerted offensive by employers (broadcasting, steel, dockwork).

For some companies an increasingly important factor in flexibility relates to its position in the supply chain, and for multi-nationals to the wider international division of labour, and the way in which this is used to influence an organization's production strategy. Evidence both from the UK (Hutchinson *et al.* 1998), and from Japanese multinationals operating in south-east Asia (Gamble *et al.* 1999) suggests that the location of a plant in a particular customer or supply chain will critically affect how it is treated by a company, with attendant implications for forms of flexibility. For example, it is widely acknowledged that German manufacturing companies in the UK tend to operate a more cost-driven approach than parent companies in Germany, with an emphasis on numerical flexibility. For some, this is seen as evidence of the willingness of German companies to break away from the 'constraints' of the German system. The argument here is that it may be more useful to look at the position of UK plants in terms of the production strategy of the parent company. The plant may occupy a particular position in the supply chain requiring the assembly of low cost, low value-added components or the production of final goods for price sensitive markets not served by the German parent.

This suggests that multinationals will tend to work with and reinforce the international division of labour. In the UK, a relatively low-skill but inexpensive workforce producing low value-added products and services will attract multi-nationals looking for such attributes. Conversely, where high quality production requiring a skilled, and functionally flexible workforce is required, such production facilities are likely to be located elsewhere. The global strategies of the major motor manufacturers, Ford, GM, Honda, Nissan and VW are illustrative of these concerns.

ISSUES AND CONCERNS

Much of the focus of critics or sceptics of the 'flexibility debate' has been the way that it has been presented both as inevitable and as unambiguously 'a good thing' (see Legge 1998 for a discussion of this). The issues explored here are that whilst flexibility may be inevitable in the context of globalization and increased competition, labour market flexibility need not be. Rather, that the focus on this aspect of flexibility has served to skew the flexibility debate and 'blind' us to both other forms of flexibility that may be available to organizations and to detract attention from the costs of labour market flexibility for individuals and for employment generally (Legge 1998). Further, it has left largely untouched broader issues surrounding the political dimension of flexibility; whose interests are served by a concern with labour market flexibility above all others and how these interests are reinforced through, for example, systems of corporate governance.

A constant theme throughout this chapter has been the restructuring of European labour markets and the associated fragmentation of the European labour force (Standing 1997). Much of which has been a result of the employer driven nature of flexibility which, in the UK, has been motivated by a desire to cut costs and extend areas of managerial regulation of the employment relationship (Legge 1998; Geary 1995). However, some of this growth has been a result of 'pull factors', from employees who wish to work more flexibly.[5] Survey data for both the UK (Sly *et al.* 1997) and the European Union (EC 1995) indicates that a significant proportion of those in such jobs are in them through choice, although the proportions differ significantly between men and women and are much less for temporary than for part-time workers (European Commission 1995). Also, apart from skilled professionals, those in part-time and temporary work are frequently concentrated in the lower grades of work available and often have limited freedom and bargaining power in the labour market. The fact that much of this work is undertaken by women is compounded by the fact that employers often appear to perceive it as 'women's work' (Hunter *et al.* 1993; Casey *et al.* 1997) and assume that if it is full-time work it must be for men. Further, for temporary workers there is 'limited evidence that it offers anything more than second class employment to employees' (Legge 1998: 289), particularly for those on short-term contracts of less than one year (Gallie *et al.* 1998).

A central thrust of the concerns raised by Legge and others is that greater flexibility has meant insecurity, stress and labour intensification for an increasing number of workers. To place these concerns in context, for those individuals employed through agencies, a lack of status and bargaining power are compounded by the insecurity and frequent absence of legal protection surrounding fixed-term contracts and contract renewal (Purcell and Purcell 1996). For those, supposedly core employees providing organizations with functional flexibility, there is evidence of greater intensification of labour (Elger 1991; Edwards and Whitson 1991; Nichols 1997) and of 'management by stress' (Garrahan and Stewart 1992; Legge 1995).

These costs are clearly difficult to quantify, but may be significant for workers and are borne disproportionately by some more than others. Even within the categories of part-timers and temporary staff there is considerable variation in the impact of policies, as some are significantly better protected by legislation or collective agreements, than others (Breugel and Hegewisch 1994).

These insecurities are compounded by the growing internationalization of capital. As was noted above, the increasing importance of transnational companies means that employee performance is now subject to ever widening orbits of comparison (Marginson and Sisson 1996). Workers in the car plants of Ford and GM in Britain face increasing competition on costs and productivity from those in Spain, Germany, Belgium and further afield. In such circumstances, terms and conditions are potentially subject to a 'whip-sawing' effect as pay and conditions are squeezed under threats of plant closure (see GM's Vauxhall plant at Luton in 1998). An illustration of this was the decision by Hoover to close its washing machine assembly operations in France and consolidate its existing activities in Cambuslang in Scotland (European Industrial Relations Review 1993) on the strength of a revised terms and conditions agreement with its Scottish workforce.

This discussion also raises profound questions about the future shape, quality and quantity of employment generally. One current dilemma is that whilst significant skills gaps are emerging in many economies, the kind of work which appears to be proliferating is that which does not encourage investment in training to be given. In the absence of effective national training schemes, the responsibility falls on individuals, who, given the often limited resources they have available to them, are presented with a 'Catch 22' scenario; the need for skills acquisition but few resources to effect this. Relatedly there is the question of the extent to which 'good jobs'[6] are available to potential employees. Recent evidence suggests that they appear to have been declining in both the USA and the UK (Tilly 1997; Guest 1997) at the expense of more peripheral work.

Gender segregation

A significant element of the case of the Hoover re-location decision was the gender composition of the workforce in the Cambuslang factory, a point which necessitates some consideration of the 'feminization' of employment more generally. Throughout this chapter the concentration of female employment in a few occupations and sectors has been noted,[7] a trend which persists due much to the expanding service sector and of associated part-time employment opportunities (Meulders *et al.* 1994). Thus, the expansion of female employment appears to have taken place where it was already well-established, where its nature has tended to characterize it as 'women's work' (Hunter *et al.* 1993; Casey *et al.* 1997), and where resistance from men has been limited or 'muted'. The effect of this has been that: 'gender segregation remains a major feature of the EU labour market' (Plantenga and Tijdens 1994: 16). However, recent evidence for the UK suggests that a more complex picture is emerging. Since the 1970s there has been a decline in the occupational concentration of full-time men and women, but that part-time work, dominated by female occupations has become significantly more segregated (Hakim 1996). As Hakim states;

> The workforce has polarised into a female-dominated secondary labour market with part-time jobs and high turnover rates, while the primary labour market consists of male dominated and mixed occupations, full-time jobs and low turnover rates (Hakim 1996: 162).

Furthermore, she suggests that this female dominated secondary labour market now accounts for around 40 per cent of the total workforce; a figure which disguises the continuing vertical segregation of women's jobs in this market and more generally. These factors have the effect of depressing wages for women, and particularly those of part-time women. One consequence of these developments is that issues of equality of treatment and opportunity may be becoming more structured along the lines of employment form, rather than, or as well as, that of gender. The differences in opportunity for advancement, and reward may now be greater as between part-time and full-time women, than between full-time women and full-time men.

This said, there are clearly differences between part-time jobs in their relative attractiveness and benefits, and some of the growth of such working is clearly 'driven' by the demand from certain groups of women. In this regard it is notable that the countries with the highest female participation rates also have the highest frequencies of part-time employment for female workers (De Grip *et al.* 1997) despite different legal and institutional frameworks. However, in general, the relatively disadvantaged position of part-timers in terms of employment rights, and the fact that this group are largely composed of women has given rise to a number of legal cases concerning indirect sex discrimination both from the UK and elsewhere within the EU. Issues concerning differential qualifying periods for full- and part-time workers and entitlement to employment rights as well as the nature of those rights have generated a large number of highly publicized European Court of Justice rulings and amendments to national legislation.[8] These led in 1997 to the passing of an EU directive on part-time working, which takes effect from mid-1999 (end 1999 in the UK). The likely impact of this on the growth of part-time working is difficult to assess and will depend on the extent to which it is largely cost considerations which 'drive' the use of such flexibility. However, where similar provisions exist already within the EU, as in Belgium, they appear to have made little difference to take-up.

New managerialism, and the 'demise' of bureaucracy

A further issue which has constituted a significant 'driver' in the language and rhetoric, if not always the substance, of moves to flexibility has been that of the 'cult of the customer' (DuGay and Salaman 1992). With this has come an attack on organizational forms that are perceived to be less responsive to such customers and their 'needs'. At the levels of both ideology and practice, the customer effectively becomes a quasi-manager, 'empowered' through greater choice and customer 'charters' with workers expected to demonstrate greater customer awareness and accountability to them. More generally, this development has been about shifting risks associated with greater competition (or some simulation of this), on to individual workers, either as employees, contract staff, self-employed temps or franchisees. These pressures have been intensified by moves towards organizational restructuring, 'downsizing' and 'becoming leaner' (Hutchinson *et al.* 1998), representing a break-up and retreat from bureaucratic organization.

For much of this century, bureaucracies have provided a degree of income and employment security to employees, emphasizing consistency, fairness and due process through established procedures and formal personnel policies based around discrete jobs (Legge 1998). Furthermore, by developing internal labour markets, bureaucracies helped to provide career paths for staff, and with this an ability to plan ahead for the future. Although the challenges to bureaucratic organization have in practice been limited (Guest 1997) the rhetoric has been pervasive, and may be an accurate indication of the general direction, if not the speed, of future change.

In the event that moves to break-up organizations gather pace, it is likely that a further consequence could be the decline of organizations as sources of identity and stability for individuals. For some, this looser attachment to organizations may have wider implications for dislocation and disruption in society (Tyson 1995). This essentially Durkheimian vision of an anomic state depicts organizational restructuring and with it, more flexible forms of working as carrying with them wider threats to the stability and sustainability of a particular form of society.

The issue here is that the pressures which encourage limited attachment of individuals to their organizations run alongside the managerial exhortations to demonstrate flexibility, customer focus, and – for some – commitment. The irony, and potential concern for organizations is that the very people who may be emerging as 'core staff' in terms of customers, are those who actually have the least attachment to their organizations. One illustration of this is provided by the case of check-out operators in retail superstores. In what are frequently impersonal structures, these staff perform a key role as the human face of the store, and as a source of information about customers. How they treat customers, smile, ask questions, package food and listen to complaints may be an important factor in customer loyalty. Yet, they are frequently one of a large number of staff on a bewildering array of contractual arrangements, working few, irregular and at times unsocial hours, with relatively poor pay, and benefits considerably below those of their full-time colleagues. It follows that even those staff with the most tenuous bonds to organizations may be of incalculable value to employers, and yet what is emerging is a significant gulf between the two in terms of expectations and treatment.[9]

CONCLUDING REMARKS: DOES LABOUR MARKET FLEXIBILITY MATTER?

In drawing this chapter to a close it is useful to place the labour flexibility issue in a wider context. Much of the debate until recently has examined the phenomenon largely from the standpoint of how the various forms meet employer 'needs', and how, if employers and shareholders benefit, this is likely to constitute a 'public good'. In this section the concern has been to explore some of the wider consequences of the organizational pursuit of flexibility, suggesting that what may be good for organizations and employers need not necessarily be good for individuals, society or the economy as a whole.

At the societal level the subject of much recent discourse has concerned the issue of inclusion and exclusion; that some individuals can effectively defend themselves and participate more effectively in the wider society than can others by virtue of the jobs they hold and the associated security that these provide in terms of income and employment (Hutton 1995). This has been a particular theme in debates surrounding stakeholding and the growth of what Hutton has termed the 40:30:30 society, with increasing numbers effectively excluded and disenfranchised from full participation in society, with potentially damaging consequences both for them and for the wider society. Within the EU, the growth of long-term unemployment points to the vulnerability of those without marketable skills who may obtain brief spells in the official labour market but find themselves increasingly marginalized. This is a characteristic also of the increasing number of casuals in many areas of employment (Beynon 1997).

These developments create additional concerns. The factors encouraging us to view ourselves as customers – and raising our expectations in this role – neglects the fact that to fully participate in this role (at least within the law) also requires us to be able to produce and the inability to satisfactorily undertake the latter may have wider dysfunctional consequences at the level of society and community. Relatedly there is already evidence that in Spain, those 'insiders' in full-time employment are using their bargaining power to achieve better terms and conditions at the expense of the increasing number of temporary staff (Argandona 1997). This development contributes to a further consequence of fragmentation; that of widening income inequality (Machin 1996), and with it a greater polarization of incomes and stratification of society.

Finally, there is a concern that the whole focus on labour market flexibility may be miscast, that it serves to divert attention away from consideration of alternative forms of flexibility and furthermore that the link between certain forms of labour flexibility and economic success is not proven (Geary 1992). In the previous section differences between countries in their use of the forms of flexibility was examined and an emphasis was placed on the relative importance accorded to shareholders as stakeholders within national, legally regulated systems of corporate governance in accounting for such differences. There is what Dore (1997) has termed a 'flexibility trade off' that:

> It is precisely because they face the inflexible demands of shareholders in financial markets that British and American firms need flexibility in their labour markets (Dore 1997: 267).

This leads to the important conclusion that labour market flexibility is neither inevitable, nor necessarily essential for longer term economic success. As Dore argues further, the exhortations of the OECD and the G7 countries that:

> globalisation makes labour market flexibility inevitable, is untrue. Globalisation and international competition make some kind of flexibility imperative – but there are other markets that can provide it (Dore 1997).

In the UK, where labour costs in manufacturing represent a significant proportion of total costs, where hiring and firing is relatively inexpensive, and where few regulations exist to constrain managerial decision-making at the enterprise level, the effective options available may be less attractive particularly for smaller organizations. But the relative ease with which greater flexibility in labour use can be achieved at this level may lead to a neglect of other forms of flexibility such as production and marketing (Rubery *et al.* 1988), and to capital investment (Ackroyd and Proctor 1998). These points are significant, and raise the question of the focus of competitive strategies and the basis on which organizations, and more generally countries, compete. With increasing organizational concerns about quality and non-price factors generally, the wisdom of focusing largely on flexibility on the external margins can be questioned, but the argument here is that the focus on such flexibility can only change through a reform of the institutional-regulationist arrangements operating within a country. That is the system of industrial order (Lane 1995), corporate governance and the legal protection and representation rights accorded to different stakeholders in a society.

Notes

1 It should be noted that if much of the overtime is unpaid, as seems to be the case (Casey *et al.* 1997), then it is likely to be a cost-effective method of flexibility.
2 1997 data from selected issues of Labour Market Trends.
3 Eurostat (1996) estimates that 51.8% of all employees in the UK work shifts, evenings or nights.
4 Notably Spain (1977 and 1984), and Belgium, France, Germany and the Netherlands in the mid-1980s.
5 Evidence of 'pull' factors are strong for some part-timers and returners, see Hakim (1996).
6 See the discussion in a special edition of *Industrial Relations Journal* December 1997.
7 See the work of Martin and Roberts (1984), Hakim (1987, 1996).
8 Particularly regarding planned reductions of the qualifying period to one year in the UK.
9 This view is confirmed for those on the employment periphery by recent IPD sponsored work on the psychological contract (Guest *et al.* 1996).

REFERENCES

ACAS (Advisory Conciliation and Arbitration Service) (1988) *Labour Flexibility in Britain. The 1987 ACAS Survey*, Occasional Paper 41, ACAS, London.

Ackroyd, S. and Lawrenson, D. (1995) Knowledge work and organizational transformation, in Fincham, R. (ed.), *New Relationships in the Organized Professions*, Avebury, Aldershot. 149–170.

Ackroyd, S. and, Proctor, S. (1998) British manufacturing organization and workplace industrial relations: some attributes of the new flexible firm, *British Journal of Industrial Relations*, 36 (2), 163–83.

Argandona, A. (1997) Spain and the European Social Charter: social harmonization with unemployment and high wage growth, in Addison, J.T. and Siebert, W.S., *Labour Markets in Europe: Issues of Harmonization and Regulation*, Dryden, London.

Armstrong, P. (1995) Accountancy and HRM, in Storey, J. (ed.), *Human Resource Management: A Critical Text*, Routledge, London.

Atkinson, J. and Meager, N. (1986) *Changing Work Patterns: How Companies Achieve Flexibility to Meet New Needs*, NEDO, London.

Beatson, M. (1995a) *Labour Market Flexibility*, Employment Department Research Series, No. 48, DfEE, Sheffield.

Beatson, M. (1995b) Progress towards a flexible labour market, *Employment Gazette*, 103, 55–66.

Beynon, H. (1997) The changing practices of work, in Brown R. (ed.), *The Changing Shape of Work*, Macmillan, London.

Blyton, P. and Trinczak, R. (1997) Renewed interest in work-sharing? assessing recent developments in Germany, *Industrial Relations Journal*, 28 (1) 3–12.

Boyer, R. (ed.) (1989) *The Search for Labour Market Flexibility: The European Labour Market in Transition*, Oxford University Press, Oxford.

Boyer, R. (1990) *Capital-Labour Relations in OECD Countries from the Fordist 'Golden Age' to Contrasted National Trajectories*. Working Paper N-9020 CEPREMAP, CNRS, Paris.

Breugel, I. and Hegewisch, A. (1994) Flexibilisation and part-time employment in Europe, in Brown, R. and Crompton, R. (eds), *The New Europe: Economic Restructuring and Social Exclusion*, UCL Press, London.

Brewster, C. (1995) HRM The European Dimension, in Storey, J. (ed.) *Human Resource Mangement: A Critical Text*, Routledge, London.

Brewster, C. (1998) Flexible working in Europe: extent, growth and the challenge for HRM, in Sparrow, P. and Marchington, M. (eds), *Human Resource Management: The New Agenda*, Pitman, London.

Brewster, C., Hegewisch, A. and Mayne, L. (1994) Flexible working practices: the controversy and the evidence, in Brewster, C. and Hegewisch, A. (eds), *Policy and Practice in European Human Resource Management: The Evidence and Analysis from the Price Waterhouse Cranfield Survey*, Routledge, London.

Brewster, C., Mayne, L., Malverde, M. and Kabut, R. (1997) Introduction: flexibility in European labour markets? the evidence reviewed, *Employee Relations*, 19 (6), 509–18.

Brown, W. (1993) The contraction of collective bargaining in Britain, *British Journal of Industrial Relations*, 31 (2).

Brown, W., Marginson, P. and Walsh, J. (1995) Management, pay determination and collective bargaining, in Edwards, P., *Industrial Relations: Theory and Practice in Britain*, Blackwell, Oxford.

Casey, B. (1991) Survey evidence on trends in non-standard employment, in Pollert, A. (ed.), *Farewell to Flexibility?* Blackwell, Oxford.

Casey, B., Metcalf, H. and Millward, N. (1997) *Employers' Use of Flexible Labour*, PSI, London.

Claydon, T. (1994) Human resource management and the labour market, in Beardwell, I. and Holden, L. (eds), *Human Resource Management: A Contemporary Perspective*, Pitman, London.

Clifford, N., Morley, M. and Gunnigle, P. (1997) Part-time work in Europe, *Employee Relations*, 19 (6), 555–67.

Cross, M. (1988) Changes in working practices in UK manufacturing 1981–88, *Industrial Relations Review and Report*, 415, 2–10.

Daniel, W.W. (1987) *Workplace Industrial Relations and Technical Change*, Frances Pinter, London.

De Grip, A., Hoevenberg, J. and Willems, E. (1997) Atypical employment in the European Union, *International Labour Review*, 136 (1), 49–71.

Dore, R. (1997) Jobs and employment: good jobs, bad jobs and no jobs, *Industrial Relations Journal*, 28 (4), 262–8.

Drucker, P. (1988) The coming of the new organization, *Harvard Business Review*, Jan–Feb, 45–53.

DuGay, P. and Salaman, G. (1992) The cult(ure) of the customer, *Journal of Management Studies*, 29 (6), 615–33.

Edwards, P. (1995) Assessment: markets and managerialism in Edwards, P. (ed.), *Industrial Relations: Theory and Practice in Britain*, Blackwell, Oxford.

Edwards, P. and Whitson, C. (1991) Workers are working harder: effort and shop-floor relations in the 1980s, *British Journal of Industrial Relations*, 29 (4), 593–602.

Elger, T. (1991) Task flexibility and the intensification of labour in UK manufacturing in the 1980s, in Pollert, A. (ed.), *Farewell to Flexibility*, Blackwell, Oxford.

Elger, T. and Smith, C. (1997) International capital, inward investment and the restructuring of European work and industrial relations, *European Journal of Industrial Relations*, 3 (3), 279–304.

Employee Relations (1997) edition devoted to 'Flexibility in European Labour Markets', 19 (6).

Employee Relations (1998) 'Labour Flexibility Revisited', special edition, 20 (5).

European Commission (1995) *Employment in Europe*, Office for Official Publications in the European Communities, Luxembourg.

European Commission (1996) *Employment in Europe*, Office for Official Publications in the European Communities, Luxembourg.

European Commission (1997) *Employment in Europe*, Office for Official Publications in the European Communities, Luxembourg.

European Industrial Relations Review (1993) The Hoover affair and social dumping, 230, 14–19.

Franks, J. and Mayer, C. (1992) Corporate control: a synthesis of industrial evidence, unpublished paper, London Business School, University of Warwick.

Gall, G. (1996) All year round: the growth of annualised hours in Britain, *Personnel Review*, 25 (3), 35–52.

Gallie, D., White, M., Cheng, Y. and Tomlinson, M. (1998) *Restructuring the Employment Relationship*, Blackwell, Oxford.

Gamble, J., Humphrey, J., Morris, J. and Wilkinson, B. (1999) Manufacturing organization in Pacific Asia: work organization and human resource management implications, Paper presented at BUIRA HRM Conference *'Researching HRM'*, Cardiff University.

Garrahan, P. and Stewart, P. (1992) *The Nissan Enigma: Flexibility at Work in a Local Economy*, Mansell, London.

Geary, J. (1992) 'Employment flexibility and human resource management: the case of three American electronics plants, *Work, Employment and Society*, 6 (2), 251–70.

Geary, J. (1993) New forms of work organization and employee involvement in two case study sites: plural, mixed and protean, *Economic and Industrial Democracy*, 14 (4), 511–34.

Geary, J. (1994) Task participation: employee's participation enabled or constrained, in Sisson, K. (ed.), *Personnel Management: A Comprehensive Guide to Theory and Practice in Britain*, Blackwell, Oxford.

Geary, J. (1995) Work practices: the structure of work, in Edwards, P. (ed.), *Industrial Relations: Theory and Practice in Britain*, Blackwell, Oxford.

Guest, D. (1997) Towards jobs and justice in Europe: a research agenda, *Industrial Relations Journal*, 28 (4), 344–52.

Guest, D., Conway, N., Briner, R. and Dickman, M. (1996) The state of the psychological contract in employment, *Issues in People Management*, No. 16, Institute of Personnel and Development.

Hakim, C. (1987) Trends in the flexible labour force, *Employment Gazette*, November, HMSO, London.

Hakim, C. (1996) *Key Issues in Women's Work*, Athlone Press, London.

Heather, P., Rick, J., Atkinson, J. and Morris, S. (1996) 'Employers' use of temporary workers, *Labour Market Trends*, September, 403–11.

Herriott, P. and Pemberton, C. (1995) *New Deals: The Revolution in Managerial Careers*, Wiley, Chichester.

Hoogendoorn, J., Haima van der Wal, T. and Spitsbaard, T. (1992) The Netherlands, in Brewster, C., Hegewisch, A., Holden, L. and Lockhart, T., *The European Human Resource Management Guide*, Academic Press, London.

Horrell, S. and Rubery, J. (1991) *Employers Working Time Practices and Women's Employment*. HMSO, EOC.

Hunter, L., McGregor, A., MacInnes, J. and Sproull, A. (1993) The flexible firm: strategy and segmentation, *British Journal of Industrial Relations*, 31 (3), 381–407.

Hutchinson, S., Kinnie, N., Purcell, J., Collinson, M., Terry, M. and Scarborough, H. (1998) *Getting Fit, Staying Fit, Developing Lean and Responsive Organizations*, Institute of Personnel and Development, London.

Hutton, W. (1995) *The State We're In*, Jonathan Cape, London.

Hyman, R. (1995) The historical evolution of industrial relations in Edwards, P. (ed.), *Industrial Relations: Theory and Practice*, Blackwell, Oxford.

Jenkins, A. (1998) The French experience of flexibility: lessons for British HRM, in Sparrow, P. and Marchington, M. (eds), *Human Resource Managament: The New Agenda*, Pitman, London.

Kanter, R. (1989) *When Giants Learn to Dance*, Unwin, London.

Lane, C. (1989) *Management and Labour in Europe: The Industrial Enterprise in Germany, Britain and France*, Edward Elgar, Aldershot.

Lane, C. (1995) *Industry and Society in Europe: Stability and Change in Britain, Germany and France*, Edward Elgar, Aldershot.

Legge, K. (1995) *Human Resource Management: Rhetorics and Realities*, Macmillan, London.

Legge, K. (1998) The gift wrapping of employment degradation, in Sparrow, P. and Marchington, M. (eds), *Human Resource Management: The New Agenda*, Pitman, London.

Liebenstein, H. (1966) Allocative efficiency v X-efficiency, *American Economic Review*, 56, 392–415.

Littler, C. (1982) *The Development of the Labour Process in Capitalist Societies*, Heinemann, London.

Machin, S. (1996) Wage inequality in the UK, *Oxford Review of Economic Policy*, 12 (1), 47–64.

Marchington, M. (1995) Employee relations, in Tyson, S. (ed.), *Strategic Prospects For HRM*, IPD, London.

Marginson, P. and Sisson, K. (1996) Multinational companies and the future of collective bargaining: a review of the research issues, *European Journal of Industrial Relations*, 2 (2), 173–97.

Martin, J. and Roberts, C. (1984) *Women and Employment: A Lifetime Perspective*, HMSO, London.

Marullo, S. (1995) *Comparison of Regulations on Part-Time and Temporary Employment in Europe*, Research Series No. 52. DfEE, Sheffield.

Meulders, D. (1993) *Position of Women in the Labour Market in the European Community*, Dartmouth, Aldershot.

Meulders D., Plasman, O. and Plasman, R. (1994) *Atypical Employment in the EC*, Dartmouth, Aldershot.

Millward, N., Stevens, M., Smart, D. and Hawes, W.R. (1992) *Workplace Industrial Relations in Transition: The ED/ESRC/PSI/ACAS Surveys*, Dartmouth, Aldershot.

Moralee, L. (1998) Self employment in the 1990s, *Labour Market Trends*, March, 121–30.

Morgan, J. (1996) Labour market recoveries in the UK and other OECD countries, *Labour Market Trends*, December, 529–39.

Nichols, T. (1997) *The Sociology of Industrial Injury*, Mansell, London.

Nolan, P. and Walsh, J. (1995) The structure of the economy and the labour market, in Edwards, P. (ed.), *Industrial Relations: Theory and Practice*, Blackwell, Oxford.

Peters, T. and Waterman, R. (1982) *In Search of Excellence: Lessons From America's Best Run Companies*, Harper and Row, New York.

Piore, M.J. and Sabel, C.F. (1984) *The Second Industrial Divide: Possibilities for Prosperity*, Basic Books, New York.

Plantenga, J. and Tijdens, K. (1994) Segmentation in the European Union: developments in the 1980s, in Van Hoot, J. and Rodots, E. (eds), *Women and the European Market*, Chapman, London.

Pollert, A. (1988) The flexible firm: fixation or fact, *Work, Employment and Society*, 2 (3), 281–316.

Pollert, A. (ed.) (1991) *Farewell to Flexibility?* Blackwell, Oxford.

Purcell, J. (1991) The re-discovery of the management prerogative in the management of labour relations in the 1980s, *Oxford Review of Economic Policy*, 7 (1), 33–43.

Purcell, J. (1993) The end of institutional industrial relations?, *Political Quarterly*, 7 (1), 6–23.

Purcell, K. and Purcell, J. (1996) Responding to competition: insourcing, outsourcing and the growth of contingent labour, paper presented at the conference on The Globalisation of Production and Regulation of Labour, University of Warwick, September.

Rajan, A., Van Eupen, P. and Jaspers, A. (1998) Britain's flexible labour market: what next?, *Labour Market Trends*, May, 171–2.

Rubery, J. and Fagan, C. (1994) Does feminization mean a flexible labour force?, in Hyman, R. and Ferner, A. (eds), *New Frontiers in European Industrial Relations*, Blackwells, Oxford.

Rubery, J., Tarling, R. and Wilkinson, F. (1997) Flexibility, marketing and the organization of production, *Labour and Society* 12 (1).

Rubery, J., Smith, M., Fagan, C. and Grimshaw, D. (1998) *Women and European Employment*, Routledge, London.

Siebert, S. and Addison, J.T., (1991) Internal labour markets: causes and consequences, *Oxford Review of Economic Policy*, 7 (1), 76–92.

Sisson, K. (1995) Human resource management and the personnel function, in Storey, J. (ed.) *Human Resource Management: A Critical Text*, Routledge, London.

Sly, F. and Stillwell, D. (1997) Temporary work in Great Britain, *Labour Market Trends*, September, 347–54.

Sly, F., Stillwell, D. and Risdon, A. (1997) Women in the labour market: results from the Spring 1996 labour force survey, *Labour Market Trends*, March, 99–120.

Sparrow, P. and Marchington, M. (eds) (1998). *Human Resource Management: The New Agenda*, Pitman, London.

Standing, G. (1997) Globalization, labour flexibility and insecurity: the era of market regulation, *European Journal of Industrial Relations*, 3 (1), 7–37.

Streeck, W. (1992) *Social Institutions and Economic Performance: Studies of Industrial Relations in Advanced Capitalist Economies*, Sage, London.

Tilly, C. (1997) Arresting the decline of good jobs in the USA, *Industrial Relations Journal*, 28 (4), 269–74.

Tuselmann, H.J. (1996) The path towards greater labour flexibility in Germany: hampered by past success? *Employee Relations*, 18 (6), 26–47.

Tyson, S. (1995) *Strategic Prospects for HRM*, Institute of Personnel and Development, London.

Wakh, J. (1991) The performance of UK textiles and clothing: recovery, *International Journal of Applied Economics*, 5 (3), 277–389.

Walsh, T. (1991) The re-shaping of 'flexible' labour? European policy perspectives, in Blyton, P. and Morris, J. (eds) *A Flexible Future? Prospects for Employment and Organisation*, De Gruyter, Berlin.

Wood, S. (1989) The transformation of work?, in Wood, S. (ed.), *The Transformation of Work?* Unwin Hyman, London.

Innovation or optimization: facing up to the challenge of the global economy

10

Andy Adcroft and Robert Willis

INTRODUCTION

The discourses of social science, like sociology, economics and management, are, more often than not, careful to place any organizational analysis into a broad environmental context where the conditions of one are reflected in the conditions within the other. Thus, economics argues that market conditions are a significant reflection of the number of firms which constitute that market and the behaviour of firms reflects the market conditions under which they operate. In the more specific discourses of management, like organizational behaviour and corporate strategy, again the emphasis is placed on the organization as a reflection of the world in which it operates and that world as a reflection of the organization itself.

In the broad and eclectic discourse of organizational behaviour, this relationship between the organization and its environment can be found in a number of debates and themes: for instance, Atkinson (1984) argues that the flexible firm is a response to a number of environmental influences such as market stagnation, job loss, uncertainty, technological advance and changes in working time; Pascale and Athos (1981) view corporate cultures as being partly reflective of a number of environmental issues such as the market in which the firm attempts to sell its products and the relationship the firm has with the society in which it operates; Bradley and Hill (1983) see quality circles and Total Quality Management in the west as a response to the competitive threat posed by Japanese firms; and Clark (1991) argues that the stress experienced by women in organizations can only be truly understood when it is not abstracted from the wider phenomenon of patriarchy and capitalism.

Whilst much of the organizational behaviour literature views the external environment simply as a collection of characteristics which influence organizations and firms, the literature on corporate strategy usually views the firm as an organization which faces a number of environmental challenges. Thus, Lynch (1997: 5) argues that 'Corporate strategy is concerned with an organisation's basic direction for the future; its ambitions, its resources and how it interacts with the world in which it operates'. On a similar theme, Certo and Peter (1994: 12) argue that strategic management is defined 'as a continuous process aimed at keeping an organisation matched to its environment'. For Chaharbaghi and Willis (1998) this is a central theme of much of the mainstream and orthodox strategy literature and draw attention to Porter's view of strategy as coping with competition, Hax's view of corporate strategy as responding to external opportunities and threats and the Prahalad and Doz view that strategy is now about global co-ordination.

The themes of this chapter lie with this view of organizations as a combination of both external circumstances and internal dynamics and, thus, the chapter has two specific points of reference. First, the global economy. As a concept, the global economy has attracted interest and debate in a number of different circles: political, industrial, commercial and academic and, for many, it is seen as the single biggest issue that will dominate policy making in the future. It has become an all-encompassing idea that will affect everyone and everything. The second point of reference is the responses of management to the changes brought about by the global economy. Management action and activity will be viewed in two paradigms: first, management as an optimizing activity where the emphasis is on gradual and incremental improvements to the workings of the organization – *doing the same things, only better*; second, management as an innovating activity where the emphasis is on radical changes to the working of the organization – *doing different and better things*.

The chapter is constructed in a fairly straightforward way. The first section provides a review of some of the literature on the global economy from a broad perspective to a narrower company based perspective. The second section introduces the concepts of management optimization and innovation. The third section considers the limitations of optimization as a generic management approach to competing globally and the final concluding section argues that a shift in paradigm from optimization to innovation is necessary for organizational success in the global economy.

THE GLOBAL ECONOMY

One of the main problems for individuals and organizations who wish to face up to, and prepare for, the challenges of globalization and the global economy is that it is a concept on which much has been written but little, of any substance or use, has been said. One of the main ways in which this problem manifests itself, is that it has become a concept which means many different things to many different people. For instance, Thurow (1996) thinks that globalization simply means that anything can be made anywhere and sold everywhere. Kanter (1995) views the processes of globalization through the creation of global consumers, Yergin and Stanislaw (1998) view the global economy as the triumph of market forces over state intervention, Yip (1989) sees the processes of globalization driven by firms and businesses, Bartlett and Ghoshal (1987) see globalization as overcoming national boundaries and Chaharbaghi and Cooper (1996) address the issue of corporate imperialism in a global economy. The problem is in making sense of the complexities of globalization; it is not a black and white issue with definite right or wrong answers. Even though everyone says something different, they can still all be correct and the result of this will always be confusion and not clarity or precision: simplification of the issues results in a loss of meaning and the maintenance of complexity results in a lack of understanding.

Much of this lack of understanding and clarity is caused by the unpredictability of the forces which are driving us inexorably towards the global economy; the only thing that we really know for sure is that the future will be very different to the past and all that is on offer to aid our understanding of this is speculation and educated, and uneducated, guesswork. For instance, Thurow (1996) argues that 'for some period of time the world economy will be played in an environment where the rules are in flux – and not clearly known', Prahalad and Doz (1986) argue that an understanding of what exactly the global economy means is 'beyond the analysis of existing rules' which will, according to Levitt (1983) create a new commercial reality. Whilst many agree on the fact that it is happening and many concur as to the causes of the phenomenon, few can agree on where it will end up: Levitt says it will allow firms to 'sell the same products in the same way everywhere', a view rejected by Douglas and Wind (1987) as 'naive and oversimplistic' and Bartlett and Ghoshal (1987) see the challenge of the global economy as 'managing across borders' whereas Ohmae (1989) sees it more as 'managing in a borderless world'. The result of this is increasingly emphatic and dogmatic consultant-speak based on banalities and generalities which involve prescriptive advice that companies should simply think about 'integrating their world-wide strategy' (Yip 1988).

There is no simple and easy way for us to delve into this mass of complexity to make sense of it all: there is no single tool of analysis or investigative model which will tell us all we need to know about the diverse and inter-related political, economic, social and technological factors which are driving the forces of globalization. In any case, even if this were possible and such a model existed, it is beyond the scope of one small chapter in a much longer book with a multiplicity of themes and, in any case, it is not the objective of this chapter. Instead, what we can do is provide a number of important and influential illustrations of the debate on globalization beginning at the broadest possible level before narrowing the terms of reference to focus on what it may all mean at the level of the firm.

One of the most celebrated explanations of what exactly is happening to the world of the late twentieth century and what it represents and signifies is Francis Fukuyama's *The End of History and the Last Man* (1992). Whilst this book, and the previous articles which contributed to it, do not have the global economy as the main object of analysis, it does provide some useful insights and a starting point for analysis if we wish to consider the big picture. Fukuyama offers a number of explanations as to what and why things happened as they did in the past and what this means for the future. He delivers four main propositions:

1 History is about the struggle between different ideas and ideologies and not about events; historical events are simply visible phenomena which punctuate and illustrate the historical battle of ideas.
2 By the end of the twentieth century, history was over because liberal democracy had won the political–ideological war and liberal, free market economics had won the economic–ideological war; this is reflected in the military defeat of fascism in the mid-twentieth century and the economic defeat of communism in the post-war years.
3 Even though the war has been won, there will still be the occasional battle to be fought. These battles will be fought in two arenas. First, there will be battles with non-liberal democratic states who have not yet caught on to the fact that they are doing the wrong thing and, second, there will be internal battles with individuals and groups, within liberal democratic states, who do not recognize that their war is already over and lost.

4 Even though history is over and the ideological war is won, the world will not necessarily be a better place for it. In the future we will move away from a world in which struggles are based on principle and ideals to a world in which the struggles are based on the best form of management for the new system.

Thus, for Fukuyama, the driving forces behind the creation of the global economy are primarily political and economic and he sees the creation of a world in which the dominant political and economic orthodoxy will triumph in all four corners of the globe. The main challenge, in this world without history, will be how best to manage the system, what Marcuse (1964) described as concerns about 'techniques, productivity and efficiency' when he argued about a similar trend three decades earlier.

As a counterpoint to these arguments, Thurow (1994) offers a different perspective. Rather than seeing the world as it stands at the end of the twentieth century in the grandiose terms of Fukuyama, Thurow offers an analysis of what these changes mean for those who want to be successful in the global economy. He argues that the effects are, first, a dramatic change in the rules of the game and, second, a logical and sequential change in how the game is to be played. His thesis is based on two points of reference. First, the past and what it took to be successful in the international economy of the last few decades. Thurow views the past as a struggle between two competing forms of capitalism. On the one hand was the British and American version, Anglo-Saxon Capitalism, where the emphasis was on consumption and the short term and, on the other, was the German and Japanese variant, Communitarian Capitalism, which was centred on investment and the long-term. Unsurprisingly, Thurow argues that German and Japanese success in the past was based on the fact that their form of capitalism was superior.

Thurow's second point of reference is the future which he says will be very different as the conditions of success will change. Societies and economies will still need to have the superior form of capitalism but this will have to be coupled with 'brainpower industries' such as robotics, avionics and telecommunications. This requires a massive shift in emphasis away from, for instance, access to natural resources as the foundation on which success is built towards access to human resources; the correct capitalism and the correct industries must be supplemented with a highly trained workforce and high calibre management.

Whichever analysis of the world in which we now live is examined, there is broad consensus on one issue; the triumph and onward march of capitalism. Previous generations saw conflict between capitalism and its contenders where the main objective of capitalism was victory and dominance. That clarity of mission is now over. The problem in the future will be that, whilst capitalism will continue to develop through globalization and the movement towards the global economy, there is no clear idea of how it will develop, what it will develop into and what it should develop into. One way in which we can overcome this global lack of signposts is to narrow the focus of our attention on to globalization at the level of the firm.

A general review of the available literature on the effects of the global economy on individual firms generates three broad themes: first, we have the acceptance that the world of tomorrow will be significantly different to the world of today; second, is the sequential argument that, under these very different conditions, managers and firms must behave in a very different manner if they want to be successful; finally, is the consultant approach which explains to firms what they have to do. We can develop these themes through investigation of four influential articles and books on the topic of surviving in the globalized world by Kanter (1995), Ohmae (1989), Bartlett and Ghoshal (1987) and Prahalad and Doz (1986).

First, the view that the world of tomorrow will be very different to the world we are currently experiencing: Kanter points out 'sweeping changes in the competitive landscape; Ohmae draws our attention to the fact that 'boundaries have largely disappeared'; Bartlett and Ghoshal begin their work by placing it into the context of 'recent changes in the international operating environment' and Prahalad and Doz give substance to these changes by emphasizing 'intense competition brought about by overseas competitors'.

Second, the common theme that firms who wish to be successful must, in a number of important and dramatic ways, change the way they behave, operate and perform: Kanter suggests that they must re-think their strategies and structures; Ohmae brings in a market focus by pointing out that 'customer needs have globalised, and we must globalise to meet them'; Bartlett and Ghoshal think that all this means 'not only a total strategic re-orientation but a major change in organisational capability as well' and Prahalad and Doz argue that we must now 'go beyond the analysis of existing rules and examine how determined companies often change those rules'.

In establishing the case for change, all four are arguing pretty much the same thing but where we do get a degree of significant diversity is in how these writers and consultants think that firms should change if they are to meet the challenges which they have drawn attention to. Kanter argues that there are four keys to success in the global economy and they all revolve around the organization's ability to think locally whilst keeping a global perspective. Thus managers, in their decision making, should take account of: diversity based on core skills (i.e. take what you already have into new areas); expansions and upgrades (i.e. invest locally to improve inputs); entrepreneurship and innovation (i.e. try doing new things not just old things); assimilation into local cultures (i.e. do not try and impose the culture of your corporation on local people). If this advice is a cross between the obvious and the specific, the advice offered by Ohmae is, perhaps, equally obvious if less specific. For success in the global economy the key is the ability of senior management for thinking globally and focusing on delivering value to customers which can only be achieved through specific and deep penetration of international markets rather than, presumably, general and shallow penetrations. Prahalad and Doz maintain the theme of the obvious by offering three guidelines to management action: global integration in the management of dispersed geographical activities; global co-ordination in the management of resource commitments; and local responsiveness in the allocation of resources to meet local needs. Finally, Bartlett and Ghoshal substitute the obvious, the specific and the general for unintelligible jargon that has no real meaning at all: firms should move from 'unidimensional to multidimensional capabilities', 'symmetry to differentiation', 'dependence or independence to inter-dependence', 'control to co-ordination and co-option' and in making these moves they need to be capable of 'overcoming simplifying assumptions'. If they can do all these things they will be successful because they are 'sustaining a dynamic balance'.

To return to an earlier theme, both this broad and narrow description of the main causes and consequences of globalization provides no real clarity and no real precision as it is such a loose concept that we can make it mean pretty much whatever we want it to: it can be driven by politics or economics or ideology; its agents are governments or firms or individuals; it will result in a world either with or without borders; consumer tastes will be differentiated or the same. The result of this lack of predictability and uncertainty about the future leads, inevitably, to fears about the future which can only trigger defensive mechanisms and responses:

Listen carefully (*The Economist*, 10 December 1994).

Four billion people enter the world's economy . . . their salaries are very low . . . goods can be manufactured anywhere in the world . . . cheap labour countries sell large quantities of their products to the developed world . . . the number of people living in poverty rises sharply . . . this is the way to national suicide (Goldsmith 1995: 122).

I can see only one emergency following upon another as wave follows upon wave (Eksteins 1989: 291)

The global landscape of the mid 1990s was unpredicted and unpredictable, and it remains in flux (Taniguchi 1995: 11).

Domestic issues are increasingly affected by international actors and events that national governments cannot hope to control . . . national policy autonomy is being undermined (Washington 1993: 3).

Globalisation reduces the effectiveness of policies at the national level (Archibugi and Michie 1997: 172).

The sovereign right of rich and poor states alike to control activities within their borders is challenged by their increasing inability to regulate global economic relationships (Clapp 1997: 136).

A flood of new entrants into world markets puts at risk the employment of persons in high wage areas (Hindley 1994).

Skilled workers watch their jobs migrate overseas (*New York Times*, 28 August 1995).

Do you hear a giant sucking sound of jobs and investment disappearing from the United States across the Rio Grande to Mexico (*The Economist*, 10 December 1994).

Globalised firms tend to locate their activities where they can be carried out in the most cost effective and productive way (Gonenc 1997:11).

Growing inequality, both within and between countries, and a threat of exclusion faced by many people are further effects of globalisation (Oman 1996: 35).

The issue is not whether we block Third World development but whether we countenance the recreation of the Third World in the First (Williams *et al.* 1995a: 92).

Globalisation causes the world-wide division of have and have-not countries to be mirrored within the borders of even the richest nations (Carlson and Goldman, 1994: 20).

The full benefits of expanding international trade can be achieved only by economies that are fully adaptable (OECD Press Release 5 June 1991).

Capitalism is not static, it's dynamic . . . clinging to old policies is a losing proposition (Perot 1993: 142).

We are already feeling the effects of globalization and it is leading to uncertainty about both the past and future. Uncertainty about the past is a result of the changing rules of the game. Nations and societies became powerful and wealthy on the back of manufacturing industries but these are conditions for past, not future, success. Williams *et al.* (1995a) point out that key, strategic manufacturing industries are facing a crisis of cost recovery caused by market saturation and the entrance of new players into established markets. Cars and electronics may have driven economic progress in the developed world for half a century but they can no longer drive progress in the future. Similarly, we are uncertain and uneasy about the rules of the game in the future, which results in what Chaharbaghi and Newman (1997) call a 'crisis of wealth creation'. Either way, whether we are looking forwards or backwards, these immediate effects of the processes of globalization mean that things have to change. The past was built on manufacturing as the engine of social and economic progress and manufacturing can no longer fulfil that role. The lesson that the British have learnt from 25 years of de-industrialization is that it is easier to manage, regulate and develop a society that has the capacity to create wealth. Just as in businesses from Hanson to Toyota, the only three things that matter are cash, more cash and even more cash (Williams *et al.* 1994a), for the global economy to deliver security and opportunity the only three things that matter are wealth, more wealth and even more wealth.

Whilst we are not there yet, the global economy is inevitable; at some point in the future it will have arrived. It is because it is both inevitable and irresistible that we should embrace it. In previous generations the rules of the different political, economic, social and technological games that society played were by and large set at the national level by governments. In the future this will be no more; it is unlikely that the rules of the games will be set by governments or national organizations but they will be set by the forces of globalization. The earlier we embrace and accept the changes that these forces will bring, the more chance we have, not of halting them in their tracks, but of shaping their direction. When asked in 1992 what he thought the main issue in the presidential election campaign was, Bill Clinton replied 'It's the economy, stupid.' He was only half right. Ask what the major issue will be in the next few years about the shape and form of society and the response must be 'It's the global economy, stupid'. To further develop these points we must now shift the focus of analysis away from the environment towards the firm itself and in particular the options available to management under these global conditions.

MANAGEMENT PARADIGMS: OPTIMIZATION AND INNOVATION

Despite the many ambiguities, occasional vagueness and frequent contradictions in the literature on the global economy, one thing is certain: The future international environment in which business will operate will be very different to the international environment of the past. If the writers cannot agree on why things are changing or what things will change into, they are all agreed that the forces of globalization will bring ever quicker and ever more dynamic change. In the mainstream literature on strategic management, for instance, organizational success is often attributed to the ability of senior management to ensure that the organization's activities are matched to the demands of the environment and so it is to management that we must now turn. This section will argue that management activity falls into one of two broad paradigms: first, is the optimization paradigm where the emphasis is on slow and gradual changes and improvements to products and processes and, second, is the innovation paradigm where the emphasis is on revolutionary change to products and processes via the creation of new market values. Just as we can only understand organizations if we do not abstract them from their environment, and recognize that they are shaped by both internal and external forces, similarly, to understand management, and the decisions that managers take, we must always examine the environmental context in which decision making occurs. When we consider these paradigms of management we must, therefore, first consider the (international) environment in which each form can prosper and succeed.

In order for optimization as a management approach to be successful, two conditions must be met in the firm's external environment. First, there must be limited competition. If strategy is about a race to one ideal position (Porter 1996) then the race must be between the few rather than the many. Second, the external conditions under which all competitors in that race operate, must be broadly similar. Williams *et al.* (1995a) use the concept of the 'social settlement' to explain, analyse and quantify these structural conditions where the social settlement under which any firm operates is a result of a combination of wages paid, hours worked and social charges levied on firms by national governments and other institutions. If these structural external conditions are met, then management does indeed become a privileged and powerful actor whose decisions really do matter and, thus, management can make the difference between success and failure.

The points raised so far can be further developed if we examine competition in the international cars business. This is an example which matters for two main reasons. First, it is an industry which has enormous economic significance; in the developed world between 20 and 40 per cent of manufacturing employment is directly and indirectly dependent on this single industry (Williams *et al.* 1994a), it is, therefore, a business which has significantly 'changed the world'. Second, cars are the biggest, most complex and expensive individual items that are traded internationally. The average family saloon contains 20 000 components and its manufacture involves upwards of 10 million individual processes and so, the broad lesson is that if you can make cars quickly and efficiently you can make any manufactured product quickly and efficiently.

Management in the cars business begins with a definition of manufacturing as a transformation activity: at the level of an industry it is the transformation of raw materials into finished goods and, at the level of the firm, it is the transformation of purchased components (and services) into the final product which is then sold in the market place. Within this transformation process the concentration is on the control of labour costs which, over the whole business cycle, usually average out at 70 per cent of the total value added generated. Put another way, 70 per cent of the total internal costs of converting a series of components into a motor car is in the wages, salaries and other financial rewards of the employees. Under these conditions, the optimization paradigm finds substance in the busting of bottlenecks, the achievement of production flow, the reduction of indirect activities, automation and so on. These activities all represent incremental changes to the physical processes and products in order to reduce labour's share of value-added and increase the cash surplus available for the renewal of products and capital stock internally and distribution, externally, to shareholders and any other rentiers. The race is a slow one where fleeting and temporary advantage passes to those with the best physical interventions.

One of the most popular explanations of this optimization approach is the Womack, Jones and Roos text, *The Machine that Changed the World* (1990). This text provided the executive summary for the much more detailed and extensive International Motor Vehicle Programme whose main aim was to discover why the Japanese motor industry systematically and comprehensively trashed the American car industry during the 1980s. The Womack *et al.* explanation focuses attention on Japanese management practices which they collectively call 'lean production'. This is explained as an holistic approach to the transformation process and involves techniques such as designing products for ease of manufacture, managing relationships with suppliers through the *keiretsu* networks, the achievement of flow in the assembly processes and a build to order system to service the market. For the purposes of this chapter, the techniques of lean production are less important than the claims made for it. Womack *et al.* (1990: 26) claim, first, that lean production 'takes half the human effort in the factory' thus fulfilling the need to reduce labour costs and, second, 'is a system the whole world should adopt, and as quickly as possible' (Womack *et al.* 1990: 225) thus providing a universal, best practice approach to manufacturing.

A more recent, non-manufacturing specific approach to optimization has come from Hammer and Champy's *Re-engineering the Corporation: A Manifesto for Business Revolution* (1993) which suggests the reconstruction of processes within organizations. Thus, in this illustration, the emphasis shifts away from the Fordist focus on activities to an holistic approach to processes which, in a manufacturing sense, would include the physical processes involved in transforming inputs into outputs and, in service industries would involve the processes from, for example, a telephone complaint through to its remedy. Again, the rhetoric of re-engineering is as significant as the techniques. Hammer and Champy (1993: 34) argue that re-engineering the corporation involves 'starting all over, starting from scratch' and that it is a collection of management practices which are essentially forward looking; 'How people and companies did things yesterday doesn't matter to the business re-engineer' (Hammer and Champy 1993: 66).

In making the shift from the optimization paradigm of management to the innovation paradigm, the first point of reference is the source of competitive advantage derived from the activities of the organization or firm. In the optimization paradigm, we are primarily considering competition amongst a relatively small number of firms who are all engaged in the delivery of a similar product which is made using roughly the same processes. In this context, small and incremental changes to the product and processes can deliver competitive advantage, albeit an advantage that is usually transient and temporary in nature. In essence, this paradigm of management involves continually doing the same things in slightly different ways. On the other hand, innovation, as a management paradigm, takes the opposite approach as it is based on the view of competitive advantage being secured through difference rather than similarity; companies compete on the basis of their uniqueness. One example of this mentioned earlier is Lester Thurow's view of participation in the global economy being dependent on brainpower industries where, he suggests, economic and industrial progress in the future will be driven by industries whose competitive advantage is secured through the application of unique and valuable knowledge.

If the source of competitive advantage is the main broad difference between these two management paradigms, we can narrow and focus the analysis by considering some of the specific characteristics of innovation as compared to optimization. The two main characteristics we need to consider are, first, the relationship between the firm and its environment and, second, the nature of the products created within each paradigm. Unlike the optimization paradigm, where the environment is usually viewed as a collection of factors and forces which influence the firm, one of the main thrusts of innovative management is to reverse this process whereby the firm seeks to influence and shape its environment. In optimization, as we shall see later, the environment is the main factor which defines the direction of the organization and what can, and cannot, be done, but in innovation decisions about future directions and possibilities originate within the firm or organization concerned.

At the level of the product, the main difference between the two paradigms is in what the product embodies and represents. In the case of optimization, and the example of cars discussed earlier, the product embodies the physical processes of transformation from raw materials into finished goods. Therefore, products like cars are a collection of materials, capital and labour and this is what we, as consumers, pay for. In the case of innovation, however, the product represents and embodies something very different. Whilst physically the product will still be a collection of materials, capital and labour, this is not what we pay for and not how we secure and attain satisfaction and value from our purchases. Consumer satisfaction and value is attained, not from the physical representation of the product, but from the knowledge that the product embodies. In explaining the concept of innovation, Chaharbaghi and Newman (1996) raise a number of interesting points:

> Innovation . . . is a term which affects all individuals within an organisation and encompasses many complex social issues. As a result, it can be interpreted too broadly or differently by individuals with different world views, thus appearing to mean everything and ultimately nothing. For innovation to become the goal of individuals and organisations it must first be understood (Chaharbaghi and Newman 1996: 1).

Perhaps the best way to start to develop this understanding is through examination of an example, in this case the pharmaceuticals industry (see Froud *et al.* 1997 for a more detailed explanation of the dynamics of this industry).

The pharmaceuticals industry has hit the headlines in 1998 through the release, into the UK market, of the latest wonder drug, Viagra. This a product which is aimed at the restoration of pride, confidence and self-esteem among certain middle-aged men who suffer from the problem of impotence. Currently, in the UK, the product retails for £27 per pill whilst the cost of manufacture of a single pill is a tiny and insignificant fraction of this amount. The drug retails for that price, at a staggering mark-up on the cost involved in actually making it, because what the middle-aged man is buying is not the materials, capital and labour in the transformation process that delivers the pill, but the knowledge that the pill embodies. This example, therefore, tells us a great deal about the external circumstances and internal dynamics of the companies in the industry from which we can draw a number of general lessons and principles about innovation.

Internally, the focus of pharmaceuticals companies is on the development of new knowledge through the research and development process. Unlike in cars, for instance, where the focus is on improvements to the manufacturing process, the transformation of ingredients into a finished drug is only an incidental and minor cost. Thus we see significant financial resources allocated to the development of new knowledge. On a global basis, the top 10 pharmaceutical companies in the world collectively allocate in excess of $10 billion per year to research and development, a figure equivalent to over 15 per cent of aggregate sales revenue. At the national level, this is a UK industry which has, over the last 20 years or so, bucked the trend of de-industrialization and hollowing out: as most of UK manufacturing has retreated into low technology product markets, the UK pharmaceuticals industry has retained its position as a major global player in a high technology industry and the most successful British companies continue to allocate up to 25 per cent of the value-added they generate to research and development.

This development of new knowledge internally is crucial because, if it is successful, it results in the creation of new market values and, therefore, gives the opportunity to companies to shape, influence and (occasionally) control the environment in which they operate. In this particular industry, this is the result of two factors. First, is the legal protection offered by the patent system which secures a dominant market position, shelter from competition for up to 10 years and all the power associated with monopoly suppliers. Second, it creates a captive market. At the crudest and simplest level, people will always get sick, find new ways of becoming sick and demand to be cured from whatever sicknesses they have contracted. In the developed world, through the provision of national systems of healthcare such as the NHS in the UK, there are agencies to meet the demand for cures through the purchasing of patent protected pharmaceuticals at premium prices. In this system, the end user is even protected from high prices as the drugs are purchased through the NHS middle man who pays the biggest chunk of the real price: over the last 10 years, the NHS has seen its spending on patent protected pharmaceuticals almost triple in real terms.

From this example the advantages of competing on the basis of knowledge are clear, straightforward and dramatic: From the development of new knowledge, substance is provided in the form of a drug that marks a significant leap forward in medical treatment and technology and the result is that the environment changes dramatically in the favour of the organization who, not only is protected from competition and imitation, but also has a guaranteed buyer to shield end users from the costs of development. None of these benefits is available to companies who attempt to secure advantage through optimization as this is a paradigm where there are no more secrets and where, as the next section explains, external circumstances can serve to frustrate any positive action that management wishes to take.

THE LIMITS OF OPTIMIZATION

The two most recent examples of optimization approaches to management discussed previously, 'lean production' and 'business process re-engineering', have been criticized on a number of fronts and in a number of different ways. For example, Williams *et al.* (1992b) suggest that the Womack *et al.* explanation of success, resulting from Japanese management techniques, is flawed for four main reasons: first, they supply no real evidence to justify the assertion that Japanese lean production is new and different compared to American mass production; second, those who argue in favour of lean production as best management practice, do so on the basis of exaggerated claims about Japanese superiority; third, there is no real explanation as to how the Japanese succeed in taking labour costs out of the manufacturing processes; finally, Womack *et al.* do not establish that the results of lean production will be balanced trade and multi-regional production.

Just as the literature which is positive about lean production contains a number of flaws and half truths, so too is it the case with business process re-engineering. For instance, Strassmann (1994) suggests that there are two significant flaws in the processes of re-engineering that Hammer and Champy do not address in sufficient detail: first, it results in corporate violence which discards any possibility of consensus management and, second, the literature is more concerned with ending the past than it is with building something positive for the future. In a similar way, Willmott (1995) argues that those within organizations who sign up both for and to the re-engineering process are acting like 'turkeys voting for Christmas' as the whole concept is more likely to result in de-motivation rather than motivation.

Whilst recognizing that these two different explanations of best practice management contain a number of technical flaws, the aim of this chapter is not to engage in a debate at that level. This is for two reasons: first, these are arguments and discussions that are well rehearsed and have been presented elsewhere and a summary of those arguments can add little, if anything, to the overall debate; second, regardless of the flaws in these two explanations, we would argue that their weaknesses are more fundamental as what they represent, management as optimization, is a strategy which can only work under a certain set of circumstances: optimization can only deliver organizational success, in whatever form that organizational success is to be defined and explained, if the external conditions faced by all firms in the particular market or industry are broadly similar. These external pre-requisites for optimization will become harder to find as we move ever closer towards the global economy. We can examine this point through the example of competition in the car industry in the 1980s between Japan and the USA.

The example of Japan verses America in the car industry is an important illustration of the themes of this chapter for a number of reasons. First, as we have previously explained, the car industry has a great deal of wider economic and industrial significance; at the height of the trans-Pacific trade battle of the 1980s, over 40 per cent of the total American trade deficit was in cars and car related products. Second, the lean production debate, as an explanation of Japanese success, is a debate which has moved out of solely academic circles and has found currency in commercial, business and political discussions. Finally, the results of the battle in this industry can be used to illustrate the shape of things to come as we move ever closer to the global economy.

The explanation that we would propose for Japanese success begins by returning to two earlier themes of this chapter: the power of management under specific external conditions and the organization as a combination of internal and external factors. In this section of the chapter we draw heavily on our previous work on this issue and present similar evidence, albeit in a slightly different setting and context (see Williams *et al.* 1992b, 1994a, 1995a, 1995b, 1996).

Our main criticism of the Womack *et al.* attribution of Japanese success to the power of Japanese management is that it largely abstracts the organization from the environment in which it operates and from which it draws a number of influences. In explaining Japanese success as a bundle of management techniques, from supplier relations to productive interventions through to market relationships, Womack *et al.* tell only half the story; we would emphasize that for a more rounded and holistic explanation we need to consider a whole series of factors that lie, not only physically outside of the organizations concerned, but also lie outside of the control of these organizations. Therefore, we will also include in our analysis an examination of three issues; product market conditions, the social settlement conditions of wages, hours worked and social costs and the industrial structure in which the companies whose names appear on the products are located. Let us, therefore, begin with an examination of the market conditions in which the Japanese and American industries operated in the 1980s.

For American car firms, there are two important characteristics of the domestic market: first it is saturated and mature and, second, it is prone to massive cyclical fluctuations. In terms of saturation and maturity, the American new car market has shown no overall growth since the early 1970s: in 1973, the market peaked at almost 13.5 million units but, in no single year since then, has that level of sales been achieved. This is due to massive levels of saturation as, by the late 1980s, the park of cars in the USA meant that there were three cars on the road for every two economically active people. This problem of saturation is compounded by the problem of cyclicality in a market that is extremely sensitive to changes in the wider economic conditions: repeat or replacement purchases can always be postponed in years when the economic outlook is less than optimistic. The pattern in the USA is for rapid and significant losses in market demand on the economic downturn and for these losses to be only gradually regained on the economic upturn which delivers, at best, demand only at the levels of the previous peak.

As a counterpoint to these market conditions, we see opposite behaviour in the domestic Japanese market. Throughout the 1980s, we saw almost uninterrupted growth in the demand for new cars such that, between 1979 and 1990, the market doubled in size to peak at over 5 million new units per year. The benefits of market growth in Japan are positively compounded by the lack of any real cyclical reductions in the total level of demand for new cars. Where there was an occasional contraction in demand, recovery was achieved within a year and movement along the trajectory of growth was resumed.

These market conditions have two main effects on companies which operate in this particular industry. First, it has significant implications for the supply and productive side of the organizations as, without increases in demand and sales, the product cannot be pulled through the transformation process at anything like the speed required for low cost, high cash generation manufacturing. The second problem is that, in saturated markets, loss of market share can have rapid and disastrous effects: in a growing market, the loss of 30 per cent of market share can, under special circumstances, be tolerated, but, in the USA where every unit increase in Japanese sales meant a unit decrease in domestic manufacturer sales, the effect of Japanese penetration was to reduce American output (and, *ceteris paribus,* employment) by almost one third.

In our earlier work we have argued that one of the main consequences of globalization is a significant and structural shift in the nature of competition. In the past, competition was viewed in terms of one product versus another product, one company versus another company or one set of management practices versus another set of management practices. In the global economy, however, an equally important dimension of competition will be between different social settlements as economies enter into international competition at a different point on this development trajectory. An examination of each of the variables of the social settlement, wages paid, hours worked and social costs, shows significant, important and influential differences between Japan and the United States throughout the 1980s:

- Between 1980 and 1990 there were large fluctuations in the wage levels of the two industries but one trend is clear; Japanese wages were always significantly lower than American wages from a high of 50 per cent lower in the mid-1980s to 10 per cent lower in the late 1980s.
- Hours worked shows a degree of similarity with the evidence on wages paid, albeit without the fluctuations. If we average total hours worked in the two industries throughout the 1980s, we see that Japanese workers typically put in 13 per cent more labour time than their American counterparts over the period of a year. Basic economic calculations mean that, *ceteris paribus,* to get the same level of output, American firms had to employ 13 per cent more workers than their Japanese competitors.
- Differences in hours worked takes on added significance if the social costs incurred by the firm are based on the number of people employed. In this area the Japanese enjoyed a twofold advantage over the Americans. First, they were operating from a smaller base for social charges given the differences in hours worked and, second, social costs were significantly lower: Throughout the 1980s, social contributions averaged just under 30 per cent of hourly labour costs in Japan compared to over 40 per cent in the USA.

In placing the two industries into this broad environmental and social settlement context, we can learn a valuable lesson about the nature of competition faced by the Americans in the 1980s. The Japanese social settlement meant that their car industry could employ less people, earning lower wages and working longer hours with less social costs than their American competitors and, in doing so, secure a significant cost advantage.

The industrial organization of Japanese firms into *keiretsu* networks is usually explained in terms of the productive benefits that result: it is often viewed in terms of the more efficient management of the whole raw materials into finished goods process. However, we can move beyond these productionist reasons and examine the hard economic case for vertical disintegration if we consider the two variables of wage gradient from final assembler to primary component manufacturer and the distribution of employment within this broad industry structure. In examining the wage gradient, we notice more that is similar between Japan and the USA than that which is different. In both cases we see a steep wage gradient where wages paid in the smallest component suppliers are about half of those paid in the largest final assemblers whose name appears on the finished product: in Japan wages at the bottom of the industry are 56 per cent of those at the top and, in the USA, the difference is slightly more acute as wages are just 51 per cent at the bottom compared to the top. This relatively small difference between the two industries takes on added significance if we add into the calculation the extra dimension of employment structures.

The advantage for the Japanese industry compared to the American industry was that they were able to load employment at the bottom of the industry into those companies whose wages were lowest. Thus, we see that over one quarter of all Japanese employment in the motor industry was contained in the firms with the lowest wages compared to just under 8 per cent of American employment in the industry being in similar firms. Thus, whilst Womack *et al.* explain Japanese vertical disintegration in terms of cross ownership, just-in-time manufacturing and close relationships, we would explain it as an economic expedient which provides and allows for access to low wage supplier networks within the domestic economy. These differences in external circumstances between the two industries, market conditions, social settlement and industrial structure, have a significant role to play in defining the nature of competition between the American and Japanese car industries during the 1980s. The effects of these differences is quantified in Table 10.1.

The net result of these three external conditions is that the Japanese industry enjoyed a cost advantage over the Americans of over $1300 per car in 1988 which, in the aggregate, delivered a $3 billion cash flow advantage to the Japanese car industry as a whole before (superior) management enters into the equation. On their own, these factors go a long way to explaining why the Japanese won and the Americans lost; with or without productive inferiority, it was always likely that the Americans would not be able to overcome these structural handicaps. The next logical step to take in this argument is that, if we can provide evidence to show that the gap between the American and Japanese industries was much smaller than Womack *et al.* suggest, then, in terms of influencing performance, external forces are much more powerful than the agency of management.

Table 10.1 US motor sector structural cost handicaps per vehicle against the Japanese motor sector, 1988

Cyclicality burden arising because fall in demand from cyclical peak of 1986 raises sector build hours by 20 hours per vehicle	**$505**
Extra social costs arising from American requirement for extra workers because each American worker supplies 2000 hours per year against 2300 hours in Japan	**$321**
Extra American wage costs arising from an industry structure which displaces less employment into small firms paying lower wages	**$543**

Source: Williams *et al.* 1994a, 1995b, 1996.

The claim for lean production is that it 'takes half the human effort in the factory' and this claim is based on a narrow analysis of a few processes in the final assembly plants of a few companies: as we have already seen, the Japanese industry is characterized by, amongst other things, vertical disintegration and so, even in examining all of the processes within companies like Honda, Nissan and Toyota, the examination is limited to between just 13 and 20 per cent of all the processes which go into the manufacture of a car. We can introduce additional measures of performance to examine productivity at the industry level and, at the company level, labour productivity and the ability to generate cash flow. Table 10.2 summarizes industry level productivity and introduces two further points of reference, the German and South Korean industries.

There are a number of significant points to draw out of this statistical exhibit. First, whilst there was a difference in productive performance between the Japanese and American industries in the 1980s, it was by no means as significant as the 2:1 difference suggested by Womack *et al.*; in the good years of market growth in the USA, when the companies in the industry were able to load their factories and plants, the gap narrows significantly. Second, the Japanese show no real improvement in industry productivity at all in the 1980s and seem stuck on industry build hours of roughly 130 per car. Finally, this evidence suggests a degree of similarity in productive performance which is reflected in more specific data from company level analysis.

We have argued elsewhere that the global car industry is characterized, in productivity terms, by similar performing companies in the developed world and poor

Table 10.2 Build hours per vehicle in the US, Japanese, German and South Korean motor vehicle manufacturing industries

Year	USA	Japan	Germany	South Korea
1969	173	280	269	n/a
1970	189	254	278	n/a
1971	762	224	270	n/a
1972	169	217	268	3033
1973	167	203	266	2244
1974	182	200	308	2378
1975	174	176	279	1475
1976	163	173	246	1360
1977	165	158	258	1270
1278	170	146	278	1006
1979	179	147	294	917
1980	202	135	318	1255
1981	204	138	271	1118
1982	204	140	267	839
1983	163	139	262	725
1984	165	141	266	670
1985	155	139	258	572
1986	154	133	266	453
1987	173	132	255	348
1988	174	132	256	352
1989	170	132	286	n/a

Source: Williams *et al.* 1995a: 78.

performing companies in the developing world. This chapter provides neither the time nor the place for a restatement of the minutiae of statistical and empirical detail and so the broad picture will have to suffice. In any case readers are both invited and encouraged to consult the more detailed articles and papers on which much of this chapter is based. In analysing labour productivity and the related ability of companies in the industry to generate cash flow for product and process investment and renewal, we concluded that 'most American and Japanese car assemblers are average performers which share common problems about cost recovery' (Williams *et al.* 1996: 128).

In all of this there is one harsh and bitter lesson for the American car industry. Optimization, in the form of lean production, will only work if it is used in competition between firms which operate under broadly the same external conditions. Japanese entry into the American car market was achieved, not on the basis of superior and excellent management of the production system, but on the basis of a more favourable set of external circumstances; the more significant the external differences, the less significant is management as a privileged agent of organizational change. The lesson we can learn about the future from the Japanese car industry is no less important: small differences in the productive characteristics of organizations and management practices can be more than offset by significant differences in external circumstances; success is possible with or without superior management.

These lessons can be explained further through analysis of the next wave of new entrants into established markets which followed the Japanese; the south-east Asian tiger economies and, in particular, the entrance of the South Koreans in the 1980s and after. If we refer back to Table 10.2, the single most striking characteristic of the South Korean car industry is its productive, and therefore, management, inferiority: compared to the established players, the Koreans' inferiority was, at worst, in the region of 10:1 and, at best, in the region of 3:1 or 4:1. Despite this overwhelming disadvantage, the Korean car industry was, during the 1980s, three times as cash generative as the German car industry and 10 per cent more cash generative than the Japanese car industry. The causes and consequences of Japanese success in the American car market during the 1980s, produce a set of events and characteristics which cannot be viewed as a one-off event but rather as an illustration of a phenomenon which will be continually replicated as more and more economies enter into established global markets for products like cars. In this case the future may very well be like the past only more amplified and this raises difficult and uncomfortable questions for social scientists about the role and influence of management.

CONCLUSION: THE CASE FOR INNOVATION

Porter (1996) argues that the key role of the strategic manager is found in the making of trade-offs between what to do and what not to do: management is, first, about the analysis of present and future circumstances, both within and outside the organization, and, second, about making informed decisions, based on the results of that analysis, about how to move the organization into the best possible position in order to secure an enduring competitive advantage. If this is the principle on which the game of management is based, our analysis suggests that the rules under which the game is played are changing rapidly as a result of the movement towards the global economy. This raises two broad possibilities at the level of the firm and elsewhere: first, if competition in industries and firms, where optimization is the dominant management paradigm, is more about external conditions than internal improvements, at the national level we can move to undermine the social settlement; second, if we wish to maintain the social settlement, then the basis on which firms secure a competitive advantage must change from optimization to innovation.

First, let us consider policies which undermine the social settlement which is, after all, the British experience of the last two decades. In broad terms these policies, at the national level, are about reducing wages, intensifying the work experience and the erosion of social fringes (Williams *et al.* 1994b). We can illustrate these aims and objectives in a number of ways. Up until recently, for instance, we have opted out of the Social Charter which was aimed at the economic expedient of improving competitiveness through an undermining of the social settlement and the political expedient of standing up for ourselves in Europe. As another example, the trade union reforms of the 1980s were all about asserting the right and ability of management to optimize within the workplace without interference from other agencies. The result of these policies was supposed to be that, first, the UK would become the first choice for any inward investment into Europe and, second, that it would create a set of external economic conditions which would allow British manufacturing to flourish and, therefore, give it the ability to conquer world markets. We would argue, however, that these sort of policies are not only socially undesirable, but that they are also economically irrational and futile as all they have, and will, serve to do is give away what we already have without securing anything new and/or better for the future.

Whilst the UK has become a relatively low wage outlying member of the European Union, the record achieved on attracting inward investment is, at best, patchy. If we exclude American investment which has, by and large, already been here for 30 years, through the 1980s and into the 1990s, employment in Japanese firms in the UK increased by just 50 000 which comes nowhere near to offsetting the loss of almost 3 million domestic manufacturing jobs (Williams *et al.* 1992). In any case, inward investment is usually about short-term market access and not long-term productive generosity and, as more recent events have shown, when the conditions of cost recovery deteriorate, foreign capital tends to retreat to a holding position back at the sheltered domestic base. Just as we have failed to attract significant inward investment, with a couple of notable exceptions we have also failed to generate products which can find a place in contested world markets: at the peak of our economic cycles, the deficit on British manufactured trade usually approaches £20 billion (Williams *et al.* 1994b).

Whatever the economic statistics of the past show, policies that are aimed at forcing wage levels to flex downwards are policies which cannot continue in the long term. For example, in order to deliver similar external conditions to those enjoyed by South Korean new entrants, British wages would have to be halved, working hours doubled and social benefits be all but removed. The problem here is that the South Korean social settlement is, by the general standards of new entrants, relatively generous and, as the past shows, new entrants always come in under significantly lower social settlement conditions than their predecessors. Erskine May suggests that the characteristics of parliamentary language should be 'good temper and moderation' and, compared to new entrants into the future global economy, we may yet come to view previous new entrants as having these characteristics.

We have consistently argued elsewhere that policies which undermine the social settlement should be replaced by policies which actively serve to defend it: at the national level this is to ensure than we do not 'countenance the recreation of the Third World in the First' (Williams *et al.* 1995a: 92). As socially worthy a goal as this may be, it can only be achieved if one of two conditions are met. First, it can be achieved if we see a movement away from global free trade back to a world where trade is limited to just those which operate with a social floor. The may be neither possible nor desirable for a number of reasons. It may not be possible as it represents a significant movement away from the forces which are driving globalization and it may be undesirable as it would, in effect, make permanent the economic exclusion of two-thirds of the world's population from the global economy. The second, and, therefore, more worthy, condition which must be met is a shift away from optimization as the dominant management paradigm towards innovation.

The advantage of innovation as a set of management principles is that, not only does it render external social settlement differences less important, but that it also creates a form of international competition which can serve to defend the existing generous social settlements without undermining the ability of others to engage in meaningful economic activity. Optimization can deliver on none of these aims and objectives because, even under similar external conditions, the do-it-yourself manuals for management like *The Machine that Changed the World* and *Re-engineering the Corporation* provide high levels of transparency of techniques, transferability of processes and replicability of outcomes and results. Innovation is crucial because it changes the basis of competition from being the same only better to being different and unique. With innovation the similarities between companies and differences in external circumstances cease to be the basis of competitive advantage.

The literature on the global economy suggests that the world of tomorrow will be fundamentally different to the world of today without ever reconciling the argument as to what exactly that world will look like. The aim of this chapter was to illustrate this argument and not to engage in it and we would much rather engage in a debate about what the world of tomorrow should look like. In a chapter of this length it is impossible to sketch anything but the broadest details and general principles and the intention, therefore, has not been to emphatically and dogmatically close one debate but rather to open a new one. The next challenge for ourselves, and other like-minded social scientists, is to move the debate forward through the addition of depth to the analysis in order that we can provide the means through which extended and permanent participation in the global economy can be achieved.

REFERENCES

Archibugi, D. and Michie, J. (1997) *Technology, Globalisation and Economic Performance*, Cambridge University Press, Cambridge.

Atkinson, J. (1984) The flexible firm, in Clark, H., Chandler, J. and Barry, J., *Organisations and Identities: Text and Readings in Organisational Behaviour*, (1994) Chapman and Hall, London.

Bartlett, C. and Ghoshal, S. (1987) Managing across borders: new organisational responses, *Sloan Management Review* 29 (1): 43–53.

Bradley, K. and Hill, S. (1983) What quality circles are, in Clark, H., Chandler, J. and Barry, J., *Organisations and Identities: Text and Readings in Organisational Behaviour*, (1994) Chapman and Hall, London.

Carlson, R. and Goldman, B. (1994) *Fast Forward*, Harper Business, New York.

Certo, C. and Peter, D. (1994) *Strategic Management*, International Thompson Business Press, New York.

Chaharbaghi, K. and Cooper, M. (1996) Corporate Imperialism, mimeo, University of East London.

Chaharbaghi, K. and Newman, V. (1996) Innovating: towards an integrated learning model, *Management Decision*, 34 (4).

Chaharbaghi, K. and Newman, V. (1997) The crisis of wealth creation, *Management Decision*, 35 (7).

Chaharbaghi, K. and Willis, R. (1998) Strategy: The missing link between continuous revolution and constant evolution, *International Journal of Operations and Production Management*, 18 (9/10).

Clapp, J. (1997) *Surviving Globalisation*, Macmillan, Basingstoke.

Clark, H. (1991) *Women, Work and Stress,* University of East London Occasional Papers on Business, Economy and Society, Number 3.

Douglas, S.P. and Wind, Y. (1987) The myth of globalisation, *Columbia Journal of World Business*, Winter Issue: 19–29.

Eksteins, M. (1989) *Rites of Spring: The Great War and the Birth of the Modern Age,* Houghton Mifflin, Boston, MA.

Fitzgerald, P. (1995) Pharmaceuticals '95: Drug delivery systems, *Chemical Marketing Reporter*, September.

Froud, J., Haslam, C., Johal, S., Williams, K. and Willis, R. (1997) British Pharmaceuticals: Exemplary Success or Cautionary Tale? Paper presented at the ESF-EMOT Workshop: Globalisation and Industrial Transformation in Europe, Malaga, 9–12 January 1997 in Hirst, P. and Thompson, G. *Globalisation in Question*, Polity Press, Cambridge.

Fukuyama, F. (1992) *The End of History and the Last Man*, Penguin Books, London.

Gerry, R. (1995) Pharmaceuticals '95: Biotech Rebounds, *Chemical Marketing Reporter*, September.

Goldsmith, J. (1995) *The Response: GATT and Global Free Trade*, Macmillan, Basingstoke.

Gonenc, R. (1997) *Industrial Competitiveness: Benchmarking Business Environments in the Global Economy*, OECD.

Hammer, M. and Champy, J. (1993) *Re-engineering the Corporation: A Manifesto for Business Revolution*, Harper Business, New York.

Hindley, B. (1994) *The Goldsmith Fallacy: Why Open Trade and GATT are Best*, Rochester Paper Number 3, Centre for Policy Studies.

Kanter, R.M. (1995) Thriving Locally in the Global Economy, *Harvard Business Review* 75 (5): 151–61.

Levitt, T. (1983) The Globalisation of Markets, *Harvard Business Review* 61 (3): 92–102.

Lynch, R. (1997) *Corporate Strategy*, Pitman Publishing, London.

Marcuse, H. (1964) *One-Dimensional Man*, Beacon, Boston, MA.

OECD Press Release, 5 June 1991.

Ohmae, K. (1989) Managing in a Borderless World, *Harvard Business Review* 67 (3): 152–62.

Oman, C. (1996) *The Policy Challenges of Globalisation and Regionalisation*, Policy Brief No. 11, OECD Development Centre.

Pascale, R. and Athos, A. (1981) Corporate cultures, in Clark, H., Chandler, J. and Barry, J. (1994) *Organisations and Identities: Text and Readings in Organisational Behaviour,* Chapman and Hall, London.

Perot, R. (1993) *Not For Sale At Any Price*, Hyperion, New York.

Porter, M. (1996) What is Strategy? Operational effectiveness is not Strategy, Harvard Business Review, November.

Prahalad, C.K. and Doz, Y. (1986*) The Multinational Mission: Balancing Local Demands and Global Vision*, The Free Press, New York.

Strassmann, P. (1994) The Rap on Re-Engineering, *Computer World* 28 (39): 119–21.

Taniguchi, M. (1995) *Linkages: OECD and Major Developing Economies*, OECD.

Thurow, L. (1994) *Head to Head: The Coming Economic Battle among Japan, Europe and America*, Nicholas Brierly Publishing, New York.

Thurow, L. (1996) *The Future of Capitalism*, Nicholas Brierly Publishing, New York.

Washington, S. (1993) *Globalisation: Challenges and Opportunities for Government*, OECD Working Papers No 28.

Wells, H.G. (1940) *The New World Order*, Secker and Warburg, London.

Williams, K., Haslam, C., Williams, J., Cutler, T., Adcroft, A. and Johal, S. (1992a) Against lean production, *Economy and Society*, 21 (3).

Williams, K., Haslam, C., Williams, J., Adcroft, A. and Johal, S. (1992b) *Factories or Warehouses: Japanese Manufacturing Foreign Direct Investment in Britain and the United States*, University of East London Occasional Papers on Business, Economy and Society, Number 6.

Williams, K., Haslam, C., Williams, J., Johal, S. with Adcroft, A. (1994a) *Cars: Analysis, History, Cases*, Berghahn Books, Oxford.

Williams, K., Haslam, C., Williams, J., Johal, S., Adcroft, A. and Willis, R. (1994b) Defend the social settlement: a memo for Labour, *Renewal*, 1 (3).

Williams, K., Haslam, C., Williams, J., Johal, S., Adcroft, A. and Willis, R. (1995a) The crisis of cost recovery and the waste of the industrialised nations, *Competition and Change: The Journal of Global Political Economy*, 1.

Williams, K., Haslam, C., Johal, S., Williams, J. and Adcroft, A. (1995b) Beyond management: problems of the average car company in Babson, S. (ed.) *Lean Work: Empowerment and Exploitation in the Global Auto Industry*, Wayne State University Press, Detroit.

Williams, K., Haslam, C., Johal, S., Williams, J. and Adcroft, A. (1996) The limits of management: problems of the average car company, in Glover, I. and Hughes, M. *The Professional Managerial Class: Contemporary British Management in the Pursuer Mode*, Avebury, Aldershot.

Willmott, H. (1995) Should personnel managers be more critical of BPR?, *People Management*, 23 (3).

Womack, J., Jones, D. and Roos, D. (1990) *The Machine that Changed the World*, Rawson Associates, New York.

Yergin, D. and Stanislaw, J. (1998) *The Commanding Heights: The Battle Between Government and the Marketplace That is Remaking the Modern World*, Simon and Schuster, New York.

Yip, G.S. (1989) Global Strategy in a World of Nations, *Sloan Management Review.*

Yip, G.S., Loewe, P.M. and Yoshino, M.Y. (1988) How to Take Your Company to the Global Market, *Columbia Journal of World Business*, Winter Issue: 37–48.

Section 4
The Politics of Organization and Management

These chapters share a concern with the relationship between business and politics. The first – by Ian Pirie – represents a critical review of the literature on business ethics. It opens with a sketch of the historical development of the subject from the early years of the twentieth century, noting a shift in emphasis since the first books on the subject were written. In the late 1960s and early 1970s, it is suggested, a concern emerged for the 'social responsibility of business' – interpreted by one writer as a question of 'institutional standards and responsibility'. More recently the emphasis is thought by Pirie to have shifted towards 'the moral capacity of individuals'.

The literature at any point in time is seen as coloured both by what is occurring (the kind of ethical problems thrown up by business) and by the wider social, economic and political context (both the structures and the values prevalent at the time). It is thought likely that changes in the socio-economic context will lead to different kinds of ethical problems and to different attitudes to the regulation of business. A fruitful exploration of 'business ethics' it is argued must, therefore, take the socio-economic context into account, and throw light on the relationship between this and the prevalent ethical values. It must also address the question of 'power', both in business and of business.

In surveying the literature from this perspective a number of viewpoints are identified. The first sees capitalism as in itself a just or ethical system; where problems occur, therefore, the explanation must lie either in some 'interference' with the market mechanism, or in the individual failings of managers. This viewpoint recognizes the individual, economic and social levels, but has little or nothing to say about the organizational level. When writers on business ethics do discuss the organization, they are seen as falling into several groups: one stresses the importance of values in organizational culture, and the need for managers to develop the 'right' values; another stresses the effects of the organization on behaviour; a third deals with ethical theories as such. These approaches are criticized not only as 'managerial', but as failing to deal with the socio-economic context.

Pirie argues that a more satisfactory viewpoint involves consideration of the social level, through either 'stakeholder' or 'contract' theories. Of these the former is found to be the least satisfactory as its scope is too limited and its approach still largely managerial. The contract approach is seen as more useful, provided it tackles the 'political' issues around conflicts of value, and enforcement. Its main strength, however, is thought to lie in its raising the question: what would such a contract between business and society be for? In other words, what are the socio-economic and political conditions which might be necessary for truly ethical business? And deeper still, what kind of society do we want to see? This broader social politics approach is the one favoured by the author.

A similarly critical approach is adopted in the second chapter. It, too, seeks to move beyond the limitations of an organizational view and connect organizational policies to wider political concerns. Like Pirie in the preceding chapter, Neale starts by setting contemporary debates in their historical context, providing a sketch of the development of social responsibility in business, this time from the nineteenth century onwards.

The chapter then examines the influence of new social movements on organizational behaviour and the translation of their demands into the language of 'stakeholding'. Taking equal opportunities policies and environmental management systems as examples, it suggests that managers selectively interpret movement demands to make them compatible with existing management assumptions and practices. The author's approach owes much to social constructionism, and its understanding of how managers shape stakeholder influence and seek control through the creation of systems devoted to monitoring the achievement of measurable targets. It recognizes, however, that social constructivist accounts can exaggerate the power of managers to determine outcomes – for if managers construct their own stakeholders, they do not construct them just as they please. In exceptional situations, as with Brent Spar in 1995, new social movements can force managements to re-consider their decisions from a different perspective, particularly if this is one that is shared by other stakeholders. Yet always, in the private sector, managers are seen as constrained by a structural framework, which gives primacy to one stakeholder group, shareholders, and recognizes other stakeholder interests only to the extent that these are compatible with the promotion of shareholder value.

Together these two chapters represent a challenge to much of the conventional literature on management and organizational behaviour. In seeking to locate managerial concerns both historically and socially they move beyond the rather narrow approach often seen in the literature. In adopting a critical perspective towards existing institutions, which conventional approaches often take as given, they also represent a more radical approach. Implicit in both chapters, too, is the presumed centrality of ethical and social considerations which are all too often marginalized; treated as a separate issue which can be turned to after the issues of profit and efficiency have been dealt with. What these chapters suggest is that business and management practices reflect the nature of the society of which they are part. And our own society is one which does not allow humans to flourish, equal opportunity to prevail, or the environment to be protected.

In separating these chapters out from others there is, of course, the danger of perpetuating the marginalization of political and ethical concerns. There are, however, many links between these chapters and others in this book. The concern with the constraints imposed by the nature of contemporary capitalism is, for example, explored in the chapters by Johnston, Murton and by Adcroft and Willis. Indeed all the other chapters, too, are concerned to connect organization and management thought and practice to wider ethical and political concerns. In this way, these chapters can be seen not as isolated from the others, which is precisely how ethics tends to be seen in the conventional management literature, but as an integral part of a book which sets out to place management and organization in its social and political context – raising questions about the nature of what it is as well as about what it might and should become.

The social politics of business ethics 11

Ian Pirie

INTRODUCTION

> It is not logic that makes men reasonable, nor the science of ethics that makes men good (Oscar Wilde: Aristotle at Afternoon Tea).

Over the last few years, there has been a growth in the number of books and articles which have appeared on the subject of business ethics, and there is a flourishing *Journal of Business Ethics*. A new academic field is clearly establishing itself, and it has the characteristics one might expect of a new and 'underdeveloped' field: in particular, lack of agreement over basic terms, methodology and boundaries (Donaldson 1989).

However, the earliest articles and books specifically addressing the topic of business ethics or social responsibility appeared in the late 1960s and early 1970s, and there has been a marked change in emphasis since then, with a clear shift from 'social' to 'ethical' concerns. As Nash (1990) says, the recent change in emphasis in the literature reflects a 'shift from problems of institutional responsibility and institutional mechanisms for encouraging conformity to high standards' to a preoccupation with the 'moral capacity of individuals'.

This chapter aims to examine this shift, by reviewing a number of books published since the 1960s. It will examine how thinking in this area relates to the historical context (for which the reader is also directed to the chapter by Alan Neale). It will primarily argue that questions of business ethics cannot be detached from social and political dimensions, nor reduced to problems of individual morality. An assessment will be made of the different positions taken, especially in some of the recent literature, in relation to business ethics.

First, below, three historical 'phases' are identified in writing about business ethics and social responsibility. These phases correspond to changes both in business and in the economic/political context, and go some way towards explaining why attitudes to business ethics have changed.

However, it is misleading to suggest that different business malpractices simply reflect 'different times', as Pearson (1995) seems to do: 'the excesses of one era produce periods of reaction', or that the literature simply reflects public reaction to the changing patterns of behaviour by business organizations or individuals; for example, Nash (1990) says: 'often discussion grows out of a major collapse of moral standards in a specific business activity'. These are both over-simplifications. On the first point: while in certain periods a particular kind of malpractice might be more prominent, there is also a fair amount of continuity; for example, while price-fixing was prevalent in the 1950s (Nash 1990), several cement companies were found guilty in August 1995 of the same offence. And on the second: we still have to explain and understand the different patterns of behaviour, as well as the changing reactions to it, in particular why we no longer stress 'institutional responsibility and institutional mechanisms'.

The aim of a historical approach should surely be to avoid the extremes of contingency and determinism. We cannot explain away or excuse poor ethical standards by attributing them to 'what was done' at the time. Nor can it be convincingly maintained that there are no patterns to business behaviour, no general trends or principles. The view taken here is that two interrelated aspects of historical change are crucial to understanding business ethics: the first is political (in the broad sense, that is shifts in the distribution of power), and the second is social (viz. changes in dominant ideas).

HISTORICAL OVERVIEW

Phase 1 – Origins

The origins of concern over ethical/responsible business go right back to the early years of the century, especially in the USA. (Luthans *et al*. 1972). Key factors were:

- the new power of large corporations and 'robber barons', (leading to anti-trust legislation in the USA);
- the inter-war depression, which many saw as caused by unregulated business;
- the growth of the trade union and socialist movements, and of social democracy in politics.

The main political responses to the dangers of corporate power and unregulated capitalism were anti-trust legislation in the USA, and government involvement in regulating the economy, through Keynesianism and the New Deal.

Phase 2 – post Second World War

The consumer boom of the 1950s was followed by a reaction against excessive materialism and inequalities in the 1960s. There was a disillusion with mere consumerism, especially on the part of middle-class youth; Sethi (1971) refers to the 'post-depression era population, whose primary concern was not economic rationality'; and there were protests against corruption, poverty, war and imperialism. In the early 1970s writers were very conscious of the 'times . . . a-changing', and the public was increasingly aware of the power and impact of the corporation – the 'corporate wall' of Sethi's title – both at home and abroad (e.g. Dow chemicals in Vietnam).

The main pre-occupations of books at this time were:

- incidents of business activity which had caused public protest – cases discussed in Sethi's book include: the Santa Barbara oil spill, resistance to the building of nuclear power plants, ITT and Chile;

- crises in the social and natural environments: Steade (1975) covers the topics: profit, business power, quality of working life, pollution, social renewal;
- challenges to the economic system of capitalism and in the political sphere – see Perrow (1972), and Heilbroner and London (1975), where Heilbroner writes of the 'long-run challenge to business civilisation'.

Some had seen a 'revolution' happening around 1968, and although this view turned out to be over-dramatic, the social and political climate undoubtedly changed with the development of the (middle class) consumer movement, and the more radical new social movements around feminism, ecology, etc.

Given this more public discussion, much of the literature at this time focuses on ways of regulating business, and making business 'accountable'. Thus Luthans, Hodgetts, Thompson (1984) includes a section on 'social activism'; Galbraith, in *The New Industrial State* (1967) writes of 'countervailing powers' that would hold big business in check. The expression 'social responsibility of business' gained ground at this point also (Donaldson 1973). In this phase, with the exception of Baumhart's (1961) *Harvard Business Review* article on 'business ethics', terms like 'social responsibility' or 'social issues' were preferred.

Phase 3 – the Thatcher/Reagan era

With the encouragement of 'enterprise', privatization, and de-regulation, public concern turned to the internal affairs of businesses, and the reprehensible behaviour of prominent businessmen, as well as – perhaps more than – the social impact of business. A list of scandals which have caused discussion would include: Guinness, Maxwell, BCCI, British Airways, and the pay awards to Directors of ex-public utilities.

With the breakdown of the Soviet economies, and the apparent worldwide dominance of capitalism, perhaps it is inevitable that criticisms of 'the system' are less often heard, and blame for problems is laid on individuals.

This brief sketch shows how changes in the political climate, as well as the changing business organizational structures led to the study of business ethics becoming separated from the wider social and ideological context. Other reasons why this has happened are more to do with the defensive attitude of business to its socio-political environment, an attitude which is reflected in the narrowness of business and management theory.

Thus, apart from the writings of social reformers such as Robert Owen or the advocates of workers' co-operatives, and apart from the activities of a few 'philanthropical' companies, *public* demand for higher standards of conduct on the part of business has arisen only *after* a crisis of some sort, or after a decision has been made which has had negative consequences. Thus, again with the exception of a few companies, business is being pushed into social/ethical considerations by *outside* factors – by popular protest, or media, group, or government pressure; there may be many more companies now, even a majority, with ethical codes of behaviour, but it is certainly possible to argue that these moves came about only as reactions to public criticism, and therefore as self-interested survival tactics.[1]

Also, as Donaldson (1989) points out, reforming figures such as Owen, Lord Shaftesbury, even the successful Quaker entrepreneurs, 'rarely feature in the management literature, and never prominently'; and he adds: 'OB books which include ethics are rare'. In other words, management studies have been concerned with, as it were, the norm – and (as will be further shown below) have kept ethics 'at a distance'; and where ethics is treated, it is regarded as being a different discipline.

PERSPECTIVES ON ETHICS

However, there is surely a danger in a focus on 'ethics' which separates individuals in business from their organizations, and the organization from its social context, in order simply to question the ethics of specific actions. To adopt such a purely 'internalist' perspective[2] means, as Shaw and Barry (1995) point out, that our ethics will be based solely on general principles and abstract reasoning – it will not help us to understand how problems have arisen and what can be done to prevent them, let alone saying anything about the kind of society in which we want to live. Such an internalist approach also stops at the level of the individual, putting aside both the organization and the 'system' as a whole,[3] and it is the contention here that this is inadequate.

The case for integrating ethics with social concerns can be made in several ways. First, as Trevino and Nelson (1995) argue: 'our ethical conduct is influenced (and, to a large degree controlled) by our environment'. These authors make this point to argue for a key role for managers in creating a highly ethical culture. However, it equally indicates that if managers or political leaders demonstrate *low* ethical standards, others will surely follow!

Second, what we *view as* ethical or unethical is often a reflection of economic/ political trends; the acceptability in the 1980s of rampant individualism and even greed is the clearest example, but the well-known view that 'what's good for General Motors is good for America' can also be seen in this light.

And finally, (as a surprisingly large number of writers in the field note) there is a conflict between the values, particularly the profit-drive, of capitalism and the requirement of socially responsible/ethical behaviour. Thus Nash (1990) notes the likely conflict between 'common-sense values' (such as 'honesty, fairness, respect for others, service, promise-keeping, prudence and trustworthiness'), and the pressures of the market place. Similarly, Jennifer Jackson (in Almond 1995) accepts that it is often more difficult for people in business to practise the virtues of temperance, compassion and a sense of justice. Other writers recognize that in the real world, lying, fraud, deception and theft sometimes lead to greater profits. What is perhaps more surprising is that, despite making these observations, the writers cited are all optimistic about the prospect of rendering business more ethical.

I would wish to argue, therefore, that understanding the issue of ethical business requires developing a method of analysis which goes beyond the traditional disciplines of management and organizational behaviour and which considers business in its socio-political context. This approach clearly identifies ethics with the question of the 'good society', as well as with questions of power and responsibility.[4]

This being said, we need now to look more closely at different approaches to business ethics in the literature, and to try to group them according to their stances on the relationship between ethics and the social context.

FIRST PERSPECTIVE: THE 'HAPPY CAPITALISTS'

The first group comprises writers who do consider the social context, but they either separate it explicitly from any problems which might be identified in regard to ethical behaviour in business, or they argue that the economic context of 'free-market capitalism and liberalism' itself creates the highest ethical standards. As they see individual self-interest as the motive force behind the market, these writers lack a theory of organizations (or, in more recent new right analyses, they view organizations as protectors of vested interests, and a threat to the just order of a liberal market economy).

The best-known advocate of free-market capitalism must be Milton Friedman, whose 1962 statement that the only responsibility business has is to its shareholders is often quoted in texts in this field. For example:

> There is only one social responsibility of business – to use its resources and engage in activities designed to increase its profits so long as it stays within the rules of the game, engages in open and free competition, without deception and fraud (Friedman 1962).

Also:

> If businessmen do have a social responsibility other than making maximum profits for their shareholders, how are they to know what it is? Can self-selected private individuals decide what the social interest is? (Friedman 1962).

The basis of his argument is, of course, that capitalism is a just system, promoting the maximum freedom, provided no one 'interferes' with the market mechanism. He identifies 'morality' as a personal matter, and argues that business is not capable of making ethical judgements.

Presumably, according to this view, when damage or harm is done by an enterprise this must either be because the market has *not* been made the supreme arbiter (i.e. the vested interests of a group such as a trade union, or a pressure group have been allowed to override the market), or because of some accident, or individual error or misdemeanour on the part of a manager. Friedman stresses the ownership rights of shareholders, and goes so far as to say that a manager who uses corporate funds for some charitable purpose is diverting the shareholders' property to uses other than those they intended, and certainly not to their benefit, and this is unethical since it is tantamount to theft!

The simplest response to this is to take a few cases of damage or harm done, and to try to find the causes. With such incidents as:[5] the Exxon Valdez oil spill; ITT's involvement in Chile (in the overthrowing of a legitimately elected government);[6] or Nestlé's sale of dried milk for babies in the third world, despite evidence that it has caused deaths from dehydration – it is hard to be convinced by explanations simply in terms of accidents, errors, individual misdeeds, or interference with the market. To take the case of the pollution caused by Exxon as an example, here were involved not only the ship's captain, and the oil company, but the oil consortium Aleyeska, and several government agencies; in addition, a major part was played by public reaction over the damage to wildlife, which the company seriously underestimated.

Similar positions to Milton Friedman's were taken by Professor H.B. Acton, and by John Wood of the Institute for Economic Affairs, in papers published by the

Foundation for Business Responsibilities in 1972 and in 1973.[7] Professor Acton also revives Samuel Smiles's victorian doctrine of self-help. In a debate with Michael Ivens of Aims of Industry, John Wood described a CBI recommendation that companies should consider an ethical dimension in corporate activities as 'a recipe for corporate hemlock'. Wood went on to describe social responsibility as diverting business into 'ill-defined, conflicting and usually transitory social objectives, in place of the pursuit of profit, or avoidance of loss.' Perhaps surprisingly, Michael Ivens' retort was that people adopting this position were 'romantic brutalists' – such splits on the political right have since become even more pronounced!

I think it is fair to say that all of these writers rely on stressing the tremendous gains made by (free-market) capitalism, and have little or nothing to say about the negative social impact of business. Acton credits capitalism with bringing:

> Free speech, free movement, free trade, free thought, exploration of the earth and oceans, an ideal of peaceful domesticity, water colour drawing, conversation pieces, the novel and domestic drama (sic!) (Acton 1972: 9).

Moreover, the model of capitalism being used surely belongs to some (mythological) point in the past? Modern patterns of ownership and control, and modern business organizations, are so much more complex, the world is so much more inter-related, while also manifesting such gross inequalities, that talk of market mechanisms treating people equally and creating equal freedom cannot be taken seriously. However, at least these writers acknowledge the impact of the social context on business.

Other writers who see a positive ethical aspect to capitalism (e.g. Burke *et al.* 1993) recognize that not all managers act ethically, and they try to identify reasons for this – such as short-term market pressures, or organizational phenomena. This position will be examined separately below.

SECOND PERSPECTIVE: ORGANIZATIONAL APPROACHES

Several recent books acknowledge that business ethics is a matter of concern, but then make the assumption that the problem can best be addressed through managers' understanding and training. Thus they set out to convey to managers an understanding of what ethics consists of, what principles might guide someone faced with an ethical dilemma, what kind of dilemmas managers may find themselves in, and how to think through problems. Such writers are usually quite keen on 'ethical codes', which are believed to help produce an ethical organizational culture. The concern with organizations here is limited to questions of how they can be adapted and used to increase ethical standards; the individual is seen in consensual terms, as a member of a team, rather than as potentially in conflict, or as in any way constrained by the organization.

There are several useful features to this approach, but many limitations. One valuable outcome is to remind us that not all ethical problems are at the 'macro' level – many arise *within* the organization, around, for example: sexual harassment and discrimination, positive discrimination/affirmative action in recruitment or promotion, 'perks' and pilfering, conflicts of interest, whistle-blowing, etc.

However, it is surely over-simplistic to say, as Solomon and Hansen (1985) do, that the problem is merely that managers and employees are not always aware of the potential harm that could arise from a decision or action, or that 'ethical errors are the result of ethical naivete' and 'most people in business who do wrong do so not because they are wicked but because they think they are trapped and do not even consider the ethical significance of their actions'. It may be that an individual really *is* trapped, especially given the increasing pressures of a competitive and insecure environment.

We must surely distinguish between situations where someone:

- is *not aware* of the likely consequences;
- is faced with more than one 'right' action, and has to choose the best, when different ethical principles are involved – what I call an ethical *dilemma*;
- knows what the right thing is to do, but *chooses* not to do it; and
- wants to act ethically, but finds themselves *unable* to, because of some constraint or other.

With the first of these kinds of situation, education or training will help, though maybe only up to a point: there is some disagreement about how people develop a moral sense, what stages they go through, whether men and women have the same moral sense, etc. (see Snell 1993; also Barry and Clark in Davies 1997 for discussion of Kohlberg, Gilligan, etc.). The second kind of situation is more difficult, and the more you 'know' about ethics the more difficult it may become! Often in the literature the recommendation to managers in this kind of situation is to do what *feels* right – a rather shaky position?

But there is a perennial philosophical and practical problem in the third situation: knowing what is right or wrong is one thing, but being convinced I *should* do what is right is another. The philosophical problem here is: how do I know I should do right? And although to philosophers an argument such as Kant's demonstration of the link between being rational and doing one's duty may be convincing, it is something of a tall order to convey to the average employee or manager! (See, however, Sorell and Hendry 1994). The practical problem here concerns motivation, for experience tells us that not everyone is motivated towards duty (the Kantian view) or happiness (the Utilitarian argument – where we should all be motivated to seek the maximum happiness for the maximum number) – some want power, excitement, revenge – and business is an ideal means to get these.

With regard to the fourth situation, where the organizational context is the most obvious constraint on individual ethical behaviour, a number of writers discuss ways of improving corporate culture to obviate this. Collins and O'Rourke (1994), for example, suggest a three-step procedure for identifying and improving an organization's ethics:

1 analyse how power is (a) obtained (b) maintained (an approach based on Machiavelli?) by managers in relation to the different stakeholders (see below);
2 make a judgement based on: are promises kept, are harms avoided, how much mutual aid is practised, are persons and property respected, how much honesty is there?
3 identify necessary changes in organizational structure, operating policies, and reward systems.

As a procedural guide this looks fine, but again it does not tell us how to ensure managers *want* 'mutual aid, respect and honesty' in an organization; and it gives the impression that once the 'necessary changes' have been identified – by the manager? – the problem is solved!

Donaldson (1992: 94) also recognizes the powerful constraints on individual behaviour in organizations, such as what he calls 'intervening processes' in the 'cultural milieu'. He goes on to discuss in some detail (ch. 5) 'ethical structures for industry', and in doing so recognizes the importance of external factors such as law enforcement. However, the main thrust of this otherwise useful book seems to be that, 'all business activity is value-driven', and that 'ethical and efficiency values can be reconciled'. Indicative of this emphasis on values is the conclusion that where there have been 'transgressions' in the financial services, this is due to either 'low values or confused ones'. Given this perspective, solutions proposed are mainly to do with 'consciousness-raising', and issues of conflicting power and interests are played down.

Within the 'organizational' perspective, moreover, there is further disagreement over what kinds of organization are in fact developing, let alone how these will affect individuals' (ethical) behaviour. Of particular concern is the new, leaner, 'post-modern' organization.

On the 'optimistic' side there is Pearson (1995). This writer is sceptical abut anything practical emerging either from using philosophy to promote ethics in business, or from any business ethics initiatives; as he puts it 'Kant never had to run a business'! He also argues that the globalization of markets and of technology is producing global corporate alliances, where each company focuses on its core competencies, and outsources in areas where other companies have advantages; this will be accompanied by loosely-coupled networks of autonomous teams and fragmented forms of organization (rather than bureaucratic hierarchies). In this world, business will depend more than ever on 'trust', and consequently managers and workers will be pushed into more professional, ethical ways of acting. A similar position is taken by Hutton (1995).

On the 'pessimistic' side, there is Nash (1990), who suggests that:

- the de-layering of management will deprive organizations of experienced managers, leaving more temptations for short-term interests to take priority;
- workers generally have less job security, and there are more low-paid workers and a bigger gap emerging between their pay and that of top management, causing resentment rather than a sense of solidarity and commitment;
- traditional methods of leadership such as personal contact and communication are all but obsolete, so ethical values cannot be passed on.

Clearly one cannot consider the 'organization' without being soon drawn into considering external factors as well. It might seem, however, that – ideological commitments aside – the only way of deciding between the optimists and the pessimists will be to watch what happens: will there be more or less ethical behaviour by and in organizations?

Those not wishing to 'wait and see' in this way may find it useful to examine the work of another group of writers who point to the psychological or cognitive factors that are at work in organizations, not all of which will promote ethical behaviour. Among such internal factors, Hartley (1993) mentions custom, groupthink, indifference and expediency – though he does not attempt to analyse or evaluate their influence.

A more thorough analysis of such factors is provided by Trevino and Nelson (1995). For example, they discuss a most revealing personal recollection on the part of D.A. Gioia, who was one of the managers at the time Ford produced the Pinto model. This car had a vulnerable petrol tank placed in a dangerous position, such that when a car was struck from the rear it could explode. Despite a number of fatal accidents, Ford refused to recall the car, (Gioia was responsible for recall decisions) and even decided, after calculations, that it would be cheaper to meet the costs of being sued for fatalities than to recall and redesign the car. Gioia discusses his own actions in terms of 'script processing' – a technique we all are said to use to get through the pressure of making many decisions: we develop a script which sets up a behaviour pattern that does away with the need to inspect each decision in detail. Gioia simply thought that the Pinto case was just like a number of others he had encountered, and he was under stress from a heavy workload, so he went on to 'autopilot'.

Trevino and Nelson (1995) also identify 'multiple ethical selves' and 'role behaviour' – where we use different ethical standards according to the situation we are in, or the role we are playing. A similar discussion can be found in Hartley (1993), who examines 'groupthink' in the case of General Motors' Corvair vs. Ralph Nader. An example here might be the common belief, that business is a particular kind of situation, more analogous to a game like poker than to other parts of life, where 'bluffing' is quite acceptable, (see Carr 1968 and Drummond and Bain 1994). With 'groupthink', an individual's ethics unthinkingly reflects the group's – just as we often take our society's ethical standards for granted.

Other writers (e.g. Donaldson 1989) refer to the disturbing findings of Stanley Milgram, who demonstrated how we are prepared to sacrifice our individual conscience when faced with a figure of authority who tells us what we are doing is right.

It would seem to me that there is considerable evidence that organizations affect individuals' ethics, and that a lot more work could usefully be done at this level. However, most of the literature, again, takes a 'managerial' approach, and this ducks the question: who ensures managers are ethical? It also assumes that managers can 'empower' employees to be more ethical – but what of the 'empowerment paradox': – is empowerment something that can be given, or do workers have to take it for themselves? (Gandz and Bird 1996). Nash (1990) questions whether the modern manager believes in empowerment, and does not want his/her workers to be 'diligent followers and functionaries many indifferent, or fearful of punishment, or desirous of a good career, or too obedient'? (the quotation is actually taken from Primo Levi's description of a typical member of the Nazi SS).

Despite the limitations of the organizational approach to business ethics, a (sometimes) useful feature lies in the 'brief guide to ethics' that most of these books contain. Unlike the apologists for 'pure capitalism' mentioned above, (who sometimes give the impression that Adam Smith said it all – or that we can simply amalgamate Adam Smith, the Utilitarians and Kant), and unlike Pearson (1995) (who, as noted above, is sceptical of philosophy), these writers at least recognize that philosophers have struggled over ethics for two millennia, and some acknowledge that there is still a good deal of disagreement.

However, these writers are not philosophers, and they naturally sometimes produce rather sketchy summaries of mainstream ethical theories. Moreover, all are constrained by the fact that, as noted, ethics and business/management studies have evolved as quite separate disciplines (since the early political economists that is). Given these constraints and the disagreements among philosophers on ethics, it is not surprising that some authors simply conclude that you should take from all the different theories whatever you can!

There is no space here to comment on these summaries of ethics, but I would not wish to suggest it is a waste of time getting to grips with the 'classical' theories of ethics. To point the reader in what I hope is a useful direction, and to give a flavour of the breadth of the field, books which are about business ethics but which contain good summaries of the philosophical aspects are (in order of publication):

- Hoffman, W.M. and Frederick, R.E. (1984 , reprinted 1995) has useful articles by: J. Rawls, R. Nozick, J.J.C. Smart, Irving Kristol and Kai Nielson; but the book raises more questions than answers as to how to apply these to the cases cited.
- Donaldson, J. (1989) has a useful glossary of terms in ethics. It is worth noting also that he includes industry and trades unions in his study. Although he has a chapter entitled 'Critical business ethics', this is more a plea for the three key principles he identifies: pluralism, the golden rule, and autonomy, rather than containing what one might expect in the way of a 'critical' stance.
- Jennings, M.M. (1993) this has a good section on a wide range of ethical theories, and makes an attempt at integrating the theories with the cases, but much of the time this feels a bit contrived.
- Hartley, R.F. (1993) is based on detailed cases, and the working-together of ethical issues and real-life events is most helpful, and the philosophical level is not too demanding.
- Snell, R. (1993) emphasizes moral reasoning, and adapts a model put forward by Kohlberg (see Davies 1997) of different levels of ethical reasoning. A useful way of 'sorting out' the many different ethical theories!
- Sorell, T. and Hendry, J. (1994) have a very high level both of clear theoretical explanation (making even Kant sound fresh!) and of integration into current problems.
- French, P.A. (1995) is at a high philosophical level, but with helpful 'philosopher-boxes'. A central concern is the corporation as an entity.

THIRD PERSPECTIVE: THE STAKEHOLDER APPROACH AND MANAGERIALISM

One perspective which begins to go beyond the business organization to the social context uses the stakeholder model.[8] This acknowledges the changed patterns of ownership and control that characterize business in the twentieth century, and argues that a business's loyalty is *not* only to its stockholders, but to all those who have a stake or interest in the firm's activities.

This model, it can be argued (Weiss 1994), may deal with the objection that an organization has no intentionality or conscience, and therefore we cannot speak of 'ethical business', but only of ethical individuals. For what is focused on here is the relationships of interest and power surrounding management. Weiss recommends a series of steps for managers: first, draw up a map of stakeholders – customers, suppliers, employees, stockholders – next, identify the interests and power of each, any coalitions that might exist or come into existence; finally, decide what responsibilities or (moral) obligations you have to each stakeholder.

The positive aspect of this procedure lies in its recognition that business affects a wide range of people, who have rights, or a kind of property claim, against the business, and that blind loyalty to stockholders may deprive others of their rights, or do them unjustifiable harm. 'Ethics' then comes in as a way of sorting out any conflicts and moral dilemmas which may arise – though how far it can help to prioritize between different stakeholders is debatable.

A further 'selling point' for some writers (including Weiss) is the argument that a business will not survive if it ignores its stakeholders' rights or needs. This provides, therefore, what philosophers call a 'prudential' obligation – you would be wise, for your own safety or self-interest, to do your duty.

A more conceptually 'loose' version of the stakeholder approach is taken by writers like Clutterbuck and Snow (1990, 1992). Here are included: customers, employees, suppliers, shareholders, the political arena, the broader community, the environment. This approach necessitates a different means of appeal to motivate managers, and the language here is of 'mutual benefit' (seen as a step on from enlightened self-interest, but clearly closely related). These writers, together with Carmichael and Drummond (1989), stress that 'good business pays', and 'ethical failures cost'. It is argued that: in a period of skills shortage, employees will prefer to work for a company with a good (ethical) reputation, and will stay longer; customer loyalty will be stronger; suppliers will meet higher standards ('good business is good to do business with'); government intervention will be avoided; relationships with legislators and bureaucrats will be improved; you will be better able to influence the (trading) environment; and that companies which are sensitive to their environment 'tend to be better and faster at perceiving and taking advantage of social and market change'.

On the face of it this is a very strong prudential case! However, no one is claiming that high ethical standards guarantee success, or even survival – profit must still come first; and, you *may* even do well with low ethical standards. Thus, even Carmichael and Drummond (1989: 77), can only go so far as to say: 'High-ethics, low-profit organisations do not survive. High-profit, low-ethics organisations *should* not survive.' It can also be argued that while there is currently a 'climate' in which ethical business may do well, this may just be a passing fashion.

Two major areas of limitation can de identified with the whole stakeholder, managerial approach. First, following from the question of who is included as a stakeholder (see also ch. 3 of Hoffman and Frederick (1995)): if narrowly interpreted, the concept is based on property or interest relationships, some of which may be enshrined in law, thus providing a strong basis for regulation; but could we then include (e.g.) the natural environment, or animals? And if not, how are they to be protected?

If, on the other hand, you interpret stakeholders in a wide sense, as Clutterbuck does, then the basis of the model is either a belief in ongoing social concern about ethical standards, or a moral position about our responsibilities to each other, and this gives less scope for enforcement and presents a weaker argument than the prudential one.

Moreover, when identifying who is affected by a business do we take into account direct effects only? For example, when the subsidiary of a multinational company does well, and improves the standard of living of the immediate community, does it have any responsibility towards the wider area or region, where standards of living will relatively decline?

The second area where this approach is open to criticism is its managerial slant. First, stakeholders as identified by management may exclude people who feel themselves affected by a business – and a powerful business organization can always manipulate the perceptions of others.[9] Second, this approach must involve prioritizing, and it is interesting to note that Weiss (1994) (whose own view is that the 'primary obligation is to the economic mandates of the owners') quotes a survey of managers, who when asked to rank their stakeholders in order of importance, put themselves at the top! No surprise? On the other hand, perhaps it is a surprise that at the bottom of the list were both shareholders and elected officials and government bureaucrats!

So we are left with the essentially political question: who decides who the stakeholders are? In the survey mentioned above it was found that only 38 per cent of the firms gather external views on business ethics, only 29 per cent have non-executive directors for this purpose, and only 25 per cent employ consultants.

If a stakeholder approach is to serve any purpose, we must clearly ensure that fair and balanced assessments are made of all stakeholders' needs – and to do this in my view necessitates more equal power-relationships between the interested parties.

In conclusion, the stakeholder/managerial approach begins to study links between organizations and society, recognizes that it is public demand that is raising the ethical stakes, and highlights interesting issues about power, interests and rights. However, the likelihood of critical examination of ethical issues is minimized by the limitations of the stakeholder concept and by the constraints of the managerial approach.

FOURTH PERSPECTIVE: SOCIAL CONTRACTS AND COVENANTS

There are similarities between the stakeholder and the social contract approach – and it is of interest that the Labour Party adopted the former in the run-up to the 1997 General Election, rather than the latter, which in one interpretation would seem closer to socialism (see below). Perhaps New Labour wouldn't want to be associated with Newt Gingrich's 'contract with America'!

There are two interpretations of the concept of a 'social contract' in political philosophy (from where it originates) – the first (and oldest, deriving from Hobbes and Locke) emphasizes the *freedoms* which citizens gain as a result of agreeing to co-operate under the law. Without some agreement to give up our absolute rights to a sovereign body, in exchange for protection, life would be, in Hobbes's words: 'solitary, poor, nasty, brutish and short' (Hobbes 1651).

A different emphasis was given later by Rousseau, for whom the social contract was an agreement which would enable *moral development* in society (Rousseau 1762). The difference can also be summarized as between 'negative' freedom (freedom *from* interference by others, insecurity, etc.) and 'positive' freedom (freedom *to* be creative, co-operate, etc.).

This distinction is mirrored in writers on business ethics. An example of the former interpretation is Cannon (1992), who says: 'There exists an implicit or explicit contract between business and the community in which it operates', and who stresses the 'voluntary and active nature of the economic and business relationship'. This leads to 'mutuality of benefits'. The emphasis on freedom is clear:

> The leaders of the enterprise will seek the minimum of external intervention by the state in the workings of the market. It is in the interests of the firm to keep the costs of state intervention to a minimum by internalising . . . the contract. It is in the interests of the state to favour those enterprises which keep the costs to the community of intervention to a minimum (Cannon 1992).

This is not far from Carmichael and Drummond's (1989) view, that 'good business' is 'an exercise in simple economics'. For Cannon, then, increased freedom will bring increased responsibility – there is a 'new climate' and 'corporate leaders in the private sector acknowledge their responsibility to respond'.

I find this a shallow and over-optimistic view. In the car industry, for example[10] there has been a long fight against being asked to exercise social responsibility in regard to pollution. Cannon at one point acknowledges this, but seems not to attach any importance to it. What is lacking is any analysis of the power of different groups in society, and any sense of how dominant ideas arise – assuming 'social responsibility' *is* a dominant idea at present. Far from this, Cannon's book gives the impression that 'new climates' just arrive ('a new paradigm seems to be emerging') – which surely equally means they could just disappear! Notions of 'hegemony' or of 'negotiation' would be useful here (see Sutton 1993), but writers like Cannon are too anxious to retain the 'freedom' they see as central to a business society.

There are, however, writers who attempt to shift the perspective. For example, Camenisch (1981) gives a more Rousseau-like version of the contract, which is based on the argument that business's main purpose, its defining feature in fact, is to 'provide goods and services which contribute to *human flourishing*' (my emphasis). If profit-making is the essence of business, then Friedman must be right to say that to make a profit is its social responsibility. But if 'contributing to human flourishing' is the purpose, then all kinds of questions arise as to what kind of life we wish to live – and the locus of decision-making (as to what specific activities business should pursue) shifts from business (or the 'market') to 'humans' who wish to 'flourish'. This viewpoint corresponds to the third model identified by Shaw and Barry (1995), where ethics is seen as a concern with 'character', 'virtue' and 'practical reasoning' – ideas derived from Aristotle.[11]

An argument with some similarities to this, though with resonances closer to the mainstream of management writing, and to the stakeholder perspective, is put by Nash (1990). This is the view that the ideas of such as Peters (1987) on 'excellence' in business have at their heart the notion of *integrity*, and of subordinating self-interest to *value-creation* and *service to others*. Nash's 'covenantal ethic' is based on 'caring and value-creation'. While pointing out that 'today's survival environment stimulates a me-first business ethic', she argues that truly enlightened self-interest looks to 'longer-term self-enhancement'. Burke *et al.* (1993) seem also to believe that 'at heart' capitalism is an ethical system, and problems only arise because of *either* lower-level phenomena, such as the way responsibility is organized, *or* short-termism, which is seen not as intrinsic to capitalism but as a temporary associated value, which can be changed without radically modifying the system.

In fact, a feature of a number of recent books is to stress the problem of long-term survival, and to argue that ethical practices are essential to this. The 'new' Labour party seems to have caught on to this approach, and a strong case in economic terms is argued by Will Hutton (1995).

However, I am not the first to suggest that Hutton's overall argument is unconvincing. Whilst Hutton argues that the British state is dominated by antiquated institutions and values, typified by the City of London, he nevertheless believes that the City is already beginning to see reason and to consider long-term rather than short-term goals. In the light of ongoing scandals about the pay of directors of large organizations, mergers of insurance companies on a global scale, and the extent to which international trade in goods is dwarfed by trade in money, my view is that Hutton is whistling in the wind.

As Hutton seems to me to underestimate the entrenched power of the City, so most of those writers on business ethics who consider the social context seem to me to underestimate such difficulties as: (a) the degree of conflict behind the surface of the modern economy, and the difficulties of meeting competing needs and values (e.g. cutting pollution but retaining jobs in the car industry); (b) questions of enforcement: if business continues to take the short-term profit-maximizing route, should the state intervene, and if so how? These writers aim to 're-moralize' capitalism; the point should be to change it.

FIFTH PERSPECTIVE: BUSINESS ETHICS AND SOCIAL POLITICS

A few writers do manage to question the ethics of both business and capitalist society. This must be done, since the dominant values of a society will be shaped by its dominant institutions – and this clearly includes business. We cannot 'tidy up the stable'[12] without changing the structures and ways of thinking that got the stable into a mess in the first place!

I believe that a philosophical approach – that is, a critical approach – to business ethics can help us get the necessary detachment in order to begin to identify alternative ways of thinking, and new values. However, the reality of power as it is now distributed has to be dealt with as well, and this is a political question – a question of 'legitimacy' (Sutton 1993).[13]

Finally, on the social front, we need to consider alternative models of society, and alternative working arrangements, which would enable 'humans to flourish'. Some of these I believe are close to hand – for example (a) workers' co-operatives such as Scott Bader, whose articles of constitution include: no outside owners, not contributing to preparations for war, minimizing wage-differentials in the firm, and democratic decision-making which involves all members on an equal basis; (b) co-operative and municipal socialism (not exactly flavour of the month, but see for example Birchall 1994).

Other social models are not so much part of our 'modern British' life: in this respect, the most useful of the business ethics books I have found are those such as: Shaw and Barry (1995), which includes (a) Desjardins: 'Virtues and Business Ethics', (p. 95) where the basic problem is identified as producing 'good' people in the (Aristotelian) sense of contributing to a 'good' society; and (b) Schumacher's 'Buddhist Economics' (p. 178) where the development of appropriate 'character' and appropriate institutions are inseparable. Similarly useful is the discussion of Sustainable Development by Carmen and Lubelski in Davies (1997).

These approaches seem much more satisfactory: there is no artificial separation of business ethics from social ethics, or personal from public ethics; there is a recognition of the way business is 'embedded' in society; and there is a questioning of the kind of society we need, to ensure ethical business. I believe that these are the basic questions, and I hope that this chapter will encourage the reader to explore them further.

Notes

1 Thus Clutterbuck and Snow (1992) give the result of a survey of companies, which suggests that between 60% and 70% have policies or codes on ethical issues. At the same time, the main factor in promoting such policy was 'to enhance corporate image' (identified by 88% of the companies) – and 26% said it was 'competitive pressure'.

Note also the title of Humble (1973) *Social Responsibility Audit, a management tool for survival* (my emphasis), and see Ivens (1970) where it is claimed (Introduction) that business is accepting its social responsibilities, and 'at the same time the *intellectual forces opposing private industry make it more and more necessary* (my emphasis) for the individual director to think through the full implications of business decisions, and to achieve a coherent business philosophy.'

2 The term is borrowed from the philosophy of science: an internalist perspective takes scientific activity as a self-contained procedure for acquiring knowledge; an 'externalist' perspective recognizes the impact of society on the activity of science, and consequently holds 'knowledge' to be provisional or even to some degree relative.

3 de George, in *Journal of Business Ethics*, April 1987, identifies three 'levels of analysis': (i) at the level of the free enterprise system, (ii) the corporation in the system, (iii) the personal level. (This is similar to Alford and Friedland (1985) who argue that pluralism focuses on the level of the individual, managerial theory on the level of the organization, and class theory on the societal level.) The argument of this chapter is that while distinguishing between the three levels is useful procedurally and conceptually, there must be interaction, in the real world, between them.

4 See Galbraith (1996), also the first two chapters in particular of Davies (1997), where issues of ecology and democracy are interwoven with economics and with business ethics.

5 For details of these cases see: Hartley (1993: ch. 16 – oil-spill by the Exxon Valdez; ch. 6 – ITT; ch. 10 – Nestlé).

6 One wonders whether Friedman didn't in fact support the ITT action, since it aimed to prevent Chile from becoming a socialist country. He later advised the new military junta on economic policies, sidestepping ethical issues this might raise by saying that his role was purely as a technical advisor.

7 The Foundation for Business Responsibilities was connected in the press with Lady Porter of Westminster Council – the allegation being that she used it to channel funds to her Conservative group on the Council.

8 William Evan and R. Edward Freeman discuss this theory, linking it with a Kantian approach, in Hoffman and Frederick (1995). However, this is not as new an idea as some would like us to think, since they refer back to an essay in Huizinga (1983), and James Robertson argued the case in *Profit or People?* (1974).

9 I am reminded of an old advertisement for 3M, a company which puts most of its money into the space/armaments industries, but which reassures housewives that it is doing something for them, because a spin-off of its work is an improved scourer for the washing-up.

10 See Neale (1995).

11 Other models take ethics as simply to do with individual moral decisions (what Shaw calls the 'standard' model), or decisions taking into account the existing social and political context (the 'political' model). Davies (1997) identifies four perspectives: (1) virtue (represented especially by Solomon (1993)), (2) Christian/theological, (3) (industrial) democracy, and (4) ecosystems.

12 See 'Tidying up the stables', or the social responsibility of business in Perrow (1972).

13 See especially the articles by Habermas on 'legitimacy', and by Boulding on the 'Ecosystem of power' in Sutton, B. (1993).

REFERENCES

Acton, H.B. (1972) *The Ethics of Capitalism,* Foundation for Business Responsibility, London.

Alford, R.F. and Friedland, R. (1985) *Powers of Theory,* Cambridge University Press, Cambridge.

Almond, B. (ed.) (1995) *Introducing Applied Ethics*, Blackwell, Oxford.

Baumhart, R. (1961) *Ethics in Business*, Reinhart and Winston, New York; also *Harvard Business Review*, 39 (1961).

Binns, D. (1992) *Administration, Domination and 'Organisation Theory'* University of London, Occasional Papers on Business Economy and society.

Binns, D. (1993), *Total Quality Management, Organisation Theory and the New Right,* University of East London, Occasional Papers on Business Economy and Society.

Birchall, J. (1994) *Co-op: the People's Business*, Manchester University Press, Manchester.

Burke, T., Maddock, S. and Rose A. (1993) *How Ethical is British Business?*, University of Westminster, Faculty of Business, Management and Social Science.

Camenisch, P.F. (1981) Business ethics: on getting to the heart of the matter, *Business and Professional Ethics Journal*, 1, reprinted in Shaw, W.H. and Barry, V. (1995) *Moral Issues in Business*, ITP/Wadsworth, Belmont, CA, p. 252.

Cannon, T. (1992) *Corporate Responsibility*, Financial Times and Pitman Publishing, London.

Carmichael, S. and Drummond, J. (1989) *Good Business*, Business Books, London.

Carr, A. (1968) Is business bluffing ethical? *Harvard Business Review*, 46 (1).

Clutterbuck, D. and Snow, D. (1992) *Actions Speak Louder Than Words*, Kogan Page, with Kingfisher, London.

Clutterbuck, D. and Snow, D. (1990) *Working with the Community*, Weidenfeld and Nicholson with Kingfisher, London.

Collins, D. and O'Rourke, T. (1994) *Ethical Dilemmas in Business*, South-Western Publishing Co., Cincinnati, OH.

Davies, P.W.F. (ed.) (1997) *Current Issues in Business Ethics*, Routledge, London.

Davis, K. (1971) *Business, Society and Environment*, McGraw-Hill, New York and London.

de George, R.T. (1987) The status of business ethics, past, present and future, *Journal of Business Ethics*, 6 (3).

Donaldson, P. (1973) *Economics of the Real World*, Penguin, Harmondsworth.

Donaldson, J. (1989) *Key Issues in Business Ethics*, Harcourt Brace Jovanovich, London.

Donaldson, J. (1992) *Business Ethics: A European Casebook*, Academic Press, London.

Drummond, J. and Bain, B. (eds) (1994) *Managing Business Ethics*, Butterworth-Heinemann, Oxford.

Editors (1969) The war that business must win, *Business Week*, 1 November, reprinted in Perrow, C. (1972) *The Radical Attack on Business*, Harcourt Brace Jovanovich, New York.

Frederick, W.C., Post, J.E. and Davis, K. (1992) *Business and Society – Corporate Strategy, Public Policy, Ethics*, McGraw-Hill, New York.

French, P.A. (1995) *Corporate Ethics*, Harcourt Brace, Orlando, Fl.

Friedman, M. (1962) *Capitalism and Freedom*, University of Chicago Press, Chicago.

Friedman, M. (1970) The Social Responsibility of Business is to Increase Its Profits, in *New York Times Magazine*, 13 September, also in Hoffman W.M. and Frederick R.E. (1995) *Business Ethics – Readings and Cases in Corporate Morality*, McGraw-Hill, New York.

Galbraith, J.K. (1967) *The New Industrial State*, Penguin, Harmondsworth.

Galbraith, J.K. (1996) *The Good Society: The Humane Agenda*, Sinclair-Stevenson, London.

Gandz, J. and Bird, F.G. (1996) The ethics of empowerment, *Journal of Business Ethics*, 15 (4), 383–92.

Hartley, R.F. (1993) *Business Ethics – Violations of the Public Trust*, John Wiley, New York.

Heilbroner, R.L. and London, P. (eds) (1975) *Corporate Social Policy*, Addison-Wesley, Reading, MA and London.

Hobbes, T. (published 1651) *Leviathan*, Cambridge University Press, Cambridge, 1991.

Hoffman, W.M. and Frederick, R.E. (1995) *Business Ethics – Readings and Cases in Corporate Morality*, McGraw-Hill, New York.

Huizinga, C. (ed.) (1983) *Corporate Governance: A Definitive Exploration of the Issues*, UCLA Press, Los Angeles.

Humble, J. (1973) *Social Responsibility Audit, a Management Tool for Survival*, Foundation for Business Responsibilities, London.

Hutton, W. (1995) *The State We're In*, Cape, London.

Ivens, M. (1970) *Industry and Values*, Harrap, with Foundation for Business Responsibilities, London.

Jennings, M.M. (1993) *Case Studies in Business Ethics*, West Publishing Co, Minneapolis/St Paul.

Klein, T.A. (1977) *Social Costs and Benefits of Business*, Prentice-Hall, Englewood Cliffs and London.

Luthans, F., Hodgetts, R.M. and Thompson, K.R. (1972) *Social Issues in Business – Poverty, Civil Rights, Ecology, Consumer*, Macmillan, New York.

Luthans, F., Hodgetts, R.M. and Thompson, K.R. (1976) *Social Issues in Business – A Text with Current Readings and Cases*, Macmillan, New York.

Luthans, F., Hodgetts, R.M. and Thomson, K.R. (1984) *Social Issues in Business – Strategic and Public Policy Perspectives*, (4th edn), Macmillan, New York/London.

Nash, L. (1990) Good intentions aside, Extract in Drummond, J. and Bain, B. (1994) Managing Business Ethics, Butterworth-Heinemann, Oxford.

Neale A. (University of East London Business Policy Group) (1995) 'Take my breath away', in Fairweather, B. *et al.* (1997) *Environmental Futures*, Macmillan, London.

Pearson, G. (1995) *Integrity in Organisations*, McGraw-Hill, London.

Perrow, C. (1972) *The Radical Attack on Business*, Harcourt Brace Jovanovich, New York.

Peters, T. (1987) *Thriving on Chaos*, Macmillan, London.

Robertson, J. (1974) *Profit or People?* Calder & Boyars, London.

Rousseau, J.-J. (published 1762) *The Social Contract*, Everyman, London, 1993.

Sethi, S. Prakash (1971) *Up Against the Corporate Wall*, Prentice-Hall, Englewood Cliffs and London.

Shaw, W.H. and Barry, V. (1995) *Moral Issues in Business* (6th edn), ITP/Wadsworth, Belmont, CA.

Snell, R. (1993) *Developing Skills for Ethical Management*, Chapman and Hall, London.

Solomon, R.C. (1993) *Ethics and Excellence: Co-operation and Integrity in Business,* OUP, New York.

Solomon, R.C. and Hansen K. (1985) *It's Good Business*, in Shaw and Barry (1995) *Moral Issues in Business,* ITP/Wadsworth, Belmont, CA and London, p. 36.

Sorell, T. and Hendry, J. (1994) *Business Ethics,* Butterworth-Heinemann, Oxford.

Steade, R.D. (1975) *Business and Society in Transition,* Canfield Press, San Francisco.

Sutton, B. (1993) *The Legitimate Corporation.* Blackwell, Oxford.

Trevino L.K. and Nelson, K.A. (1995), *Managing Business Ethics,* John Wiley, New York.

Van Dam, C. (1978) *Trends in Business Ethics,* Nijhoff, Leiden, Boston.

Weiss, J.W. (1994) *Business Ethics, a Managerial Stakeholder Approach,* Wadsworth Publishing Co, Belmont, CA.

Wood, J. and Ivens, M. (1973) *Is a Preoccupation with Business Responsibility a Betrayal of Capitalism?* Foundation for Business Responsibilities, London.

12 Responsible organizational behaviour?: business responses to new social movements

Alan Neale

INTRODUCTION

Mahatma Gandhi was once asked what he thought about British civilization. He paused for a moment, and then replied: 'I think it would be a good idea.'

Social responsibility, like British civilization, is a problematic and contested concept. For Marxists, competition between capitalist firms dictates that absolute priority is given to capital accumulation and control over the labour process, making pursuit of other goals impossible. At the other end of the political spectrum, Milton Friedman has argued that the sole responsibility of business is to maximize profits. Between these positions, it is increasingly suggested that businesses can and should respond positively to demands that they become more socially responsible. This new orthodoxy derives from Berle and Means (1932), who argued that a separation of ownership and control in the modern corporation frees professional managers to take on wider responsibilities. Recent versions, like Clutterbuck (1992), Cannon (1994), or Kay (1997), claim that many interest groups have a stake in modern business – not just shareholders, but employees, customers, suppliers, the broader community, and future generations. As stakeholders become more aware of issues like job discrimination and environmental damage, it is suggested, their demands grow in intensity. In this situation, social responsibility is not only desirable, but also a potential source of competitive advantage.

Yet how real are social responsibility initiatives by business? The social responsibility literature quotes from corporate mission statements which stress values like giving 'proper regard to the conservation of the environment' (Shell) or providing 'equal opportunity in all aspects of employment' (PowerGen). There is, however, little analysis of how such statements translate into practice, and a frequent confusion of description with prescription.

This chapter aims to provide a more critical assessment, identifying possibilities and limits of socially responsible business behaviour in different institutional contexts. A brief history of ideas about social responsibility leads into a discussion of new social movements and their influence on management thought. This is followed by an assessment of the extent to which equal opportunities and environmental management policies actually meet the concerns raised by new social movements. The chapter concludes that fundamental changes in corporate governance and trade regulation would be needed to make socially responsible business a real possibility.

NINETEENTH-CENTURY BUSINESS AND SOCIAL RESPONSIBILITY

As early nineteenth-century entrepreneurs single-mindedly pursued profits and capital accumulation, many accepted negative environmental and social impacts, in the form of dislocation of traditional links to the land and widespread poverty and alienation, as a necessary price for 'progress'. Political economists like Malthus and Ricardo lent ideological support by suggesting that attempts at social reform would be self-defeating, as this would encourage population growth to outstrip food supply.

Not all industrialists ignored the social consequences of their activities. A notable exception was Robert Owen, the part-owner and manager of the largest and most advanced cotton mill of the time, at New Lanark, near Glasgow. He provided schooling, model housing, and healthcare for his employees, while achieving significant increases in profitability. Owen tried to sell his reforms to fellow capitalists on the grounds of financial self-interest. 'Many of you have long experienced in your operations the advantages of substantial, well-contrived, and well-executed machinery', he wrote.

> If then due care as to the state of your inanimate machines can produce such beneficial results, what may not be expected if you devote equal attention to your vital machines, which are far more wonderfully constructed? When you shall acquire a right knowledge of these . . . you will be readily induced to turn your thoughts more frequently from your inanimate to your living machines; you will discover that the latter may be trained and directed to procure a large increase of pecuniary gain (Owen, 1813).

Owen's suggestions that manufacturers would profit from treating their workers better met with little direct response at the time, although similar policies were developed later in the century by Quaker employers, particularly in the chocolate industry. His calls for legislation to improve working conditions had more immediate influence, with successive Factory Acts, from 1833 on, limiting the length of the working day. Owen came, however, to see his social ideals as incompatible with the commercial reality of capitalist competition, and chose to prioritize the former. He left New Lanark, and turned his attention to establishing classless communities and co-operatives. Owen and his followers were influential in promoting women's rights, and developing the trades unions which, later in the century, were to become more powerful agents for improving working conditions than either paternalist employers or legislators.

SOCIAL RESPONSIBILITY IN THE TWENTIETH CENTURY

By the early twentieth century, the position of owner/managers as 'captains of industry' was being eroded by the superior economic performance of large scale enterprises with access to external funding. Dependence on share capital encouraged a professionalization of management, with key management personnel appointed for their expertise rather than their relationship to the owner. For Max Weber, the essential feature of capitalism was 'rational calculation' – this was achieved by bureaucratic organization which ensured both impersonality in decision-making and dominance over the market place and workforce (Weber 1968). Bureaucratic managers, Weber suggested, do not pursue goals of their own – rather, they inhabit an 'iron cage' (Weber 1967), impersonally following rules and procedures designed to prize predictability from the chaos of market competition, and ensure accountability to providers of capital.

Although Weber did not refer to corporate social responsibility, his iron cage left little room for managers to indulge in welfare initiatives, and his analysis of bureaucracy in political organizations even threw doubt on the capacity of legislative change to achieve social reform. Weber's pessimism was not shared by all organization theorists. The 'human relations' approach, which Elton Mayo popularized in the 1930s, drew on studies at Western Electric's Hawthorne plant in Chicago to argue, *contra* Taylor's ideas of 'scientific management', that human emotions are important. Labour productivity, Mayo (1960) argued, would improve if managers encouraged their workers to feel that they belong, by creating 'pleasanter, freer, and happier working conditions'. Mary Parker Follett, an inter-war pioneer of personnel management, suggested that business managers could learn from their counterparts in social welfare administration that success in promoting 'integrative unity' – making employees feel that they were 'partners in the business' – would have positive effects on work quality and productivity (Follett 1941).

Also in the 1930s, Berle and Means asserted that shareholders were becoming less influential in the running of corporations, delegating control to professional managers. They suggested that managers were becoming a 'purely neutral technocracy', but, unlike Weber, who identified this as an instrument of domination in the interests of the providers of capital, they argued that one outcome might include 'balancing a variety of claims by various groups in the community and assigning to each a portion of the income stream on the basis of public policy rather than private cupidity' (Berle and Means 1932: 356). The idea that managers are neither faceless agents of shareholder interests nor an elite group pursuing its own self-interest, but can be freed (and, in Berle's later writings, are freed) by shareholder quiescence to act in the interest of society as a whole, has been enormously influential. Where Weber saw the 'disenchantment of the world', Carl Kaysen could claim, half a century later, that 'The modern corporation is a soulful corporation' (Kaysen 1957).

If the ideological message of the Berle and Means study has been powerful, empirical support remains weak. Most of the examples of 'soulfulness' cited by Kaysen, for example, were corporate image building exercises like charitable donations or architectural patronage. Similarly, developments such as 'human relations' and 'scientific management' can be viewed, from a labour process perspective, as alternative ways of organizing labour relations in the interests of company profitability, depending more on technological and labour market conditions, or the militancy of trade union demands, than on any exercise of social responsibility. While the assumption of neo-classical economists that corporations are unitary organizations, single-mindedly pursuing profit maximization, has been discredited, institutional arrangements, in the UK and USA at least, continue to inhibit any significant pursuit of interests which might conflict with those of shareholders. Indeed, many recent changes – globalization, growth of institutional shareholding, development of stock option bonus schemes, increased takeover activity, and financial engineering, for example – have had the effect of re-inforcing managerial prioritization of shareholder value.

NEW SOCIAL MOVEMENTS

Since the early 1960s, established political cultures in many countries have been shaken by the activities of new social movements, giving a different twist to the social responsibility debate. The US Civil Rights movement, formed to assert basic social and political rights for black people, spawned, in quick succession, movements for Black Power, Women's Liberation, and Gay Liberation. As ideas of 'identity politics' spread geographically, additional movements emerged – including those of people with disabilities, for the natural environment, and for animal rights. Within each movement, there were differences between a 'liberal' wing, seeking accommodation by established institutions to new demands, and a 'radical' wing, issuing a fundamental challenge to those institutions. While divisions between these wings, and sometimes between these movements, have been intense, they unite in questioning a wide range of assumptions underlying the existing social order, from the perspective of groups or interests which have traditionally been oppressed or marginalized by it.

Many writers contrast these 'new' social movements with the 'old' movement of the industrial working class. Alberto Melucci, for example, sees the difference between old and new as characterized by a shift from material to cultural concerns. 'Contemporary social movements, more than others in the past,' he suggests, 'have shifted towards a non-political terrain: the need for self-realisation in everyday life' (Melucci 1989: 23). Melucci's categorization can be challenged on a number of counts. It is often forgotten that many old social movements had an important cultural dimension. The utopian socialists of the early nineteenth century, for example, challenged *all* aspects of social hierarchy, including the patriarchal family as well as the class system, and they attempted to put egalitarian ideals into practice in communities which were similar in many respects to those established by participants of new social movements in the late 1960s and early 1970s.

If cultural aspects of old social movements are often underplayed, so are historical antecedents of new social movements. The first wave of feminism, for example, may, before the First World War, have prioritized a narrow political objective (votes for women), but contemporary documents reveal the extent of both its militancy and its challenge to patriarchal culture. It is notable, too, that the new second wave described itself, in the late 1960s and 1970s, as a women's *liberation* movement – it transcended the dualism of Melucci's categorization by combining material demands with cultural innovations, and by insisting that 'the personal is political'.

Whatever the accuracy of a strict delineation between old and new, there is no doubt that, over the past three decades, many people have sought, in Melucci's words, 'a complementarity between private life, in which new meanings are directly produced and experienced, and publicly expressed commitments' (Melucci 1989: 206). This has affected people's relationships to business organizations in many different ways – not just as workers, but as citizens, customers, and even, sometimes, entrepreneurs or shareholders. One implication for business is that, to be perceived as socially responsible, it must reconsider its policies across the board – not just in personnel management and public relations, but in all its operations.

LIBERATION MANAGEMENT?

There has been widespread resistance on the part of business managers to addressing deeper issues of corporate social responsibility, particularly where these conflict with shareholder value. At a more superficial level, however, many management consultants and writers now promote organizational changes which, while oriented primarily to improving competitiveness, at the same time refer to concerns raised by new social movements, and indeed suggest positive links between the two.

In the corporate strategy field, Johnson and Scholes (1997) suggest that assessing stakeholder expectations should become an integral part of strategy formulation and evaluation. Relationships with stakeholder groups, they propose, should be actively managed by mapping their power and interests, with the aim of converting potential threats into business opportunities. This political calculation is given an economic gloss by Michael Porter, who argues that conflicts between business and environmental interests can be resolved by innovations which bring about economies in resource use (Porter and van der Linde 1995).

A more evangelical tone is struck by management 'gurus' like Rosabeth Moss Kanter and Tom Peters, who employ the language of new social movements to reinforce their message that success in a global market place requires constant organizational change. Kanter's first management book (1977), for example, identified structural factors institutionalizing unequal power relationships between men and women in large corporations, and encouraged constructive responses by managers to the challenge of equal opportunity legislation. Kanter says that writing this book was motivated by her involvement in the women's movement, and she acknowledges 'a debt to debates within feminism' (Kanter 1977: preface). Although much of Peters' early work owes more to the New Right than to new social movements (Silver, 1987), there is an ambivalence around this in his more recent writings, as is suggested by the title of one of his books, *Liberation Management* (Peters 1992), and by his emphasis on 'putting employees first'.

These writers stress that a successful business needs not only to meet changing customer demands, but to surpass and anticipate them. This, they suggest, requires managers to exercise intuitive more than calculative skills, and it needs a workforce which is highly motivated, through empowerment of individual workers and flattening of organizational hierarchies. Control, they argue, should come from a shared culture and vision, rather than bureaucratic procedures, the aim being to encourage innovative and rapid responses to changing market threats and opportunities.

Underlying this is a perception that bureaucratic organizations could prosper only in the special circumstances of the post-war economic boom, when domestic demand ensured that few firms could fail. In the more competitive, and uncertain, global market place of the period since the early 1970s, by contrast, only giants who 'learn to dance' (Kanter 1989) will survive. Firms which can respond nimbly to the challenges of market fragmentation, it is suggested, will also be well equipped to respond positively to social and political demands for outcomes such as equality of opportunity and environmental protection.

CONSTRUCTING STAKEHOLDERS

Despite dissimilarities in style and approach between management strategists and gurus, they share a conviction that threats from new social movements can be converted into business opportunities, and that stakeholder interests are objective 'facts' waiting to be discovered. What gets downplayed is the active role which managers play in *constructing* their stakeholders. Construction occurs directly, of course, in relation to a company's supply chain, where, increasingly, suppliers are selected according to their ability to satisfy precise criteria (on price, quality, delivery, etc.).

With wider social responsibilities, construction is more indirect, but no less real. Fineman and Clarke (1996) have shown how British managers systematically play off one set of stakeholders (campaigners, for example) against another (customers, for example), to legitimate corporate environmental strategies which are consistent with their own values and personal identities. Far from reacting passively to environmental protest, managers actively select which demands they meet, and promote their own vision of corporate greening.

As Mary Douglas and Aaron Wildavsky (1982) have reminded us, 'to organize means to organize some things in and other things out'. It is easy to see how selective interpretation of stakeholder demands leads to the promotion of initiatives like 'clean technology', which allow companies to demonstrate some commitment to environmental improvement, while avoiding deeper concerns raised by green activists which might require a more fundamental transformation of existing structures of production and consumption (Neale 1997b).

EQUAL OPPORTUNITIES POLICIES

Pressure from new social movements has led many governments to adopt legislation outlawing certain forms of discrimination (particularly by ethnicity and gender). Examples include the Civil Rights (1964) and Equal Employment Opportunity (1972) Acts in the USA, and the Sex Discrimination (1975) and Race Relations (1976) Acts in Britain. Quangos, such as the Equal Employment Opportunities Commission in the USA and the Equal Opportunities Commission (EOC) and Commission for Racial Equality (CRE) in Britain, were appointed to promote good practice, including the establishment of equal opportunity policies by organizations. In the USA, adoption of these policies has been fairly widespread. In Britain, where legal requirements are less stringent, the pace of change was slower, but by the early 1990s most large organizations claimed to have equal opportunities policies.

Jewson and Mason (1986a) have distinguished between 'liberal' and 'radical' models of equal opportunity. The liberal perspective views discrimination as resulting from the prejudice of individual managers who deny some people the chance of competing on equal terms for available jobs. Here, the emphasis is on changing personnel procedures to eliminate 'subjective' bias from selection procedures, so that the 'best' person for the job is chosen. This ignores structural obstacles, embedded within social institutions and operating independently of the mindsets of individual managers, to the advancement of disadvantaged groups. Radical approaches, Jewson and Mason suggest, focus not on procedures by which individuals are selected and promoted, but on social outcomes – whether or not the distribution of rewards between different groups fairly represents their distribution in society. To compensate for the legacy of past injustice, radical approaches often advocate positive discrimination. An example might be quota systems to increase the representation of disadvantaged groups, as has been adopted by some organizations in the USA. In Britain, employers are encouraged to set targets for the representation of identified groups (particularly women and ethnic minorities) and to monitor progress towards those targets. Only certain types of positive action (reserved training courses, for example) are allowed, however, and using quotas to achieve targets is illegal.

In the predominant liberal approach, the underlying assumption is that formalized personnel procedures can remove job discrimination, without any need to change organization structures or job design. Although some middle management posts have been opened to women, equal opportunities policies in Britain have had little overall effect on improving employment outcomes for disadvantaged groups. Most of the recent growth in women's employment, for example, has been in jobs which are both part-time and low paid. Many policies exist only on paper, and often little attention is given to implementing action plans. Yet even in cases where equal opportunity policies are real, the outcomes are still disappointing, and many researchers suggest that the problem lies in the liberal assumptions on which most policies are based. A typical model of a 'fair' selection procedure involves non-discriminatory adverts, screening of applications and interviews, and monitoring of outcomes. This is based on professional jobs, where, in principle, it is possible to identify the 'best' person for the job, and devise procedures to minimize prejudice in the selection process. This model does not easily translate to most manual jobs, however, where a number of applicants may be equally suitable and recruitment may be informal. Attempts to implement equal opportunities by formalizing recruitment procedures can make line managers, who see the new requirements as unnecessarily time consuming, resentful, and may be experienced by intended beneficiaries as an additional discriminatory burden. At a Midlands engineering plant studied by Jewson and Mason (1986b), Asian workers felt threatened by an equal opportunities initiative which replaced a traditional arrangement, where they were represented by a community 'broker', with more formal procedures.

Monitoring, the collection of statistical information on the composition of the present workforce, job applicants, appointments and promotions, is needed to measure progress in meeting equal opportunity objectives, and this can pose problems even where there is a formal recruitment system. Monitoring of gender and age is fairly straightforward. 'Race', on the other hand, is not a category which has any 'objective' scientific meaning (Miles 1993). Here, self-classification is required, but the ways different individuals describe themselves are not necessarily consistent, making the interpretation of responses inherently unreliable. Monitoring of disability, too, is affected by differing perceptions of what constitutes a disability, and how this affects the individual's ability to perform particular work tasks. Monitoring is particularly problematic in the case of sexual orientation. Informal homophobic attitudes and harassment are rife in many work situations, and many lesbians and gay men would feel safer concealing their sexual identity than openly acknowledging it in a monitoring exercise, unless their employer was actively promoting a workplace culture in which they felt able to be open about their sexuality.

Accurate monitoring requires not only detailed information about who does what job, but a clear definition of job content and status. This is not a problem in traditional, hierarchical organizations, operating in stable markets. Where organizations are downsizing in response to changed market conditions, however, job re-structuring makes equal opportunities monitoring impossible (Woodall *et al.* 1997). In many high-innovation organizations, too, job demarcations are breaking down, as employees are grouped in short-term project teams and rewarded according to performance rather than position. Perhaps, as Kanter (1984) suggests, these companies 'tend to go further toward an egalitarian, *meritocratic* ideal than their counterparts', but the lack of rigid job structures which, it is claimed, produces this outcome, at the same time makes equality of opportunity difficult to substantiate.

The most important limitation of the liberal ideology which underpins most equal opportunities policies is its individualizing of discrimination, to the neglect of the institutional and social factors which condition individual behaviour and affect individual life chances. Gender discrimination at work, for example, is closely related to inequalities at home. On the demand side of the labour market, managers, in assessing a candidate's likely work commitment, often act on sexist assumptions about men as 'bread-winners' and women as 'homemakers' (Collinson *et al.* 1990), while, on the supply side, the constraints of domestic responsibilities dictate much of the concentration of women in low paid segments of the labour market (Burchell and Rubery 1994).

Managers increasingly assume that personal commitment is demonstrated by working long hours, and account is rarely taken of how this can discriminate against people with caring responsibilities or disabilities. Tom Peters was not being ironic when he noted that it is not possible to combine full and satisfying personal *and* professional lives – 'the price of excellence is time, energy, attention and focus, at the very time that energy, attention and focus could have gone toward enjoying your daughter's soccer game' (Peters and Austin 1985: 419).

Collinson *et al.* (1990) suggest that 'only when domestic responsibilities are no longer treated negatively and are rendered compatible in *practice* with full-time employment will the ideological partial truths and conventional gender identities that underpin men's domination of the labour market be undermined. At minimum, this requires, first, the development and extension of *career-break schemes*; second, increased opportunities for *flexible working patterns*; and third, the provision of *crèche facilities*, available to the children of all employees' (Collinson *et al.* 1990: 210). Reforms have been introduced, but they tend to be limited to high status staff, or concentrated on areas of skill shortage. Firms may contemplate such innovations to protect their investments in training and on-the-job experience, but they are reluctant to extend them to all staff, and, indeed, they may at the same time be pursuing labour market strategies which drive down pay levels for lower status jobs by exploiting many women's need to organize jobs around domestic responsibilities.

Reforms which make it easier for women to combine paid jobs with domestic responsibilities only scratch at the surface of the problem, however, because they challenge neither the culture of working long hours nor the gender division of labour at home. In British organizations where 'family friendly' policies have been introduced for core workers, for example, take-up by men of opportunities to work fewer hours has been minimal, and women with promotion ambitions have also been reluctant to take advantage of them, for fear of being seen as not committed to their career (Lewis 1997). Ultimately, equal opportunities for women in employment depend on changing attitudes to time at work and on men assuming equal responsibilities at home. As Cynthia Cockburn emphasizes, men's relationship to work would have to change. 'There is no room in this scenario for fetishised masculine careers. A requisite of course is that employing organizations make available to fathers too the flexibilities that some are just now offering to mothers. More, however, they have to direct their personnel policies towards the expectation that men will really use them' (Cockburn 1991: 98).

The importance of looking beyond access to jobs to job content in a social context has been highlighted by disability rights campaigners in Britain. They argue that disability is in large part socially constructed; individuals are literally 'disabled' by working and other environments which do not accommodate them (Oliver 1990; Lunt and Thornton 1994). From this perspective, it is not enough for employers to make (in the words of the 1995 Disability Discrimination Act) 'reasonable adjustment' to the physical environment of the workplace. If, as in almost all cases, jobs are designed with able-bodied persons in mind, then they will often be 'disabling' to people who are not able-bodied. To avoid discrimination, the employer would need to be prepared to rewrite job specifications and change work practices, customizing them to take into account the (potential) employee's individual circumstances.

Cockburn argues that there are major differences between a 'short agenda' of equal opportunities, which focuses narrowly on recruitment procedures and is supported by top management, and a 'long agenda', which goes beyond positive discrimination to encompass a more fundamental transformation of the organization's structure and culture, and is pushed by equality activists (Cockburn 1989, 1991). Equal opportunities are promoted by governments, and supported by many top managers, on the grounds that they can help organizations make the most of the individual talents of their employees, reduce recruitment and training costs, and improve customer relations (the short agenda).

Even these limited aims are threatened at times of recession (Donaldson 1993), and top managers are much less willing, at any time, to contemplate changes that do not directly further what they see as the main aim of the organization – in the private sector, to make profits. Thus organizational changes are often promoted to reduce costs or promote sales, but rarely to 'humanize' the structure, despite claims by Kanter and Peters that the latter will help bring about the former. And corporate strategy can continue to attack labour costs by downsizing and by exploiting labour market segmentation, at the same time that it promotes equal opportunities to reduce turnover of its remaining full-time workers (in retail banking, for example).

Whatever the motives of top management in introducing equal opportunities policies, the posts that have been created to implement them have, in some organizations (particularly in the public sector), attracted new social movement activists, who see themselves as responsible to the disadvantaged groups they represent as well as to senior management. Setting up interest groups and consulting with them on policy development encourages a lengthening of the equal opportunities agenda, to encompass wider issues such as harassment and bullying, the existence of informal social networks which exclude members of disadvantaged groups, and the possibility of re-designing jobs to make them more compatible with the domestic responsibilities or disabilities of individual employees. Without senior management support or trade union action, however, positive measures to tackle such issues are rarely put into place.

Lengthening the equal opportunities agenda typically exposes conflicts of interest which the short agenda conceals. This, it is sometimes suggested, risks provoking a 'backlash' by aggrieved white males. Some of the most vehement expressions of backlash have, in fact, come from far right religious groups in the USA, who want women back in the home and are opposed to even the most basic civil rights for lesbians and gay men, and from free market ideologues, who oppose any regulation of business. When jobs and careers are under threat, such political opposition can encourage some white men to blame women and minorities, rather than de-industrialization or re-structuring, for their redundancy, particularly if, as in some US organizations, affirmative action includes preferential treatment for disadvantaged groups.

It is partly in response to the threat of 'backlash' that many US organizations are shifting their emphasis from countering discrimination to 'managing diversity', which by ostensibly valuing difference appears to offer something for everyone. The new approach can be related theoretically to post-structuralist deconstruction of unitary social identities, but its practical application owes more to recent shifts from personnel management (emphasizing formal procedures) to human resource management (actively matching individual employees to the strategic needs of the business). Diversity management can improve on more bureaucratic approaches, if it highlights the role of organizational cultures in encouraging or stifling diversity, or illuminates dimensions of difference which might be ignored by many equal opportunities policies. Black women managers, for example, face particular problems that are not addressed by making them identify as *either* black people *or* women, and Liff and Dale (1994) have suggested that diversity policies, by emphasizing the multi-faceted nature of discrimination, could tackle these issues more effectively than conventional equal opportunities approaches.

The danger, which Liff and Dale acknowledge, is that diversity management can further individualize collective problems, and be interpreted narrowly in terms of advantages for the organization. The terminology is significant – managing diversity, not celebrating it. Certainly in the USA, most diversity plans stress factors like improving effectiveness of team operation, adding value to the organization, or matching the diversity in the market place, while making little or no reference to social justice. In Britain, too, consultants promoting diversity policies emphasize advantages to the organization, and downplay challenges to social inequality. As Kandola *et al.* (1995) put it: 'Diversity takes individuals as the primary focus of concern, not groups. Such an approach, however, will mean that certain group-based equal opportunity actions need to be seriously questioned: in particular positive action and targets.'

Denying the social structuring of discrimination, and giving discretion to line managers (who remain overwhelmingly white, male, heterosexual and able-bodied) to determine what forms of diversity are to be promoted and in what circumstances, diversity management strays far from the original demands of new social movements. What might, in other circumstances, have been a constructive response to the backlash, has become, all too frequently, a subtle expression of it.

ENVIRONMENTAL MANAGEMENT

Environmental regulation has been around for much longer than anti-discrimination legislation. In Britain, the Alkali Act of 1863 was introduced in response to pressure from landowners concerned about the damage caused to their crops by emissions from Merseyside chemical factories producing alkalis for the soap and glass industries. The controls introduced by the Act stimulated technological innovations which cut toxic emissions by producing chlorine (a by-product of the process) in a more utilizable, and cleaner, form. This pacified the landowners, whose crops were no longer damaged, and it benefited the manufacturers as well, as they could now develop new products, based on chlorine, which became more profitable than the alkalis their factories had originally been set up to produce.

The chlor-alkali experience, with pollution control stimulating new technology to the advantage of producers as well as the immediate environment, apparently justified a cosy relationship between regulators and industry which the Alkali Inspectorate (the forerunner of the Pollution Prevention and Control division of the Environment Agency) set up, and which pervaded subsequent British approaches to pollution control. It was also used to support the idea that business, at first resistant to environmental controls, eventually supports them (if applied sensitively), to its own as well as nature's benefit.

Environmental movements in the early 1970s were sceptical about business reconciling private profits with environmental protection. They were critical not only of industry's record in complying with regulatory controls, but also of the whole emphasis of the industrial system on economic growth, which they saw as conflicting with finite resources and with the capacity of ecosystems to absorb pollutants. Business, in this period, tended to react defensively to the environmentalist critique – in some cases denying the significance of environmental damage, in others promoting technical fixes which solved some environmental problems but created additional ones (nuclear power as a replacement for fossil fuels, for example).

In the 1980s, attention shifted from issues of resource depletion and local pollution to global problems such as acid rain, global warming and destruction of the ozone layer. For many 'dark greens', intensification of global environmental problems confirmed that industrial technology was the problem rather than the solution – for them, nature had an intrinsic, spiritual value which transcended human interests, and nothing less than dismantling the industrial system was required to restore the balance between ecosystems and human communities on which survival depends. While the business community continued to oppose deep ecology perspectives which stress natural limits on economic activities, certain sections of it allied with the 'light green' wing of the environmental movement, to argue that industrialism could be made more compatible with the natural environment, by emphasizing principles like 'sustainable development' and 'ecological modernisation' (Neale 1997b).

For environmental groups like the World Wide Fund for Nature (WWF) and Greenpeace, partnership with certain sections of business has moved beyond communication about the aims of environmental policy to a joint search for solutions to environmental problems (Murphy and Bendell 1997). WWF, for example, worked closely with B&Q and other timber product retailers to develop a certification scheme for sustainably managed forests, as a practical step towards halting rainforest destruction, and Greenpeace collaborated with refrigerator manufacturers and Calor Gas to develop hydrocarbon refrigerants which are less damaging than the HFC greenhouse gases which the chemical industry wanted to use in place of ozone-depleting CFCs.

For the small number of businesses which are co-operating with environmental groups like WWF and Greenpeace, there are immediate advantages in terms of improved public image and increased sales to environmentally-conscious consumers. More generally, many larger firms are responding to greater public awareness of environmental issues by instituting environmental policies which combine a more systematic approach to internal environmental management with some public reporting of environmental performance. The form these environmental policies take usually reflects the specific circumstances of the industry, but again, there can be both public relations and marketing advantages, as well as opportunities for cost reduction.

In chemicals, a key motive has been damage limitation – disasters, like the 1984 release of toxic gas from a pesticide plant in Bhopal, India, have been costly for the firm involved as well as the victims, and they have shaken public confidence in the industry. Reacting to public concern about management failures at Bhopal, and the scale of the disaster, national associations in many countries set up 'Responsible Care' programmes. These encourage (and sometimes require) members to improve their environmental and safety performance, and to publish indicators which measure that performance.

While adoption of environmental policies by companies and industry associations is an advance on previous practice, doubts remain about the quality of the information presented – with few exceptions, there is no independent verification, and information on environmental performance is selected to present the company in a good light. Under Responsible Care in the UK, for example, the Chemical Industries Association requires each production site to report releases to the environment, but not all sites do this, and releases are aggregated into an index (weighted according to management's judgement of their significance) rather than identified separately. The policy focus is on process modification (reducing waste production to yield both environmental and financial benefit, for example), rather than product re-design to reduce life-cycle environmental impact (which involves more short-term cost but greater scope for long-term environmental improvement).

In the chemical industry, the very firms which are pioneering 'eco-innovation' remain vehemently opposed to demands from environmental groups that they should develop replacements for chlorine products such as PVC because of their health and ecosystem risks. The industry views chlorinated compounds (originally developed, as we have seen, as a by-product of alkali production) as creating lucrative market opportunities, and favours assessment of environmental risks on a case by case basis, reflecting current scientific evaluations of likely damage. Particular compounds should be banned only if there is clear evidence of unacceptable risk, and if alternative substances can be found to fulfil the same function without significant increases in cost. From an ecological perspective, however, chlorine is an inherently toxic substance, and the presumption is that chlorine compounds should not be developed, until there is clear evidence that no long-term environmental damage will result (the 'precautionary principle'). For the industry, taking 'reasonable' risks with the environment is acceptable, while for environmental groups, producers have a duty of care, covering the life-cycle of their products (which can be many decades when chemical compounds resist bio-degradation).

Concern, particularly from insurers, about lack of common standards encouraged the development of more formal Environmental Management Systems. In Britain, the introduction in 1994 of an environmental standard, BS 7750, was a landmark in this process, and acquiring BS 7750 certification became a focus for many firms in a number of industries. BS 7750 was modelled on the international quality management standard ISO 9000 (formerly BS 5750), and, like that standard, it emphasized documented procedures and 'continual improvement.' Businesses chose which of their sites to enter, and determined their own objectives and targets. External certifiers, most with quality assurance rather than environmental expertise, checked that the documentation was in order, that the management system operated as specified, and that the firm was making progress in meeting its targets. If they were satisfied, the firm had its claims to environmental excellence endorsed by possession of the standard.

BS 7750, like its quality management predecessor, was mechanistic and bureaucratic, yet it gave firms total freedom to determine their own objectives. If they chose improvements to boost short-term profits (energy efficiency, for example), they could achieve certification, providing there was some environmental payoff. From a green perspective, the main problems were the lack of any attempt to assess the firm's objectives and targets in relation to its most significant environmental impacts (or even to the performance achieved by competitors), and an absence of any public reporting requirement.

The latter objection is removed in the 1995 EU Eco-Management and Audit Scheme (EMAS), but in other respects EMAS is similar to BS 7750. In each scheme, a poor environmental performer can be certified, providing its procedures have been approved and it has demonstrated continual improvement. ISO 14001, the international standard which has superseded BS 7750, is even weaker, in that it emphasizes management systems rather than performance. The aim is to make the standard as inclusive as possible, in order to minimize trade barriers. As with diversity management, the standard is being actively promoted as an alternative to legal regulation.

Richard Welford, who co-authored an enthusiastic text on the subject (Welford and Gouldson 1993), has since re-considered the value of environmental management systems. He now suggests that 'self-imposed environmental objectives and targets devalue the standards and do little to guarantee a sustainable future' (Welford 1995: 76). Sustainability is the key environmental issue business will have to face in the twenty-first century, and this, Welford argues, will require a 'transcendent organisation', which will 'reject dominant management paradigms associated with environmental management systems as not going far enough and it will institute change consistent with ecological management practices. The transcendent organization will audit for sustainability and introduce wide-ranging culture change programmes to make the values and actions of the firm consistent with sustainable development' (Welford 1995: 198).

Welford is vague as to how such a 'transcendent organisation' might be created, but suggests that the technique of life-cycle analysis (LCA) might point a way forward, by providing analytical underpinning for product stewardship. LCA involves evaluating environmental impacts of products at each stage of their life-cycle – raw material extraction and processing, component manufacture, assembly, distribution, use, and disposal – so they can be re-designed to lessen environmental impacts. 'The concentration on the product, rather than the system,' Welford suggests, 'facilitates direct measurement of environmental impact . . . LCA also widens the environmental analysis beyond management systems and site-specific production attributes which can so easily hide environmental damage up or down the supply chain' (Welford 1995: 100).

There are major methodological problems with LCA, which enthusiasts like Welford skate over. These include where to draw the boundaries of the analysis (the cost of tracking every element of a product from cradle to grave would be prohibitive, but limiting the scope could bias the result), how to deal with location-specific impacts (options with low impacts in one location might have high impacts in another), and how to evaluate impacts at different stages of the life-cycle (how, for example, might damage to rivers from disposal of phosphate detergents compare with damage from opencast mining of the bauxite needed for the zeolite builders in phosphate-free detergents?). Such problems allow firms to select data for an LCA which present their products in a favourable light. Independent assessment, as in the EU eco-labelling scheme, reduces dishonest application of LCA, but, unless firms foresee significant marketing advantage, there is little incentive to participate. At the end of the day, judgements have to be made, and no refinement of the technique can avoid this.

The pitfalls of relying on management techniques to 'solve' environmental problems, and possible bottom-line consequences of getting it wrong, are highlighted in the case of Brent Spar, the redundant North Sea oil storage buoy which Shell UK decided, in 1995, to dump at sea. Shell UK did not see any need to debate the issues publicly, despite widespread international opposition to marine dumping of hazardous waste. It claimed, on the basis of internal studies, that deep sea dumping was the Best Practical Environmental Option, and consulted marine biologists who suggested that the toxics on board would be safely dispersed. Greenpeace challenged this view, and argued that the platform should be dismantled onshore and re-used. Effectively combining direct action and media management, it occupied the Spar, and persuaded many Europeans that Shell was behaving irresponsibly. Car users boycotted Shell products, and Shell UK was made to re-consider, following concerns within the Shell group about lost revenues and diplomatic pressure from European governments.

Brent Spar raised important issues, common to many business decisions involving significant environmental impacts. Each disposal option involved environmental damage, but the risks and uncertainties were such that impacts could not be precisely measured or compared. No management technique could determine an optimal decision – evaluation necessarily included a large element of judgement. Many environmentalists claimed that the technical evaluation was biased. The UK government, they suggested, was committed to sea dumping as the cheapest option (because disposal costs could be offset against Petroleum Revenue Tax), and made sure that the 'independent' assessments were commissioned from scientists who would support them, and not from those whose research might cast doubt on optimistic assumptions that surface ecosystems would not be contaminated.

Reducing 'bias' is important, but a more fundamental lesson is that the environment is not something out there, capable of being understood 'objectively' by scientists – we humans are part of nature, and our evaluation of how our activities affect it is a contested one (Neale 1997a). Many business decisions involve significant environmental impacts. If they do not take into account how environmental issues are perceived by different groups, the outcomes will often damage both nature and the medium-term commercial interests of the business.

CONCLUSION

Many businesses are, in their equal opportunities and environmental management policies, starting to address some of the issues posed by new social movements. What they offer, however, usually falls far short of what these movements demand. Business selects what is compatible with medium-term profitability, and jettisons even this in a recession. Equality of opportunity, after all, is not the same as equality – differences in access to higher paid jobs can be reduced at the same time as differentials widen between higher-paid and lower-paid jobs, and between those in employment and those without earnings (as occurred in the British labour market throughout the 1980s). Environmental improvement, too, does not necessarily mean good environmental performance, and it rarely promotes sustainability.

Top management often feels that, in establishing its policies, it has 'solved the problem', making demands for tighter regulation irrelevant. Yet, often, this reveals how little it listens to what new social movements are saying. Even arguments from management writers like Rosabeth Moss Kanter and Tom Peters, that innovation requires flexibility and empowerment, have, on the whole, been ignored, and the bureaucratic mechanisms which firms have installed to implement their policies remain, from the perspective of new social movements, more part of the problem than part of its solution. The language of targets and monitoring, central to both equal opportunities programmes and environmental management systems, is employed to facilitate acceptance by managers, not challenge the way they operate.

Cynthia Cockburn, promoting a long equal opportunities agenda, identifies a space within organizations where disadvantaged groups can press for change. Richard Welford, anticipating a 'transcendent organisation' capable of genuinely sustainable development, appeals to the higher selves of top managers. Both Cockburn and Welford see a need for fundamental change, but there is little sense, in their work, of what the institutional barriers to such change might be, and how they might be eroded.

Managerial preferences for a short equal opportunities agenda, or for environmental management systems, reflect social values which oppose anything more fundamental, and an institutional framework which gives primacy to short-term profits and punishes managements whose financial performance capital markets deem unsatisfactory. Despite talk of multiple stakeholders, the structure of corporate governance, in the UK and USA at least, recognizes only shareholders, and it allows them, through takeovers, to sell control to another firm where this offers a better financial deal. At the same time, the ability of national governments to promote social welfare and environmental quality through regulation is jeopardized by a free trade regime which gives competitive advantage to firms locating in regions of the global economy which offer low unit labour costs or lax environmental controls.

Organizational behaviour always takes place within a wider structural context, and social responsibility is no exception. Without institutional change which widens corporate governance and accountability to include other stakeholders as well as shareholders, and protects social and environmental settlements from the ravages of 'free' trade, significant advances in social responsibility are likely to remain thin on the ground.

REFERENCES

Berle, A. and Means, G. (1932) *The Modern Corporation and Private Property,* Macmillan, London.

Burchell, B. and Rubery, J. (1994) Divided women: labour market segmentation and gender segregation, in A.M. Scott (ed.), *Gender Segregation & Social Change* Oxford University Press, Oxford.

Cannon, T. (1994) *Corporate Responsibility,* Pitman, London.

Clutterbuck, D. (1992) *Actions Speak Louder: a Management Guide to Corporate Social Responsibility,* Kogan Page, London.

Cockburn, C. (1989) Equal opportunities: the short and long agenda, *Industrial Relations Journal,* 20 (3), 213–25.

Cockburn, C. (1991*) In the Way of Women: Men's Resistance to Sex Equality in Organizations,* Macmillan, London.

Collinson, D., Knights, D. and Collinson, M. (1990) *Managing to Discriminate,* Routledge, London.

Donaldson, L. (1993) The recession: a barrier to equal opportunities?, *Equal Opportunities Review,* 50.

Douglas, M. and Wildavsky, A. (1982*) Risk and Culture: an Essay on the Selection of Technical and Environmental Risks,* University of California Press, Berkeley.

Fineman, S. and Clarke, K. (1996) Green stakeholders: industry interpretations and response, *Journal of Management Studies,* 33 (6), 715–30.

Follett, M.P. (1941) *Dynamic Administration,* Pitman, London.

Jewson, N. and Mason, D. (1986a) The theory and practice of equal opportunities policies: liberal and radical approaches, *Sociological Review,* 34.

Jewson, N. and Mason, D. (1986b) Modes of discrimination in the recruitment process: formalisation, fairness and efficiency, *Sociology,* 20 (1), 43–63.

Johnson, G. and Scholes, K. (1997) *Exploring Corporate Strategy* (4th edn), Prentice-Hall, Hemel Hempstead.

Kandola, R. Fullerton, J. and Ahmed, Y. (1995) Managing diversity: succeeding where equal opportunities has failed, *Equal Opportunities Review,* 58, 31–6.

Kanter, R.M. (1977) *Men and Women of the Corporation,* Basic Books, New York.

Kanter, R.M. (1984) *The Change Masters,* George Allen & Unwin, London.

Kanter, R.M. (1989) *When Giants Learn to Dance,* Simon & Schuster, New York.

Kay, J. (1997) The Stakeholder Corporation, in Kelly, G., Kelly, D. and Gamble, A. (eds), *Stakeholder Capitalism,* Macmillan, London.

Kaysen, C. (1957) The social significance of the modern corporation, *American Economic Review,* May, 310–19.

Lewis, S. (1997) 'Family friendly' employment policies: a route to changing organizational culture or playing about at the margins?, *Gender, Work and Organization,* 4 (1), 13–22.

Liff, S. and Dale, K. (1994) Formal opportunity, informal barriers: black women managers within a local authority, *Work, Employment and Society,* 8 (2), 177–98.

Lunt, N. and Thornton, P. (1994) Disability and employment: towards an understanding of discourse and policy, *Disability and Society,* 9 (2), 223–38.

Mayo, E. (1960*) The Human Problems of an Industrial Civilization,* Harvard Business School Press, Boston, MA.

Melucci, A. (1989) *Nomads of the Present: Social Movements and Individual Needs in Contemporary Society,* Hutchinson Radius, London.

Miles, R. (1993) *Racism After 'Race Relations',* Routledge, London.

Murphy, D. and Bendell, J. (1997) *In the Company of Partners: Business, Environmental Groups and Sustainable Development Post-Rio,* Policy Press, Bristol.

Neale, A. (1997a) 'Organisational learning in contested environments: lessons from Brent Spar', *Business Strategy and the Environment,* 6 (2), 93–103.

Neale, A. (1997b) 'Organizing environmental self-regulation: liberal governmentality and ecological modernization in Europe', *Environmental Politics,* 6 (4), 1–24.

Oliver, M. (1990) *The Politics of Disablement,* Macmillan, Basingstoke.

Owen, R. (1813) *A New View of Society,* AMS Press, New York.

Peters, T. (1992) *Liberation Management,* Macmillan, London.

Peters, T. and Austin, N. (1985) *Passion for Excellence,* Random House, New York.

Porter, M. and van der Linde, C. (1995) Green and competitive: ending the stalemate, *Harvard Business Review,* 73 (5), 120–34.

Silver, J. (1987) The ideology of excellence: management and neo-conservatism, *Studies in Political Economy,* 24, 105–29.

Weber, M. (1967) *The Protestant Ethic and the Spirit of Capitalism,* Allen & Unwin, London.

Weber, M. (1968) *Economy and Society,* Vol. 2, Bedminster Press, New York.

Welford, R. (1995*) Environmental Strategy and Sustainable Development: the Corporate Challenge for the 21st Century,* Routledge, London.

Welford, R. and Gouldson, A. (1993) *Environmental Management and Business Strategy,* Pitman, London.

Woodall, J., Edwards, C. and Welchman, R. (1997) Organizational restructuring and the achievement of an equal opportunity culture, *Gender, Work and Organization,* 4 (1), 2–12.

Subject index

Author index